organizations:
structure and process

SECOND EDITION

organizations: structure and process

RICHARD H. HALL

University of Minnesota

Prentice-Hall, Inc., *Englewood Cliffs, New Jersey* 07632

58625

Library of Congress Cataloging in Publication Data

HALL, RICHARD H (date)
   Organizations: structure and process.

   Includes bibliographical references and index.
   1. Organization. 2. Organizational change. I. Title.
HM131.H237 1977   301.18′32   76-45743
ISBN 0-13-642025-7

Printed in the United States of America

10   9   8   7   6   5   4   3   2

Prentice-Hall International, Inc., *London*
Prentice-Hall of Australia Pty. Limited, *Sydney*
Prentice-Hall of Canada, Ltd., *Toronto*
Prentice-Hall of India Private Limited, *New Delhi*
Prentice-Hall of Japan, Inc., *Tokyo*
Prentice-Hall of Southeast Asia Pte. Ltd., *Singapore*

contents

FOUR

organizations and society   301

preface to the second edition

The motivations for revising a book are complex. The most immediate occurs when the first edition comes out. At that time, I realized that there were several important omissions in the literature reviewed. I wished that I could get the manuscript back and improve it, which of course could not be done. The desire, and the need, for revision are compounded by the rapid increase in the amount and quality of research on organizations in the past few years.

An additional motivation comes from being in and thinking about organizations, whether from teaching in a classroom, working in organizations, talking with colleagues, conducting research, or reading newspapers. The pervasiveness of organizations in our society, in their beneficial qualities and their perverse qualities, continues to hit me between the eyes—and elsewhere. I felt that the role of organizations in society needed to be stressed much more sharply.

Since the publication of the first edition, my own ideas about organizations have changed. I think that people familiar with the first edition will see some important shifts in perspective. In addition to placing greater emphasis on the role of organizations in society, the present volume emphasizes the importance of the political processes within organizations as crucial decisions are made in regard to the directions organizations will take. There is a movement away from the "technological determinism" of the first edition. The impetus for these changes comes from reviewers of the first edition, colleagues, and students. I hope that our knowledge and understanding of organizations will continue to grow so that this edition, too, will become dated. One change that was consciously *not* made was the addition of a great deal of illustrative material. I continue to believe that the contents are more meaningful if readers refer to illustrations of organizations with which they are already familiar.

I would like to thank Peter Blau, Jerald Hage, Mark Lefton, Charles Perrow, Robert Rothman, Neil Smelser, and Mayer Zald for their useful criticisms of the manuscript, and Carolyn Davidson and Ed Stanford of Prentice-Hall for their conscientious work on behalf of this edition. As always, of course, the credit and blame rest with the author.

organizations:
structure and process

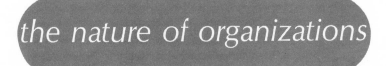

the nature of organizations

1

the role of organizations

The easiest way to develop an understanding of the role of organizations is to pick up a newspaper. It need not be one of the great national papers such as the *New York Times* or the *Washington Post*. It can be a suburban or smalltown weekly. Try to find an article, or an editorial for that matter, that does not deal with organizations. On the front page we can find such events in recent history as the payments made by the oil corporations to foreign political parties—both organizations. The U.S. Department of Agriculture, a government organization, is explaining its sale of grain to farmers' organizations. Labor unions are threatening a strike against construction organizations. Arab and Israeli officials, playing organizational roles, are negotiating some agreement.

Moving through the newspaper, we come to the sports section. Teams, leagues, professional and amateur associations, and tournaments are the dominant items here and each is an organization. The family section reports on organized activities for family members. Travel and recreation sections have glowing or condemning reports on restaurants, hotels, or resorts. They also contain reports on new forms of recreation, which soon become organized into such phenomena as hang-gliding clubs or associations of collectors of old beer bottles. The arts section similarly reflects the organizational influence. Rarely is any artistic work without organizational presentation or sponsorship.

Aside from the want ads, which themselves are almost totally organizational with the exception of individual people selling their cars or old appliances, the final section of the newspaper is the comics. Here we see strong bastions of individualism, such as Snoopy or Mary Worth. But while professing individualism, these characters are products of corporate enterprises.

It should be clear from this exercise that organizations dominate our

3

lives. What, then, are the alternatives or exceptions? The alternatives are also organizational. Protests against organizations themselves become organized. Such alternative forms of grouping as communes are organizations in their own right, and have most of the characteristics of "straight" organizations. The individual can attempt to escape the organization by returning to nature, but except for a few successful hermits, the return to nature is probably doomed to failure as an alternative precisely because most people have grown up in organizations and are habituated to using what organizations can provide. The individual creative artist or scientist was an actuality in the past, but is very unlikely in the present.

While the alternatives to organizational living are limited, the exceptions are not. Our private thoughts and actions may not be organizational, but nevertheless there are organizational intrusions. If we think about our work, our education, or our shopping, we once again enter organizational roles. On the other hand, our thinking about our relationships with other people or about ourselves or about ideas is not organizational. Similarly, spontaneous interactions among people are not organizational. When we are in love with someone or spontaneously dislike someone it is hardly an organizational experience. Here we can find happiness, joy, hate, and sorrow.

Yet, how much time in a day or week is spent in such private and individualized moments? How much of what goes on in a community, in a nation or between nations is of this order? When we turn and face outside ourselves, an organizational reality confronts us.

What is this organizational reality like? This is the question to which this book is addressed. The question will not be answered in its entirety, nor can it be, given the present state of knowledge of organizational analysts. However, at least a partial answer will be given, which, it is hoped, will serve as a basis for developing more complete answers as more research and experience are accumulated and explanatory theories developed.

The focus of the analysis is on organizations *qua* organizations. That is, organizations (human collectivities designed to achieve some goal) will be studied as phenomena in their own right—as actors in society. The organization will be seen as composed of individuals who play critical roles and make critical decisions, but the focus is on what organizations themselves do and don't do. Similarly, society has many problems and many rewards. The focus again will be on the role of organizations in society.

To introduce the topic, the analysis will first be turned to a consideration of organizations and their role in the international order. The focus will then shift to a national system, the United States. Finally, the interrelationships between organizations and the individual will be considered.

ORGANIZATIONS AND INTERNATIONAL RELATIONS

The major reason for beginning the analysis with an examination of organizations at the international level is that information about organizations and international relations illustrates a major point to be developed throughout this book—organizations are affected (manipulated) by their environment and in turn attempt to affect (manipulate) the environment.

It is commonly thought that organizations are subject to the rules of the government under which they operate. It is less commonly realized that international politics can deeply affect an organization. In August 1975, the *Minneapolis Star* reported that the German automobile firm Volkswagen had presented evidence to the Arab countries that it had severed business ties with Israel. This was done in the hopes that the Arab countries would lift their boycott of Volkswagen products. In analytic terms, the organization was affected by its environment to the extent that it had to make a response to this threat to its profit and survival.

Another example of this general point is the well-documented situation of the International Telephone and Telegraph Company's involvement in the domestic politics of Chile. Here the organization was attempting to influence the environment in its behalf.

Not only business corporations are operative on the international scene. The Central Intelligence Agency is an organization, as are its counterparts of all nations. International terrorist groups are also organizations, apparently highly disciplined, with a full complement of ranks and division of labor like most other organizations. Other government units, including the military, narcotics-regulation units, departments or ministries of agriculture, and state or foreign offices, operate at the international level. Universities have overseas branches, as do religious organizations.

The multinational corporation has received the most attention in recent years, and for good reason. These organizations obviously have an impact on local economies. In 1968, Jean Jacques Servan-Schreiber forecast that American-owned firms and subsidiaries in Europe, plus U.S. stockholdings in European firms, would soon rival the combined powers of domestic European industrial and commercial firms.[1] As Charles

---

[1] Jean Jacques Servan-Schreiber, *The American Challenge* (New York: Atheneum, 1968).

McMillan has pointed out, however, not all multinational firms are American.[2]

There are many explanations for the emergence of the multinational corporation. All have a strong element of truth. The first such explanation is imperialism or the attempt to expand corporate markets and reduce costs through the use of economic power over a weaker nation. The nation could be weaker in terms of pay scales and thus provide cheap labor; it could be weaker in terms of political dependence and thus give corporations of the more powerful nations tax breaks and incentives. Robert Heilbroner sees technology as the key to the growth of multinationals.[3] Mass-production systems and computer information-handling have pushed all societies to larger and larger units of production. An inevitable consequence of this is expansion to overseas markets and production facilities.

Arnold Toynbee offers another explanation: multinational firms overcome the problem that sovereignty is dispersed over 140 local states, many of which can have antiquated political arrangements.[4] Toynbee believes that because local economic independence is impossible for many nations, the multinational firm could become the dominant economic and political form of organization, superseding the traditional nation–state.

McMillan's explanation is more complex. He suggests that the multinational corporation is a consequence of corporate choices made to implement product-market strategy:[5] as corporations begin to produce a complex range of products, these are to be sold in different markets through multiple channels of distribution. McMillan's explanation, which, as will be seen later, is solidly within contemporary organizational theory, suggests that multinational corporations are in essence inevitable. Even in a no-growth economic situation, the desire to cut costs or maintain the share of the market would lead to international expansion.

Each of the above explains part of the international growth of organizations. Each also explains why organizations in general seek to expand their influence over the environment as a means of protecting their flanks and expanding their operations.

These explanations have a strong aura of the inevitable about them. But there are conditions that could drastically alter this impression. Na-

[2] Charles J. McMillan, "Corporations without Citizenship: The Emergence of Multinational Enterprise," in Graeme Salaman and Kenneth Thompson, eds., *People and Organisations* (London: Longman Group Limited, 1973), 25–43.

[3] Robert Heilbroner, "Nobody Talks about Busting General Motors in 500 Companies," *Forbes*, 113 (May 15, 1974), 61.

[4] Arnold Toynbee, "As I See It," *Forbes*, 113 (April 15, 1974), 68.

[5] McMillan, "Corporations without Citizenship," 36.

tional revolutions or elections can turn the host country around to the point that all industries are nationalized, or at least foreign investments are confiscated. Not all multinational ventures are successful, and failure of sufficient magnitude could lead to reduced multinational development. Nevertheless, the combination of factors discussed above strongly suggests that multinational organizations of all sorts will be an increasing part of the international scene, and will in turn influence international events.

ORGANIZATIONS AND THE NATIONAL ORDER

The discussion, which focuses on the United States, could equally well have been written about any industrialized nation. Most readers will probably find the discussion depressing, once they realize how pervasive and extensive organizations are in national life. Equally depressing, to some, is the realization that organizations determine the direction (or nondirection) of the society, and that they block social change but are also the very basis of change.

Perhaps one of the best places to begin is with beer. One of the real pleasures of the not-too-distant past was sampling local brands of beer in different sections of the country. These local beers were organizationally produced, to be sure, but frequently had very distinct tastes—good and awful. Today there are very few local breweries; most of them are owned by large national breweries and only retain the local label. For the person who likes beer, this is sad. The situation is sadder in Europe, where first Britain was forced to alter its ingredients and process drastically to join the EEC, and now Bavaria is fighting similar demands. (The threat to its native brewing methods was one source of votes in Britain against joining the Common Market.) The situation is also indicative of the directions that organizations take in all spheres of life.

Organizations tend to grow. As Robin Morris points out, organizational growth is organizational success.[6] Even in a no-growth economy, public and private organizations try to grow at one another's expense. The purchase of additional breweries on the part of a beer company or the amalgamation of all state universities within one system in the interest of economy are part of the orientation toward growth. Such growth is a major way in which organizational decision makers or elites demonstrate their contributions to the organization.

In addition to their growth in size, another important consideration

[6] Robin Morris, "Is the Corporate Economy a Corporate State?" *The American Economic Review* (May 1972), 103–15.

gives contemporary organizations an unprecedented role in contemporary society: the modern organization is a *legal* entity, just like the individual person, as James S. Coleman has pointed out in a perceptive set of essays.[7] The legality is granted by the state, itself a legal creation. While the individual is given a set of rights and responsibilities by the state, these same rights and responsibilities are extended to organizations. These rights, coupled with size, give organizations an enormous amount of power within the state. Coleman also points out that the state or government is more comfortable dealing with other organizations than with individual persons, and thus tends to provide more preferential treatment in terms of taxation or rights to privacy.

The point here is not to ask whether organizations use this power wisely—people on various positions of the political spectrum differ on this issue—but rather to demonstrate the inexorable power of organizations regardless of the directions in which it is used. Not much can happen without an organizational basis.

How do organizations wield their power? Several ways are immediately evident. Charles Perrow has documented the manner in which Litton Industries grew from a very small operation into a major conglomerate with tentacles into such diverse areas as shipbuilding, aerospace, education, and poverty.[8] This growth resulted from a conscious effort by Litton's management to expand their method of operations into as many market areas as possible. Robert Kharasch's analysis of the federal government bureaucracy illustrates another way in which power is wielded.[9] Here there was less concern with growth of market and more with organizational maintenance—that is, with a continuation of what the organization was presently doing. If the organization was to receive a report by a certain date and the report did not arrive on time, the reporting organization was penalized even when the report contained nothing of importance either to the federal agency or to the reporting organization. The government organization has power through its mandate from the legislature and will seek to maintain that power even if no purpose is being served.

Organizations tend to grow; they also tend to maintain themselves. By these conditions and processes a nation becomes organizationally dense.

---

[7] James S. Coleman, *Power and the Structure of Society* (New York: W. W. Norton and Company), 1974.

[8] Charles Perrow, *The Radical Attack on Business: A Critical Analysis* (New York: Harcourt Brace Jovanovich, Inc.), 1972.

[9] Robert N. Kharasch, *The Institutional Imperative: How to Understand the United States Government and Other Bulky Objects* (New York: Charterhouse Books, 1973).

Yet another factor is at work: organizations are created to bring about social change. Organizations oriented to social change rely on other organizations for funding and other support. Having analyzed social movements in the United States, John D. McCarthy and Mayer N. Zald note that the support for many movements comes from churches and private foundations.[10] The government also has supplied funds for movements such as the National Welfare Rights Organizations. Similarly, business corporations have contributed funds directly and indirectly to social movements. While many motivations surround the funding activity, social movements have an increasingly common component, according to McCarthy and Zald: they are increasingly professionalized, with paid professional staffs. Thus, whether the issue be the environment, poverty (government employees, university professors, social workers, and poverty organizers alike have made money on poverty), prostitution, welfare rights, or minority groups, the movement to improve conditions and change society is an organized one. Like other organizations, these seek to maintain themselves and grow. In an organizationally dense society, it obviously takes an organization to fight an organization.

An additional implication in this discussion should be made explicit: organizations grow, maintain themselves, and continue their operations regardless of the motivations of their members. If we judge a given organizationally dense society to have bad policies, it is easy to say that this is the consequence of evil people. The more difficult, but more accurate, conclusion is that it is a consequence of the nature of organizations. While there are evil people, careful thought will bring one to the realization that it is the operation of organizations that brings society to its many crisis points. The Vietnam war was in reality a consequence of the ongoing operations of several military and diplomatic organizations of several nations. In the United States, it also occurred under different administrations of quite different political persuasions.

Similarly, a mining company has been ordered to stop dumping mine tailings into Lake Superior. The organization persisted in doing this even though public sentiment (except in the mining community) and the law were against continued dumping. Are there evil executives and workers? Probably no more than in the federal court structure or the state pollution control agency. The decisions that were made in the organization were in behalf of the organization. This is not to suggest that decisions are not made on the basis of a profit motive or for the self-advancement of the individuals involved. The key factor is that through the organiza-

[10] John D. McCarthy and Mayer N. Zald, *The Trend of Social Movements in America: Professionalization and Resource Mobilization* (Morristown, N.J.: General Learning Press, 1973).

tion and its survival and growth, individual desires are met. In effect, it does not matter whether decisions are made in behalf of an organization or for the benefit of an individual or set of individuals. To maintain or enhance the strength of the organization is the critical motive from which decisions are made.

Another aspect of organizations should be noted at this point. We have been discussing decision makers or elites within organizations, but other people in organizations are influential in the directions that organizations take. These are the individuals who process and interpret the information that is passed on to people in decision-making positions. As will be discussed in more detail later, in all organizations people tend to pass on information that they believe their superiors want to hear. In addition, established roles, lines of communication, and ranks in organizations virtually force certain things to be communicated and suppress other things. For example, many organizations utilize management-information systems, which are essentially computerized systems of information selection and transfer. In a business corporation or government agency that utilizes such a computerized system, the personnel in the management-information department tend to select information most suitable to the computer. Thus quantitative information enters the communications lines and passes up through the organization, at the expense of qualitative nuances in information, which are downplayed.

Another aspect of this same point is that organizational procedures are established in advance to deal with most possible events. For example, all colleges and universities have established admissions procedures, permitting them to process the large number of applicants for each incoming class. By establishing minimum standards in terms of test scores and grades, the schools attempt to control the inputs into their systems. This typically means that they continue to do what they have been doing, creating a momentum that is hard to stop. All organizations have similar procedures in regard to personnel inputs and the inputs of other raw information materials. When these procedures are added to other organizational procedures—the communications process, differences in rank, and the decision-making process—a great deal of momentum has accumulated; the organizations continue to do what they have been doing—dumping waste into a lake, expanding markets, waging a war, trying to alter the conditions of those in poverty by means of an established program, and so on. It is this reality of organizations that is so frequently missed in most analyses of contemporary society.

Thus far we have not dealt with the important issue of how extensively large organizations are interconnected to form societal control systems. As will be seen in later discussions, there is ample, well-documented evidence of interlocking corporate directorships, and of strong linkages between industry and government and among universities, industry, and government.[11] Whether such linkages are judged to be conspiratorial or merely convenient, they exist. And they exist because of the nature of the organizations involved. Organizations, as part of the behavior that leads to their growth and survival, form linkages with other organizations that serve to enhance their own position.

Given a high organizational density and a momentum toward greater organizational size and density, what alternatives are available to the society? There appear to be very few, and this is at the heart of the pessimism noted earlier. One alternative is to eliminate organizations and all that they stand for—hierarchy, competition, momentum, linkages, rules.[12] Although this has been successfully accomplished in many communal situations, unfortunately, relatively simple technologies and low population densities appear to be prerequisites for success. A nonorganized approach to the delivery of water in San Francisco or the removal of waste in New York is very hard to envision. More complicated technological issues, ranging from police protection, through agricultural production for urban citizens, and on to the complexities of such issues as eliminating poverty, make it impossible to think of a nonorganizational basis for action. Even if the problems of production of physical goods were assumed to have been solved—and they have not been for those without—the production and distribution of social services in areas such as medicine, the judiciary, general social services to many segments of the population, and education would still remain organizational. In essence, the populations of industrialized nations have grown too large and the problems therein too complex for a step backward (or forward) to a nonorganized society.

Another alternative is to break large organizations apart into smaller units. The basic problem here is to decide who would do the dividing and enforce its continuance. If it were an organization such as the government, there would be no advance. If division were not enforced, it would not be long until the pattern of growth, merger, and acquisition would begin again, given the organizational pressures which have been briefly described above.

A potentially more feasible alternative is suggested by the noted

---

[11] See Perrow, *The Radical Attack on Business;* Michael Patrick Allen, "The Structure of Interorganizational Elite Cooptation: Interlocking Corporate Directorates," *American Sociological Review*, 39, 3 (June 1974), 393–406; and C. William Domhoff, *Who Rules America?* (New York: Random House, 1970).

[12] See Frederick C. Thayer, *An End to Hierarchy! An End to Competition!: Organizing the Politics and Economics of Survival* (New York: New Viewpoints, 1973).

French sociologist Michel Crozier.[13] After documenting that industrial societies are basically stalled by the weight and inertia of contemporary organizations—organizations that are virtually incapable of adapting to pressures for change from within them or from outside—Crozier suggests that we use these very organizations to turn society around. To do so, individuals would have to participate in the affairs of their organizations more than they now do. Crozier suggests that this is more possible now than in the past, since individuals are less rigid and moralistic in their cultural and political stances than they used to be.

The participation of workers or members in the management of organizations is not a new idea. Many organizations, particularly in Europe, have governmentally or privately mandated participation plans. But such participation has not been a panacea for the organizations or for society; complex problems, specialized skills, and differences in rank within organizations apparently tend to lessen the degree of participation from all segments of organizations. Nevertheless, it appears to be a means of creating change within organizations.

An additional difficulty with participatory schemes is determining who should participate. To what extent should prisoners run prisons, patients run hospitals, or students run universities? (But should they be run exclusively by wardens, physicians, or administrators?) The question comes down to who shall decide what is humane. Past and present decision-making systems seem to have been less than successful. While alternatives like that suggested by Crozier appear to offer the possibility for some incremental improvements, their likelihood is limited, considering the nature of organizations as we know them.

A final—and probably the most likely—alternative is to do nothing and let organizations run as they have always run. This also contains its own seeds of change, for although alliances among various forms of organizations are typically stressed—business with government or universities with business—the truth is that organizations do oppose each other. Some government programs, such as those involving automobile pollution emission standards, are anathema to the automobile industry. Federal programs for school integration run into stiff opposition. Business firms, except perhaps the very large and very unsuccessful ones such as Lockheed and Penn-Central, can go out of business in the face of competition. Unions and management have bitter, to-the-death confrontations. Social movement organizations do threaten established procedures, such as when they halt the construction of electrical generating plants or off-shore oil drilling. How long this alternative will remain feasible in the

[13] Michel Crozier, *The Stalled Society*, Rupert Swyer, trans. (New York: The Viking Press, 1973).

future is questionable, since it is conceivable that all dissent could be suppressed or that there is so much dissent that the whole system stops. Perhaps the participatory model is the most potentially reasonable alternative to the current situation.

ORGANIZATIONS AND THE INDIVIDUAL

The fate of the individual in the organization is a hotly debated topic. Several recent studies have examined how individuals react to their lives as employees of organizations.[14] The conclusion shared by all is that work that is highly routinized, repetitive, and dull is highly alienating for the individual. This is not to say, of course, that work in pre-organizational societies was *not* alienating. Subsistence farming or hunting and gathering is hardly enlightening if it is a matter of survival. That which provides challenge, potential for advancement, and the use of creative or expressive capabilities is enjoyable and even enlightening. As will be discussed in detail later, the way in which people react to their work is essentially an organizational phenomenon, because organizational structures are determined by the technology employed in carrying out the organizational tasks; in few cases are alternative structures of work entertained by the organizational decision-making framework. The individual is thus confronted with a work situation over which little individual control can be exercised.

There is another side to working in organizations. In an important study, Melvin Kohn found small but consistent tendencies for people who work in more bureaucratized organizations to be more intellectually flexible, more open to new experiences, and more self-directed than those working in nonbureaucratized settings.[15] Kohn attributes these findings to the fact that bureaucratized organizations require their work force to be better-educated and also provide more job protection, higher salary, and more complex work. The implication of this study is that work in organizations is not necessarily alienating or deadening to the individual.

---

[14] See Studs Terkel, *Working* (New York: Pantheon Books, 1974); Jerome M. Rosow, ed., *The Worker and the Job: Coping with Change* (Englewood Cliffs, N.J.: Prentice-Hall, Inc., 1974); Stanley Aronowitz, *False Promises* (New York: McGraw-Hill Book Company, 1973); *Work in America: Report of a Special Task Force to the Secretary of Health, Education, and Welfare* (Cambridge, Mass.: M.I.T. Press, 1973); *Survey of Working Conditions* (Survey Research Center, University of Michigan, Ann Arbor, 1970); and Richard H. Hall, *Occupations and the Social Structure*, 2nd ed. (Englewood Cliffs, N.J.: Prentice-Hall, Inc., 1975).

[15] Melvin L. Kohn, "Bureaucratic Man: A Portrait and Interpretation," *American Sociological Review*, 36, 3 (June 1971), 461–74.

Indeed it is likely that for exactly the same work some organizations demand more creativity and flexibility than other organizations do. The work of a secretary or an executive can be challenging and have potential for advancement in one organization and not in another. Here again, organizational characteristics are critical variables as they interact with those of the individual.

People not only work in organizations, they have extensive contacts with them as customers or clients. The recent growth of consumer and client-advocacy organizations is testimony to the fact that those who come to the organization for products or services are not totally satisfied with what they receive. Aside from the frequently ignored fact that advocacy organizations share the same pitfalls as the very organizations they are fighting, relatively little is known about how people react to their meetings within organizations.

A recent study by Daniel Katz et al. sheds some light on how people react to their encounters with organizations.[16] In a survey of people's reactions to their contacts with government agencies in the areas of employment, job training, workmen's compensation, unemployment compensation, welfare services, hospital and medical services, and retirement services it was found that the majority of these clients were satisfied with the service and treatment they received. Thus, widespread discontent with the "system" in this regard appears to be a myth, because common stereotypes about encounters with government bureaucracies are contradicted by the data. Nevertheless, the fact that most people are satisfied does not mean that the organizations are operating as effectively as possible. Katz et al. note:

> A majority of satisfied clients may leave a sizable minority dissatisfied. Even a 75 percent level of satisfaction may be low for some programs in which 90 percent or higher is desirable and feasible. In a population of 200 million, small percentages are large numbers.[17]

In a related study of the same phenomenon, this time among juveniles who have had contact with the juvenile justice system, Peggy Giordano found "something less than a seething rage against the professionals who staff the juvenile justice system."[18] Apparently even in this population, which is thought to have very negative encounters with the establish-

[16] Daniel Katz, Barbara A. Gutek, Robert L. Kahn, and Eugenia Barton, *Bureaucratic Encounters* (Ann Arbor, Mich.: Institute for Social Research, 1975).
[17] *Ibid.*, p. 115.
[18] Peggy C. Giordano, *The Juvenile Justice System: The Client Perspective* (unpublished Ph.D. thesis, University of Minnesota, 1974), p. 147.

ment, organizations are not viewed with the distaste that is generally believed to be present.

An element in the Giordano research is worth noting: if a client feels close to an individual in an organization, his or her interpretation of the total organization appears to be affected. Individuals coming to an organization do so as individuals. The person in the organization may or may not be able to respond in a personal way. Many organizations prescribe the manner in which their employees are to respond to outsiders. Even if the prescribed manner is warm and friendly, as is the case of airline cabin attendants, it is still an organizational prescription. In the case of the professional staffs with which Giordano dealt, and which formed the bulk of the services studied by Kahn et al., the professional is granted some latitude in interpersonal interactions. Such latitude is less likely at the clerical or retail sales level, where many individual contacts with organizations are made.

PLAN OF ANALYSIS

The overview of the subject presented in this chapter was intended to convey the critical importance of organizations in society. No single book will explain all there is to know about organizations; the sociology of organizations, presented in this book, is only one perspective on the subject matter. A composite view of organizations requires inputs from psychology, economics, management, anthropology, political science, mathematics, and industrial relations. The sociological perspective is central to what is called organizational theory because sociological research has provided important evidence and perspectives on the nature of organizations. The analysis of organizations in this book is designed to extend our understanding of the nature and role of organizations.

The next two chapters are general in nature. Chapter 2 deals with the alternative perspectives or theories of organizations that scholars and practitioners have presented in their attempts to understand organizations. Also in Chapter 2 the difficult subject of whether organizations can be classified into usable typologies will be discussed. A perspective from which all organizations can be analyzed will be developed. Chapter 3 deals with the important issue of organizational goals and effectiveness.

Part 2 deals with organizational structure. Chapters 4 through 7 are on the structure, complexity, formalization, and centralization, respectively, of organizations. These will seem to be dry topics if it is not realized that the structure of organizations determines much of what goes on inside them and what happens to them. For example, the consequences for the individual in a highly formalized structure that spells out the person's behavior in advance are very different from situations in which a great deal of individual discretion is possible. Similarly, a highly centralized organization permits little decision making, and thus less autonomy, for the units within it than does a centralized structure. A major focus of the second section will be on the joint impacts of size and technology on particular organizational forms.

Part 3 is concerned with the processes that occur within organizations. As will be explored in Chapter 8, the development and exercise of power within organizations take a variety of forms and are critical to the operation of organizations, as they are to the lives of the individuals within them. Although conflict is not the inevitable consequence of the exercise of power, it is a distinct possibility. Thus, also in Chapter 8, we will examine conflict as it occurs between individuals and groups within the organization. Some conflict can involve entire departments, as when the custodial staff of a prison is practically at war with the rehabilitative staff. The consequences of differing forms of power and conflict will also be examined. Chapter 9 deals with leadership and decision making, where it will be argued that leadership is not as important as it is sometimes thought to be. Common sense and experience would seem to tell us this—how many football or basketball teams are really turned around with new coaches or managers?—but there tends to be a strong belief that leadership is really what the organization or nation needs. This view will be challenged. The discussion of decision making will focus on what actually occurs rather than on prescribing how it ought to occur. (There is a big difference.) Chapter 10 deals with communications in organizations, how information-flows are blocked or distorted, and what are the implications of this for the organization. Also discussed is organizational change, or the ways in which organizations, due to internal or external sources, take on new activities and assume new forms.

Finally, Part 4 returns to the topic of this introductory chapter. Chapter 11 reverses the pattern of analysis and looks at the impact of organizational environments on the organization itself. Because organizations, like individuals, exist in physical and social environments, there are important linkages between environmental and organizational conditions, as well as crucial interorganizational relationships. Organizations compete, cooperate, communicate, and conflict with each other. Just as organizations are an important component of the lives of individuals, so other organizations are critical to the lives of a single organization. A manufacturing firm has suppliers and wholesalers with which it does business. It also deals with a series of local, state, and federal government agencies as it conducts its business. All of these relationships are important for the parties involved. Finally, Chapter 12 is concerned with organizations and social change. The ways in which organizations contribute to social stability or inertia, actively block change, and serve as agents of change will be considered.

SUMMARY AND CONCLUSIONS

The purpose of this chapter has been a simple one—to indicate the importance of organizations. Organizational analysis is dull until it is realized that organizations are a vital, indeed central, component of the social order. Whether we like the social order or not, it is therefore important to understand its organizational underpinnings—as a condition for either changing the order or strengthening it.

2

perspectives on organizations

In this chapter organizations will be defined. The discussion will then turn to ways in which organizations might be typed or classified for ease in understanding. Following this, alternative perspectives or theories of organizations will be evaluated. Finally, the perspective to be followed in the rest of the book will be presented.

DEFINITIONS

Discussions of definitions can be quite deadly; but they also yield a good deal of insight into the phenomena under investigation.[1] And they provide a basis for understanding the approach taken by their developer in his own discussion of these phenomena.

Weber   Like any other field of study, and like organizations themselves, the analysis of organizations has a tradition, one that in many ways centers on Max Weber. Weber has become known in the field primarily for his discussions of bureaucracy, a topic we will discuss later, but he also concerned himself with the more general definitions of organizations. Weber first distinguishes the "corporate group" from other forms of social organization. The corporate group is a "social relationship which is either closed or limits the admission of outsiders by rules, . . . so far as its order is enforced by the action of specific individuals whose regular function this is, of a chief or 'head' and usually also an administrative staff."[2]

---

[1] James G. March and Herbert A. Simon with Harold Guetzkow, in *Organizations* (New York: John Wiley & Sons, Inc., 1958), p. 1, suggest that definitions of organizations do not serve much purpose. I disagree.

[2] Max Weber, *The Theory of Social and Economic Organization*, A. M. Henderson and Talcott Parsons, trans. (New York: The Free Press, 1947), pp. 145–46. Weber also has a specific definition of organizations: "A system of continuous purposive activity of a specified kind" (p. 151). This is actually too concise for this discussion.

This aspect of the definition contains a number of elements requiring further discussion, since they are basic to most other such definitions. In the first place, organizations involve social relationships. That is, individuals interact within the organization. However, as the reference to closed or limited boundaries suggests, these individuals are not simply in random contact. The organization (corporate group) includes parts of the population and excludes others. The organization itself thus has a boundary. A major component of this definition, the idea of order, further differentiates organizations from other social entities. Interaction patterns do not simply arise; a structuring of interaction is imposed by the organization itself. This part of the definition also suggests that organizations contain a hierarchy of authority and a division of labor in carrying out their functions. Order is enforced with specific personnel designated to perform this function.

To the idea of the corporate group, Weber adds some additional criteria for organizations. In organizations, interaction is "associative" rather than "communal."[3] This differentiates the organization from other social entities, such as the family, which would share the other, aforementioned characteristics of the corporate group. Weber also notes that organizations carry out continuous purposive activities of a specified kind.[4] Thus, organizations transcend the lives of their members, and have goals, as "purposive activities" suggests. Organizations are designed to do something. This idea of Weber's has been retained by most organizational analysts.

Weber's definition has served as the basis for many others, in part because it is close to reality. His focus is basically on legitimate interaction patterns among organizational members as they pursue goals and engage in activities.

Barnard A different focus has been taken by Chester Barnard and his followers. While in agreement with Weber on many points, Barnard stresses a different basis for organizations. His basic definition of an organization is "a system of consciously coordinated activities or forces of two or more persons";[5] that is, activity accomplished through conscious, deliberate, and purposeful coordination. Organizations require communications, a willingness on the part of members to contribute, and a common purpose among them. Barnard stresses the role of the individual. It is he who must communicate, be motivated, and make decisions. While Weber emphasizes the system, Barnard is concerned with mem-

---

[3] *Ibid.*, pp. 136–39.

[4] *Ibid.*, pp. 151–52.

[5] Chester I. Barnard, *The Functions of the Executive* (Cambridge, Mass.: Harvard University Press, 1938), p. 73.

bers of the system. The relevance and implications of these contrasting approaches will be taken up later.

ORGANIZATIONS AND SOCIAL ORGANIZATION

One of the major problems in discussing or thinking about organizations is that the very term is so similar to the broader term of "social organization." Most analysts conceive of social organization as the "networks of social relations and the shared orientations . . . often referred to as the social structure and culture, respectively."[6] Social organization is the broader set of relationships and processes of which *organizations* are a part. The analysis of social organization can be at the macro or total societal level, or at the micro or interpersonal or intergroup level. Experimental anaylses of dyads or triads, for example, contribute to the understanding of social organization. Organizations, as we are using the term here, are part of the more general social organization, being affected by it and, reciprocally, affecting it in turn.

Other Definitions   Some writers have attempted to alleviate these terminological problems by adding the adjective "complex," "large-scale," or "formal" as a prefix to organizations. Peter M. Blau and W. Richard Scott, for example, note that:

> Since formal organizations are often very large and complex, some authors refer to them as "large-scale" or as "complex" organizations. But we have eschewed these terms as misleading in two respects. First, organizations vary in size and complexity, and using these variables as defining criteria would result in such odd expressions as a "small large-scale organization" or a "very complex complex organization." Second, although formal organizations often become very large and complex, their size and complexity do not rival those of the social organization of a modern society, which includes such organizations and their relations with one another in addition to other nonorganizational patterns. (Perhaps the complexity of formal organizations is so much emphasized because it is man-made, whereas the complexity of societal organization has slowly emerged, just as the complexity of modern computers is more impressive than that of the human brain. Complexity by design may be more conspicuous than complexity by growth or evolution.)[7]

[6] Peter M. Blau and W. Richard Scott, *Formal Organizations* (San Francisco: Chandler Publishing Co., 1962), p. 4. For an overview of the scope of social organization, see Marvin E. Olsen, *The Process of Social Organization* (New York: Holt, Rinehart and Winston, Inc., 1968). Olsen defines social organization as "the process of merging social actors into ordered social relationships, which become infused with cultural ideas."

[7] Blau and Scott, *Formal Organizations*, p. 7.

While few would argue with Blau and Scott's points regarding the difficulties in the use of "complex" or "large-scale," the same criticism can be made of "formal" as a prefix. Organizations also vary in their formalization, and we would thus have to talk about more-or-less-formal formal organizations, which is not a great leap forward. With these considerations in mind, the simple term "organization" will be used here. "Social organization" will refer to the broader context.

The discussion becomes more concrete when we consider Amitai Etzioni's and W. Richard Scott's definitions and examples. Etzioni states:

> Organizations are social units (or human groupings) deliberately constructed and reconstructed to seek specific goals. Corporations, armies, schools, hospitals, churches, and prisons are included; tribes, classes, ethnic groups, and families are excluded. Organizations are characterized by: (1) divisions of labor, power and communication responsibilities, divisions which are not randomly or traditionally patterned, but deliberately planned to enhance the realization of specific goals; (2) the presence of one or more power centers which control the concerted efforts of the organization and direct them toward its goals; these power centers also continuously review the organization's performance and re-pattern its structure, where necessary, to increase its efficiency; (3) substitution of personnel, i.e., unsatisfactory persons can be removed and others assigned their tasks. The organization can also recombine its personnel through transfer and promotion.[8]

Scott's definition contains some additional elements. He says:

> . . . organizations are defined as collectivities . . . that have been established for the pursuit of relatively specific objectives on a more or less continuous basis. It should be clear, . . . however, that organizations have distinctive features other than goal specificity and continuity. These include relatively fixed boundaries, a normative order, authority ranks, a communication system, and an incentive system which enables various types of participants to work together in the pursuit of common goals.[9]

This definition appears to correspond quite well with reality. However, two problems are evident in this and the other definitions: the place of goals in the nature of organizations, and the issue of the distinctiveness of boundaries. It is clear that a widely varying proportion of organizational

---

[8] Amitai Etzioni, *Modern Organizations* (Englewood Cliffs, N.J.: Prentice-Hall, Inc., 1964), p. 3.

[9] W. Richard Scott, "Theory of Organizations," in Robert E. L. Faris, ed., *Handbook of Modern Sociology* (Chicago: Paul McNally and Co., 1964), p. 488.

activity is unrelated to goals.[10] Perhaps it is preferable to say that organizations are established for the pursuit of goals but engage in activities that may or may not be related to them. This acknowledges the role of goals, but at the same time points to the importance of other activities that are not goal-related.

The problem of the distinctiveness of the boundary is evident in some easily recognized cases. The local political party, for example, often has a small paid staff to answer phones, collect mail, and so on. However, the true power belongs to nonpaid members of the organization, some of whom may not even be known to the paid members. During election campaigns, the membership in the organization swells rapidly as people are enlisted to make telephone calls, deliver posters, and make speeches. This addition of voluntary and part-time personnel really throws the boundary issue up in the air. Many similar kinds of organizations could be identified—religious, fraternal, and others. These voluntary organizations may in this way be so different from other organizations that they form a unique, distinct type. Organizations dealing with emergencies often have their ranks expanded by volunteers—even organizations with very distinct boundaries, such as police or fire departments. Such unusual cases call for further provisions of openness in the definition.

Then again, none of the definitions discussed has included the organization's environment, a point that should be made explicit in the definition, since environment plays a major role in what goes on in organizations. The conception of environment to be used here includes everything "outside of" a particular organization. Climatic and geographical conditions, other organizations, the state of the economy, and the stage of development of the nation—these are but a few of the environmental factors that all organizations must face and contend with.

Environmental factors affect organizations from two directions. First, environmental factors are a major part of an organization's input. The organization, as described in the definitions above, then does something with this input, producing an output. The output goes back into the environment, thus again affecting the organization as the output is consumed, utilized, and evaluated in the environment.[11]

With all these considerations in mind, the definition of organizations to be used in this analysis can now be stated. *An organization is a collec-*

[10] For a concise statement of this position, see Alvin W. Gouldner, "Organizational Analysis," in Robert K. Merton, Leonard Broom, and Leonard S. Cottrell, Jr., *Sociology Today* (New York: Basic Books, Inc., 1959), pp. 405–6.

[11] This discussion and terminology correspond to that of James D. Thompson, *Organizations in Action* (New York: McGraw-Hill Book Company, 1967), pp. 19–20; and Daniel Katz and Robert L. Kahn, *The Social Psychology of Organizations* (New York: John Wiley & Sons, Inc., 1966), pp. 16–17.

tivity with a relatively identifiable boundary, a normative order, ranks of
authority, communications systems, and membership-coordinating sys-
tems; this collectivity exists on a relatively continuous basis in an en-
vironment and engages in activities that are usually related to a goal or a
set of goals.

This definition is admittedly cumbersome. But the discussion thus far
has indicated the reasons for this. Organizations are complex entities that
contain a series of elements and are affected by many diverse factors. To
convey an understanding of the nature and the consequences of these
internal and external factors is the task of the remaining chapters of this
book. Before turning to these and other matters, however, an important
but often overlooked question must be asked.

ARE ORGANIZATIONS REAL?

At first glance, this question probably seems inane; it was stated at the
outset that organizations surround us and that we are a part of them
most of our lives. But a second look at the question will reveal a very
basic issue: whether organizations are anything more than individuals
who have come together in an interaction system.

Many organizational analysts say that organizations can be understood
only by taking the interaction perspective;[12] that is, since humans make
decisions and react to situations, the actions and reactions of individuals
form the heart of the organization, and therefore nothing in an organization can be understood apart from the individuals involved. Blau provides a good example of this perspective when he states:

> Within the organization, indirect exchange processes become substituted for
> direct ones, although direct ones persist in interstitial areas, such as informal
> cooperation among colleagues. The development of authority illustrates the
> transformation of direct into indirect exchange transactions. As long as
> subordinates obey the orders of a superior primarily because they are
> obligated to him for services he has rendered and favors he has done for
> them individually, he does not actually exercise authority over the
> subordinates, and there is a direct exchange between him and them, of the
> type involving unilateral services. The establishment of authority means that
> normative constraints that originate among the subordinates themselves

---

[12] Herbert A. Simon makes a succinct statement of this position when he warns
against reifying the concept of organization—". . . treating it as something more
than a system of interacting individuals." In Simon, "On The Concept of Organizational Goal," *Administrative Science Quarterly*, 9, No. 1 (June 1964), 1. The position
taken here is the exact opposite. The organization is not reified, because it is reality.

effect their compliance with the orders of the superior—and indirect exchanges now take the place of the former direct ones. The individual subordinate offers compliance to the superior in exchange for approval from his colleagues; the collectivity of subordinates enforces compliance with the superior's directives to repay its joint obligations to the superior; and the superior makes contributions to the collectivity in exchange for the self-enforced voluntary compliance of its members on which his authority rests.[13]

Blau then notes that:

. . . in return for offering services to clients without accepting rewards from them, officials receive material rewards from the organization and colleague approval for conformity with accepted standards. The clients make contributions to the community, which furnishes the resources to the organization that enable it to reward its members.[14]

Blau's analysis places primacy on the interaction between individuals as the heart of the organization. The position taken in this book is that this is an incomplete view of organizations in two ways.

ORGANIZATIONS AND THE INDIVIDUAL

In the first place, individuals in organizations frequently behave *without* engaging in direct or indirect exchange. When the captain of the defensive platoon of a football team shouts "Pass!" both the linemen and defensive backs react immediately in their stance and their entire approach to the play. When an item to be charged in a department store costs more than $100, the clerk routinely calls the credit office to check the credit of the prospective purchaser. Both these illustrations involve routine learned behavior. Although the learning has taken place in a direct-interaction situation, the actual behavior takes place without mental reference to the interaction process. It has become a type of learned stimulus–response mechanism, with the intervening interaction variable deleted as a consideration. Much behavior in organizations is of this type. The organization trains, indoctrinates, and persuades its members to respond on the basis of the requirements of their position. This

[13] Peter M. Blau, *Exchange and Power in Social Life* (New York: John Wiley & Sons, Inc., 1967), p. 329.
[14] *Ibid.*, p. 330.

response becomes quite regularized and routinized and does not involve the interaction frame of reference.

The argument that behavior in organizations is organizationally based, rather than individually or interactionally, is not intended to mean that *all* behavior in organizations is so determined. Instead, the intent here is to demonstrate that organizational factors play an important part in determining how an individual will act in a variety of situations. The particular impact of organizational factors will vary according to the situation. In some situations, organizational factors are dominant; in others, individual or interaction effects. Even in the case of individually or interactionally based behavior, however, organizational considerations play a role. In discussing the factors that contribute to the kinds of role expectations one organization member holds toward another (role expectations are of vital importance in any interaction situation), Robert Kahn et al. note:

> To a considerable extent, the role expectations held by the members of a role set—the prescriptions and proscriptions associated with a particular position—are determined by the broader organizational context. The organizational structure, the functional specialization and division of labor, and the formal reward system *dictate the major content of a given office.* What the occupant of that office is supposed to do, with and for whom, is given by these and other properties of the organization itself. Although other human beings are doing the "supposing" and rewarding, the structural properties of organization are sufficiently stable so that they can be treated as independent of the particular persons in the role set. For such properties as size, number of echelons, and rate of growth, the justifiable abstraction of organizational properties from individual behavior is even more obvious [Italics added].[15]

Therefore, in answer to the question posed at the beginning of this section we can say that organizations are real. They are real to the extent that strictly organizational factors account for part of the behavior of individuals at all times in organizations. The exact proportion of the variation in individual behavior accounted for by the organizational factors, as opposed to interactional or individual factors, cannot be exactly specified at the present time. The position taken here is that organizational factors can account for *all* the variation in behavior in some circumstances (this is the purpose of training and indoctrination pro-

[15] Robert L. Kahn, Donald M. Wolfe, Robert P. Quinn, J. Diedrick Snoek, and Robert A. Rosenthal, *Organizational Stress* (New York: John Wiley & Sons, Inc., 1964), p. 31.

grams in many kinds of organizations). In others, organizational factors interact with other behavioral determinants. It is hoped that research in organizations will begin to provide data on the conditions under which these factors operate. At present, unfortunately, the analysis must rest on these incomplete descriptions.

ORGANIZATIONS AS ACTORS

The treatment of organizations as realities has thus far been concerned with the behavior of individuals. An even more basic issue is whether organizations have an existence of their own, above and beyond the behavior and performance of individuals within them. The question becomes, "Do organizations act?" The answer is again in the affirmative and is the second reason that viewing organizations just as interacting individuals is too narrow a conceptualization.

Some characteristics of the definitions discussed above provide indications of the existence of organizations. The fact that organizations persist over time and replace members suggests that they are not dependent on particular individuals. When a new member enters an organization, he is confronted with a social structure—which includes the interaction patterns among organizational members and these members' expectations, toward him—and a set of organizational expectations for his own behavior. It does not matter who the particular individual is; the organization has established a system of norms and expectations to be followed regardless of who its personnel happen to be, and it continues to exist regardless of personnel turnover. This is not to suggest that personnel do not have an impact on organizations. Rather, the contributions of individuals are incorporated into the organizational system. But the system persists over time and beyond the membership of individuals.

There is another sense in which organizations have an existence. When we think about decision making, it is typically at the level of the individual using a variety of techniques to arrive at a decision. Many decisions in organizations, however, are organizational decisions. That is, the organization has set the parameters for decision making and the individual simply follows the procedures that have been prescribed for him. These rather programmed types of decisions are usually at a low level. But more important decisions about future organizational directions and policies are also strongly influenced by organizational factors. The whole area of tradition and precedent, power position within the organization, and the organization's relationship with its environment have an impact on how individuals within the organizational hierarchy make decisions on behalf of the organization. Organizational considerations thus pervade the decision-making process.

When we hear statements such as "It is company policy," "Z State University never condones cheating," or "Trans–Rhode Island Airline greets you with a smile," these are recognizable as being about organizations. Organizations do have policies, do and do not condone cheating, and may or may not greet you with a smile. They also manufacture goods, administer policies, and protect the citizenry. These are organizational actions and involve properties of organizations, not individuals. They are carried out by individuals—even in the case of computer-produced letters, which are programmed by individuals—but the genesis of the actions remains in the organization. The answer to our basic question, then, is: Organizations are real.[16]

Organizational characteristics are crucial determinants of the behavior of individuals in them. That is, if organizations have characteristics of their own, and if these characteristics deliberately affect the behavior of members, then organizational characteristics must be understood if we are to understand human behavior. The same point is relevant to understanding how a society functions; if we are to understand a society that depends upon organizations, we must understand its organizations.

TYPES OF ORGANIZATIONS

The discussion of the different definitions of organizations could lead to the conclusion that all organizations share common characteristics and are thus of one class or type. In one sense that is true, just as there are

---

[16] A basic difficulty in answering the question of whether organizations are real is methodological in nature. Since we tend to think of information about organizations as coming from individuals, it is difficult to conceptualize organizations as entities. Paul F. Lazarsfeld and Herbert Menzel ("On the Relationship Between Individual and Collective Properties" in Amitai Etzioni, ed., *Complex Organizations: A Sociological Reader* [New York: Holt, Rinehart & Winston, Inc., 1961]) (see also Allen H. Barton, *Organizational Measurement* [New York: College Entrance Examination Board, 1961] for a related discussion) have developed a framework from which distinctions between individual and collective (organizational) properties may be drawn. They note that information from individuals can be utilized to determine organizational properties by using averages, standard deviations, correlation coefficients, and other such figures. Information about the relationships between members of the organization also describes the organization. Information can also be gathered that is *not* dependent upon individuals. Information bearing directly on organizational characteristics can be obtained from records, informants, national data sources, etc. The informants may be organizational members, but they relate characteristics of the organization and not of themselves. Examples of these kinds of research will be utilized throughout the analysis that follows. The organizational "realist" position which is taken here is consistent with the argument that groups are real as proposed by Charles K. Warriner, "Groups Are Real: A Reaffirmation," *American Sociological Review* 21, No. 5 (October 1956), 549–54.

defining characteristics that enable us to differentiate humans from other forms of life. In many cases, only the simple classification of human versus nonhuman is required for thought or action. In other cases, this simple classification does not tell us enough and we begin to classify.

Classification schemes are designed to indicate a meaningful difference between the types or classes identified. Classification enables a person to view the world; without classification the individual is surrounded by a chaos of stimuli. Without classification a person would be unable to function at all.

There is a basic difficulty in classifying anything; a classification that works marvelously in one situation might be disastrous in another. For example, the typology based on sex is one of the most useful that we have available. It is nice to be able to distinguish between women and men. This distinction becomes useless, however, if we need to distinguish between a qualified or unqualified person as a lawyer, accountant, chef, or automobile mechanic. Here, a different classificatory scheme is required.

The same problem is faced when organizations are considered: a usable classification system in one instance may be unusable in the next. In some instances, knowing whether an organization is a good place to work or not is sufficient. In others, we may want to classify on the basis of which parties benefit from the actions of the organization. In still others it is useful to know how formalized or structured the organization is so that we can understand or predict the amount of autonomy given to individual workers.

Organizational analysts are well aware of the need for typologies.[17] But at the same time they are convinced that the relatively simple, prima facie typologies probably add more confusion than clarity. Charles Perrow, for example, notes:

> . . . types of organizations—in terms of their functions in society—will vary as much within each type as between types. Thus, some schools, hospitals, banks, and steel companies may have more in common, because of their routine character, than routine and nonroutine schools, routine and

---

[17] Some analyses of organizations (e.g., that of March and Simon) do not deal with the problem of typologies. The March and Simon approach, while treating organizations as a generic entity, makes generalizations difficult, since it is not clear how one set of findings might apply in another situation. For the purposes of the discussion that follows, we will assume that the terms *classification, typology,* and *taxonomy* are synonymous, even though in a strict sense they are not. For a discussion of this, see Tom Burns, "The Comparative Study of Organizations," in Victor H. Vroom, ed., *Methods of Organizational Research* (Pittsburgh: University of Pittsburgh Press, 1967), p. 119.

nonroutine hospitals, and so forth. To assume that you are holding constant the major variable by comparing several schools or several steel mills is unwarranted until one looks at the technologies employed by the various schools or steel mills.[18]

While we may argue about Perrow's emphasis on technology as the key variable, his point is very important. It is *organizational characteristics* that should serve as the classificatory basis. The great danger in most classificatory schemes is oversimplification; they are based on a single characteristic. Typologies thus derived ". . . can be expanded indefinitely as some new factor is seized upon to indicate an additional class."[19] Such problems with typologies are not limited just to the study of organizations. Tom Burns notes, ". . . the history of sociology, from Montesquieu through Spencer, Marx, and up to Weber himself, is littered with the debris of ruined typologies that serve only as the battleground for that academic street-fighting that so often passes for theoretical discussion."[20]

Typologies that end in debris did not stop at Weber's era. A generally accepted typology of organizations is nonexistent in spite of the general agreement that a good typology or set of typologies is desperately needed. While simple typologies can be used for limited analyses, such as comparing organizations in their turnover rates, growth rates, or rates of investment in research and development, classifications of this sort have only a limited usefulness.[21] We end up knowing only one thing about organizations, not understanding them in their rich complexity.

The essence of the typological effort really lies in the determination of the critical variables for differentiating the phenomena under investigation. Since organizations are highly complex entities, classificatory schemes must represent this complexity. An adequate overall classification would have to take into account *the array of external conditions, the total spectrum of actions and interactions within an organization, and the outcome of organizational behaviors.* A review of some of the efforts made to classify organizations will indicate the diversity of variables that have been considered, the relative fruitlessness of the schemes, and some possible future directions for typological efforts.

---

[18] Charles Perrow, "A Framework for the Comparative Analysis of Organizations," *American Sociological Review,* 32, No. 2 (April 1967), 203.

[19] Daniel Katz and Robert L. Kahn, *The Social Psychology of Organizations* (New York: John Wiley & Sons, Inc., 1966), p. 111.

[20] Burns, "Comparative Study of Organizations," p. 119.

[21] See *ibid.,* p. 123.

SOME TYPOLOGIES

By Goal or Function

This review will move from some relatively simple schemes to more elaborate formulations. Typical of the simple schemes is that of Talcott Parsons,[22] based on the type of function or goal served by the organization. In this analysis, Parsons is concerned with the linkages between organizations and the wider society. He distinguishes four types of organizations, according to what they contribute to the society.

The first type is the *production organization,* which makes things that are consumed by the society. The second type is that oriented toward *political goals;* it seeks to ensure that society attains its valued goals; and it generates and allocates power within the society. The third type is the *integrative* organization, whose purposes are settling conflicts, directing motivations toward the fulfillment of institutionalized expectations, and ensuring that the parts of society work together. The final form is the *pattern maintenance* organization, which attempts to provide societal continuity through educational, cultural, and expressive activities.

While each of these functions is clearly important for society (other societal goals could be identified), this type of classificatory scheme does not really say much about the organizations involved. In the first place, some organizations can be placed in more than one category. A large corporation, such as General Motors, is clearly a production organization. But it is also important in the allocation of power. Through public relations, corporate contributions to foundations and colleges, and attempts at working with disadvantaged youths, the same corporation falls into the other categories. Its prime effort is undoubtedly production, but these subsidiary concerns make such a classificatory scheme less than totally useful. Even more important, such a typology does not differentiate among the characteristics of organizations themselves. As Perrow noted, there can be as much—or more—organizational variation within such categories as between them.

Katz and Kahn

An elaboration of this same type of approach is provided by Katz and Kahn.[23] Their first type of organization is the *production* or *economic*

---

[22] Talcott Parsons, *Structure and Process in Modern Society* (New York: The Free Press, 1960), pp. 45–46.

[23] Katz and Kahn, *Social Psychology,* pp. 111–28.

organization, which is concerned with "the creation of wealth, the manu-facture of goods, and the providing of services for the general public or for specific segments of it." These production organizations can then be subdivided into primary, secondary, and tertiary forms. They provide instrumental integration for the society as a whole through their produc-tion of an output that is consumed, often as a basic survival need, by members of the society. The rewards these organizations offer serve as inducements "to keep the collective order working."

The second type is the *maintenance organization,* which is "devoted to the socialization of people for their roles in other organizations and in the larger society." This type can be subdivided into those organizations directly involved in maintenance, such as the church and school, and those concerned with restoration, either through health and welfare ac-tivities or rehabilitation and reform. These organizations provide norma-tive integration for the society.

The third type, *adaptive* organizations, "create knowledge, develop and test theories, and, to some extent, apply information to existing prob-lems." The most obvious examples are universities, through their research functions, and other research organizations. Some artistic organizations would also qualify for this category because of their extension of human understanding and experience. These organizations provide a part of the informational integration that exists in a society.

The final type is the *managerial* or *political* organization, concerned with the "adjudication, coordination, and control of resources, people, and subsystems." The state is obviously the most central and visible such organization. Through its power to use and control force, the state is the central power source. Other organizations in this type would be govern-ment subsystems, pressure groups, labor unions, and special-interest or-ganizations that represent such diverse groups as doctors, educators, and farmers. When penal institutions are viewed as law-enforcement agen-cies, they, too, are political organizations.

This last point illustrates a difficulty with this formulation. Many penal institutions are also clearly maintenance organizations. Both law-enforce-ment and rehabilitation orientations can be found within the same or-ganizations, suggesting that the differentiations are something less than clear-cut. Katz and Kahn recognize the likelihood that a single organiza-tion will engage in more than one major function, either as an explicit program, as in the case of universities with their split between teaching and research, or as an adjunct to their major function, as in the case of oil companies seeking protective tax legislation (a political activity) so that they may more effectively engage in production.

Katz and Kahn go beyond classifying organizations according to their major functions. They look at organizational characteristics as they interact with these major functions. Noting the seemingly limitless dimensions along which organizations can vary, they select four characteristics that seem to them basic for organizational operations. The first of these is the nature of the "through-put." Here the differentiation is between organizations that transform *objects* and those that transform *people*. A basic distinction here involves the fact that the people being transformed, even in prison-like situations, must be motivated to participate in the organization. The organization's staff must be able to react to an acting object. A second major difference is that people-processing organizations do not sell their outputs directly in the marketplace. Support comes indirectly, through taxes, subsidies, or gifts; and the output is consumed indirectly, through hiring practices or the return of well patients to the community.

Even the distinction between people versus objects is not all that simple. Yeheskel Hasenfeld suggests that a further distinction should be made between organizations that simply process people and those that seek to change them.[24] The former seek to confer a new public status on people and relocate them in a new social environment. Examples include university admissions offices (the individual is processed from the role of high school or college graduate to that of college or graduate student) and juvenile courts (juvenile to juvenile offender). People-changing organizations attempt to bring about behavioral changes in individuals. The teaching units of universities are people-changing organizations, as are the probation or institutionalized treatment organizations associated with juvenile courts. Hasenfeld maintains that this distinction is linked to other important organizational characteristics, which suggests that the original people-versus-object distinction is not revealing enough.

The second organizational differentiation is between *expressive* and *instrumental orientations* on the part of organization members. Expressive orientations are characteristic of organizations in which members participate for some intrinsic satisfaction gained from their participation, while an instrumental orientation is one in which participation is for the purpose of receiving some reward that will then allow intrinsic satisfactions to be sought outside the organization. The expressive end of the continuum can be represented by organizations whose members come together for the sole purpose of engaging in a commonly enjoyed activity, such as model railroading or weightlifting, while the extreme of the instrumental orientation is characterized by a simple desire to receive a paycheck at the end of the week. Here again, there are relatively few pure types, since more instrumental orientations can enter almost any

[24] Yeheskel Hasenfeld, "People Processing Organizations: An Exchange Approach," *American Sociological Review*, 37, 3 (June 1972), 256–63.

type of expressive activity (note the wide variety of motivations that people express for attending religious services), and people can come to enjoy even the most repetitious of assembly-line tasks.[25]

The third basis of differentiation concerns the *organizational structure* itself. Katz and Kahn suggest that organizations vary according to the degree to which their boundaries are open and permeable; the degree to which the structure is elaborated, both horizontally and vertically, into subunits and hierarchical levels; and the nature of the allocation system within the organization. This last differentiation refers to the extent to which rewards are distributed equally to organization members; the cooperative would lie at one end of the continuum, while the private organization that operates solely for the benefit of owners would lie at the other. Most organizations, again, fit somewhere between these extremes. The allocation process is, of course, a source of conflict within the organization, and the presence of conflicting groups (management–labor) is another aspect of structural differentiation.

The final basis of differentiation is the manner in which organizations attempt to *utilize the energy or resources at their disposal.* This ranges from those organizations seeking to maintain an equilibrium by neither expanding nor contracting the amount of input or output, to those that seek to maximize the utilization of input so that more resources are retained in the organization than are expended. An example of the former extreme would be a corporation with an unchanging supply and market situation, which attempts to return a consistent profit to the owners over time. The latter extreme is represented by organizations that attempt to capture larger and larger shares of their market at increasingly lower costs. In a rapidly changing social environment, there would be a strong tendency for organizations to fall at the nonequilibrium end of the continuum.

Katz and Kahn then discuss the interplay between these organizational dimensions and the categorization based on societal functions performed. They argue that the societal functions have an impact on how the organizational factors form configurations. While the relationships between the larger society and organizations are certainly important, the overlap and ambiguities present in the classification by major functions are so great that the distinction itself becomes practically meaningless. Later in this chapter, we will turn to a consideration of factors that appear to make more of a difference than those in the approach of Parsons and Katz and Kahn. Although the organizational characteristics that Katz and Kahn discuss are quite relevant dimensions along which organizations

[25] See Charles R. Walker and Robert Guest, *The Man on the Assembly Line* (Cambridge, Mass.: Harvard University Press, 1952), p. 77.

vary, the goals-and-functions approach does not seem to be a sufficiently discriminating classificatory basis.

Etzioni and Blau and Scott

The next set of typology schemes moves away from the reliance on an a priori differentiation between major societal functions. These schemes, two of which will be considered here, utilize different sets of classificatory bases—each, however, also involving a single principle.

Etzioni and Blau and Scott made almost simultaneous attempts to provide classification systems for organizations using very different bases. The Etzioni classification uses *compliance* as the major source of differentiation between organizations.[26] Compliance is the manner in which lower participants in an organization respond to the authority system of the organization. The compliance is expressed through the nature of the lower participant's involvement in the organization. When coercion is the basis of authority, compliance is alienative; when remuneration is the basis of authority, compliance takes the form of a utilitarian (instrumental or calculative) orientation toward the organization; and when the authority basis is moral or normative and expressed through persuasion, compliance is moral. The three types of authority and three types of compliance are combined in a three-by-three classificatory scheme. Most organizations would fall into "congruent" types, in that they would be *coercive–alienative, remunerative–utilitarian, or normative–moral.* The incongruent types (e.g., coercive–utilitarian) would tend to move toward congruency, according to Etzioni.

The Blau and Scott formulation is based on a different principle.[27] The major criterion here is who is the prime beneficiary of the organization's actions. This is related to, but not the same as, the functions approach discussed above. In this case, the basis of differentiation is the output of the organization as it is directly consumed by some segment of society. The nature of the output is not the important thing, but who benefits, or *cui bono.* The nature of the beneficiaries helps determine the nature of member participation and the central problems faced by each organization type.

Blau and Scott derive four basic organization types. The first is the *mutual-benefit association,* in which the members themselves are the prime beneficiaries of the organization's actions. The second type is the

[26] Amitai Etzioni, *A Comparative Analysis of Complex Organizations* (New York: The Free Press, 1961), pp. 23–67.

[27] Peter M. Blau and W. Richard Scott, *Formal Organizations* (San Francisco: Chandler Publishing Co., 1962), pp. 40–58.

business concern, with the owners as prime beneficiaries. The *service organization* is the third type, with the clients that are served as the prime consideration. The final type is the *commonweal organization,* in which the public at large receives the major benefits. Blau and Scott also recognize the possibility of mixed types, but their major emphasis is on the pure types.

Analysis of the Etzioni and Blau and Scott Systems

At first glance, both these typologies seem quite intrinsically satisfying. They utilize variables that are important in organizations. The question is, however, are they adequate typologies? Two critiques suggest that they are not. (The critiques themselves, coincidentally, also appeared almost simultaneously.) In an analysis of the Etzioni system, Burns notes that insofar as the environment allows, Etzioni believes that organizations will tend to shift their compliance structure toward the congruent types and congruent-type organizations will resist factors that push them toward incongruent compliance structures, since congruent types are more effective than incongruent types and organizations are under pressure to be effective. Burns then asks, "First, if there is so much pressure towards congruence, how do organizations get to be 'incongruent' in the first place? Second, what is the 'environment' doing in there if it is not to afford blanket cover for all contingencies which might weaken or wreck the hypothesis? And, third, for whom and for what are organizations reckoned to be 'effective'?"[28]

Burns is saying essentially that the Etzioni typology leaves too many things unexplained and utilizes some unwarranted assumptions. His criticisms of the Blau and Scott formulation take a different tack. He notes first that in many large businesses the managers actually control the organization, with the stockholders receiving benefits based on the discretion of the real controllers. He also notes that the hospital "operated as a business enterprise by a consortium of medical practitioners [may not be] fundamentally different from a hospital [that is] publicly maintained or privately endowed.[29] Burns makes a more fundamental criticism of the prime-beneficiary approach when he states that it is extremely difficult to isolate an explicit, stable, and coherent group served by any organization. The beneficiaries themselves have factions, disagree, and engage in power struggles. This is closely related to the issue of organizational goals, which is similarly fraught with the lack of explicitness, stability, and coherence. Burns concludes that neither of these typologies, based as

[28] Burns, "Comparative Study of Organizations," p. 121.
[29] *Ibid.,* p. 122.

they are on single principles, sufficiently deals with the complexities of organizational existence.

A quite different but equally critical approach to these typologies is taken by Richard Hall, J. Eugene Haas, and Norman Johnson.[30] This analysis is empirically based, and it is at the empirical level that the first problems with the typologies are evident. This study used 75 organizations as the basis for examining the utility of the typologies. In most cases, placement of the organizations into the suggested classifications was relatively easy. Business organizations generally fell into the "utilitarian" or "business" categories, prisons were classified as "coercive" and "commonweal," and so on. Problems in each typology arose, however. Public school systems, for example, are suggested by Etzioni to be primarily "normative" organizations, with the likelihood of "coercive" overtones. Since students must attend by law and can be adjudged delinquent if they do not, coercion is often a strong basis for attendance. At the same time, the student who utilizes the school system as a means of social mobility or vocational training is rather clearly treating it as an instrumental entity. Grades and knowledge are used as a means to an end. The diversity of the involvement on the part of the organization members makes placement in the three major types extremely difficult in many cases.

Similar difficulties were encountered with the Blau and Scott system. A basic issue was whether to use short-run or long-run benefits. Using schools again as the example, the client group—students—receives both short-run and long-run benefits. The society at large also receives important benefits from the operation of schools. A similar case exists with mass-media organizations, such as newspapers or television stations. While the owners are a major beneficiary, assuming a profitable operation, the public at large also benefits. In the case of welfare agencies, the client groups receive benefits, but so again do the public and the welfare workers. A basic difficulty with both classificatory systems is, therefore, the fact that real organizations just do not fit into the suggested categories with the ease that would be desirable in a truly definitive typology.

Mere placement of the organizations into the classifications does not really test the typologies. The critical function of a typology is to "allow us to combine a number of variables into a single construct, and thus allow us to deal with extremely complex phenomena in a relatively sim-

---

[30] Richard H. Hall, J. Eugene Haas, and Norman J. Johnson, "An Examination of the Blau–Scott and Etzioni Typologies," *Administrative Science Quarterly*, 12, No. 1 (June 1967), 118–39.

ple fashion."[31] In order to determine whether these typologies do in fact provide some ordering of organizational phenomena, a series of organizational characteristics were cross-tabulated with the classification schemes.

Analysis of data from the 75 organizations indicated that the typologies did not differentiate clearly among the organizations in terms of such important structural variables as complexity or formalization; nor did they predict well in regard to changes in the organizations. The typologies did yield insights into the aspects of organizations which served as the original basis—compliance patterns and beneficiaries. A subsequent reanalysis of this data by Peter Weldon suggests that Hall et al. may have exaggerated the extent to which these typologies are inadequate.[32] Weldon found that the two typologies had statistically significant correlations with many important organizational characteristics. They did not, however, deal at all well with the crucial issue of organizational dynamics or change.[33]

Etzioni has compiled the results of some 60 studies that utilized his framework.[34] They generally support the compliance patterns that the typologies predict: normative organizations have members who are morally and strongly committed to the organizations, and remunerative and coercive organizations have weaker commitments of the sort predicted. The Etzioni typology thus appears to "work" in terms of compliance patterns of members. It is not, however, an inclusive typology.

An Empirically Derived Typology

A very different approach to the classification of organizations was attempted by Haas, Hall, and Johnson.[35] This approach tried to develop a taxonomy of organizations, similar to the taxonomy used in zoology to

[31] David Mechanic, "Methodology of Organizational Studies," in Harold J. Leavitt, ed., *The Social Science of Organizations* (Englewood Cliffs, N.J.: Prentice-Hall, Inc., 1963), p. 158.

[32] Peter D. Weldon, "An Examination of the Blau–Scott and Etzioni Typologies: A Critique," *Administrative Science Quarterly*, 17, No. 1 (March 1972), 76–78.

[33] Richard H. Hall, J. Eugene Haas, and Norman J. Johnson, "Reply to Weldon," *Administrative Science Quarterly*, 17, No. 1 (March 1972), 79–80.

[34] Amitai Etzioni, *A Comparative Analysis of Complex Organizations: Revised and Enlarged Edition* (New York: The Free Press, 1975).

[35] J. Eugene Haas, Richard H. Hall, and Norman J. Johnson, "Toward an Empirically Derived Taxonomy of Organizations," in Raymond V. Bowers, ed., *Studies on Behavior in Organizations* (Athens: University of Georgia Press, 1966), pp. 157–80. See also Norman J. Johnson, "Toward a Taxonomy of Organization" (unpublished Ph.D. dissertation, The Ohio State University, 1966), pp. 186–234.

differentiate vertebrata at the phyla level (amphibia, mammalia, aves, and reptilia), at the class level, and so on. Using data from 75 organizations and some 100 different organizational variables, this study was able to generate some nine major classes of organizations. Unfortunately, the bases for differentiation among the classes were seemingly trivial as organizational properties. The reason for the rather unusable findings may have been the type of measurement used or it may have been the fact that certain key variables were not included in the analysis. In any event, this initial effort at developing a classification scheme from empirically based characteristics did not produce usable classifications. Future research may be able to do so.

A Structural Typology

The final classification effort is an attempt to type organizations according to important structural characteristics.[36] It is also empirically based and uses the following structural dimensions: (1) the *structuring of activities,* or the degree of standardization of routines, formalization of procedures, specialization of roles, and stipulation of specific behavior by the organization; (2) the *concentration of authority,* or the centralization of authority at the upper levels of the hierarchy and in controlling units outside the organization; and (3) the *line control of workflow,* or the degree to which control is exercised by line personnel as opposed to control through impersonal procedures. Using a sample of 52 English organizations and the three bases of classification, D. S. Pugh, D. J. Hickson, and C. R. Hinings suggest the following types:

1. Full Bureaucracy: ". . . relatively high scores on both structuring of activities and concentration of authority, a high dependence score . . . , and a relatively low score on workflow integration of technology. . . . It has high scores on both standardization of procedures for selection and advancement, etc., and formalization of role definition. . . ."
2. Nascent Full Bureaucracy: Possesses the same characteristics, but not to such a pronounced degree.
3. Workflow Bureaucracy: "High scores on structuring of activities combined with relatively low scores on the remaining two structural factors. Their use of impersonal control mechanisms is shown by the high scores on formalization of recording of role performance as well as a high percentage of nonworkflow personnel and clerks . . . high scores of workflow integration."

---

[36] D. S. Pugh, D. J. Hickson, and C. R. Hinings, "An Empirical Taxonomy of Work Organizations," *Administrative Science Quarterly,* 14, No. 1 (March 1969), 115–26.

4. Nascent Workflow Bureaucracy: ". . . show the same characteristics to a less pronounced degree, and are considerably smaller."
5. Preworkflow Bureaucracy: ". . . are considerably lower on scores of structuring of activities, but have the typical workflow–bureaucracy pattern of dispersed authority and impersonal line control."
6. Implicitly Structured Organizations: ". . . have low structuring of activities, dispersed authority, and high line control."
7. Personnel Bureaucracy: ". . . low scores on structuring and high scores on line control . . . high scores on concentration of authority."[37]

This scheme is graphically shown in figure 2-1. The authors suggest that a developmental sequence occurs on two of their dimensions. More highly structured organizations develop as the organizations grow in size over time, and growth in size is in turn related to general economic development. The control dimension tends to move from line control— that is, control exercised by the workflow personnel themselves and their subordinates—to impersonal control. As technology develops, more and more of the control system is passed to "procedures dictated by stan-

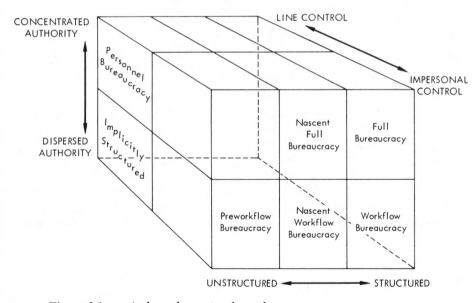

Figure 2-1   A three-dimensional typology

Source: D. S. Pugh, D. J. Hickson, and C. R. Hinings, "An Empirical Taxonomy of Work Organizations," Administrative Science Quarterly, 14, No. 1 (March 1969), 123.

[37] *Ibid.*, pp. 121–23.

dardization and the new specialists who devise the procedures."[38] No such developmental sequence is seen in the case of the concentration of authority; the patterns here are linked to historical factors and the auspices under which the organization operates.

Like the other typologies discussed, this one has problems. The basic problem is that there is no indication of how or why the shifts between types take place. Such shifts would not occur on a random basis or in a vacuum. A second problem is that once the typology is available, what does it predict? What consequences flow from the organization's being one type or another?

This review indicates that attempts to develop typologies have not gotten very far, and one may wonder why the issue was brought up at all. The basic reason was to indicate the difficulties with such classification schemes. The problem is not that they are useless, but that they are not comprehensive. Because it is undoubtedly impossible to develop an inclusive typology, the organizational analyst is forced to utilize whatever classification scheme is *most* useful—that is, the one that will allow the analyst to categorize organizations so that meaningful predictions can be made. For example, if we wished to predict the productivity of professional workers in organizations (engineers, scientists, lawyers, accountants), we would need to know something about the professions involved, since there are differences in work and cognitive styles among the professions. We then would probably want to classify the organizations on the basis of the degree of autonomy from organizational constraint given these workers. For some professionals, a high degree of autonomy is related to high productivity. If our professionals happened to be lawyers, they could be found in *all* of the types of organizations so far discussed.

A usable classification scheme is thus actually a *set* of classification schemes. In some cases, we may want to predict something about the organization itself; in other cases we may want to predict something about the organization's outputs; while in still others we may want to know something about organizational members. Each of these situations requires a separate classification scheme, based on which variables are dependent or independent.

THE VOLUNTARY ORGANIZATION

Most of the discussion thus far has utilized organizations with paid members or employees as the basis. Another set of organizations further confuses the typological (and general theoretical) issue: voluntary or-

38 *Ibid.*, p. 124.

ganizations. These organizations have unclear boundaries, since a person can be a member of many voluntary organizations without ever being active in any of them. Involvement in such organizations can range from revolutionary or missionary zeal to total passivity. The organizations can be huge or minute. To further complicate matters, many voluntary organizations have paid staff members, e.g., labor unions, professional associations, religious organizations, consumer movements, political parties, and so on. When there are paid employees, the paid staff can be treated as in any other organization, except that mobilizing and utilizing volunteers is crucial to the organization's activities.

Voluntary organizations are not a separate type of organization; they are confronted with the same problems as other organizations and share many of the same properties. They do exhibit important differences in certain phases of their activities, since member participation is sporadic and primarily based on the members' varying levels of commitment to the organization. In this sense, Etzioni's distinction becomes critical because "moral" involvement is at the heart of participation in voluntary organizations.

PERSPECTIVES ON ORGANIZATIONS

Most people who deal with organizations, either as practitioners or as analysts, attempt to bring some order to the complexity of the subject by adapting perspectives or theories. The notion of perspectives will be used in the present discussion because "theory" has a specific set of meanings that do not fit our present state of knowledge about organizations.[39]

The development of organizational analyses has generated numerous schools of thought. According to Paul Lawrence and Jay Lorsch, each of these is attributable to the analyst's own experiences in organizations;[40] others link them to variations in training and discipline. Derek Pugh has provided a categorization of these schools that will be the basis for the present discussion.[41] The six approaches are management theory, struc-

[39] According to Paul Davidson Reynolds, *A Primer in Theory Construction* (Indianapolis: The Bobbs-Merrill Company, Inc., 1971), pp. 10–11, there are three meanings of theory: (1) well-supported empirical generalizations or laws, (2) interrelated definitions, axioms, and propositions, and (3) a set of descriptions of causal processes.

[40] Paul R. Lawrence and Jay W. Lorsch, *Organization and Environment: Managing Differentiation and Integration* (Cambridge, Mass.: Harvard Graduate School of Business Administration, 1967), pp. 159–210.

[41] Derek S. Pugh, "Modern Organization Theory: A Psychological and Sociological Study," *Psychological Bulletin*, 66, No. 21 (October 1966), 235–51.

tural theory, group theory, individual theory, technology theory, and economic theory.

Management theory has been largely derived from practicing managers who have attempted to put their experiences on paper for the benefit of other practitioners. The major representatives of this approach are Henri Fayol, Lyndall F. Urwick, Luther Gulick, James Mooney, and Frederick W. Taylor.[42] These writers have offered numerous prescriptions on how organizations ought to be set up for maximum productivity and efficiency. Their major concern has been with principles of specialization, hierarchical arrangements, delegation of authority and responsibility, span of control, and the arrangement of organizational subunits.

Because these authors are concerned with getting the most out of the organization and its employees, they attempt to develop techniques that are applicable to all organizations. They suggest, for example, that "each five to six workers . . . need one first line supervisor; every six first line supervisors, and hence, every forty workers, need one second line supervisor, and so on."[43] Various principles of specialization are offered, such as by purpose, process, clientele, or geographical concentration.

Management theory has been criticized on many grounds. The nature of the specialization within an organization can be affected by the general culture in which the organization is found, the kinds of personnel employed, the availability of personnel, and the restrictions imposed by labor legislation and union contracts. Management theory tends to ignore or oversimplify the motivations of all levels of employees, assuming at one extreme that all manual workers should be viewed as extensions of the machines with which they are working, or, at the other extreme, that higher-level employees should be guided solely by job descriptions. These writers also assume only one type of authority—that based on hierarchical position. The role of expertise is almost totally ignored or is assumed to coincide perfectly with position.

A more basic problem with this approach is highlighted by Pugh:

> The . . . difficulty with management theorists, particularly the common sense ones, is that not being scientists, their statements do not have sufficient precision to enable crucial experiments to be undertaken to test their

---

[42] Henri Fayol, *General and Industrial Management* (London: Sir Isaac Pitman, 1949); Lyndall F. Urwick, *The Elements of Administration* (London: Sir Isaac Pitman, 1947); Luther Gulick and Lyndall F. Urwick, eds., *Papers on the Science of Administration* (New York: Institute of Public Administration, Columbia University, 1937); James D. Mooney and Allan C. Reilly, *Onward Industry!* (New York, Harper & Row, Publishers, 1931); and Frederick W. Taylor, *Principles of Scientific Management* (New York: Harper & Row, Publishers, 1911). Pugh places Taylor in another category, but he is as easily and more traditionally placed here.

[43] Etzioni, *Modern Organizations*, p. 23.

validity. This is their attraction for the layman, since the proverbs appear to be wise and true for all occasions. But scientific statements are precisely *not* true for *all* occasions, and it is an integral part of the process of science to look for occasions for which they are not true. A scientific hypothesis is essentially a falsifiable statement. When the statements of the management theorists are subject to the same scrutiny, and attempts made to operationalize them, it is usually found that they do not stand up to such analysis very well.[44]

Pugh then notes that the proverb, "Increased specialization will lead to greater efficiency," sounds fine, but the basis for specialization remains unspecified.

Etzioni pinpoints the difficulties inherent in this approach when he raises the questions: "Take, for example, building missiles for military use. Should the missile program be assigned to one branch of the armed forces or all three, since missiles can be used on land, sea, and air? Should we have a single missile force because all missile-building requires a common fund of knowledge? Should we build a number of different regional forces because some missiles are built for Europe's defense and some for U.S. defense?"[45]

Thus, while management theorists deal with issues that are central to the understanding of organizations, their treatment is insufficiently based in reality. While the theorists themselves have real experiences that serve as the basis for their own formulations, the generalizability and basis for the formulations are highly suspect. Since management theory is in many ways a very specific form of the closed-system perspective, it suffers from the same weaknesses of that perspective, which will be discussed later.

Structural theorists are the next group identified by Pugh.

Regularities in such activities as task allocation, the exercise of authority, and coordination of function are developed. Such regularities constitute the organization's structure, and sociologists have studied systematic differences in structure related to variations in such factors as the objectives of ownership, geographical location, and technology of manufacture, which produce the characteristic differences in structure of a bank, a hospital, a mass production factory or a local government department.[46]

Weber, of course, is identified most closely with this approach in his discussions of bureaucracy. Later examinations of the extent to which or-

[44] Pugh, "Modern Organization Theory," p. 238.

[45] Etzioni, *Modern Organizations*, p. 24.

[46] Pugh, "Modern Organization Theory," p. 239. The work of Pugh et al., which will be discussed in some detail later, falls in this category for the most part.

ganizations do or do not conform to the bureaucratic model are in the structuralist tradition.

The major problem in the utilization of the structuralist approach appears to be due to historical developments within the field of organizational analysis itself. Many earlier studies that have become "classics" in their own right came to the justified conclusion that when the pure bureaucratic model is applied to real organizations, it leads to a whole series of dysfunctions.[47] These dysfunctions exist at both the organizational and individual behavior levels. In retrospect, it is not surprising that there are differences in power among organizational subunits, that some tasks cannot be organized in the same way as other tasks within the organization, or that individuals may overconform to rules and procedures. If organizational structure is assumed to be based only on the bureaucratic model, the structuralist approach is certainly a dead-end street. If, on the other hand, variations in structure are assumed and the sources of variations can be pinpointed, the structuralist approach remains a relevant component for organizational analysis. Burns and Stalker and Lawrence and Lorsch have demonstrated rather clearly that major differences in structure are related to environmental, technological, and internal considerations.[48] These differences are also related to organizational effectiveness.

Pugh points out that the traditional structuralist approach does not take the individual and his motivations and contributions to the organization into consideration. The individual is assumed to be "programmed into" appropriate organizational behaviors. Here again this may have been the case in the past. Few contemporary analysts ignore the individual. He is considered in conjunction with the other factors that are significant for understanding organizations. Organizational structure is one of these factors.

Using just one structural yardstick, whether it be the bureaucratic model or anything else, is clearly rather futile. At the same time, the past misuse of the structural approach should not result in its dismissal for the present analysis. In the present analysis the structuralist approach will remain as one of the important and powerful tools, because structural regularities are an important contributor to the differences between organizations.

[47] See, for example, Phillip Selznick, *TVA and the Grass Roots* (New York: Harper Torchbook Edition, 1966); Alvin W. Gouldner, *Patterns of Industrial Bureaucracy* (New York: The Free Press, 1954); and Robert K. Merton, "Bureaucratic Structure and Personality."

[48] See Tom Burns and G. M. Stalker, *The Management of Innovation* (London: Tavistock Publications, 1961); and Lawrence and Lorsch, *Organization and Environment.*

Partially as a reaction to an extreme emphasis on structure and partly from its own impetus, the third school of theorists, the *group theorists*, arose. Elton Mayo, who directed the now famous (or infamous, depending on one's point of view) Hawthorne studies, and Kurt Lewin and his associates, who followed up with further research, are most directly responsible for, and advocates of, this approach.[49] The major premise of this set of theorists is that the work group exerts a tremendous amount of influence on individual behavior, overriding both the organizationally based norms and the individual's own predispositions. Some of the principal conclusions from this approach are:

> . . . the amount of work carried out by a worker is determined not by his physical capability but by his social capacity; non-economic rewards are most important in the motivation and satisfaction of workers, who react to their work situations as groups and not as individuals; the leader is not necessarily the person appointed to be in charge, informal leaders can develop who have more power; the effective supervisor is "employee-centered" and not "job-centered," that is, he regards his job as dealing with human beings rather than with the work; communication and participation in decision making are some of the most significant rewards which can be offered to obtain the commitment of the individual.[50]

These findings, which are correct to some degree for all organizations, have been taken as the basis for an overall organizational theory and also for many prescriptions on how managers ought to manage and how organizations ought to organize.[51] But there are several drawbacks to this use. Foremost is the fact that there is contradictory evidence in regard to group bases of behavior as compared with individual or organizational bases for behavior.[52] Under some conditions, the factors that seem to be the major determinants of behavior are the exact opposite of what the group theorists propose. Pugh points out that these theorists

---

[49] See Elton Mayo, *The Human Problems of Industrial Civilization* (New York: The Macmillan Company, 1933); Fritz J. Roethlisberger and William J. Dickson, *Management and the Worker* (Cambridge, Mass.: Harvard University Press, 1939); and Kurt Lewin, "Forces Behind Food Habits and Methods of Change," *Bulletin of the National Research Council*, 108 (1943), 35–65.

[50] Pugh, "Modern Organization Theory," p. 241.

[51] See, for example, Rensis Likert, *New Patterns of Management* (New York: McGraw-Hill Book Company, 1961), and Douglas McGregor, *The Human Side of Enterprise* (New York: McGraw-Hill Book Company, 1960).

[52] For a particularly devastating critique of the major empirical basis for this perspective, see Alex Carey, "The Hawthorne Studies: A Radical Criticism," *American Sociological Review*, 32, No. 3 (June 1967), 403–16.

have ignored the important dimension of power in organizational rela-tionships.[53] The evidence used as the basis of the approach comes largely from case studies, and these case studies, according to Lawrence and Lorsch, have generally been carried out in organizations that would pro-vide support for the group theorists' perspective.[54] The group theorists argue that organizational theory ought to be built around the concept of the group and its effects on the individual and on his behavior in the organization. The group and the processes of group interaction become tools for better organizations, management, and, in the long run, society, according to this perspective. But because this approach ignores many other highly salient factors, it cannot stand alone as an organizational theory. But the findings of the research and the perspective taken do contribute to our overall understanding of organizations and thus must be incorporated in any form of systematic overview that is taken.

The next set of theorists is also concerned with the individual—in this case, as an individual. Pugh labels as *individual theorists* those who focus their major concern upon the individual and his predispositions, reac-tions, and personality within the organizational setting.[55] A basic issue in such an approach is what view of personality is taken. On the one hand are those of a psychoanalytical bent who see organizations as staffed by members with varying kinds of relationships to their parents, and who, acting in a continual state of development, behave in organizations on the basis of their individual predispositions alone. Others, such as Mas-low and Herzberg, view the organization as a means of providing the individual with a set of rewards of varying levels of satisfaction, with the implication that organizations should continually attempt to provide members with the highest (self-growth and self-development) level of motivation and reward possible.[56] While these and other such approaches

[53] Pugh, "Modern Organization Theory," p. 241.

[54] Lawrence and Lorsch, *Organization and Environment*, pp. 179–82. This is not meant to imply that the researchers "stacked" their data. It rather represents the kinds of organizations that are receptive to research by university-based scholars.

[55] See Chris Argyris, *Understanding Organizational Behavior* (Homewood, Ill.: Dorsey Press, 1960); *Integrating the Individual and the Organization* (New York: John Wiley & Sons, Inc., 1964); and "Personality and Organization Theory Revisited," *Administrative Science Quarterly*, 18, No. 2 (June 1973), 141–67. Barnard, *Functions of the Executive*, could also be placed in this category. Much of this writing could also be placed under the "management theory" rubric, again indicating the difficul-ties and overlap inherent in attempts to classify multidisciplinary approaches to or-ganizations.

[56] See Frederick Herzberg, Bernard Mausner, and Barbara Snyderman, *The Moti-vation to Work* (New York: John Wiley & Sons, Inc., 1959); and Abraham H. Mas-low, *Eupsychian Management* (Homewood, Ill.: Richard D. Irwin, Inc., 1956).

to individual personality contain elements of plausibility, they have not been sufficiently documented with empirical evidence to allow their total acceptance as the final theory of personality. More important for our purposes, they obviously ignore or totally discount the impact of organizational, wider societal, and, generally, even group influences on individual behavior.

The work of March and Simon, a modern classic in the field of organizations, utilizes the individual perspective. They regard the organization as a set of individuals engaged in the decision-making process. While they recognize the importance of organizational constraints on the decision-making process, their framework is built around individual motivations. Their important discussion of the "cognitive limits on rationality" is at the individual psychological level, with important organizational modifiers such as hierarchical and task differentiation.[57] The potential from such an approach is great. It has not been realized to its fullest because of the absence of an empirically grounded set of psychological principles around which individual behavior can be organized. Nevertheless, any total analysis of organizations must include the individual human element. Too frequently, sociologists tend to assume that individual differences are randomly distributed and therefore do not matter in their analyses. The viewpoint taken here is that they do in fact matter. Although the focus will not be psychological and there will be little mention of the individual as an individual, the impact of different types of individuals will be included in the perspective developed. In our discussion of types of individuals, the primary focus will be on occupational types, and differences will be considered within a narrow range of variation. Since there is not yet a firm basis on which to align individual differences, it seems appropriate to note that they do exist and make a difference, but not to try to account for every possible individual permutation.

The next perspective is represented by the *technology theorists*. Much of the gist of this approach will be discussed later, with the implication that technology is a major factor in the development and form of organizations. Technology is part of the environment, in that organizations can bring technological developments into their systems.[58] It is also part of the internal system of the organization. Woodward's work graphically illustrates the influence of differing forms of technological systems on organizational structure. Thompson's concern with the "core technology" of the organization also emphasizes the importance of this variable, as

---

[57] March and Simon, *Organizations*, pp. 136–71.
[58] See Lawrence and Lorsch, *Organization and Environment*.

does Perrow's analytical framework.[59] As would be expected, technology will be included as a component of the perspective to be advanced here. It cannot be given a primary position in the analysis, however, since technology is in interaction with organizational structure, group structure, individual factors, and so on. The work of Trist and his associates has demonstrated that the technical system of an organization interacts with the ongoing social system.[60] In their studies of coal mining operations, these researchers from the Tavistock Institute conclude that a changed technical system does not immediately alter the organization. Its effect is moderated by what has existed before. The introduction of a similar technological change in an organization with a different basis would have different results. From this standpoint, technology will be a major determinant of the nature of organizations, but not *the* determinant.

The final set of theorists considered by Pugh is that of the *economic theorists*. Their approach typically uses business firms as its basis, but the ideas can be extended to other organizational forms. The basic premise in this perspective is that the organization is an active participant in the economic process, seeking to enhance its position and make economically sound (rational) decisions. Much of the work in this area is an attempt to specify how economically rational decisions can be made under conditions of psychological and sociological variations.[61]

Despite the fact that it is based on simulation models that lack empirical verification,[62] the approach is valuable because it forces the organizational analyst, and particularly the sociologist, to pay attention to economic factors. At face value, economic factors are important to organizations simply as necessary for survival, but they are too often ignored in organizational analyses. It is true that we have no clear understanding of the exact role that economic factors play. If too much attention is given to such factors, many of the dangers of an overly rational view of organizations come into play. If they are ignored, an important component is eliminated. Again, additional information is needed.

Although each of the six perspectives discussed so far has something of importance to say about organizations, none is completely usable by

---

[59] By "core technology," Thompson means the operations within the organization, or what the organization does, regardless of its nature.

[60] E. L. Trist and K. W. Bamforth, "Some Social and Psychological Consequences of the Longwall Method of Goal-Getting," *Human Relations*, 4, No. 1 (February 1951), 3–38; and F. E. Emery and E. L. Trist, "The Causal Texture of Organizational Environments," *Human Relations*, 18, No. 1 (February 1965), 21–32.

[61] See Richard M. Cyert and James G. March, *A Behavioral Theory of the Firm* (Englewood Cliffs, N.J.: Prentice-Hall, Inc., 1963).

[62] Pugh, "Modern Organization Theory," p. 247.

itself. These perspectives can be combined into two inclusive perspectives. These two overriding perspectives can then be combined into the single perspective on which the analysis that follows will be based.

TWO INCLUSIVE PERSPECTIVES

Organizations can be approached from a *closed-* or *open-*system perspective.[63] The closed-system model views organizations as instruments designed for the pursuit of clearly specified goals, and thus directing organizational arrangements and decisions toward goal achievement and toward making the organization more and more rational in the pursuit of its goals (management, structural, and aspects of economic theory). The open-system model (technology, group, individual, and some aspects of economic theory) views organizations as not only concerned with goals, but as also responding to external and internal pressures. In some cases, the open perspective virtually ignores the issue of goals.

THE ORGANIZATION AS A CLOSED SYSTEM

The closed-system perspective is traditionally tied to Max Weber's early writings on bureaucracy. While Weber has been overly criticized for ignoring factors that would deflect an organization from a pure closed system, much of his writing is concerned with how organizations can structure themselves for the utmost rationality.

Weber's ideal type of bureaucracy is one in which the goals and purposes are clear and explicit. Organizational rules, procedures, and regulations are derived from the goals in a manner that says in effect, "If this is the goal, then, this is the most rational procedure for achieving it." The tasks to be performed in the achievement of this goal are subdivided among the members of the organization so that each member has a limited sphere of activity that is matched to his own competence. Offices (positions) are arranged in a pyramidal hierarchy, with each office having more authority than those below it. Decision making is based upon officially established rules and criteria that are attached to the position. If a decision is required that is beyond the realm of a position at a particular level, it is passed up to the next level. Members participate in the organization on the basis of contractual (written or otherwise) agreements, and the participation is based upon remuneration, typically in the

---

[63] This distinction and terminology follows Thompson, *Organizations in Action*, pp. 4–7.

form of a wage or salary. (Voluntary organizations are obviously another matter. They have not been examined carefully from this perspective.) The person fills the office or position, so that in an important way it does not matter who the person is, since his behavior is guided by the organizationally established normative order. Selection for membership is based on the person's technical competence—the combination of the individual's skills and the requirements of the position determining who shall be employed and in what position. Interpersonal relationships are maintained on an impersonal basis, so that socio-emotional elements do not intrude into organizational operations.

It has been demonstrated that these elements do not appear together in reality.[64] It is also clear that this is too limited a perspective on organizations from any other bases as well. Nonetheless, this approach to organizations persists in the literature. An example is Jerald Hage's attempt to develop an "axiomatic theory of organizations."[65] The variables selected for inclusion in the theory and the indicators used to measure these variables reflect a closed-system approach, although Hage's other work does not take a closed-system view of the world.

Hage considers four organizational ends or goals.[66] The first is adaptiveness, or flexibility, and is to be measured by the number of new programs per year and the number of new techniques adopted per year. Flexibility in other contexts usually refers to adaptation to external influences or other disturbing factors, and Hage suggests that environmental influences are important. At the same time, however, new programs and new techniques can be developed on the basis of internal considerations. The second organizational end is production, or effectiveness, measured by the number of units produced per year and the rate of increase in the number of units produced per year. This is clearly an internal consideration. The third goal is efficiency, or the cost factor, and is measured by the cost per unit of output per year and the amount of idle resources per year. The final end is job satisfaction, or morale. This is measured by the employees' satisfaction with working conditions and by the turnover rate of job occupants per year. These ends involve more than just output; basically, they reflect internal organizational factors, with only minimal concern paid to external considerations. They are also part of a con-

[64] See Richard H. Hall, "The Concept of Bureaucracy: An Empirical Assessment," *American Journal of Sociology*, 69, No. 1 (July 1963), 32–40.

[65] Jerald Hage, "An Axiomatic Theory of Organizations," *Administrative Science Quarterly*, 10, No. 3 (December 1965), 289–320.

[66] *Ibid.*, p. 293.

ceptual model that views the organization as a system in and of itself. The "closedness" of this approach is emphasized when the means to these ends are discussed. Hage gives four organizational means.[67] The first is complexity, or specialization, which is measured by the number of occupational specialties and the level of training required for them. Complexity is necessary because "organizations must divide work into jobs in order to achieve their specific objectives." This statement is, of course, extremely close to Weber's position. The second means is centralization, or hierarchy of authority, and is measured by the proportion of occupations or jobs whose holders participate in decision making and the number of areas in which they participate. The third means is formalization, or standardization, measured as the number of jobs that are codified and the range of variation allowed within jobs. The final means is stratification, or the status system. This is measured by the differences in income and prestige among jobs and the rate of mobility between low- and high-ranking jobs or status levels. As might be expected, these means are totally internal to the organization.

From these ends and means, Hage develops a set of propositions and corollaries, indicated in Table 2-1. Whether these are empirically valid is not the issue at this point. What is important is the perspective taken that organizations can be understood on the basis of these basically internal factors. As we shall demonstrate, many of the factors that Hage labels as means are in fact related. The ends part of the equation is probably too internally oriented to satisfy most organizational analysts. Nevertheless, Hage's supporting evidence is strong and provides partial substantiation for the propositions and corollaries he derives. Undoubtedly, however, factors other than the means and ends discussed have an effect on them, and thus while the theory is axiomatic, it is also incomplete.

Organizations are not closed systems for the sake of being closed systems. It is at this point that the idea of rationality within the closed system must be introduced. The closed-system perspective is a way of approaching and optimizing organizational rationality—linking means to ends. Thompson captures the essence of this point when he notes, "The rational model of an organization results in everything being functional —making a positive, indeed an optimum, contribution to the overall result. All resources are appropriate resources, and their allocation fits a master plan. All action is appropriate action, and its outcomes are predictable."[68]

[67] *Ibid.*, pp. 293–94.
[68] Thompson, *Organizations in Action*, p. 6.

TABLE 2-1   MAJOR PROPOSITIONS AND COROLLARIES OF THE THEORY

Major Propositions:

   I. The higher the centralization, the higher the production.
  II. The higher the formalization, the higher the efficiency.
 III. The higher the centralization, the higher the formalization.
  IV. The higher the stratification, the lower the job satisfaction.
   V. The higher the stratification, the higher the production.
  VI. The higher the stratification, the lower the adaptiveness.
 VII. The higher the complexity, the lower the centralization.

Derived Corollaries:

   1. The higher the formalization, the higher the production.
   2. The higher the centralization, the higher the efficiency.
   3. The lower the job satisfaction, the higher the production.
   4. The lower the job satisfaction, the lower the adaptiveness.
   5. The higher the production, the lower the adaptiveness.
   6. The higher the complexity, the lower the production.
   7. The higher the complexity, the lower the formalization.
   8. The higher the production, the higher the efficiency.
   9. The higher the stratification, the higher the formalization.
  10. The higher the efficiency, the lower the complexity.
  11. The higher the centralization, the lower the job satisfaction.
  12. The higher the centralization, the lower the adaptiveness.
  13. The higher the stratification, the lower the complexity.
  14. The higher the complexity, the higher the job satisfaction.
  15. The lower the complexity, the lower the adaptiveness.
  16. The higher the stratification, the higher the efficiency.
  17. The higher the efficiency, the lower the job satisfaction.
  18. The higher the efficiency, the lower the adaptiveness.
  19. The higher the centralization, the higher the stratification.
  20. The higher the formalization, the lower the job satisfaction.
  21. The higher the formalization, the lower the adaptiveness.

Limits Proposition:

VIII. Production imposes limits on complexity, centralization, formalization,
      stratification, adaptiveness, efficiency, and job satisfaction.

Source: Jerald Hage, "An Axiomatic Theory of Organizations," Administrative
Science Quarterly, *10, No. 3 (December 1965), 300.*

A CRITIQUE OF THE CLOSED-SYSTEM PERSPECTIVE

Approached from a purely rational viewpoint, the organization must
make a perfect link between ends and means. In the closed-system per-

spective, it can do so internally; it can arrange itself so that the conditions Thompson suggests can be achieved. But obviously, this is more easily said than done. In developing his critique of the rational model, Thompson says that in order to be as rational as possible, organizations must "buffer" themselves from environmental influences, anticipate those environmental changes that cannot be buffered against, and ration their resources when the environmental influences cannot be controlled.[69] This suggests strongly that *organizations are forced to move away from a purely rational model.* It also brings up the importance of environmental factors as they impinge upon the organization, a point that will be taken up shortly.

Organizations must grapple with their environment. In addition, there are two "internal" factors that cast doubt on the utility of a closed-systems perspective. The first of these internal factors is the failure of the organizational characteristics that are supposed to vary together or to characterize rational organizations to do so. Stanley H. Udy, Jr., found that "rational" and "bureaucratic" elements of organizations tended to "be mutually inconsistent in the same formal organization."[70] The presence of a hierarchy or a specialized administrative staff was not related to a performance emphasis or other indicators of an emphasis on goal attainment. Udy's data came from 150 nonindustrial societies. In a study of contemporary organizations, Hall found that the elements within organizations that were supposed to be arranged in a neat, harmonious fashion instead had weak and negative relationships with each other.[71] Both sets of findings suggest that the patterning found within organizations is based on more than conditions internal to organizations.

The second factor internal to the organization that throws doubt on the total utility of the closed-system approach is the nature of the organizational members themselves. The closed-system approach tends to assume that people will act in accordance with the organization's desires. Most of the time, this is probably the case. However, there is enough deviation from norm and role expectations to expose as extremely naive the idea that organizational members are well-oiled machines.

The James March and Herbert Simon discussion of the shortcomings of viewing humans as machines in a closed-system perspective has become a classic in the field.[72] March and Simon note that an individual must be motivated to participate and produce in the organizational setting. The individual is confronted with a series of action alternatives that

---

[69] *Ibid.*, p. 19.

[70] Stanley H. Udy, Jr., " 'Bureaucracy' and 'Rationality' in Weber's Organization Theory," *American Sociological Review*, 24, No. 6 (December 1959), 794.

[71] Hall, "Concept of Bureaucracy."

[72] March and Simon, *Organizations*, pp. 34–171.

he could pursue. Each of these alternatives has consequences for the individual, and the consequences in turn are valued differentially by the individual. These values are affected by the identification patterns of the individual. For instance, there can be work group identity, which may or may not have values that coincide with those of the organization. The individual is also confronted with the dynamics of the group, perhaps in a situation in which competition is required by the organization or develops on its own. In either case, individual behavior is different from what it would be under conditions of cooperation.

At the same time, the individual has external sources of identification, such as family, union, or professional organization. The literature on professionals in organizations strongly suggests that membership in a profession influences the individual employed in an organization.[73] Professional values are brought into the organization, and if the organization wants the professional to do something that is in violation of professional norms and values, the professional is apt to reject or substantially alter the organizational requirements. Professionals or trade union members are usually in the "enviable" position of being able to leave an organization for another very readily, because there are probably many other organizations ready and willing to pay for their services.

The organization member can also identify with the organization itself. This is fine, but only up to a point. If it is carried too far, or if the identification is with organizational means and not ends, it can be dysfunctional for the organization as well as for the individual. Merton's concept of the bureaucratic personality, with its rigid adherence to rules, inflexibility with clients, and unadaptability, and Victor Thompson's concept of "bureaupathology," with many of the same characteristics, are indicative of the manner in which overadherence to and identification with organizational means can deflect the individual from the behavior that is most beneficial to the organization.[74]

March and Simon also point out that there are limits to individual cognitive abilities, thus limiting the extent of rational decisions in or out of the organizational context. March and Simon propose that decisions are *satisficing* rather than optimal.[75] That is, given human limitations, even when assisted by computers, the decisions that are made in an or-

[73] See, for example, William Kornhauser, *Scientists in Industry* (Berkeley: University of California Press, 1963); *Administrative Science Quarterly*, 10, No. 1 (June 1965), entire issue; and Eliot Freidson, ed., *The Professions and their Prospects* (Beverly Hills, Calif.: Sage Publications, 1973).

[74] Robert K. Merton, "Bureaucratic Structure and Personality," *Social Forces*, 18, No. 4 (May 1940), 560–68; and Victor Thompson, *Modern Organizations* (New York: Alfred A. Knopf, Inc., 1961), pp. 152–77.

[75] March and Simon, *Organizations*, pp. 140–41.

ganization are not as optimal as they would be if humans had access to, and the ability to interpret, all relevant information before making a decision. The norm of rationality itself cannot therefore be viewed as a set standard, but rather as a guideline from which deviation is expected.

The criticism of the closed-system perspective thus far has concentrated on factors that limit its utility from within the organization. As implied earlier, the major problem with this approach is that it tends to ignore external considerations. Katz and Kahn state:

> The major misconception is the failure to recognize fully that the organization is continually dependent upon inputs from the environment and that the inflow of materials and human energy is not constant. The fact that organizations have built-in protective devices to maintain stability and that they are notoriously difficult to change should not obscure the realities of the dynamic interrelationships of any social structure with its social and natural environment. The very efforts of the organization to maintain a constant external environment produce changes in organizational structure. The reactions to changed inputs to mute their possible revolutionary implications also results in changes.[76]

Katz and Kahn go on to note that there are additional misconceptions inherent in the closed-system model. They mention that there are more ways than one to produce a given outcome, and thus internal arrangements could vary rather widely to give rise to a common end. They also suggest that it is erroneous to view environmental influences as "error variances."[77] The environmental factors cannot be controlled in research or practice. Further, the closed-system approach ignores the importance of feedback for the information system of an organization.

Experience and practice in organizations indicate that the environment *does* play a major role in what happens within an organization. Since both input and output are directly related to the environment and are major components in any analysis, the closed-system perspective is, almost by definition, inadequate for a comprehensive understanding of organizations. From an empirical standpoint, too little of the variance within organizations is explained by internal factors. But despite all these shortcomings, the perspective persists in the literature and in practice, apparently for the reason that the closed-system approach does explain some of what organizations do. Organizations do try to maximize rationality, even if they are aware that they can attain only "satisficing" decisions. They do try to buffer, level, and smooth out environmental

[76] Katz and Kahn, *Social Psychology of Organizations*, p. 26.
[77] *Ibid.*, p. 27.

fluctuations. Since organizational actions are at least partially based on a closed-system perspective, it is a necessary component of the organizational analyst's repertoire, even though he recognizes that the technique will not be totally successful. Furthermore, the relationships found by Udy and Hall and suggested by Hage, whether positive or negative, are relationships. That is, an increase or decrease in the intensity of one internal factor is related to an increase or decrease in the intensity of another. Whether the source of the change is internal or external to the organization is thus irrelevant if the relationship is predictable. Predictable relationships are a prerequisite for theory or practice. The closed-system perspective would seem to be a similar prerequisite for the insights provided by other perspectives. With this in mind, let us examine the open-system perspective.

THE ORGANIZATION AS AN OPEN SYSTEM

The distinction between the closed- and open-system approaches to organizations has its modern roots in the work of Alvin Gouldner. Gouldner distinguished between the "rational" and the "natural-system" models of organizations, the terms largely corresponding to our closed- and open-system perspectives, respectively. Gouldner describes the open-, or natural-, system approach as follows:

> The natural-system model regards the organization as a "natural whole," or system. The realization of the goals of the system as a whole is but one of several important needs to which the organization is oriented.[78]

One of these important needs is survival, which can lead to neglect or distortion of goal-seeking behavior. Organizational changes are seen as relatively unplanned, adaptive responses to threats to organizational equilibrium. The organization is seen as emergent, with organizational goals playing a relatively minor role in the directions in which the organization emerges. The natural-system approach also stresses the interdependence of the parts of organizations, noting that even a planned change in one part will have important, and usually unanticipated, ramifications for the rest of the system.

Gouldner's major concern is with developments within the organization that deflect it from the rational model. In a sense, this approach still views the organization as a closed system, since the emphasis is on de-

[78] Gouldner, "Organizational Analysis," p. 405.

velopments and attempts to maintain homeostatic conditions within the organization. Gouldner hints at the importance of environmental factors but does not develop this consideration very far. From studies such as Michel Crozier's analysis of two French organizations, it is clear that the *general environment* surrounding an organization has a tremendous impact on how it is structured and operated, as well as on the goals it purports to seek.[79] The role of *other organizations* on the behavior of a focal organization has been clearly documented in the analyses of William Evan, J. Kenneth Benson, Howard Aldrich, Sol Levine and Paul White, and others.[80] Organizations are confronted from inside and outside with conditions that lead to the "natural" forms of development described by Gouldner. Survival is thus based on adaptation to both internal and external forces.

The open-system perspective has been more fully developed in the work of Katz and Kahn. They suggest nine common characteristics shared by all open systems:

1. *The importation of energy.* New supplies of energy are brought into the organization in the form of people and materials. This energy is supplied by other organizations or the general environment.
2. *The throughput.* This is simply the work that is done in the system (organization). The input is altered in some way as materials are processed or people are served.
3. *The output.* Whatever emerges from an organization is utilized, consumed, rejected, etc., by the environment.

---

[79] Michel Crozier, *The Bureaucratic Phenomenon* (Chicago: The University of Chicago Press, 1964).

[80] William M. Evan, "The Organization-Set," in James D. Thompson, ed., *Approaches to Organizational Design* (Pittsburgh: University of Pittsburgh Press, 1966), pp. 173–91; J. Kenneth Benson, "The Interorganizational Network as a Political Economy," *Administrative Science Quarterly*, 20, No. 2 (June 1975), 229–49; Howard Aldrich, "An Organization-Environment Perspective on Cooperation and Conflict between Organizations in the Manpower Training System" in Anant Negandhi, ed., *Conflict and Power in Complex Organizations* (Kent, Ohio: Center for Business and Economic Research, Kent State University, 1972). See also Eugene Litwak and Lydia F. Hylton, "Interorganizational Analysis," *Administrative Science Quarterly*, 6, No. 4 (March 1962), 395–420; Sol Levine and Paul White, "Exchange and Interorganizational Relationships," *Administrative Science Quarterly*, 5, No. 4 (March 1961), 583–601. See also Burton R. Clark, "Interorganizational Patterns in Education," *Administrative Science Quarterly*, 10, No. 2 (September 1965), 224–37; Harold Guetzkow, "Relations Among Organizations," in Raymond V. Bowers, ed., *Studies on Behavior in Organizations: A Research Symposium* (Athens, Ga.: University of Georgia Press, 1966), pp. 13–44; and Roland L. Warren, "The Interorganizational Field as a Focus for Investigation," *Administrative Science Quarterly*, 12, No. 3 (December 1967), 369–419.

4. *Systems as cycles of events.* Products sent into the environment are the basis for the source of energy for the repeating of the event. Industry uses labor and materials to produce a product that is sold. The income derived is used to buy more materials and labor. The voluntary organization can do something for its members that leads them to continue to contribute energy to the organization. In both cases the importation of new energy into the organization triggers a new cycle. Each cycle may be composed of subsystems or be a part of a larger system. At the same time, the cycles themselves are affected by changes in the total system.

5. *Negative entropy.* Organizations attempt to import more energy than they expend. Energy can be stockpiled to avoid the condition of using more energy than is imported. (The latter situation leads to organizational death.)

6. *Information input, negative feedback, and the coding process.* The information coming into an organization is coded and selected so that the organization is not inundated with more than it requires. Information provides signals from the environment, and negative feedback indicates deviations from what the environment desires. It is a control mechanism.

7. *The steady state and dynamic homeostasis.* Systems tend to maintain their basic character, attempting to control threatening external factors. As growth and expansion occur, basic system characteristics tend to remain constant. Under conditions of extreme growth or expansion, a new character may develop that will serve as a new homeostatic basis.

8. *Differentiation.* There is a tendency toward elaboration of roles and specialization of function.

9. *Equifinality.* Multiple means to the same ends exist within organizations. As knowledge increases, the number of relevant means may be reduced, but there will still be more than one way to accomplish objectives.[81]

The Katz and Kahn approach is built around the general systems model that is finding favor in many disciplines.[82] Although some of the terminology and concepts are obviously difficult to operationalize and use, the development of their system demonstrates the essence of the open-system approach. Organizations are affected by what comes into them in the form of input, by what transpires inside the organization, and by the nature of the environmental acceptance of the organization and its output. Understanding organizations involves much more than understanding goals and the arrangements that are developed for their accomplishment. At a later point, we will consider in depth the nature of the

[81] Katz and Kahn, *Social Psychology of Organizations,* pp. 19–26.
[82] See Walter Buckley, *Sociology and Modern Systems Theory* (Englewood Cliffs, N.J.: Prentice-Hall, Inc., 1967); and Walter Buckley, ed., *Modern Systems Research for the Behavioral Scientist* (Chicago: Aldine Publishing Company, 1968).

impact on organizations of both internally and externally based influences. Meanwhile, we must recognize the open-system perspective for its relevance in directly specifying these elements as important for organizational analysis.

A CRITIQUE OF THE OPEN-SYSTEM PERSPECTIVE

The open-system model is obviously much broader in its conceptual scope than is the closed-system approach. This breadth is vital for better understanding and operation of organizations. At the same time, as Etzioni suggests, the model is much more "exacting and expensive" when used for research.[83] Few researchers have the tools or the ability to take into account all the various components that must be included in even a relatively simple open-system model. The measurement of the various forms of inputs and the consequences of outputs has not been even moderately developed. For the practitioner, a full utilization of the model involves comprehending and evaluating the multiple factors that impinge upon his organization. March and Simon have stated that decision making in organizations is based on "bounded rationality." When the full implications of the open-system perspective are taken into consideration, the bounds on rationality become even more apparent.

The open-system perspective suggests that rationality within organizations is, or can be, drastically impaired and also that events occur without organizational intent—that interaction patterns, norms, and structure show tendencies to grow in number and complexity beyond what is foreseen or intended for the "official," formal system. A total acceptance of the open-system approach, especially as proposed by Gouldner, would make it appear that there is actually little need for organizations at all, since things just seem to happen. Rather obviously, this is too extreme a position. The very nature of organizations signifies that they do accomplish certain things. They do alter their inputs and produce outputs and make decisions; and these things are done on a relatively predictable and relatively stable basis. The Katz and Kahn notion of cycles of action suggests that organizational work is not composed of random actions. A basic question therefore is: Can the open-system and the closed-system perspectives be reconciled? Can the insights provided by each be combined in some way to yield more insights than does either perspective taken alone? At least partial answers to these questions are provided by James Thompson's work.

Thompson develops a set of propositions that describe how organiza-

---

[83] Etzioni, *Modern Organizations*, p. 17.

tions act (or should act), given the fact of external and internal constraints on rationality. These propositions specify what organizations can do, in the face of threats to rationality, to stay as rational as possible. For example, "The more sectors in which the organization subject to rationality norms is constrained, the more power the organization will seek over remaining sectors of its task environment."[84] If an organization is constrained in one area, it will seek to reduce constraints in others, giving it more power in the total system than if it did not make such an attempt. For example, during an inflationary cycle, an organization with rising costs will seek power to increase its income through raising the prices for its goods and services. This is essentially a trade-off situation. The organization that is unable to gain power in other sectors and is thus totally dominated by the situation around it cannot operate in a rational manner. Most organizations have areas in which they can operate at their own discretion and therefore can subject themselves to the norm of rationality.

Thompson develops similar propositions about most areas of organizational operations. The content of these propositions is subject to empirical verification, but for our purposes, it does not really matter if the propositions are valid or not. What is important is that they form a basis for bringing the insights of the closed- and open-system approaches together. In essence, *organizations attempt to be rational, controlling their internal operations and environment to the greatest extent possible, but never achieving a totally closed, rational system.* How well the organization achieves rationality depends upon the strength of the internal and external pressures and the organization's capability of control.

In the next section, the perspective that serves as the basis for the balance of the analysis will be presented. It contains elements of the closed and open perspectives, but puts both within a single analytical framework.

A CONTINGENCY–CHOICE PERSPECTIVE

To derive a perspective by which the actions of organizations can be understood, three factors must be taken into account: the individuals within the organization; the environment of the organization; and the form of the organization. The basic assumption of the perspective is Thompson's, namely that organizations try to behave rationally in the

---

[84] J. Thompson, *Organizations in Action*, p. 32. The concept of task environment was first proposed by William R. Dill to indicate those components of the environment that are significant or potentially significant for goal setting and goal attainment. The task environment, according to Dill, includes customers, suppliers, competitors, and regulatory groups. See Dill, "Environment as an Influence on Managerial Autonomy," *Administrative Science Quarterly*, 2, No. 4 (March 1958), 409–43.

face of multiple conflicting pressures, and thus attempt to control those aspects of their existence, both internal and external, that pose threats to rational actions.[85]

In this perspective the concern with individuals within the organization is limited to those of their actions that have organizational relevance; the individual is seen as the mechanism through which environmental and organizational characteristics are shaped. Karl Weick states: "Rather than talking about adapting to an external environment, it may be more correct to argue that organizing consists of adapting to an enacted environment, an environment which is *constituted* by the actions of interdependent human actors."[86] How individuals conceptualize what is happening in the environment around their organization is critical to how the organization then responds or does not respond. It is critical to note that the responses of the individuals are shaped and even determined by their position within an organization. An individual has a distinct rank and a position within the organization. Ranks and positions are not equal in their power or access to power and it is thus the perceptions of the organizational elite or key decision makers (plus the perceptions of those who are in a position to observe and interpret organizationally relevant information and pass it on to the elite) that are critical to the operations of the organization.

The perceived environment is not the same for all organizations. In some cases it is stable and highly predictable; in other cases it is fluid, changing, and almost impossible to understand. This is why "contingency" is a component of the perspective. Organizations attempt to "fit" their structure and processes to the perceived environment.[87] The form of the organization is thus contingent upon the environment.

---

[85] James Thompson, *Organizations in Action.*

[86] Karl Weick, *The Social Psychology of Organizing* (Reading, Mass.: Addison-Wesley Publishing Co., 1969), p. 27. David Silverman, *The Theory of Organizations: A Sociological Framework* (New York: Basic Books, 1971), also uses this basic framework, but emphasizes the differences among the shared definitions of the situation within organizations.

[87] This approach is most closely associated with the work of Lawrence and Lorsch, *Organization and Environment.* The conclusions are based on their own research on business organizations and on the work of Tom Burns and G. M. Stalker, *The Management of Innovation* (London: Tavistock Publications, 1961); Joan Woodward, *Management and Technology* (London: Her Majesty's Printing Office, 1958); and others. Henry Tosi, Ramon Aldag, and Ronald Storey, "On the Measurement of the Environment: An Assessment of the Lawrence and Lorsch Environmental Subscale," *Administrative Science Quarterly*, 18, No. 1 (March 1973), 27–36, have criticized Lawrence and Lorsch's measurement of the degree of environmental uncertainty that organizations face, but the thrust of their findings continues to be replicated. See, for example, Anant R. Negandhi and Bernard C. Reimann, "A Contingency Theory of Organization Re-examined in the Context of a Developing Coun-

As will be demonstrated in later chapters, the forms that organizations take vary rather systematically with environmental constraints, so that the organization must be viewed as a responding entity. The organization also attempts to manipulate the environment to its own advantage, whether in such indirect ways as advertising and public relations, or through direct manipulations of political and economic events, as when attempts are made to ensure that political parties are maintained in office or supplies of raw materials are guaranteed through legal or illegal acquisitions of sources of supply.

The technique by which organizations respond to their environments depends upon the choices made within the organization; John Child calls these the "strategic choices."[88] Child argues that the internal politics of organizations determine the structural forms, the manipulation of environmental features, and the choice of relevant performance standards that are selected by the organization. The internal politics in turn depend upon the power distributions within the organization, which are themselves a structural condition subject to alteration over time.

While it is clear that such strategic choices are made as a response to the environment and to internal conditions, the number of available alternative responses by the organization is limited. Katz and Kahn suggest that organizational systems are characterized by "equifinality," or the possibility of several means available to achieve the organization's goals. The range of means available through strategic choice mechanisms is limited by the environmental constraints, the perceptual and cognitive predispositions of organizational decision makers, and the existing form of the organization, which limits the possible organizational response patterns.

Rationality is still a key factor in the contingency–choice perspective. Organizations attempt to make their structure and operations rational by their strategic choices in regard to the environment. When the organization is threatened, the strength of the threat must be evaluated.[89] It is one thing if a few consumers are angry at an organization, but quite another when national consumer groups publish widely read attacks on an organization's product or service, and still another—and worse one—when legis-

---

try," *Academy of Management Journal,* 15, No. 2 (June 1972), 137–46; Peter M. Blau and Richard A. Schoenherr, *The Structure of Organizations* (New York: Basic Books, 1971, especially Chapters 6–8); and Johannes M. Pennings, "The Relevance of the Structural Contingency Model for Organizational Effectiveness," *Administrative Science Quarterly,* 20, No. 3 (September 1975), 393–407.

[88] John Child, "Organization Structure, Environment, and Performance: The Role of Strategic Choice," *Sociology,* 6, No. 1 (January 1972), 1–22.

[89] When decisions between alternative goals within the organization are made, the power process is also operative. See Aaron Wildavsky, *The Politics of the Budgetary Process* (Boston: Little, Brown and Company, 1964), for a discussion of the political processes involved in determining federal budgets.

lation is pending that would severely regulate an organization in the private sector or eliminate an organization in the public sector. Thus, firms in the petroleum industry fight legislation that would prohibit offshore oil exploration, and government agencies fight policies that would eliminate them or absorb them into another agency. Ironically, organizations such as airlines fight the deregulation of their market. Such deregulation is seen as a severe threat to their stable environment.

The perspective that has been derived, therefore, is that organizations do operate generally under norms of rationality. Under pure rationality norms, the organization's energies would be deployed as illustrated in figure 2-2. Since it has been amply demonstrated in the discussion that

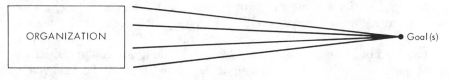

Figure 2-2   Deployment of organizational structure and processes under pure rationality model

both external and internal considerations lead to a deflection from the closed rational system, organizations under most conditions will deploy themselves in the manner indicated in figure 2–3. Under severe external threat, the deployment will be in the form indicated in figure 2–4. The power of the external and internal pressures and threats is the key variable. Unfortunately, there are no available systematic measures of the power of such threats. The perceived severity of the threat is a key to the decision making within the organization. The decision-making process itself is carried out under less than fully rational conditions.

Figure 2-3 indicates how organizations actually operate under most conditions. The figure is truncated, in that it ignores the transactions at

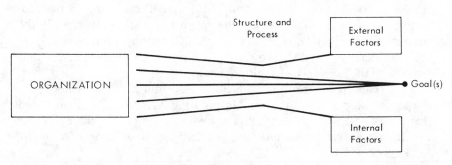

Figure 2-3   Deployment of organizational structure and processes under typical open system model

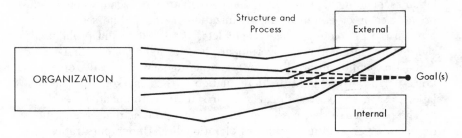

Figure 2-4   Deployment of organizational structure and processes under powerful threat conditions (external)

the organization's input and output ends and the feedback mechanisms from these transactions, as well as the power-distribution and decision-making processes within the organization itself—all of which are important factors. Nevertheless, figures 2-3 and 2-4 do illustrate the distillation of the perspectives that have been discussed and that will be followed in the analysis.

A NOTE ON RATIONALITY

The contingency–choice perspective emphasizes that organizations have goals and attempt to be rational in their attainment. These efforts take place in an environment that prevents some organizational efforts from being goal-directed. Moreover, rationality is less than perfect, since people, individually and collectively, have less than perfect skills and judgment. Two additional aspects of rationality should be discussed before the perspective on organizations is further developed.

The first point has been implicit in the previous discussion: organizations have multiple goals (the next chapter will more fully develop this point). Multiple goals are typically conflicting goals. Universities, for example, have the goals of teaching and research, among others. While these are usually presented as compatible activities leading to the ultimate goal of knowledge, in fact the pursuit of one works against the pursuit of the other. An organization rationally set up to maximize good teaching does not facilitate research, and vice versa. Rationality is thus limited by the very fact of multiple goals.

The second point is a more difficult one: "rationality" does not mean the same thing in all cultures. Martin King Whyte has demonstrated that organizations in China attempt to be just as rational as those in other countries.[90] Table 2-2 summarizes his findings. It is obvious from the

---

[90] Martin King Whyte, "Bureaucracy and Modernization in China: The Maoist Critique," *American Sociological Review*, 38, No. 2 (April 1973), 149–63.

TABLE 2-2   SIMILARITIES AND CONTRASTS BETWEEN WESTERN AND CHINESE ORGANIZATIONS

CONTRASTS

Western Conceptions	Maoist Conceptions
1. Use criteria of technical competence in personnel allocation	1. Use both political purity and technical competence
2. Promote organizational autonomy	2. Politics takes command, and openness to outside political demands
3. Legal-rational authority	3. Mass line participative-charismatic authority
4. Informal social groups unavoidably occur	4. Informal groups can and should be fully coopted
5. Differentiated rewards to office and performance encouraged	5. Differentiated rewards to office and performance deemphasized
6. Varied compliance strategies needed, depending on the organization	6. Normative and social compliance should play the main role everywhere
7. Formalistic impersonality	7. Comradeship
8. Unemotionality	8. Political zeal encouraged
9. Partial inclusion and limited contractual obligations of office-holders	9. Near total inclusion and theoretically unlimited obligations
10. Job security encouraged	10. Job security not valued, and career orientations not encouraged
11. Calculability through rules and established procedures	11. Flexibility and rapid change valued, rules and procedures looked on with suspicion
12. Unity of command and strict hierarchy of communications	12. Collective leadership and flexible consultation

SIMILARITIES

1. Organizations have specific goals	1. Same
2. Organizations utilize a hierarchy of specialized offices	2. Same
3. Authority and rewards greater at the top of an organization	3. Same, although efforts to deemphasize
4. Universalistic hiring and promotion criteria	4. Same, although criteria differ
5. Files, rules, and written communications regulate organizational life	5. Same, although not always viewed positively
6. Offices separated from office-holders	6. Same

Source: Martin King Whyte, "Bureaucracy and Modernization in China: The Maoist Critique," *American Sociological Review*, 38, No. 2 (April 1973), 157.

similarities that organizations have common properties, regardless of culture. The contrasts, on the other hand, suggest that it is feasible to pursue very different means toward these similarities. The emphasis on political processes and emotionality indicates another route to rationality. As Whyte concludes,

> Activities which seem irrational to Western eyes may have a rational justification. For example, weekly sessions for the study of Mao's thought for factory workers may not simply interfere with production by tiring people out. Insofar as this activity strengthens organizational cohesion and identification, it may contribute to production. At the same time, it is not clear that the Maoist ideal is a panacea for all organizational problems, or that it can even very easily be applied. In real Chinese organizations its application may result in some cases in both political involvement and internal efficiency, in others in political involvement without greater efficiency, or perhaps in failure in both areas.[91]

Rationality is thus not a singular thing. All organizations seek to be rational within the limits set by multiple goals and alternative modes of rationality. Nonetheless, it is impossible to understand organizations without including the rationality component.

SUMMARY AND CONCLUSIONS

Chris Argyris has argued that much of organizational sociology is inapplicable to the real world.[92] Focusing only on the formal properties of organizations, ignoring the role of the individual, and having a pro-managerial bias are some of the claims which Argyris makes and demonstrates. The contingency–choice perspective is an attempt to indicate that the sociological analysis of organizations need not commit the sins it is accused of by Argyris and does not omit crucial variables for understanding organizations.

Beginning with the difficulties in defining organizations and developing a usable typology, the emphasis has been on organizations *in* an environment, acting to achieve important organizational goals. Individuals make up an organization, but within structural constraints. Organizations change, as a result of external and internal forces, but the changes themselves occur within the limits of the preexisting organizational structure and the environment in which the organization is operating.

---

[91] *Ibid.*, p. 162.

[92] Chris Argyris, *The Applicability of Organizational Sociology* (London: Cambridge University Press, 1972).

3

goals and effectiveness

Every consumer hopes that the organizations from which goods and services are purchased are effective. If I buy a pair of skis, for example, I hope that the manufacturer was effective in making the skis and that there are no hidden flaws. I also hope that the manufacturer remains effective and in business so that if something does go wrong the guarantee on the skis can be honored. Similarly, most citizens want government services to be delivered effectively, whether they be fire and police protection, refuse removal, or taxation. Employees of organizations are concerned with what the organization can provide them, and may also be concerned that the organization do a good job. We show a concern with goals whenever we ask questions about where our organization is going, what its purpose is, and so on.

Despite the universal importance of goods and effectiveness, they remain *the* problematic issue in organizational analysis, for three reasons: first, all organizations have multiple and usually conflicting goals; second, the multiplicity and conflict among goals, plus other constraints, prevent any organization from being fully effective; third, organizations that are effective for one set of constituents may be ineffective or dangerous for another. The purpose of this chapter is to examine the nature of organizational goals and effectiveness, to indicate some of the problems associated with the conceptualization and measurement of these phenomena, and to try to develop some understanding of how these issues can be dealt with in theory and in practice.

ORGANIZATIONAL GOALS

"An organizational goal is a desired state of affairs which the organization attempts to realize."[1] This desired state of affairs is by definition

[1] Amitai Etzioni, *Modern Organizations* (Englewood Cliffs, N.J.: Prentice-Hall, Inc., 1964), p. 6.

many things to many people. In a large organization, top executives may see the organization as seeking one kind of state while those in the middle and lower echelons may have drastically different goals for the organization and for themselves personally. Even in an organization in which there is high participation in decision making and strong membership commitment, it is unlikely that there will be a total consensus on what the organization should attempt to do, let alone on the means of achieving these ends.

At first glance the goal idea seems simplest in the case of profit-making organizations. Indeed, much of the research on effectiveness has used this type of organization because of goal clarity. The readily quantifiable profit goal is not such a simple matter, however. It is confounded by such issues as the time perspective (long-run or short-run profits); the rate of profit (in terms of return to investors); the important issue of survival and growth in a turbulent and unpredictable environment that might in the short run preclude profit making; the intrusion of other values, such as providing quality products or services or benefiting mankind; and the firm's comparative position vis-à-vis others in the same industry. Even the nature of profit itself has multiple meanings. It can involve return on stockholders' equity, return on total capital, sales growth, earnings per share growth, debt to equity ratio, and net profit margin. These are not well correlated,[2] which alone makes the idea of goals extremely complex. If something as straightforward and quantifiable as profit turns out not to be so straightforward and quantifiable, then all goals must be analyzed with much caution.

The difficulties apparent in the straightforward profit-making firm are indicative of the difficulties inherent in determining what the goals of any organization really are. When the subject of analysis is shifted to a government agency, university, or church, determining the organization's goals becomes almost impossible.

Take, for example, the case of a government regulative agency charged with administering the public-utilities laws and regulations of a state. A casual view suggests that this is a unitary goal, assuming that the laws and regulations are clearly stated. However, this assumption is seldom validated, given the large number of lawyers and other technical experts employed by the agency for the purpose of developing and defending interpretations of the existing laws. Administration in such a case is not a simple matter either, since the choice between active and passive administration is a political and organizational football. The well-known distinction between the letter and the intent of the law becomes an issue for such agencies as they develop their operating procedures. What is the

[2] "Measuring Management 1974," *Forbes*, 115 (January 1, 1975), 38.

goal for the agency? If it is staffed by personnel who have values above and beyond simply administering the existing laws (every organization contains personnel with differing values), their own values toward social action or inaction can clearly modify the stated goals of the organization. In the case of the public utilities agency, beliefs in such diverse areas as air and water pollution, the nature of the publics served by the agency (the public, segments of the public, or the organizations involved), the desirability of maintaining certain public services despite their unprofitability (as in the case of railroad service), and competition versus monopoly in public services—these merely exemplify the range of alternatives available as goals for this organization aside from those found in its formal charter.

The three commonly stated goals of colleges and universities—teaching, research, and public service—are almost by definition too vague to serve as much of a guide for organizational analysis or practice. It can also be seen that they have become essentially incompatible in practice. Universities and colleges tend to concentrate on one of the three goals to the exclusion of the others. While emphases change, the basic issue of deciding among these goals remains. And also, since each contains vast uncertainties—exactly what is meant by good teaching, research, or service?—the use of the goal concept in this setting becomes excruciatingly difficult.

With an understanding of some of the difficulties in the utilization of the goal concept, let us examine the concept more systematically.

THE MEANING OF ORGANIZATIONAL GOALS

Organizational goals can be approached from a variety of perspectives. Parsons has cogently pointed out that organizational goals are intimately intertwined with important and basic societal functions, such as integration, pattern maintenance, and so on.[3] From this point of view, organizational goals are really an extension of what the society needs for its own survival. At the other extreme is the position that organizational goals are nothing more than the goals of the individual members of the organization. Petro Georgiou, for example, argues that organizations can be understood through a focus on individuals exchanging incentives and pursuing a variety of goals.[4] But this position appears extreme. Organiza-

[3] Talcott Parsons, *Structure and Process in Modern Societies* (New York: The Free Press, 1960), pp. 17–22, 44–47.

[4] Petro Georgiou, "The Goal Paradigm and Notes toward a Counter Paradigm," *Administrative Science Quarterly*, 18, No. 3 (September 1973), 291–310.

tional goals may not be the things around which individuals in organizations base all of their actions, but the organization does structure their activities and set limits on the incentives that can be exchanged.

An exclusive focus on societal functions or individual predispositions obscures more than it illuminates. If the level of analysis is kept in the broad societal-function framework, the variations in goals and activities among organizations performing the same basic functions are ignored. If the level of analysis focuses on just the variety of individual goals, the whole point of organizations is missed—if there were only individual goals, there would be no point in organizing. Clearly, many individuals may have the same goal, such as making a profit, furthering a cause, or destroying an enemy. But also clear is that when these people come together in the form of an organization, the profit, cause, or destruction becomes an abstraction toward which they work together.

Organizational goals by definition are creations of individuals, singly or collectively. At the same time, the determination of a goal for collective action becomes a standard by which the collective action is judged. As we will see, the collectively determined, commonly based goal seldom remains constant over time. New considerations imposed from without or within deflect the organization from its original goal, not only changing the activities of the organization, but also becoming part of the overall goal structure. The important point is that the goal of any organization is an abstraction distilled from the desires of members and pressures from the environment and internal system. While there is never 100 percent agreement among members as to what organizational goals are or should be, members can articulate a goal that is a desired state for the organization at some future point in time.

This approach is in some ways similar to that of Herbert Simon. Simon's major focus is on decision making within the organization. He notes that:

> When we are interested in the internal structure of an organization, however, the problem cannot be avoided. . . . Either we must explain organizational behavior in terms of the goals of the individual members of the organization, or we must postulate the existence of one or more organizational goals, over and above the goals of the individuals.[5]

Simon then differentiates between the goals or value premises that serve as inputs to decisions and motives, and the causes that lead individuals

[5] Herbert A. Simon, "On the Concept of Organizational Goal," *Administrative Science Quarterly*, 9, No. 1 (June 1964), 2.

to select some goals over others as the basis for their decision making. He keeps the goal idea at the individual level, but offers the important notion that the goals of an organization at any point in time are the result of the interaction among the members of the organization.

To this we would add that external conditions also affect the nature of an organization's goals. An example is the case of some military organizations. The official goal is typically to protect the state and its people from external threats. The leaders of the military organization may come to believe, for any number of reasons, that the goal is to be victorious over a wide variety of enemies (this is not necessarily the same as protecting the state). This then becomes the goal until it is modified by interactions or conflicts with lower-level personnel, or with external forces in the form of some type of civilian control, with the goal again becoming altered to engagement in limited wars without winning or protecting the state. In this hypothetical and oversimplified example, the goals of individual organization members, particularly those in high positions, are crucial in goal setting. These goals are modified in the course of internal and external interactions.

In Simon's approach, goals become constraints on the decision-making process. The constraints are based on abstract values around which the organization operates. Decisions are made within the framework of a set of constraints (goals), and organizations attempt to make decisions that are optimal in terms of the sets of constraints they face. While the approach taken here is not based solely on the decision-making framework, the perspective is the same. Organizational actions are constrained not only by goals, but also by the external and internal factors that have been discussed. Probably in the great majority of cases, goals are one, if not the only, relevant constraint.

OPERATIVE GOALS

Treating goals as abstract values has the merit of showing that organizational actions are guided by more than the day-to-day whims of individual members. At the same time, abstract values are just that— abstract. They must be converted to specific guides for the actual operations of an organization. Perrow takes this position when he distinguishes between "official" and "operative" organizational goals.[6] Official goals are "the general purposes of the organization as put forth in the charter,

---

[6] Charles Perrow, "The Analysis of Goals in Complex Organizations," *American Sociological Review*, 26, No. 6 (December 1961), 855.

annual reports, public statements by key executives and other authoritative pronouncements." Operative goals, on the other hand, "designate the ends sought through the actual operating policies of the organization; they tell us what the organization actually is trying to do, regardless of what the official goals say are the aims."

This distinction is grounded in reality. Two organizations, both with the official goal of profit making, may differ drastically in their actual emphasis on making profits. Blau's examination of two employment agencies with the same official goals shows wide variations between the agencies in what they were actually trying to accomplish.[7] In his discussion of this point, Perrow states:

> Where operative goals provide the specific content of official goals, they reflect choices among competing values. They may be justified on the basis of an official goal, even though they may subvert another official goal. In one sense they are means to official goals, but since the latter are vague or of high abstraction, the "means" become ends in themselves when the organization is the object of analysis. For example, where profit making is the announced goal, operative goals will specify whether quality or quantity is to be emphasized, whether profits are to be short run and risky or long run and stable, and will indicate the relative priority of diverse and somewhat conflicting ends of customer service, employee morale, competitive pricing, diversification, or liquidity. Decisions on all these factors influence the nature of the organization, and distinguish it from another with an identical official goal.[8]

From this perspective, operative goals become the standards by which the organization's actions are judged and around which decisions are made. In many cases these operative goals reflect the official goals, in that they are abstractions made more concrete. However, operative goals can evolve that are basically unrelated to the official goals. In this regard, Perrow notes:

> Unofficial operative goals, on the other hand, are tied more directly to group interests, and while they may support, be irrelevant to, or subvert official goals, they bear no necessary connection with them. An interest in a major supplier may dictate the policies of a corporation executive. The prestige that attaches to utilizing elaborate high-speed computers may dictate the reorganization of inventory and accounting departments. Racial prejudice may influence the selection procedures of an employment agency.

[7] Peter M. Blau, *The Dynamics of Bureaucracy* (Chicago: University of Chicago Press, 1955).
[8] Perrow, "Analysis of Goals," pp. 855–56.

The personal ambition of a hospital administrator may lead to community alliances and activities which bind the organization without enhancing its goal achievement. On the other hand, while the use of interns and residents as "cheap labor" may subvert the official goal of medical education, it may substantially further the official goal of providing a high quality of patient care.[9]

Operative goals thus reflect the derivation and distillation of a set of goals from both official and unofficial sources. These operative goals are developed through interaction patterns within the organization, but persist after the interactions are completed. They reflect the "desired state of affairs," or abstract official goals, the modifications and subversions of these by personnel in decision-making positions, and the force of pressures from the external environment. It is the combination of official goals with internal and external factors that leads to an existing set of operative goals.

If the use of unofficial goals is carried too far, of course, every organization could be viewed as having a huge, perhaps infinite, number of such goals. The distinction must be made, therefore, between goals and operating policies and procedures. The latter are the exact specifications, formally or informally stated, of what individual actors at all levels are to do in their daily activities. Goals, on the other hand, remain at the abstract level, serving as constraining or guiding principles from which policies and procedures can be derived. Operative goals are abstractions in the same way as official goals; they are a set of ideas about where the organization should be going, which are operationalized into specific plans and procedures.

THE DETERMINATION OF ORGANIZATIONAL GOALS

How does one find out exactly what the goals of an organization are? From the research point of view, this is a vital step if there is to be any concern with issues such as effectiveness, personnel and resource allocation, or optimal structuring. In a very real sense, if organizational research is to be anything more than simply descriptive, it must be concerned with goals. For the member of the organization at any level, goal determination is similarly vital. If he misses what the goals really are, his own actions may not only fail to contribute to the organization, they may contribute to his own organizational demise. Members of organizations must know the "system" if they are to operate within it or to change it.

[9] *Ibid.*, p. 856.

From the discussion above, it should be clear that the actual "system" is much more than official statements about it.

The vital importance of understanding operative goals can perhaps best be exemplified by an actual case.[10] The case in point is the familiar one of the goals of a university. The University of Minnesota *Faculty Information* booklet contains the following statements:

Teaching. The University emphasizes excellence in teaching. The first duty of every faculty member engaged in instruction is the communication of knowledge and values to students, and the stimulation of their intellectual ability, curiosity, and imagination.

Research. Research is the second strong arm of the University. The faculty member is aided in obtaining funds and facilities for research, and is encouraged to contribute to the ever-expanding realms of human knowledge.

Public Service and Professional Commitments
. . . .

University Service
. . . .

Community Service and Extension Education
. . . .[11]

As everyone must know, these goals are not equally stressed, even though the official pronouncement would lead one to believe otherwise. If a new (or old) faculty member actually believed what he read, he would probably soon find himself at a distinct disadvantage. One of the questions asked of the faculty, in at least one department, when salary increases for the coming year were being considered was the number of offers from other universities that each had received. The larger the number of offers, apparently, the greater the likelihood of receiving a substantial raise, and vice versa. But the vast majority of such offers are forthcoming to those who are active in the research side of the goal equation, since the other factors cannot be readily visible to other institutions. This is not an unusual case, nor is the meaning of it limited to colleges and universities. Knowledge of operative goals is imperative for effective functioning and for the effective implementation of one's own ideas. At the extreme, such knowledge is necessary for individual survival in organizations.

[10] Cases and case studies are useful as examples, but they cannot be used as bases for generalizations concerning other organizations, even of a very similar type.
[11] *Faculty Information* (Minneapolis: University of Minnesota, 1972), pp. 8–11.

Operative-goal determination for the individual is obviously important. It is plainly part of the ongoing organizational system, also, and thus central to organizational functioning. It is equally important for the organizational analyst. The significance of operative goals forces the analyst to go beyond the more easily determined official goals. The key to finding out what are the operative goals lies in the actual decisions of the top decision-makers in the organization. The kinds of decisions they make about allocation of resources (money, personnel, equipment, etc.) are a major indicator. In a study of juvenile correctional organizations, Mayer Zald found that resources were consistently allocated to the custodial and traditional aspects of the institutions rather than to professional treatment personnel, despite official pronouncements that rehabilitation was the goal.[12] Although lower-level personnel influence the decisions made in the organization, it is the people near or at the top who have the major and sometimes final say.

The emphasis on the major decision makers within the organization is underscored by James Price in his discussion of techniques for identifying organizational goals.[13] Price also suggests that the focus should be on organizational goals, rather than on the personal goals of these top decision makers. The emphasis should be on both the intentions and the activities of the organizations.[14] Intentions involve what the participants believe the organization is trying to accomplish, while activities are what the individuals in the organization are actually doing. From both interview and observation, then, organizational goals can be determined.

The discussion of the determination of organizational goals has omitted an important component: the fact is that there may not be agreement among the top decision makers about the priorities or content of the identified goals. Factions within organizations push for their own advantage. Different philosophies can be represented. The priorities among goals can change, as can the content of the goals themselves.

One operative goal probably would not emerge from discussions with organizational decision makers—the goal that all organizations seek: to survive. Survival activities are usually linked to other goal-related activities, but at times survival becomes the overriding issue. John Kenneth Galbraith suggests that the guiding principle in large business firms is

[12] Mayer N. Zald, "Comparative Analysis and Measurement of Organizational Goals: The Case of Correctional Institutions for Delinquents," *The Sociological Quarterly*, 4, No. 2 (Spring 1963), 206–30.

[13] James Price, "The Study of Organizational Effectiveness," *The Sociological Quarterly*, 13, No. 1 (Winter 1972), 3–15.

[14] Edward Gross, "The Definition of Organizational Goals," *British Journal of Sociology*, 20, No. 3 (September 1969), 277–94.

not profit maximization or social good, but the interests of people who possess the power and who believe that "a large organization is rewarded by its own expansion."[15] This permits more promotions, jobs, challenge, pay, and prestige. While survival and growth are of great importance, a total focus on these aspects would ignore the essential operative goals around which organizational activities are based. General Motors may want to survive and grow, but it also seeks a profit, builds automobiles, and responds to innovations. To be sure, these goals contribute to survival, but General Motors could not be understood just on a survival-growth perspective.

Since operative goals reflect what the major decision makers believe to be the critical areas and issues for the organization, it follows that the operative goals will shift as internal and external conditions impinge upon the organization. It was argued in the last chapter that these conditions can deflect the organization from a pursuit of its goals. In a real sense, the operative goals are deflected by these threats or conditions during period of severe stress. At the same time, *the operative goals will usually reflect some variation on the theme of the official goal.* That is, operative goals are generally based on the official goals, even though there is not perfect correspondence. Profit-making organizations vary in their emphases; colleges and universities pay more or less attention to teaching, research, and so on; and hospitals are concerned to varying degree with teaching, patient care, and research. If the official goals remain the same when pressures, conditions, and priorities change, the shift in operative goals will be mainly in emphasis.

CHANGES IN ORGANIZATIONAL GOALS

Organizational goals change for three major reasons. The first reason, direct pressure from external forces, leads to a deflection from the original goals. The second, pressure from internal sources, may lead the organization to emphasize quite different activities than those originally intended. The third, changed environmental and technological demands, leads the organization to redefine its goals. While this is similar to the first reason, the factors here occur in *indirect* interaction with the organization, whereas in the first case the organization is in *direct* interaction with the relevant environmental factors.

The impact of external relationships on goals is best seen in Thompson

---

[15] John Kenneth Galbraith, "The U. S. Economy is not a Free Market Economy," *Forbes,* 113 (May 15, 1974), 99.

and McEwen's analysis of organization–environmental interactions.[16] They note that organizational goal setting is affected by competitive, bargaining, co-optative, and coalitional relationships with the environment. In the competitive situation—"that form of rivalry between two or more organizations which is mediated by a third party"—organizations must devote their efforts toward gaining support for their continued existence. Competition is most easily seen among business firms that compete for the customer's dollar, but it is also very evident among government agencies as they compete for a share of the tax dollar or among religious organizations as they compete for members and their support. (Religious and other voluntary organizations must also compete with alternative organizations for membership and money.) Competition partially controls the organization's "choice of goals" in that its energies must be turned to the competitive activity. Continuous support is vital for continued survival as an organization.

Bargaining also involves resources, but in this case the organization is in direct interaction with supplier, consumer, and other organizations. In the bargaining situation, the organization must "give" a little to get what it desires. Bargaining takes place in standard relationships between two organizations, as when a routine supplier is asked to alter its goods for the organization. This "custom" order will cost the supplier more money and hence he bargains for a better price, with the organization bargaining to get its custom equipment at the old price. Thompson and McEwen note that universities will often bargain away the name of a building for a substantial gift. Government agencies may bargain by not enforcing certain regulations in order to maintain support for the seeking of other goals. The impact of bargaining is more subtle than that of competition, but it has a similar impact on goal setting.

Co-optation is "the process of absorbing new elements into the leadership or policy-determining structure of an organization as a means of averting threats to its stability or existence."[17] The classic study of co-optation is Selznick's *TVA and the Grass Roots,* in which he documents the impact of bringing new societal elements into the governing structure of the TVA.[18] The organization shifted its emphases partially as a result of the new pressures brought to bear in the decision-making system. It is no accident that boards of directors or trustees contain mem-

[16] James D. Thompson and William J. McEwen, "Organizational Goals and Environment: Goal Setting as an Interaction Process," *American Sociological Review,* 23, No. 1 (February 1958), 23–30.

[17] *Ibid.,* p. 27.

[18] Phillip Selznick, *TVA and the Grass Roots* (New York: Harper Torchbook Edition, 1966).

bers from pressure groups important to the organizations involved.[19] If a member of a group that is antipathetic to the organization can be brought into the organization, the antipathy can be minimized. At the same time, the presence of that person on a controlling board has an influence on decisions made, even though the hostility rate may be down. Co-optation is thus a two-way street. Both those co-opted and those doing the co-opting are influenced.

The final type of external relationship is coalition, or the "combination of two or more organizations for a common purpose. Coalition appears to be the ultimate or extreme form of environmental conditioning of organizational goals."[20] While seeking common purposes, coalitions place strong constraints on the organizations involved, since they cannot set goals in a unilateral fashion.

Although it is clear that other environmental factors also affect the nature of organizational goals, Thompson and McEwen's analysis centers on transactions with other organizations. They suggest a very important consideration in the determination of the operative goals of an organization: organizations operate in a "field" of other organizations,[21] and these affect what the focal organization does. While this has been amply demonstrated in economic analysis of market competition, the impact goes further. The interactions we have described are direct evidence that the use of official-goal statements would be misleading, since the transactions with other organizations by definition would deflect an organization from its official goal.

Operative goals are also affected by what goes on inside an organization. A given set of goals may be altered drastically by changes in the power system of the organization, new types of personnel, as in the case of a sudden influx of professionals, and the development of new standards that supersede those of the past. Etzioni has called this phenomenon "goal displacement."[22]

Goal displacement is clearly evident in Robert Michels' analysis of Socialist parties and labor unions in Europe in the early twentieth century.[23] In this study he developed the idea of the "iron law of oligarchy."

[19] See Jeffrey Pfeffer, "Size and Composition of Corporate Boards of Directors: The Organization and its Environment," *Administrative Science Quarterly*, 17, No. 2 (June 1972), 218–28.

[20] Thompson and McEwen, "Organizational Goals and Environment," p. 28.

[21] For a further discussion of this point, see Roland L. Warren, "The Interorganizational Field as a Focus for Investigation," *Administrative Science Quarterly*, 12, No. 3 (December 1967), 396–419.

[22] Etzioni, *Modern Organizations*, p. 10.

[23] Robert Michels, *Political Parties* (New York: The Free Press, 1949).

Goals and Effectiveness 79

Michels pointed out that these revolutionary groups began as democratic organizations. The need for organization to accomplish the revolutionary purposes (operative goals) led to the establishment of leaders of the organizations. The leaders, tasting power, did not want to relinquish it, and therefore devoted much of their energies to maintaining their positions. Since members of most voluntary organizations, even revolutionary parties, are politically indifferent, and since the skills necessary for leading the parties are not universally distributed, the leaders could rather easily perpetuate themselves in power—in part by co-opting or purging the young potential leaders. The emphasis in the parties shifted to organizational maintenance, at the expense of militancy and revolutionary zeal. Close parallels to this situation exist in contemporary revolutionary and militant movements of every political and social persuasion.

A different form of goal displacement can be seen in Robert Scott's analysis of the "sheltered workshop for the blind."[24] When these workshops were formed in the early twentieth century, the overall goal was to integrate the blind into the industrial community. However, because it was recognized that many blind people could not work in regular factories, the sheltered workshops were developed to provide the blind with work (making brooms and mops, weaving, chair caning, etc.) as a social service. Owing to a series of events, the workshops began to define themselves as factories in competition with nonblind producers of goods. The emphasis shifted from helping the blind to employing competent workers (not necessarily mutually exclusive categories), and the social-service function largely fell by the wayside. Part of the reason for the shift in emphasis lay in changed environmental conditions, with an increased demand for the workshops' products. But it appears that these demands could have been resisted and the original intent of the workshops maintained intact. The internal decision-making process led to the development of clearly different goals from those professed at the outset.

Still another type of displacement can be seen in what Etzioni calls "over-measurement" and Bertram Gross labels "number magic."[25] Both refer to the tendency for organizations of all types to organize their energies (goals) around activities that are easily quantified. Easy quantification leads to counting publications of university faculty rather than evaluating classroom performance, looking at output per worker rather

[24] Robert A. Scott, "The Factory as a Social Service Organization: Goal Displacement in Workshops for the Blind," *Social Problems*, 15, No. 2 (Fall 1967), 160–75.
[25] Etzioni, *Modern Organizations*, pp. 8–10; and Bertram M. Gross, *Organizations and Their Managing* (New York: The Free Press, 1968), p. 293.

than "diligence, cooperation, punctuality, loyalty, and responsibility,"[26] and counting parishioners in a church rather than assessing the spiritual guidance of the parishioners.[27] These examples could be multiplied many times for many organizations. The obvious solution to this problem is to use multiple indicators for determining the extent to which organizations are achieving their goals. When this is not done and the easily quantifiable measure is stressed, organizational goals become deflected toward the achievement of the easily measured aspect.[28] This may in turn actually defeat the purpose for which the organization was designed. These internal sources of goals change can be found in any organization and are a basic part of the determination of the operative goals. In the extreme cases discussed here, the changes are rather clearly dysfunctional in terms of the official and original operative goals; but the processes inherent in these changes are a normal part of the goal-setting process.

The final source of goal change is a more generalized environmental pressure—generalized, that is, in terms of falling within abstract categories such as technological development, cultural changes, and economic conditions; however, the impact on the organization is direct. Several studies are available that provide direct evidence for this basis of goal change. Perhaps the most dramatic evidence comes from David L. Sills' analysis of the National Foundation for Infantile Paralysis.[29] Although the study was completed before the transition to be discussed was accomplished, the change in operative goals is very evident. The foundation was formed to assist in the prevention and treatment of polio through research, coordinating, and fund-raising activities. At the time the foundation was organized, polio was a major health problem, highlighted by Franklin D. Roosevelt's crippled condition as a result of the disease. Roosevelt himself founded the organization in 1938, at the height of his own popularity and the seriousness of the polio problem. The organization grew rapidly, and its March of Dimes became a very successful volunteer fund-raising effort.

In less than two decades, the organization accomplished its primary goal. Through the development of the Salk and Sabine vaccines, polio has largely been eliminated as a serious health hazard. Rehabilitation facilities have been consistently improved to assist those who suffer from

[26] Gross, *Organizations and Their Managing*, p. 295.

[27] Etzioni, *Modern Organizations*, p. 10.

[28] For an extended discussion of this point, see W. Keith Warner and A. Eugene Havens, "Goal Displacement and the Intangibility of Organizational Goals," *Administrative Science Quarterly*, 12, No. 4 (March 1968), 539–55.

[29] David L. Sills, *The Volunteers* (New York: The Free Press, 1957).

the effects of polio contracted in the past (the number of new cases at present is insignificant). For the organization, these events presented a clear dilemma. The choice was between going out of business and developing a new goal. The latter alternative was chosen, as the organization decided to concentrate on "other crippling diseases," with particular emphasis on birth defects. Sills suggests that the presence of a strong national headquarters together with committed volunteers should maintain the organization over time. The historical evidence seems to confirm this, although the organization does not appear to be as strong as it was during the polio epidemics.

The volunteer and nonvolunteer members of this organization had a vested interest in its maintenance. At the same time, technological developments outside the organization made its continuation questionable because of its operative goals at that time. The focus of the organization shifted to adapt to the changed technology. While some of the operative goals remained the same, others shifted to meet the new concerns.

The impact of technological shifts can also be seen in Lawrence and Lorsch's analysis of firms in the plastics industry. In this case, technological change, in the form of a rapidly changing "state of the art," is an ever-present and pressing factor of the environment. In discussing the performance of organizations in this industry, Lawrence and Lorsch comment:

> The low-performing organizations were both characterized by their top administrators as having serious difficulty in dealing with this environment. They had not been successful in introducing and marketing new products. In fact, their attempts to do so had met with repeated failures. This record, plus other measures of performance available to top management, left them with a feeling of disquiet and a sense of urgency to find ways of improving their performance.[30]

This sense of urgency would be translated into altered operative goals for the organization as it seeks to cope more effectively with the rapidly changing technological system.

Technology is not the only environmental factor impinging upon the organization, despite its apparent centrality. The general values in the environment surrounding an organization also affect its operation. Burton Clark's analysis of the adult-education system in California indicates

[30] Paul R. Lawrence and Jay W. Lorsch, *Organization and Environment: Managing Differentiation and Integration* (Cambridge, Mass.: Harvard Graduate School of Business Administration, 1967), p. 42.

clearly that an organization is vitally affected by the values of those whom it serves and whose support it seeks.[31]

The official goals of the adult-education system are concerned with relatively lofty matters, such as awareness of civic responsibilities, economic uplift, personal adjustment in the family, health and physical fitness, cultural development, broadened educational background, and the development of avocational interests. This educational system suffers from a number of handicaps. It is part of the public educational system but not part of the normal sequence. It is a "peripheral, nonmandatory" part; and this marginality is heightened by the fact that the system operates on an "enrollment economy." That is, school income is determined largely by attendance (paid) in classes. If attendance declines, support for the program from tax revenues is likely also to decline. Course enrollments become "*the* criterion by which courses are initiated and continued."[32]

Courses are offered only if they are popular. It is not surprising, therefore, to find classes in cake decorating, rug making, and square dancing. While these are legitimate avocational activities, the pressure for courses such as these precludes much attention being paid to the other official goals and increases the criticisms of the adult-education program from other segments of the educational enterprise. The adult-education administrators are thus caught in the bind of trying to maintain attendance in the face of competing demands for the potential student's time, and trying to satisfy the pertinent criticism of other educators and members of the legislature. The values of the clientele are inconsistent with those of the system itself. The organization adapts to their demands, but then finds itself out of phase with another part of its relevant environment.

Organizations in the service area are constantly confronted with changed values that make their services in greater or lesser demand. Colleges and universities were unprepared for the rise in enrollments caused by the increased valuation placed on education during the early 1960s. While demographic conditions would have led to a prediction of some increase, more than the expected proportions of high school graduates opted for college as opposed to other endeavors (for whatever reason). These changed values obviously affected the goals of the organizations as they were forced to "process" students at the expense of some of the traditional goals. When college-going became somewhat devalued in the early 1970s, colleges and universities responded by emphasizing

[31] Burton R. Clark, "Organizational Adaptation and Precarious Values," *American Sociological Review*, 21, No. 3 (June 1956), 327–36.
[32] *Ibid.*, p. 333.

or starting programs for people who are older than the traditional student.

Shifts in cultural values and their impact on the goals of organizations are obvious in the profit-making sector also. While the goal of profit may remain, the operative goals shift as more energies are put into market research, and as organizations redefine themselves as "young" organizations for the "now" generation. These are often more than advertising slogans, in that internal transformations have occurred to refocus the organizations' activities.

Shifts in the economic and political systems surrounding an organization would have similar influences on the goals of the organization involved. While much more than goals are affected by these interactions with the environment, it should be clear that organizational goals, like the organizations for which they serve as constraints and guides for action, are not static. Internal and external factors affect them. The relative strength of the various factors affecting goals, which would include the decision-making and power processes within the organization, have not yet been determined.

THE UTILITY OF THE GOAL CONCEPT

The factors that affect goals, and the fact that the meaningful goals for an organization are not necessarily those officially pronounced, might lead us to reject the goal concept altogether. However, there is still the simple but basic fact that the organization would not exist if it were not for some common purpose. Except in the case of conscription, as in some military systems or the public schools, members come to the organization voluntarily, if not enthusiastically. In all cases, the organization engages in some activity. This activity is not simply random behavior; it is based on some notion of what the purpose of the action is.

This purpose or goal is the basis for organizational activities. It is true that means can come to be emphasized more heavily than the goal itself, that members of the organization may have no idea of why they are doing what they are doing, and that ritualistic adherence to outmoded norms may become the norm; but these behaviors would be impossible without the presence of a goal. Even when forgotten or ignored, the goal is still the basis for the organization, since the means would not have developed without it in the first place.

From the discussion above, it is clear that most organizations have more than one goal. These multiple goals may be in conflict with one another; even then, they are still a basis for action. The action itself may or may not conflict with other goals. The relative importance of the goals can be determined by the way the organization allocates its resources to them. Since both external and internal pressures affect goals, along with the more rational process of goal setting, goals cannot be viewed as static. They change, sometimes dramatically, over time. These changes, it should be stressed, can occur because of decision making within the organization. This decision making is almost by definition a consequence of internal or external forces. Goal alterations decided within the organization are a consequence of the interactions of members who participate in the goal-setting process. Goal alteration can be done by an oligarchic elite or through democratic processes (in very few organizations would a total democracy prevail).

Shifts in goals can also occur without a conscious decision on the part of organization members—that is, as a reaction to the external or internal pressures without a conscious reference to an abstract model of where the organization is going. While this is not goal-related behavior, the persistence of such activities leads to their becoming operative goals for the organization, as where the organization focuses its efforts on achieving easily measured objectives at the expense of more central but less easily measured goals.

It is at this point, of course, that the goal concept is most fuzzy. If an organization is oriented toward some easily quantifiable objective for the sake of measuring its achievements, the analyst can stand back and say, "Aha, this organization isn't doing what it is supposed to do!" At the same time, the easily quantified goal is no less of an abstraction than is the possibly more lofty objective that serves as the analyst's point of departure. The analyst can also point out the deflections that occur as a result of the external and internal pressures discussed. Concentration upon deflections from official goals, whether they are due to quantification or external and internal pressures, can lead to the decision that goals are really not relevant for organizational analysis. It is at this point that the work of Perrow and Simon is most pertinent. Perrow's emphasis on the operative goals, however they are developed, and Simon's notion that goals place constraints on decision making both suggest that goals are relevant, even central, for organizational analysis. It does not matter what the source of operative goals might be; what does matter is that they come into the decision-making and action processes of the organization. They are still abstractions upon which the organization and its members behave.

The goal concept, with the modifications we have discussed, is vital in organizational analysis. The dynamics of goal setting and goal change do not alter the fact that goals still guide what happens in an organization. If the concept of goals is not used, organizational behavior becomes a random occurrence, subject to whatever pressures and forces exist at any point in time. Since organizations have continuity and do accomplish things, the notion that goals are abstractions around which behavior is organized remains valid.

The analysis of goals, however, is a rather empty exercise until the second part of the equation is added: because a goal is something that is sought, the seeking leads to the issue of goal accomplishment, or effectiveness. Since goals are seldom accomplished, except in rare cases such as that of the National Foundation for Infantile Paralysis, *effectiveness* is a more usable term than *accomplishment*. The discussion of effectiveness that follows is based on the goal notion that has been developed, and also on the perspective taken in the previous chapter—that organizations attempt to be rational and goal-seeking, but are deflected by the kinds of pressures and forces that have been described.

EFFECTIVENESS

Effectiveness has been defined as the "degree to which [an organization] realizes its goals."[33] From the discussion of goals it should be clear that effectiveness is not a simple issue. The basic difficulty in analyzing it is the fact of multiple and often conflicting goals in many organizations. Effectiveness in one set of endeavors may lead to ineffectiveness in another.

Effectiveness is a difficult issue from another standpoint. *Efficiency* is often confused with effectiveness. Etzioni defines efficiency as the "amount of resources used to produce a unit of output."[34] Clearly, an organization can be efficient without being effective, and vice versa. Controversies regarding certain poverty programs illustrate this point. The costs (efficiency) of producing a well-trained and well-adjusted person who came from a disadvantaged background were higher than those of producing a college graduate at some elite universities. The programs may have been effective—although this was never directly confirmed—but they were not efficient, at least from the point of view of many legislators. Efficiency and effectiveness are often closely related, but it is dangerous to assume, without careful investigation, that they are identical.

Yet an additional difficulty with the concept of effectiveness is the question, effectiveness for whom? It does not take a Marxist to realize that high profits can be at the expense of workers or consumers. Nor

[33] Etzioni, *Modern Organizations*, p. 8.
[34] *Ibid.*, p. 8.

does it require a capitalist to recognize that at times continued profit can be accomplished only through the conservation of resources. The question of who determines effectiveness cuts to the heart of the role of organizations in society. As with goals, the people at or near the top of organizations make the most critical judgments of effectiveness. At the same time other groups in contact with an organization, such as regulatory or licensing organizations, competitors, and consumers, assess an organization for its effectiveness.

The easiest solution to the problem of who assesses effectiveness is to use the perspective of Basil Georgopoulos and his associates.[35] They argue that effectiveness should be determined on the basis of organizational criteria rather than externally derived criteria. The organizational criteria are thus defined as legitimate. This procedure is satisfactory only when other criteria are acknowledged to be legitimate in viewing organizations for their role in society. Organizational effectiveness is typically approached from one of two alternatives—the goal approach and the systems-resource approach.

THE GOAL APPROACH

The goal approach is relatively simple and is exemplified by Etzioni's definition of effectiveness given at the start of this discussion.[36] The difficulties in determining organizational goals (which have already been discussed) and the multiple and conflicting nature of the goals of many organizations require that the goal approach be used with caution. When there is a single goal or a clear hierarchy of them, use of the goal approach is relatively simple, but when there is no clear hierarchy or there is conflict over goal priorities, use of the goal approach becomes more

[35] Basil S. Georgopoulos and Arnold S. Tannenbaum, "A Study of Organizational Effectiveness," *American Sociological Review*, 22, No. 5 (October 1957), 534–40; and Basil S. Georgopoulos and Floyd C. Mann, *The Community General Hospital* (New York: The Macmillan Company, 1962).

[36] See James L. Price, *Organizational Effectiveness: An Inventory of Propositions* (Homewood, Ill.: Richard D. Irwin, Inc., 1968); James L. Price, "The Study of Organizational Effectiveness," *The Sociological Quarterly*, 13, No. 1 (Winter 1972), 3–15; comments on this research by Leland C. McCormick, J. Kenneth Benson, and James L. Price in *The Sociological Quarterly*, 14 (Spring 1973), 271–78; and Jaisingh Ghorpade, ed., *Assessment of Organizational Effectiveness* (Pacific Palisades, Calif.: Goodyear Publishing Co., 1971). The goal approach taken here is also congruent with the conclusions of Richard M. Steers, "Problems in the Measurement of Organizational Effectiveness," *Administrative Science Quarterly*, 20, No. 4 (December 1975), 546–58. Steers' conclusions are based on a review of 17 studies of organizational effectiveness.

complicated. Moreover it is often difficult if not impossible to determine the extent to which some goals are or are not realized. Quantifiable goals such as profit are relatively easy to measure but less-quantifiable goals are exceedingly difficult to evaluate.

For organizational theory, the absence of general measures of effectiveness is a severe limitation.[37] Ideally, with a general, uniform measure or set of measures, the conditions that lead to effectiveness in a variety of conditions could be determined. Except for profit-making organizations, no such general measures are now available.

One technique that shows some promise is to ask persons in superordinate positions over organizational subunits or total organizations themselves to estimate the effectiveness of the subordinate organizations. This technique has been used with success by Thomas Mahoney and William Weitzel and by Robert Duncan.[38] Even here, however, the superordinate managers utilize different criteria for determining the effectiveness of the units they supervise. Mahoney and Weitzel note:

> General business managers tend to use productivity and efficient performance. These high-order criteria refer to measures of output, whereas lower-order criteria tend to refer to characteristics of the organization climate, supervisory style, and organizational capacity for performance. The research and development managers, on the other hand, use cooperative behavior, staff development, and reliable performance as high-order criteria; and efficiency, productivity, and output behavior as lower-order criteria.[39]

A major conclusion to be drawn from this research is that effectiveness criteria as developed by the organization itself do not vary together. The complex organization cannot be effective by any global or ultimate definition of effectiveness. The organization can be effective on one or several goals but must be less effective or ineffective on others. The fact

[37] Price, "The Study of Organizational Effectiveness, *ibid.*, 3–15.

[38] Thomas A. Mahoney and William Weitzel, "Managerial Models of Organizational Effectiveness," *Administrative Science Quarterly*, 14, No. 3 (September 1969), 357–65; Robert B. Duncan, "Multiple Decision-Making Structures in Adapting to Environmental Uncertainty: The Impact on Organizational Effectiveness," *Human Relations*, 26, No. 4 (April 1973), 273–91.

[39] *Ibid.*, p. 362. David A. Tansik, "Influences of Organization Goal Structure upon Participant Evaluations," *Academy of Management Journal*, 16, No. 2 (June 1973), 265–76, suggests that more visible goals are measured by output criteria, while less-visible goals are measured by other criteria. This is in line with Mahoney and Weitzel's findings. Similarly, there is evidence that the criteria of effectiveness vary with the type of technology utilized by organizational units: Thomas A. Mahoney and Peter J. Frost, "The Role of Technology in Models of Organizational Effectiveness," *Organizational Behavior and Human Performance*, 11 (February 1974), 122–38.

TABLE 3-1	**DIFFERING PERCEPTIONS OF EFFECTIVENESS**		

GOAL	Staff Score	Youth Score	Parent Score
1. Making decisions about what action (if any) this organization should take in regard to a specific problem youth.	3.95	2.89	3.50
2. Conducting case evaluations by gathering information and attempting to fully understand each problem youth.	4.00	2.96	3.44
3. Communicating this information about the problem youth and the understanding of his problems to the court.	4.10	3.26	3.62
4. Protecting the rights of problem youth.	4.19	3.16	3.82
5. Aiding in the adjustment of problem youth through case supervision and other forms of treatment.	3.62	2.94	3.06
6. Working with other agencies in gathering or providing information and/or treatment.	3.29	3.15	3.31
7. Protecting the community from problem youth through prevention and control of problem behavior.	3.10	2.87	2.98
8. Conducting research and planning programs.	2.67	3.04	3.24

that choices among criteria must be made reinforces the utility of the goal concept, however, since these choices are made among the operative goals.

As noted earlier, a major issue in analyzing effectiveness is the question, effectiveness for whom? A study conducted by the author and some colleagues addressed this question[40] with respect to organizations that deal with problem youth. One of the organizations, a county juvenile probation department, will serve as the basis for discussion. The goals of this organization were determined by interviews with key personnel at the top of the agency. The professional staff of the agency, as well as a sample of the youths who had been served or treated ($N = 50$) and their parents, were asked to rate the performance of the organization on each of the organization's goals. This rating was on a five-point scale, with a higher score meaning higher performance on a particular goal. Table 3-1 indicates the results of the effectiveness ratings.

[40] Richard H. Hall, John P. Clark, and Peggy C. Giordano conducted the research at the University of Minnesota under NIMH Grant #2 R01 MH17508–03MHS.

Several points emerge from these findings. First, there are clear differences in effectiveness as perceived by the staff itself; the organization does better on some goals than others. Second, the clients, both youths and parents, rate the organization more poorly than the staff, although none of the ratings are extremely negative. Third, although not shown on the table, there is a strong relationship between the importance attached to a goal and the performance rating by the staff. The important goals are those on which performance is highest in the staff's view. An obvious problem with this approach, of course, is the fact that the clients are likely to know little about goals, such as 6 and 8, that do not involve direct interaction with them. This research does demonstrate that it is important to know who is judging effectiveness on which goals.

Before turning to an alternative to the goal approach to effectiveness, an additional piece of evidence regarding the approach should be noted. William Rushing examined both profit and nonprofit hospitals.[41] The profit-making hospitals were more oriented to economic outcomes. The economic factor was found to affect decision making and the characteristics of the organizations. Aside from the profit-vs.-nonprofit consideration, the goals of these organizations were similar. This strongly suggests that goals are in fact critical for the form and actions of organizations. One major approach to effectiveness, however, does not utilize goals.

THE SYSTEM-RESOURCES APPROACH

Stanley Seashore and Ephraim Yuchtman[42] have attempted to avoid some of the pitfalls of the goal approach by essentially ignoring organizational goals in their analyses of effectiveness. They criticize those who use the goal approach on the ground that the determination of goals is extremely difficult, if not impossible. Their criticism is largely of those who advocate the use of the official, rather than operative goals. Where they do consider the operative goals, they note that there are often conflicting goals for the same organization. Instead of the goal model, Sea-

[41] William Rushing, "Differences in Profit and Nonprofit Organizations: A Study of Effectiveness and Efficiency in General Short-Stay Hospitals," *Administrative Science Quarterly*, 19, No. 4 (December 1974), 547–62.

[42] Stanley E. Seashore and Ephraim Yuchtman, "Factorial Analysis of Organizational performance," *Administrative Science Quarterly*, 12, No. 3 (December 1967), 377–95; and Yuchtman and Seashore, "A System Resource Approach to Organizational Effectiveness," *American Sociological Review*, 32, No. 6 (December 1967), 891–903. See also Thomas E. Drabek and Judith B. Chapman, "On Assessing Organizational Priorities: Concept and Method," *The Sociological Quarterly*, 14, No. 3 (Summer 1973), 359–75.

shore and Yuchtman suggest the use of a "system-resources" model for the analysis of organizational effectiveness.

The system-resources approach is based on the idea of the organization as an open system. As such, it engages in exchange and competitive relationships with the environment. Effectiveness becomes the "ability of the organization, in either relative or absolute terms, to exploit its environment in the acquisition of scarce and valued resources."[43] These resources are acquired in the competitive and exchange relationships. An organization is most effective when it "maximizes its bargaining position and optimizes its resource procurement." This approach links the organization back into the society by noting that it is in interaction with the environment and thus must gain resources from that source.

In an empirical examination of this approach, Seashore and Yuchtman used data from 75 insurance-sales agencies located in different communities throughout the United States. Data from these agencies were factor-analyzed. The analysis yielded 10 factors that were stable over time. These were:

1. Business volume
2. Production cost
3. New member productivity
4. Youthfulness of members
5. Business mix
6. Manpower growth
7. Management emphasis
8. Maintenance cost
9. Member productivity
10. Market penetration[44]

These factors are not taken as indicators for all organizations. The factors of youthfulness of members, for example, while related to performance in this case, may be part of a phase or cycle in the life of these organizations. In interpreting the results of this analysis, Seashore and Yuchtman note that factors such as business volume and penetration of the market could be considered goals, but member productivity and

[43] Yuchtman and Seashore, "A System Resource Approach," p. 898.

[44] Seashore and Yuchtman, "Factorial Analysis," p. 383. Factor analysis is a technique that allows the researcher to arrange or reduce a large set of data into factors or components. It involves the use of the correlation coefficients for a set of variables and the determination of the underlying patterns among them. Each factor is intended to represent a unique aspect of the phenomenon being measured, in this case indicators of effectiveness.

youthfulness certainly cannot. They conclude that while not all the factors associated with performance can be considered as goals, they can be regarded as important resources gleaned from the environment.

This approach would essentially do away with goals as a component of the analysis of effectiveness. It also suggests that there is no universal standard by which effectiveness can be judged, requiring that the issue of effectiveness be handled organization by organization, or at least type of organization by type of organization.[45]

Viewed from another perspective, the Seashore and Yuchtman approach does not differ markedly from the one that has already been discussed. The acquisition of resources from the environment is based upon the official goal of the organization (Seashore and Yuchtman use the term *ultimate criterion*[46]). Movement toward this goal, or ultimate criterion, is difficult if not impossible to measure. The next step is to specify the operative goals (*penultimate criteria* in the Seashore-Yuchtman approach) and other activities in which the organization engages. Performance or effectiveness according to these criteria is more easily assessed. Growth in business volume is an operative goal in this sense, while youthfulness in members is merely a cyclical factor associated with performance on the other factors. The issue of goals versus resource allocation is therefore in many ways an argument over semantics. The acquisition of resources does not just happen.[47] It is based on what the organization is trying to achieve—its goal—but is accomplished through the operative goals. The Seashore and Yuchtman perspective is very useful in its attention to environmental transactions and its use of organizationally based data. Although they argue against the goal model, their own work is not that much different from the perspective taken here. Their approach is an empirical verification of the importance of the operative-goal concept.

We have seen that organizational effectiveness ultimately revolves around organizational goals, even when the system-resources implications are considered. At times, however, organizational goals are too vague to be usable as criteria for effectiveness. Organizations are then

---

[45] For additional criticisms of this approach, see Price, "The Study of Organizational Effectiveness."

[46] Seashore and Yuchtman, "Factorial Analysis," p. 378.

[47] Mayer N. Zald, in "Urban Differentiation, Characteristics of Boards of Directors, and Organizational Effectiveness," *American Journal of Sociology*, 73, No. 3 (November 1967), 261–72, uses the acquisition of resources as the criterion for effectiveness. In this case, the presence of high-status members on the boards of directors of YMCA branches is related to effectiveness because of their success in bringing in resources. Pfeffer, in "Size and Composition of Corporate Boards of Directors," also finds that boards of directors are important means by which corporations deal with critical aspects of their environment, such as financial considerations.

very likely to compare themselves with other similar organizations.[48] When colleges and universities compare themselves with other such institutions on the basis of faculty salaries, number of books in the library, or proportion of faculty with advanced degrees, they indicate that other effectiveness criteria are not available.

Although effectiveness is thus a difficult issue and one for which there are no universal criteria, all organizations attempt to maximize their effectiveness. In the next section, findings presented in regard to effectiveness indicate the extent to which effectiveness is *contingent* upon factors internal and external to the organization. The findings also indicate that *choices* are made within the organization on the issue of effectiveness.

STUDIES OF EFFECTIVENESS

The first study to be discussed is the landmark research of Lawrence and Lorsch.[49] The organizations studied were in the plastics, food, and container industries. Effectiveness was determined by change in profits, change in sales volume, and introduction of new products in the five years prior to the study. In addition, the chief executive in each organization gave a subjective appraisal of that organization's effectiveness. These effectiveness measures correlated well together.

The organizations operated in diverse environments. The plastics firms had to deal with the most dynamic and diverse environment, primarily because of the rate of technological development in the field. The container firms had a relatively stable environment, with the food firms falling in between. Because of the environmental conditions, integration within the plastics firms was problematic. The high-performing plastics firm

> had developed an elaborate set of formal devices (both an integrating unit and cross-functional teams) to facilitate the resolution of conflict and the achievement of integration. Because market and scientific factors were uncertain and complex, the lower and middle echelons of management had to be involved in reaching joint departmental decisions; these managers were centrally involved in the resolution of conflict. This organization also met all the determinants of effective conflict resolution.[50]

---

[48] Carl J. Schramm, "Thompson's Assessment of Organizations: Universities and the AAUP Salary Grades," *Administrative Science Quarterly*, 20, No. 1 (March 1975), 87–96.

[49] Lawrence and Lorsch, *Organizations and Environment.*

[50] *Ibid.*, pp. 151–52.

Conventional wisdom is usually that conflict within organizations is bad. In the high-performing plastics firms, there was a great deal of differentiation and conflict. Both contribute to performance. In the container firms, in contrast, the environment was relatively stable and homogeneous. High performance here was associated with little intrafirm differentiation, and integration was carried out by the managerial hierarchy itself. Influence was concentrated at the top of the organization. There was much less emphasis on conflict resolution, for which there were no formal mechanisms.

Thus, effectiveness in these two kinds of organization was related to organizational characteristics quite different from those of the third organizational type. Organizational structures and processes that were effective in the container industry would be ineffective in the plastics industry, and vice versa. Effectiveness is *contingent* upon the environment and the structure of the organization.

Much evidence corroborates this approach. In an earlier study, Tom Burns and G. M. Stalker found that more appropriate to stable conditions were "mechanistic" or formal and hierarchical managerial styles, while more appropriate to unstable conditions were "organic" or less formal styles, with lateral interactions rather than hierarchical command.[51] Robert Duncan found that effective decision-making units within organizations structured themselves differently according to whether environmental certainty or uncertainty was perceived.[52] The same units would use different mechanisms, depending on the situations being confronted.

A slightly altered contingency approach is taken by Selwyn W. Becker and Duncan Neuhauser in their analysis of the efficiency of hospitals and insurance firms.[53] They suggest that there are two kinds of procedures within organizations—production procedures and visibility procedures. Production procedures are those concerned with the output of the organization, while visibility procedures are designed to make the owner or controller of the organization aware of just how well the organization is achieving its goals. Becker and Neuhauser maintain that production procedures should be highly specified when tasks, both individually and in the aggregate, are simple, and less specified when the aggregate of tasks is more complex. In both cases, however, efficiency is achieved when the visibility of consequences within the organization is high. Thus

[51] Tom Burns and G. M. Stalker, *The Management of Innovation* (London: Tavistock Publications, 1961).

[52] Robert B. Duncan, "Multiple Decision-Making Structures in Adapting to Environmental Uncertainty," *Human Relations*, 26 (July 1973), 273–91.

[53] Selwyn W. Becker and Duncan Neuhauser, *The Efficient Organization* (New York: Elsevier Scientific Publishing Company, Inc., 1975).

the contingency model remains usable, but with the addition of internal auditing or performance-recording mechanisms.

The contingency approach which has been discussed does not answer all questions regarding effectiveness. Studies based on this approach have primarily used profit as the single goal and ignored other considerations. Moreover, contingencies may take different forms than environmental complexity. Richard N. Osborn and James G. Hunt found that the effectiveness of social service agencies was related to the degree of dependency on the task environment and interorganizational interactions.[54] Organizations that are highly dependent can be threatened with failure (total ineffectiveness) if an important part of this environment, such as the federal government, pulls the financial plug.

In a related study, Stanley Lieberson and James F. O'Connor studied the sales, earnings, and profit margins of 167 large U.S. corporations.[55] They found that the critical determinants of sales and net earnings of an organization were such environmental factors as: which industry the organization was in; its position within that industry; and general economic conditions. The impact of top leadership on these indicators of effectiveness was minimal, although leadership was important in terms of profit margins. Again, the link to the environment is important, but in both of the last two studies cited the environment is conceived more in terms of general political and economic conditions rather than of its complexity or dynamics.

One problem with the contingency approach is that it can lead to a conclusion that organizations simply react to the environment whereas, in reality, organizations try to control their environment to their own advantage in order to increase effectiveness. Paul M. Hirsch has examined effectiveness in the phonograph record and the pharmaceutical industries.[56] The typical pharmaceutical firm is far more profitable than the typical phonograph record firm. Much of the difference is accounted for by the pharmaceutical firms' ability to control pricing and distribution, by the patent and copyright laws, and by external opinion leaders such as the American Medical Association. The environment is thus made more favorable for the organization by its own manipulations.

---

[54] Richard N. Osborn and James G. Hunt, "Environment and Organizational Effectiveness," *Administrative Science Quarterly*, 19, No. 2 (June 1974), 231–46.

[55] Stanley Lieberson and James F. O'Connor, "Leadership and Organizational Performance: A Study of Large Corporations," *American Sociological Review*, 37, No. 2 (April 1972), 117–30. This research will be discussed more fully in the chapter on leadership.

[56] Paul M. Hirsch, "Organizational Effectiveness and the Institutional Environment," *Administrative Science Quarterly*, 20, No. 3 (September 1975), 327–44.

The contingency approach to effectiveness can be criticized from another standpoint. Johannes Pennings has pointed out that the model may best be used on organizations within which there is a high degree of interdependence.[57] Manufacturing firms exhibit such interdependence among the units within the organization. Pennings found that in stock brokerage offices the individual brokers could operate independently. In this situation, the contingency approach was poor at predicting effectiveness. We thus have the irony that the contingency approach is itself contingent upon the organizational situation.

The studies discussed have focused primarily on the environment of organizations, but decisions made within organizations also determine effectiveness. As was pointed out in the previous chapter, strategic choices in regard to the direction an organization will take must be added to the contingency framework. Child has suggested that poor performance or ineffectiveness can lead to attempts to change the organizational structure or to manipulate the environment, or to the adaptation of alternative performance standards.[58] This is done in a decision-making framework of coalitions and internal organizational politics.

This review of studies of effectiveness was intended to demonstrate that there are no single models or prescriptions for effectiveness. Certainly, organizations respond to the environment and some responses are more appropriate or effective than others. There are also efforts to shape the environment to increase organizational effectiveness, and decisions are made in regard to the best methods of achieving effectiveness. The presence of multiple and conflicting goals, however, makes effectiveness an ideal rather than a reality. Nevertheless, organizations attempt to be effective, and some forms of organizing are more effective than others. If the "one best way" for all organizations could be developed there would be no need for additional studies, and the possessor of the one best way could control the world.

SUMMARY AND CONCLUSIONS

Organizations have definitive goals that serve as bases for their activities. The operative goals are set by the key decision makers within the organization. These goals can be in conflict with each other, but priorities

[57] Johannes M. Pennings, "The Relevance of the Structural-Contingency Model for Organizational Effectiveness," *Administrative Science Quarterly*, 20, No. 3 (September 1975), 393–410.

[58] John Child, "Organizational Structure, Environment, and Performance: The Role of Strategic Choice," *Sociology*, 6, No. 1 (January 1972), 1–22.

among them are established. Survival of the organization is a continuing operative goal. Effectiveness, whether in the eyes of the organization participants, clients or consumers, or superordinates in the organization, can best be understood in terms of these operative goals. To maximize its effectiveness, an organization must deal with its environment, which it can try to manipulate to its own advantage. At the same time, to be effective, the organization has to respond to the environment in terms of its structure and internal operations, particularly when there is a high degree of interdependence within the organization.

The next section of the book deals with organizational structure, a topic that has been alluded to but not fully developed in the present discussion. It should already be clear that there is not a single structural form for all organizations and that structure is a consequence of contingencies and choice.

TWO

organizational structure

During the 1960s and the first half of the 1970s, the sociological study of organizations has been dominated by the analysis of organizational structure. There have been some positive and some negative consequences. On the positive side, research results have permitted some firm conclusions to be drawn in regard to many correlates of different structural forms, and some limited theories have emerged. On the negative side, the analysis of organizational structures just isn't all that exciting, except to researchers in the area. The lack of excitement stems from two conditions. First, structural analysts have been unable to convey the importance of structure in the operation of organizations. Second, they have been largely unable to deal with the dynamics of organizations. The second problem derives largely from the methodological approaches used, while the first is a matter of style of presentation. It is up to the reader to decide whether this first problem has been solved in the next four chapters.

What is structure? In the next chapter a formal definition will be developed. Here, a few examples will be used to indicate the importance of structure to the operation of organizations. About a year ago, this author was involved in a research project which required a fair amount of travel within the United States. On several of the trips it was necessary to obtain a travel advance. This took the form of a check made out by the University of Minnesota. The check was handwritten rather than computer-produced. Upon arriving at the bank, I was told by the teller that he could not cash the check, since it was for over $100. I had to see his superior, Ms. Smith, for her approval before the check could be cashed. This simple event illustrates several things about organizational structure. First, there is an obvious division of labor. There is also a hierarchy in operation. The organization has specified procedures for handling situations like this. The teller could not use his own judgment on whether to cash the check. Even if the teller had been an old friend, he would still be required to obtain authorization for a check exceeding a certain amount. The supervisor also has a list of procedures to follow in deciding whether to approve of the person cashing the check. This is a highly structured situation.

A very different situation is found when the activities associated with writing this book are considered. No specification of procedures or hierarchy are involved. The background research and the writing itself are accomplished at the discretion of the writer. There may be some division of labor in terms of help with some of the typing. There is a great deal of discretion in terms of content. It is a highly unstructured situation.

These examples should indicate some of the characteristics of organizational structure (although the examples should not be taken too seriously as bases for generalizations). It would be a mistake to conclude that banks are more structured than universities; in some areas they are but in others they are not. There are highly structured components of universities and minimally structured components of banks. This intraorganizational structural variation should be kept in mind throughout the discussion of structure.

The elements of organizational structure that will be analyzed here are complexity, formalization, and centralization. Each of these will be treated as a variable ranging from high to low. In the examples given above, the bank would score high on each structural variable, while the university example is one of low complexity, formalization, and centralization.

To repeat, although the examples discussed above are useful in identifying the characteristics of organizational structures, they are of little use in developing systematic knowledge about such structures. A brief consideration of research strategies and techniques is in order so that the research and the conclusions derived therefrom can best be critically appreciated.

Almost all of the research to be considered is comparative in that data are collected from more than one organization.[1] This compara-

---

[1] See Wolf V. Heydebrand, ed., *Comparative Organizations: The Results of Empirical Research* (Englewood Cliffs, N.J.: Prentice-Hall, Inc., 1973).

tive approach sometimes extends to data collected from different societies, but most comparative organizational research is limited to studies within one nation. Comparative research has enabled organizational researchers to generalize beyond the particular set of organizations being studied. Most researchers try to make their findings as widely usable as possible.

Such generalizing remains problematic, however, for two major reasons. First, even though research data come from more than one organization, there is almost no way of knowing the extent to which the organizations studied are representative of the universe of organizations about which generalizations are to be made. The important research conducted in Great Britain by Woodward and the Aston Group (Pugh, Hickson, Hinings, et al.)[2] has been largely of industrial firms. In the United States, the work of Blau and his associates has been primarily among government agencies; that of Aiken and Hage among health and welfare organizations; and that of Hall and his associates among sets of heterogeneous organizations that cannot be thought of as a sample of organizations. A basic problem is that there is no universe of organizations from which a sample can be drawn. There is no organizational census to serve as a sample base analogous to the census of private citizens. There are directories of manufacturers, lists of schools, and the like, but no overall listings.

Moreover, there is no usable classification scheme to permit generalizations within the limits of a particular "type" of organization. For example, although few researchers would suggest that research in a government employment security office cannot be generalized to an industrial research laboratory, probably none of the researchers would be sure as to exactly what can be so generalized.

The second major problem is measurement. Two approaches to measurement have predominated: the institutional method and the survey method.[3] The institutional method relies upon documents and records of the organization together with information gathered

---

[2] Specific references will accompany discussion of the research.

[3] Johannes Pennings, "Measures of Organizational Structure: A Methodological Note," *American Journal of Sociology*, 79, No. 3 (November 1973), 686–704. See also Koya Azumi and Charles J. McMillan, "Subjective and Objective Measures of Structure," New York, American Sociological Association Annual Meetings, 1974.

from key informants about the organization. The focus of this method is upon the formal or official characteristics of the organizations. The survey method, on the other hand, relies on information from all or a sample of organizational participants, using interviews or questionnaires. In the survey approach, the questions asked are about the organization rather than about the individual. Both approaches are designed to measure elements of organizational structure.

The problem is that measures intended to measure the same thing—formalization, for example—apparently do not, since organizational scores on the two types of measurement are either weakly or negatively correlated. Pennings suggests that this may be due to the fact that the structural elements are multidimensional. That is, elements such as formalization and centralization probably include several components that themselves may or may not be correlated.

This discussion of some of the methodological problems is intended to indicate that the research findings in regard to structure are not complete. As will be seen, many of them, regardless of the organizations studied or the measurement technique used, make a great deal of sense. The materials to be presented should be understood as tentative (as is the case with all research).

4

the nature and consequences of structure

The idea of structure is basically simple. Buildings have structures, in the form of beams, interior walls, passageways, roofs, and so on. The structure of a building is a major determinant of the movements and activities of the people within it. Buildings are supposed to have structures that fit the activities that go on within them. An office building is different from a factory. Factories where automobiles are made are different from those where computers are made. Architects design buildings to fit the needs of the activities that are to be carried out within them. They are designed to accommodate populations of various sizes— no architect would design a huge cathedral for a small congregation—and to withstand the environment in which they are located. Buildings in Minnesota are different from those in Arizona. While the size, major activity or technology to be used, and environment are all important in building design, so too is the element of choice—of decor, color, and so on.

The analogy of organizational structures to those of buildings is not perfect, since organizations are not built by architects but by the people within them. But the factors that affect or determine the structure of buildings do the same for organizations. This chapter will examine the interacting influences of size, technology, environment, and choice on organizational structures.

By organizational structure we mean ". . . the distributions, along various lines, of people among social positions that influence the role relations among these people."[1] This simple definition requires amplification. One implication of the definition is the division of labor: people are given different tasks or jobs within organizations. Another implication is that organizations contain ranks, or a hierarchy: the positions that people

[1] Peter M. Blau, *On the Nature of Organizations* (New York: John Wiley & Sons, Inc., 1974), p. 12.

fill have rules and regulations that specify, in varying degrees, how incumbents are to behave in these positions.

Organizational structure serves two basic functions. First, structures are designed to minimize or at least regulate the influence of individual variations on the organization. Structure is imposed to ensure that individuals conform to the requirements of the organization and not vice versa. Second, structure is the setting in which power is exercised (structure also sets or determines which positions have power in the first place), in which decisions are made (the flow of information which goes into a decision is largely determined by structure), and in which the organization's activities are carried out.

Many discussions of structure do not take the individual into account. It was just noted that one function of structure is to regulate the influence of individual variations. This regulation can be severe or hardly noticeable. In some cases every individual action is monitored, while in others the individual is encouraged to utilize the utmost discretion possible. It should be noted that when discretion is emphasized, the organization typically has exercised strong initial control in its processes of selecting the individuals.[2]

Organizational structures have impacts on individuals above and beyond this determination of the amount of discretion exercised. For example, the position of an individual in an organization, such as clerk, supervisor, middle manager, or whatever, shapes that individual's reactions to the organization.[3] Although such demographic factors as age or sex are also determinants, the position of the individual appears to be more important. Similarly, the satisfaction of the individual with work is related to organizational structure.[4] Although the difficulties in classifying both individuals and organizations make the evidence inconclusive, it appears that some kinds of workers are more satisfied in one kind of organizational structure while others prefer a different kind. In the Ivancevich and Donnelly study, for example, the research subjects, salesmen, were

[2] See Peter M. Blau and Richard A. Schoenherr, *The Structure of Organizations* (New York: Basic Books, 1971), 347–57.

[3] Jeanne B. Herman, Randall B. Dunham, and Charles L. Hulin, "Organizational Structure, Demographic Characteristics, and Employee Responses," *Organizational Behavior and Human Performance*, 13, No. 2 (April 1975), 206–32. See also Melvin L. Kohn and Carmi Schooler, "Occupational Experience and Psychological Functioning: An Assessment of Reciprocal Effects," *American Sociological Review*, 38, No. 1 (February 1973), 97–118.

[4] John M. Ivancevich and James H. Donnelly, Jr., "Relation of Organizational Structure to Job Satisfaction, Anxiety-Stress, and Performance," *Administrative Science Quarterly*, 20, No. 2 (June 1975), 272–80.

found to be more satisfied and less anxious in "flat" organizational structures, ones with few hierarchical levels.

Structural characteristics and individual characteristics interact. Indeed, things that might appear to be a consequence of individual actions can turn out to have important structural linkages. For example, the capacity for innovation, generally thought to be crucial for organizational survival, would seemingly be based on the capabilities of the individuals in the organization. This may not be the case, however; J. Victor Baldridge and Robert A. Burnham found that structural factors, such as organizational size and complexity, together with environmental characteristics, were more related to organizational innovations than were individual factors such as age, attitudes, and education.[5] Once again, the point is not that individuals are unimportant, but rather that individual characteristics *interact* with organizational structural characteristics to produce the events within organizations.

In the discussion that follows, there is an unfortunate problem with much of the literature to be discussed: the overwhelming majority of studies of organizational structures wittingly or unwittingly make the assumption that there is *a* structure in an organization; but there is ample evidence that this is not the case.[6] There are structural differences between work units, departments, and divisions. There are also structural differences according to the position on the hierarchy. For example, a hospital admissions unit has explicit rules and procedures so that all persons who are admitted are treated the same way and so that employees are guided by a clear set of organizationally prescribed expectations. The physical rehabilitation unit of the same hospital has many fewer specific guidelines concerning what it is to do. Similarly, the behavior of lower-level workers, such as orderlies and kitchen workers, is prescribed to a much higher degree than is that of nurses and physicians. There is intra-organizational variation both across organizational units and up and down the hierarchy.

[5] J. Victor Baldridge and Robert A. Burnham, "Organizational Innovation: Individual, Organizational, and Environmental Impacts," *Administrative Science Quarterly*, 20, No. 2 (June 1975), 165–76.

[6] Eugene Litwak, "Models of Organization Which Permit Conflict," *American Journal of Sociology*, 76, No. 2 (September 1961), 177–84; Richard H. Hall, "Intraorganizational Structural Variation: Application of the Bureaucratic Model," *Administrative Science Quarterly*, 7, No. 3 (December 1962), 295–308; Andrew Van de Ven and Andre Delbecq, "A Task Contingent Model of Work Unit Structure," *Administrative Science Quarterly*, 19, No. 2 (June 1974), 183–97; and Andrew Van de Ven, "Equally Efficient Structural Variations within Organizations," in L. Pondy, D. Slevin, and R. Killman, eds., *The Management of Organization Design: Research and Methodology* (New York: Elsevier Publishing Company, 1976).

It is unfortunate that this intraorganizational structural variation is not more frequently considered in research, for the general findings in regard to size, technology, environment, and choice would have as much applicability—if not more—to the divisions within organizations as they do to the total organizations studied. In other words, if large size, a routine technology, a calm environment, and a choice to leave the organization unchanged are assumed, the impact on the structure of a unit within an organization would probably be greater than the impact of these same factors upon the total organization. The ideas to be developed thus fit both total organizations and the units therein.

THE SIZE FACTOR

Size is obviously the number of employees in an organization. Or is it? This is an adequate definition only in those cases where the organization is composed solely of full-time paid employees.[7] The issue is much more complex, however, when volunteer and/or part-time personnel comprise a major part of the organization. For example, a county political party organization may have five or six paid employees between elections. During the heat of an intense political campaign, the number might be multiplied by a thousand or more volunteer and unpaid people, all of whom work varying numbers of hours. Similarly, a grocery-store chain may have several thousand full-time employees, but its effective size is much larger because of the great number of part-time workers. In both cases, using just the number of full-time paid employees would be extremely misleading in any kind of comparative research.

The Conceptual Issue

The problem of numbers can be resolved, as we will see shortly. A more basic issue in regard to size is the conceptual one, in terms of who is counted as an organization member in the first place. Again, in the

---

[7] Several authors prefer to deal with size in terms of "scale of operation," noting that an organization with a small number of members may have huge assets or sales or add a great deal to the number of employees through capital investment. While this is undoubtedly the case, few studies have utilized such an approach and, in general, the scale of operations will be closely related to size as defined here. Seymour Melman, "The Rise of Administrative Overhead in the Manufacturing Industries of the United States, 1899–1947," *Oxford Economic Papers* (*New Series*), 3 (January 1951), 62–112, uses several measures of scale of operation. Oscar Grusky, "Corporate Size, Bureaucratization, and Managerial Succession," *American Journal of Sociology*, 67, No. 3 (November 1961), also uses scale of operation.

case of organizations with paid employees, the issue is a rather simple one, although even here, customers, clients, and stockholders could be included within the organization. Since it has been amply demonstrated that these "outsiders" can have an important impact on the organization, they could legitimately be included in analyses. However, their primary interests lie outside the organization, and so they can be excluded for the present purposes. The issue is more complicated when some nonemployees are included within the organization.

Many prisons present a striking example of the difficulties inherent in this situation. Prisoners, unlike the other members of such an organization, are in the organization all the time. For them it is a "total institution," in Goffman's terms.[8] Prisoners also work in the laundry, kitchen, shops, and so on. Further complicating the issue is the fact that the number of paid employees per prisoner can vary according to differing emphases on custody, rehabilitation, and level of security. The same issue, with perhaps the exceptions of security, custody, and rehabilitation, is seen in colleges and universities, where the clients served are an integral part of the organization and also work in the organization, as research assistants, secretaries, janitors, and so forth.

The Methodological Issue

These conceptual difficulties are eased when research on size is examined. While various research efforts have utilized different measures of organizational size in settings containing clients, inmates, or students, there is a high correlation among the different possible measures. In an examination of general and tuberculosis hospitals, Theodore Anderson and Seymour Warkov found correlations of .966 and .977 between average daily patient load and the total hospital labor force.[9] In a study of colleges and universities, Amos Hawley, Walter Boland, and Margaret Boland found a correlation coefficient of .943 between student enrollment and the size of full- and part-time faculty.[10] While the conceptual issue is not resolved by these data, measures of size do appear to be largely interchangeable for research and operational purposes.

Hall, Haas, and Johnson resolved the difficulty with part-time and volunteer workers by computing the number of full-time equivalent

[8] Erving Goffman, "On the Characteristics of Total Institutions," in *The Prison*, ed. Donald R. Cressey (New York: Holt, Rinehart and Winston, Inc., 1961).

[9] Theodore Anderson and Seymour Warkov, "Organizational Size and Functional Complexity," *American Sociological Review*, 26, No. 1 (February 1961), 25.

[10] Amos Hawley, Walter Boland, and Margaret Boland, "Population Size and Administration in Institutions of Higher Education," *American Sociological Review*, 30, No. 2 (April 1965), 253.

workers in the total labor force of an organization. This involves determining the number of hours per year contributed to the organization by such workers, divided by the number of hours a full-time employee normally works in a year.[11] The use of the full-time equivalent size permits comparisons to be made among organizations engaging in widely different activities.

One additional component of the size factor should be noted. In an analysis of 46 English organizations, Pugh et al., utilizing the number of employees in a standard fashion, also looked at the net assets of the organizations. As in the relations between numbers of employees and total number of members, a high correlation (.78) was found between number of employees and net assets. Thus, we can conclude that an organization's membership size is closely related to its financial size; large organizations are large in terms of both their membership and their resources.

In the discussion that follows, the size factor will be referred to as "organizational members" rather than "number of employees," because of the relationships we have mentioned. Since the purpose of the total analysis is a better understanding of organizations of all types, the use of members as the basis for discussion allows more kinds of organizations to be included. As we shall see, the findings in regard to size appear to be quite consistent across a wide spectrum of "types" of organizations.

If there is some agreement on the nature and measurement of organizational size, there is little as to the impact of size on structure. There is some compelling evidence that size is the major determinant of structure; but there is compelling evidence that size is *not* of critical importance.[12] In the discussion that follows, we will try to make some sense out of this evidence.

The major proponent of the importance of size as a determinant of structure has been Peter M. Blau and his associates.[13] Blau's data come

[11] Richard H. Hall, J. Eugene Haas, and Norman J. Johnson, "Organizational Size, Complexity, and Formalization," *American Sociological Review*, 32, No. 6 (December 1967), 905.

[12] For general discussions of the importance of size, see Theodore Caplow, "Organizational Size," *Administrative Science Quarterly*, 1, No. 4 (March 1957), 484–505; Theodore Caplow, *Principles of Organization* (New York: Harcourt Brace Jovanovich, Inc., 1965), pp. 25–28; Oscar Grusky, "Corporate Size"; F. Stuart Chapin, "The Growth of Bureaucracy: An Hypothesis," *American Sociological Review*, 16, No. 6 (December 1951), 835–56; and John E. Tsouderos, "Organizational Change in Terms of a Series of Selected Variables," *American Sociological Review*, 20, No. 2 (April 1955), 206–10.

[13] See Peter M. Blau, Wolf V. Heydebrand, and Robert E. Stauffer, "The Structure of Small Bureaucracies," *American Sociological Review*, 31, No. 2 (April 1966),

primarily from studies of government agencies, such as state employment services and municipal finance divisions, and from universities and department stores. The data reveal some fascinating anomalies about organizations and also some important considerations about the role of organizations in contemporary society. There are also some problems with the data, which will be discussed later in this section.

Blau's studies are concerned primarily with organizational size and differentiation. Differentiation is measured by the number of levels, departments, and job titles within an organization. The research findings indicate that increasing size is related to increasing differentiation.[14] The rate of differentiation decreases, however, with increasing size. On the other hand, administrative overhead is lower in larger organizations, and the span of control for supervisors is greater. Since administrative overhead is inversely related to size and the span of control is directly, or positively, related to size, larger organizations are able to achieve an economy of scale. It is here that the anomaly is demonstrated. Size is related to differentiation, and differentiation, bringing increased need for control and coordination, is related to increased requirements for administrative overhead. Size and differentiation thus work at cross purposes. Blau concludes that the size factor is more critical and that economy of scale still results from large size.

The second major set of studies that find size to be the major determinant of organizational structure are those of the Aston group.[15] These

---

179–91; Blau, "The Hierarchy of Authority in Organizations," *The American Journal of Sociology*, 73, No. 4 (January 1968), 453–67; *The Organization of Academic Work* (New York: John Wiley and Sons, Inc., 1973); *On the Nature of Organizations;* Blau and Richard A. Schoenherr, *The Structure of Organizations* (New York: Basic Books, 1971); "A Formal Theory of Differentiation in Organizations," *American Sociological Review*, 35, No. 2 (April 1970), 201–18; "Interdependence and Hierarchy in Organizations," *Social Science Research*, 1, No. 1 (April 1972), 1–24. See also Marshall W. Meyer, "Automation and Bureaucratic Structure," *American Journal of Sociology*, 74, No. 3 (November 1968), 256–64; "The Two Authority Structures of Bureaucratic Organization," *Administrative Science Quarterly*, 13, No. 2 (September 1968; "Some Constraints in Analyzing Data on Organizational Structures," *American Sociological Review*, 36, No. 2 (April 1971), 294–97 (see Blau's Reply, 304–7); "Size and the Structure of Organizations: A Causal Analysis," *American Sociological Review*, 37, No. 4 (August 1972), 434–40; and Sheila Klatzky, "The Relationship of Organizational Size to Complexity and Coordination," *Administrative Science Quarterly*, 15, No. 4 (December 1970), 428–38.

[14] These conclusions are summarized from Blau, "A Formal Theory of Differentiation."

[15] See Derek S. Pugh, David J. Hickson, C. R. Hinings, K. M. Lupton, K. M. McDonald, C. Turner, and T. Lupton, "A Conceptual Scheme for Organizational Analysis," *Administrative Science Quarterly*, 8, No. 3 (December 1963), 289–315;

studies have been carried out primarily in Great Britain, with some supporting evidence from international comparisons. The major conclusions of these studies are that increased size is related to increased structuring of organizational activities and decreased concentration of authority. Most of the data come from manufacturing organizations, but some are based on studies in government agencies and labor unions.

There is still other evidence in regard to the importance of size. Thomas Mahoney et al. report that managerial practices are related to the size of the unit being supervised.[16] Flexibility in personnel assignments, the extent of delegation of authority, and an emphasis on results rather than procedures were related to larger unit sizes.

SIZE AND THE ADMINISTRATIVE COMPONENT

One structural characteristic that has received extensive study is the administrative component of organizations. The proportionate size of this component is frequently taken by organizational analysts as an indicator of an organization's efficiency, since a high proportion of resources spent on administration could mean a lower proportion spent on other organizational activities.

Early research and speculation tended to suggest that as organizations increased in size, the relative size of the administrative component increased disproportionately.[17] Later research has tended to contravene

---

Pugh, Hickson, Hinings, and Turner, "Dimensions of Organizational Structure," *Administrative Science Quarterly*, 13, No. 1 (June 1968), 65–105; "The Context of Organization Structures," *Administrative Science Quarterly*, 14, No. 1 (March 1969), 91–114; Hickson, Pugh, and Diana C. Pheysey, "Operations Technology and Organization Structure: An Empirical Reappraisal," *Administrative Science Quarterly*, 14, No. 3 (September 1969), 378–97; and J. Inkson, Pugh, and Hickson, "Organization Context and Structure: An Abbreviated Replication," *Administrative Science Quarterly*, 15, No. 3 (September 1970), 318–29. These works represent the original Aston studies. More recent replications and extensions include John Child and Roger Mansfield, "Technology, Size, and Organization Structure," *Sociology*, 6, No. 3 (September 1972), 369–93; Lex Donaldson and Malcolm Warner, "Bureaucratic and Electoral Control in Occupational Interest Associations," *Sociology*, 8, No. 1 (January 1974), 47–57; and David J. Hickson, C. R. Hinings, C. J. McMillan, and J. P. Schwitter, "The Culture Free Context of Organization Structure: A Tri-National Comparison," *Sociology*, 8, No. 1 (January 1974), 59–80.

[16] Thomas A. Mahoney, Peter Frost, Norman F. Crandall, and William Weitzel, "The Conditioning Influence of Organization Size upon Managerial Practice," *Organizational Behavior and Human Performance*, 8, No. 2 (October 1972), 230–41.

[17] The speculative efforts are typified by the semiserious work of C. Northcote Parkinson, *Parkinson's Law* (Boston: Houghton Mifflin Company, 1957), pp. 2–13.

this, suggesting that the relationship is either in the opposite direction or is curvilinear.[18] Some of the confusion in the information on this subject is linked to definitional problems. A common definition for these purposes is "staff versus line," with the staff composing the administrative component. Unfortunately, these terms are not used consistently even in industrial practice, let alone in organizations where line (production) activities are less clear. Other research has utilized occupational titles derived from the Bureau of the Census.[19] The use of occupational titles in this way has been restricted to examinations of the size of the administrative component by broad industrial classifications, and can lead only to generalizations about the overall proportion of personnel devoted to administration within broad industry categories, since information about specific organizations is not available. A futher difficulty with the use of census-based data is that they have been limited to production organizations. Since much, if not most, of the organizational "action" occurs outside private industry, this is a severely limited perspective.

In their analysis of hospitals, Anderson and Warkov used the "percent of all employees classified in the category, 'General Hospital Administration.' "[20] This is a sound measure for hospitals, but it obviously cannot be used in other settings. Furthermore, other kinds of organizations may define their administrative component differently. This would lead to extreme difficulties in generalization. Since the important issue here for both practice and research is really administrative overhead, in terms of costs and energies expended, a more generally applicable definition is preferable. Haas, Hall, and Johnson have proposed that the definitional and conceptual problem can be resolved by taking account of all the

---

Research in this area is exemplified by Fred C. Terrien and Donald C. Mills, "The Effect of Changing Size upon the Internal Structure of an Organization," *American Sociological Review*, 20, No. 1 (February 1955), 11–14.

[18] See Anderson and Warkov, "Organizational Size"; Hawley et al., "Population Size"; J. Eugene Haas, Richard H. Hall, and Norman Johnson, "The Size of the Supportive Component in Organizations: A Multi-Organizational Analysis," *Social Forces*, 42, No. 1 (October 1963), 9–17; Gerry E. Hendershot and Thomas F. James, "Size and Growth as Determinants of Administrative-Production Ratios in Organizations," *American Sociological Review*, 37, No. 2 (April 1972), 149–53; and Blau and Schoenherr, *The Structure of Organizations*.

[19] See William A. Rushing, "The Effects of Industry Size and Division of Labor on Administration," *Administrative Science Quarterly*, 12, No. 2 (September 1967), 273–95; and Louis R. Pondy, "Effects of Size, Complexity, and Ownership on Administrative Intensity," *Administrative Science Quarterly*, 14, No. 1 (March 1969), 47–60. This approach is based on and extends the earlier work of Melman, "Rise of Administrative Overhead."

[20] Anderson and Warkov, "Organizational Size," p. 25.

personnel in an organization who engage in "supportive" activities.[21] Thus, custodial workers, some drivers, cafeteria employees, clerical help, and so on, are included in the administrative component, regardless of whether they are directly employed in "staff" or "general administrative" divisions.

This approach is based on the idea that the crucial factor is the number of workers engaged in tasks centered on the organization's major activities. That is, organizational personnel can be divided into those who contribute directly to the attainment of the organization's goals and those who do not. As we have said, not *all* of anyone's activities are directly goal-related, but most personnel can be easily placed into the direct or indirect (administrative component) categories. Such a definition has the advantage of being applicable to all types of organizations, and this is particularly important when we consider administrative types of organizations. Government bureaus, for example, can thus be compared with manufacturing organizations or hospitals in a reasonable way. The "administrator" in a government agency is equivalent to the "production manager" in industry, as are some clerical workers to assembly-line workers.

Findings from research that uses this approach to the administrative component indicate that the relationship under discussion is curvilinear. That is, the size of the administrative component is "*greater* for the smaller (0–700 employees) and larger (over 1400 employees) organizations than for those of moderate size."[22] Since the number of organizations used in this study was quite small, these findings cannot be taken as conclusive. However, the same general findings were reported by Hawley et al. in their study of colleges and universities, so that the curvilinear relationship suggested may be the true one.

The studies by Haas et al. and Hawley et al. also suggest that the relative size of the administrative component decreases as organizational size increases. The tendency toward curvilinearity is slight, and the increase among the large organizations does not reach the level found in the smaller organizations. The strong tendency for the administrative component to decrease in size is consistent with the findings of Anderson and Warkov and of Reinhard Bendix.[23] Organizations do apparently achieve an economy of scale, in that the proportion of persons engaged in administration decreases as the organization increases in size.

There are a number of explanations for such economies. It is clear that

---

[21] Haas, Hall, and Johnson, "Size of the Supportive Component," p. 12.

[22] *Ibid.*, p. 14.

[23] Anderson and Warkov, "Organizational Size"; and Reinhard Bendix, *Work and Authority in Industry* (New York: John Wiley & Sons, Inc., 1956), p. 222, Table 7.

certain tasks are required for organizational existence in contemporary society. Personnel administration, accounting, janitorial services, and so on, must be performed regardless of organizational size. In the extremely small organization, these may all be performed by the same person, but in organizations of even moderate size (the exact numbers are not known), separate personnel are needed for each of these functions. In the smaller organizations, "the personnel engaged in such activities may be 'underused' in the sense that full use is not made of their efforts in their particular areas of specialization. As organizations become larger, these same persons can perhaps continue to handle the supportive work load without the addition of other personnel. In other words, more complete use is made of such persons, thus reducing the proportion of the total personnel needed to maintain supportive activities."[24] Larger organizations would also be the most likely, from a financial point of view, to install computers and other labor-saving devices and thus reduce the size of the administrative component.

According to some analysts, organizational size is not the critical factor in understanding the size of the administrative component. Louis Pondy, in reviewing the literature on this issue, concludes that technology is a major contributor to the administrative configuration. He notes that task complexity and an intensive division of labor require administrative personnel for coordination.[25] Anderson and Warkov's findings that spatial dispersion and multiple departments of the same organization increase the size of the administrative component is also taken as an indicator of the effects of heightened technological development. In addition, it would appear that organizations whose activities require technological innovations through research and development would almost by definition have proportionately more personnel involved in the administrative (supporting-activities) component.

Pondy's own research confirms the importance of technological factors, but adds to the equation the factor of the form of organizational control. Pondy's data are taken from census information by industry, and are thus subject to the limitation that they are not based on data from organizations per se. However, his research yields useful insights into the processes leading to differential patterning of the administrative component. Consistent with the argument presented here, he finds that the administrative-component size decreases with increased organizational size. He includes an additional variable: the form of ownership of the organization. The data suggest that owner-managers and partnerships are less

---

[24] Haas et al., "Size of the Supportive Component," p. 16.
[25] Pondy, "Effects of Size," p. 47.

likely to add professional and administrative personnel, probably owing to their unwillingness to dilute their personal power.[26] Although this might lead to less profitability, it maintains the existing organizational stability. But incorporated firms, by the addition of professionals and administrators, while increasing costs, also appear to increase profits.

These findings and interpretations suggest that in nonprofit organizations the same processes would probably operate. Organizations controlled by a "strong" administrator (college president, hospital administrator, government agency chief, etc.) would be expected to have a lower proportion of personnel engaged in administrative tasks. It also appears that administrative costs, if they are incurred by the utilization of skilled personnel, would actually lead to increased organizational effectiveness, since profits in industry are an indicator of effectiveness.

By and large, the studies discussed have been cross-sectional, with the data based on one point in time. Thus, organizational size is stable for the brief duration of the study. It may well be that when dealing with numbers the more interesting issue is growth or decline.[27] This appears to be true of the administrative component. Hendershot and James, for example, found that school districts that had undergone rapid growth had the common negative relationship between size and administrative intensity.[28] The districts that had experienced slow growth had an opposite relationship. In another analysis, John Freeman and Michael T. Hannan suggest that growth and decline patterns may be more complicated than most analysts had thought.[29] They suggest that the direct (or production) component of organizations will respond to changes in demand; if the demand for the organization's product or services increases or decreases, the direct component will accordingly increase or decrease in size. But this response to the environment does not hold for the supportive component; when the demand for services declines, there is a smaller decline in the supportive component than in the direct. The supportive component, having relatively high rank in the organization, is able to protect itself from cuts in numbers. Members of the supportive component are more able to protect their positions than are those in the direct component.

[26] Ibid., p. 57.

[27] Exceptions are Mason Haire, "Biological Models and Empirical Histories of the Growth of Organizations," in Mason Haire, ed., Modern Organization Theory (New York: John Wiley & Sons, Inc., 1959), pp. 287–93; and William H. Starbuck, "Organizational Growth and Development," in James G. March, ed., Handbook of Organizations (Chicago: Rand McNally & Co., 1965).

[28] Hendershot and James, "Size and Growth as Determinants."

[29] John Freeman and Michael T. Hannan, "Growth and Decline Processes in Organizations," American Sociological Review, 40, No. 2 (April 1975), 215–28.

SIZE AND THE INDIVIDUAL

Before turning to some problems with the relationships between size and structure, we will touch upon the impact of organizational size on the individual. For anyone who has any contact with an organization as an employee, client, or customer, its size has an immediate reality. A large organization confronts the individual with many unknowns, and size is probably the first thing that a person notices. There are sheer numbers of people doing things that are at first beyond comprehension. Unfortunately, the impact of organizational size on the individual has not been systematically investigated. A subjective impression is that the size factor has an immediate impact that then diminishes the longer a person is in the organization or in contact with it.

This impression comes from two indirectly related sorts of studies. The first type of evidence is from the investigations of the "informal work group," a phenomenon that has been universally found in all types of organizations and at all levels within them. It involves the interaction patterns that develop on the job among coworkers. These interaction patterns may or may not represent deviations from official expectations—for the present analysis this issue is unimportant. What is important is that members of organizations, large and small, are found in such groups. These groups become a meaningful part of the organization for their members. The impact of size is therefore probably strongly moderated by such groups. The person who is for whatever reason an isolate would not have the effect of size moderated and would probably face the impact continually (which in this case cannot be categorically considered either positive or negative for the mental health of the individual).

The second source of indirect evidence about the impact of size on the individual comes from studies in the community. Here the evidence suggests that although in a large community an individual does not know or interact with the majority of those with whom he comes in contact, he still maintains primary relationships with many persons in and out of his own family.[30] A smaller proportion of his relationships are warm and open, but the total number is probably not too different in a large community from that in a small one. This same point would appear to be true in organizations. Without the research that is needed for verification of these ideas, it seems clear that the immediate effects of size on the in-

---

[30] For a discussion of this issue, see Joel I. Nelson, "Clique Contacts and Family Orientations," *American Sociological Review,* 31, No. 5 (October 1966), 663–72.

dividual are moderated by the processes discussed. Studies of membership participation in voluntary organizations of varying sizes usually conclude that there is less participation in larger organizations.

Research evidence is inconclusive regarding the relationships between size and individual performance and reactions to the work situation. Leo Meltzer and James Salter report that among the physiological scientists they studied, no relationship was found between size of the employing organization and scientific productivity as measured by number of publications. On the other hand, there is a curvilinear relationship between size and job satisfaction. Satisfaction is greater in medium-sized (21 to 50 employees) than in either larger or smaller organizations.[31] Meltzer and Salter suggest that variables other than size are probably more important in accounting for morale and satisfaction.[32]

In respect to the *stress* felt by the individual in the organization, the comprehensive research of Kahn et al. comes to the same conclusion. They note:

> Americans are accustomed to thinking of growth as synonymous with organizational life, and of large size as a condition for maximum efficiency. Against these assertions must be placed the finding that stress and organizational size are substantially related. The curve of stress begins to rise as we turn from tiny organizations to those of 50 or 100 persons, and the rising curve continues until we encounter the organizational giants. Only for organizations of more than 5,000 persons does the curve of stress level off—perhaps because an organization so large represents some kind of psychological infinity and further increases are unfelt.[33]

The authors then suggest that stress cannot be eradicated by shrinking organizations to small size, since the economic consequences of such a move would be "tragic." They suggest that the reason for stress in large organizations is the need for coordination among the many members, and that the way to reduce stress is by reducing coordination requirements.

[31] Leo Meltzer and James Salter, "Organizational Structure and the Performance and Job Satisfaction of Physiologists," *American Sociological Review*, 27, No. 3 (June 1962), 351–62.

[32] *Ibid.*, pp. 360–62. See also Arlyn J. Melcher, *Structure and Process of Organizations: A Systems Approach* (Englewood Cliffs, N.J.: Prentice-Hall, Inc., 1975), pp. 31–60, for additional discussion of studies of morale, absenteeism, and other categories of individual reaction.

[33] Robert L. Kahn, Donald M. Wolfe, Robert P. Quinn, J. Diedrick Snoek, and Robert A. Rosenthal, *Organizational Stress: Studies in Role Conflict and Ambiguity* (New York: John Wiley & Sons, Inc., 1964), p. 394.

This can be done, in their opinion, by giving subunits more autonomy. The research findings discussed suggest that size is related to morale. Larger organizations do present their members with situations that lead to stress and lowered morale. The effects of size are undoubtedly different on different types of members.[34] A subjective impression, for example, is that students who come to a large university from a small town with a small high school face a much more stressful situation than those from large urban schools. The same would appear to be true for other kinds of members in other kinds of organizations. The kinds of expectations and general background a person brings to the organization will be a major factor in determining how he reacts to the organization.

The issues being discussed here are obviously important in any broad conception of human values. Some of the unrest of the late 1960s can be attributed to the size of the organizations involved. Charges of depersonalization, of being treated like an IBM card, of regimented learning, and so on, are essentially true. Large organizations necessitate that members to some degree be treated as members of categories, rather than as separate individuals. At the same time, large organizations can and do vary in structure and performance. The negative effects of size can be minimized, if not eliminated, through such devices as granting more subunits autonomy and decentralization. Except for some attempts at communal living among those who choose to "drop out" of society, a return to the "good old days" of small, intimate organizations is impossible. It is impossible for two major reasons. The first is that contemporary technology for all kinds of organizations is such that it is probably impossible to keep an organization at a small size. (It is hardly conceivable that a moratorium would be called on technological development and that a society would be forced to go back to an earlier technological state.) The second reason is that human values themselves have undoubtedly shifted. Whether for better or worse, most members of the contemporary large organization are probably more satisfied there than they would be in a smaller, more intimate setting.

Size affects not only the people who work in organizations but also those who have contact with it as "outsiders." Even supposedly impersonal and professional people such as accountants apparently are awed by organizational size and give larger business firms more favorable audits than smaller ones.[35]

---

[34] For some suggestions regarding alternative reaction patterns, see Robert Presthus, *The Organizational Society* (New York: Alfred A. Knopf, Inc., 1962).

[35] "The Numbers Game: The Larger the Company the More Understanding the Accountant?" *Forbes*, 112 (July 1973), 33–35.

SIZE AND STRUCTURE

This excursion into the impact of organizational size on the individual has taken us away from our major concern—that of the impact of size on structure. The evidence presented has emphasized the strong, positive relationship between size and structure. Other researchers question this emphasis. For one thing, both Blau and the Aston group utilize the institutional approach to measurement of structure. In a study that used the subjective approach, Richard Hall and Charles Tittle found only a modest relationship between size and perceived degree of bureaucratization.[36] In another study, utilizing the institutional approach, Hall, Haas, and Johnson came up with mixed findings in regard to size and structure.[37] Using data from a set of 75 organizations of highly varied types, they concluded:

> In general, the findings of this study in regard to size are similar to those of previous research which utilized size as a major variable; that is, the relationships between size and other structural components are inconsistent. . . . there is a slight tendency for larger organizations to be both more complex and more formalized, but only on a few variables does this relationship prove to be strong. On others, there is little, if any, established relationship.

> The complexity indicators related to size fall within three major categories. The first of these is spatial dispersion. This conclusion, in which both physical facilities and personnel are considered, is congruent with the suggestion of Anderson and Warkov that the relative size of the supportive component is also related to spatial dispersion. On a common-sense basis, such dispersion is possible only for sufficiently large organizations. A decision to add dispersed facilities may require a secondary decision to add more personnel, rather than the reverse. It also appears that a very large or extensive market is more easily or economically reached through physical dispersion. Thus, it could be argued that both size and complexity are dependent upon available economic "input," and to the extent to which such potential "input" is dispersed, large organizations will also be more complex in regard to physical dispersion.

> A second set of significant relationships is found in regard to the hierarchical differentiation. Although Woodward has noted differences in

---

[36] Richard H. Hall and Charles R. Tittle, "Bureaucracy and Its Correlates," *American Journal of Sociology*, 72, No. 3 (November 1966), 267–72.

[37] Hall, Haas, and Johnson, "Organizational Size."

the "width" of the span of control according to the technological stages of industry, the generally accepted principle of limiting the number of subordinates supervised by one person seems to be operative here. More hierarchical levels are found in larger organizations.

The third set of significant relationships is in the area of intradepartmental specialization or the specific division of labor. While the number of divisions is not related to size, this form of internal differentiation is. Performance of the major organizational activities plus such prerequisites as accounting and personnel management apparently are accomplished by departmentalization regardless of organizational size. Further specialization may take place within the existing departmental structure as the organization grows in size.

In general, the relationships between size and the complexity indicators appear to be limited to a few factors. Even in those relationships found to be statistically significant, enough deviant cases exist to cast serious doubts on the assumption that large organizations are necessarily more complex than small organizations.

The same general conclusion can be reached in regard to the formalization indicators. . . . Relatively strong relationships exist between size and the formalization of the authority structure, the stipulation of penalties for rule violation in writing, and the orientation and in-service training procedures. A general association does exist to the extent that larger organizations tend to be more formalized on the other indicators, even though the relationship is quite weak.

The most immediate implication of these findings is that neither complexity nor formalization can be implied from organizational size. A social scientist conducting research in a large organization would do well to question the frequent assumption that the organization under study is necessarily highly complex and formalized. If these two general factors are relevant to the focus of his research, he will need to examine empirically, for each organization, the level of complexity and formalization extant at that time. The ideal research procedure would be to have standardized measures of these phenomena to allow comparative research. At the minimum, the degrees to which these phenomena are present should be specified, at least nominally.

A second implication of these findings lies in the area of social control. Increased organizational formalization is a means of controlling the behavior of members of the organization by limiting individual discretion. At least one aspect of complexity, hierarchical differentiation, also is related to social control in that multiple organizational levels serve as a means of maintaining close supervision of subordinates. It seems rather clear, on the basis of this evidence, that a large organization does not necessarily have to rely upon impersonal, formalized control mechanisms. At the same time, the fact that an organization is small cannot be taken as evidence that a *gemeinschaft* sort of social system is operating. An organization need not turn to formalization if other control mechanisms are present. One such control mechanism is the level of professionalization as Hage and Blau et al. have suggested. The organizations with more professionalized staffs probably exhibit less formalization.

These findings suggest that size may be rather irrelevant as a factor in determining organizational structure. Blau et al. have indicated that structural differentiation is a *consequence* of expanding size. Our study suggests that it is relatively rare that the two factors are even associated and thus the temporal sequence or causality (expanding size produces greater differentiation) posited by Blau and colleagues is open to question. In these cases where size and complexity are associated, the sequence may well be the reverse. If a decision is made to enlarge the number of functions or activities carried out in an organization, it then becomes necessary to add more members to staff and new functional areas.[38]

These findings do not suggest that size is unimportant, but rather that factors other than size must be taken into account to understand structure. Some of these additional factors will be discussed in the sections that follow.

Research on size has met with additional criticisms. Chris Argyris has analyzed Blau's research and found it wanting in several regards.[39] He first questions the reliance on official descriptions of organizational structures. Citing several studies that have found that organization charts are nonexistent or inaccurate, and that members of top management cannot always accurately describe their own organization, Argyris wonders if the approach that Blau has taken might not invalidate the results.

Moreover, Blau's results are open to interpretations other than Blau's. Much of the data come from civil service organizations in which there are budget limitations, distinct geographical limits or boundaries, and predetermined staff sizes. These organizations also would probably adhere most rigorously to traditional organizational forms:

> . . . civil service organizations are designed directly from such
> organizational principles as task specialization, span of control, and unity
> of command, etc. As employees are hired they are, in accordance with
> unity of command and task specialization, grouped together into a
> functional unit. Given the notion of chain of command each unit has to
> have a boss. Given span of control each boss may supervise a certain

[38] *Ibid.*, pp. 111–12.
[39] Chris Argyris, *The Applicability of Organizational Sociology* (Cambridge, Mass.: Cambridge University Press, 1972), pp. 1–19.

number of subordinates. As the organization grows larger the number of units increases and so does the number of bosses increase, but given the span of control regulations, so does the need to coordinate the bosses. So we have super bosses. . . . *Size may be correlated with, but may not be said to generate or to cause, structural differentiation* [italics in original].[40]

The contention of Argyris is that factors other than size should be considered as determinants of organizational structure. Civil service organizations take the form that they do primarily because of civil service regulations. It also appears that the nature of the personnel in the organization affects its shape.[41] If the personnel are highly professionalized, for example, more administrators are needed for coordination than if the personnel are not so professionalized.

Another major criticism of viewing size as the determinant of structure comes from Howard Aldrich.[42] In a reanalysis of the Aston data, Aldrich suggests that size is actually a dependent variable: ". . . the more highly structured firms, with their greater degree of specialization, formalization, and monitoring of role performance, simply need to employ a larger work force than less structured firms."[43] In Aldrich's reanalysis, *technology* emerges as the major determinant of structure.

TECHNOLOGY AND STRUCTURE

The idea of technology in organizational analysis involves much more than the machinery or equipment utilized in production. The interest in technology has been sparked by the separate work of Joan Woodward, James Thompson, and Charles Perrow.[44] Woodward's work is particu-

---

[40] *Ibid.*, pp. 11–12.

[41] John D. Kasarda, "Effects of Personnel Turnover, Employee Qualifications, and Professional Staff Rations on Administrative Intensity and Overhead," *The Sociological Quarterly*, 14, No. 3 (Summer 1973), 350–58.

[42] Howard E. Aldrich, "Technology and Organizational Structure: A Reexamination of the Findings of the Aston Group," *Administrative Science Quarterly*, 17, No. 1 (March 1972), 26–43. See also Gordon Hilton, "Causal Inference Analysis: A Seductive Process"; Howard Aldrich, "Reply to Hilton: Seduced and Abandoned"; and David R. Heise, "How Do I Know My Data? Let Me Count the Ways," in the same issue of *Administrative Science Quarterly*.

[43] Aldrich, "Technology and Organizational Structure," p. 38.

[44] Joan Woodward, *Management and Technology* (London: Her Majesty's Stationery Office, 1958); and *Industrial Organization: Theory and Practice* (London: Oxford University Press, 1965); James D. Thompson, *Organizations in Action* (New York: McGraw-Hill Book Company, 1967); and Charles Perrow, "A Framework for the

larly interesting because she stumbled on the importance of technology during the course of a research project. She found that several critical structural variables were directly linked to the nature of the technology of the industrial firms being studied. The organizations were categorized into three types: first, the small-batch or unit-production system, as exemplified by a ship-building or aircraft-manufacturing firm; second, the large-batch or mass-production organization; third, the organization that utilizes continuous production, as do chemical or petroleum manufacturers.

Woodward's findings show that the nature of the technology vitally affected the management structures of the firms studied. The number of levels in the management hierarchy, the span of control of first-line supervisors, and the ratio of managers and supervisors to other personnel were all affected by the technology employed. Not only was structure affected, but the success or effectiveness of the organizations was related to the "fit" between technology and structure. The successful firms of each type were those that had the appropriately structured technical systems.

Thompson attempts to go beyond Woodward by developing a technology typology that encompasses all organizations. Again, a threefold system is derived. The first type is the long-linked technology, involving "serial interdependence in the sense that act Z can only be performed after successful completion of act Y, which in turn rests upon act X, and so on."[45] The most obvious example is the assembly line, but many office procedures would involve the same serial interdependency. The second form of technology is the mediating technology. This links "clients or customers who are or wish to be interdependent."[46] Telephone companies, banks, employment agencies, and post offices are examples here. The final type is the intensive technology in which "a variety of tech-

---

Comparative Analysis of Organizations," *American Sociological Review*, 32, No. 2 (April 1967), 194–208; and *Complex Organizations: A Critical Essay* (Glenview, Ill.: Scott, Foresman and Co., 1972). Other seminal works on technology include Tom Burns and G. M. Stalker, *The Management of Innovation* (London: Tavistock Publications, 1961); Robert Blauner, *Alienation and Freedom* (Chicago: University of Chicago Press, 1964); F. W. Emery and E. L. Trist, "The Causal Texture of Organizational Environment," *Human Relations*, 18, No. 1 (February 1965), 21–31; and E. L. Trist and E. K. Bamforth, "Some Social and Psychological Consequences of the Long-Wall Method of Coal-Getting," *Human Relations*, 4, No. 1 (February 1951), 3–38. Lawrence and Lorsch, *Organizations and Environment*, is another major piece of research which basically utilized the technology approach. Woodward's findings were replicated in the United States by William Zwerman, *New Perspectives on Organizational Theory* (Westport, Conn.: Greenwood Publishing Company, 1970).

[45] Thompson, *Organizations in Action*, pp. 15–16.
[46] *Ibid.*, p. 16.

niques is drawn upon in order to achieve a change in some specific object; but the selection, combination, and order of application are determined by feedback from the object itself."[47] This form of technology is found in work with humans, as in hospitals or universities, in construction work, and in research.

Thompson does not explicitly link these types of technology with organizational structure in the sense that it has been discussed here. It is these technologies, however, upon which all of the organization's actions are based as the organization attempts to maximize its goal attainment. Thus, "Under norms of rationality, organizations group positions to minimize coordination costs . . . , localizing and making conditionally autonomous, first . . . reciprocally interdependent positions, then . . . sequentially interdependent ones, and finally, . . . grouping positions homogeneously to facilitate standardization."[48] Such groupings are also linked through hierarchical arrangements.

Perrow's approach to technology is based on the "raw material" that the organization manipulates. This raw material:

> . . . may be a living being, human or otherwise, a symbol or an inanimate object. People are raw materials in people-changing or people-processing organizations; symbols are materials in banks, advertising agencies and some research organizations; the interactions of people are raw materials to be manipulated by administrators in organizations; boards of directors, committees and councils are usually involved with the changing or processing of symbols and human interactions, and so on.[49]

The nature of the raw material affects how the organization is structured and operated. According to Perrow, the critical factors in the nature of the raw material, and hence the nature of the technology employed to work on it, are the number of "exceptional cases encountered in the work" and the nature of the "search process" that is utilized when exceptional cases are found.[50] Few exceptional cases are found when the raw material is some object or objects that do not vary in their consistency or malleability over time. Many exceptions are found in the obvious cases of human beings and their interactions, or the less obvious

---

[47] *Ibid.*, p. 17.

[48] *Ibid.*

[49] Perrow, "A Framework for Comparative Analysis," p. 195. See also Williams A. Rushing, "Hardness of Material as Related to Division of Labor in Manufacturing Industries," *Administrative Science Quarterly*, 13, No. 2 (September 1968), 229–45, for data on the relationship between raw materials and organizational forms.

[50] *Ibid.*, pp. 195–96.

cases of many craft specialties or frontier areas within the physical sciences. Search processes range from those that are logical and analytical to those that must rely upon intuition, inspiration, chance, guesswork, or some other such unstandardized procedure. Examples of the first form of search would be the engineering process in many industries and computer programming in most instances. The second form of search would involve such diverse activities as advertising campaigns, some biomedical research, or many activities of the aerospace industry. The examples in both cases have been chosen to suggest the manner in which both the nature of the exceptions and the search process can vary across traditional organizational types.

Both the variables discussed take the form of continua along which organizations vary. These continua interact.

> On the one hand, increased knowledge of the nature of the material may
> lead to the perception of more varieties of possible outcomes or products,
> which in turn increases the need for more intimate knowledge of the
> nature of the material. Or the organization, with increased knowledge of
> one type of material, may begin to work with a variety of related materials
> about which more needs to be known, as when a social service agency or
> employment agency relaxes its admission criteria as it gains confidence,
> but in the process sets off more search behavior, or when a manufacturing
> organization starts producing new but unrelated products. On the other
> hand, if increased knowledge of the material is gained but no expansion
> of the variety of output occurs, this permits easier analysis of the sources of
> problems that may arise in the transformation process. It may also allow
> one to prevent the rise of such problems by the design of the production
> process.[51]

Perrow's framework has been tested several times with mixed results. In a study of welfare organizations, Jerald Hage and Michael Aiken found good support for relating routineness of the work with structure.[52] Lawrence and Lorsch's study of effectiveness in the plastics, food, and container industries utilized the basic technological approach.[53] On the other hand, among a series of health departments Lawrence B. Mohr found only a weak relationship between technological manageability and

[51] *Ibid.*, p. 197.

[52] Jerald Hage and Michael Aiken, "Routine Technology, Social Structure, and Organizational Goals," *Administrative Science Quarterly*, 14, No. 3 (September 1969), 366–77.

[53] Lawrence and Lorsch, *Organizations and Environment*.

the participation of subordinates in decision making.[54] Further, the original Aston studies did not find a strong relationship between technology and organizational structure.

The mixed results in regard to technology appear to be based on several factors. In the first place, there has been uncertainty in regard to the level at which technology is operative in the organization. The Aston group sheds some light on the subject.[55]

These authors break down the general concept of technology into three components: *operations technology,* the techniques used in the workflow activities of the organization; *materials technology,* the materials used in the workflow (a highly sophisticated technique can conceivably be applied to relatively simple materials); *knowledge,* the varying complexities in the knowledge system used in the workflow. In their own research, these authors have been concerned with operations technology.

In the English organizations they studied, operations technology had a secondary effect in relationship to size. They conclude:

> *Structural variables will be associated with operations technology only where they are centered on the workflow. The smaller the organization, the more its structure will be pervaded by such technological effects; the larger the organization, the more these effects will be confined to variables such as job-counts of employees on activities linked with the workflow itself, and will not be detectable in variables of the more remote administrative and hierarchical structure* [italics in original].[56]

These findings mean that operations technology will intervene before the effects of size in these work organizations. They also imply that the administrative element in large organizations will be relatively unaffected by the operations technology. It is here that the form of the knowledge technology, which was not examined, becomes important. Marshall Meyer has found that the introduction of automated procedures into the administrative structures of state and local departments of finance results in more levels of hierarchy, a wider span of control for first-line supervisors, fewer employees under the direction of higher

---

[54] Lawrence B. Mohr, "Organizational Technology and Organizational Structure," *Administrative Science Quarterly,* 16, No. 4 (December 1971), 444–59.

[55] D. J. Hickson, D. S. Pugh, and Diana C. Pheysey, "Operations Technology and Organizational Structure: An Empirical Reappraisal," *Administrative Science Quarterly,* 14, No. 3 (September 1969), 378–97.

[56] *Ibid.,* pp. 394–95.

supervisors, and fewer responsibilities—with more communications responsibilities—for members who are nominally in supervisory positions.[57] In these particular organizations, the introduction of automation would be found in relatively simple knowledge technologies.

If the converse of the Meyer findings is considered, a very different picture emerges. If administrative and organizational procedures are highly nonroutine and are laden with problems and new issues, a less complex, less formalized system would be expected. It is thus very possible, as has been previously suggested, that each of the various segments of an organization can have a structure quite different from those of other segments. The operations of some units of an organization could be highly formalized and complex, while other units take an entirely different form. Analyses of intraorganizational structural variations empirically verify that different units of the same organizations have different structural forms.[58] Variations in knowledge technology would affect the administrative units of manufacturing organizations, just as operations technology affects the workflow in manufacturing. For organizations devoted wholly to administration, the knowledge technology would be of paramount importance.

Another basic problem with the studies on technology has been the kinds of organizations studied. The Aston group is most confident of its data when service and administrative units are removed from the sample.[59] John Child and Roger Mansfield have noted that the type of industry and its technology are related—for example, the steel industry versus the computer industry—so that sampling differences between studies could increase or decrease the relationship between technology and structure.[60]

The technology approach has also been criticized by Chris Argyris[61] on the ground that it is static, since change cannot be accounted for. Because organizations change, albeit slowly, there must be a reason for change. If technology is the sole source of structure, then technology must change before structure. If the technology is imported into the organization from outside, then someone or some set of individuals within the organization must decide to import the technological change. If the change is from

[57] Marshall W. Meyer, "Automation and Bureaucratic Structure," *American Journal of Sociology*, 74, No. 3 (November 1968), 256–64.

[58] Richard H. Hall, "Intraorganizational Structural Variation: Application of the Bureaucratic Model," *Administrative Science Quarterly*, 7, No. 3 (December 1962), 295–308.

[59] Correspondence from D. J. Hickson, November 25, 1969.

[60] John Child and Roger Mansfield, "Technology, Size, and Organizational Structure," *Sociology*, 6, No. 3 (September 1972), 369–93.

[61] Chris Argyris, *The Applicability of Organizational Sociology*, pp. 20–45.

within, again decisions have to be made. In addition to this, the technological approach does not include considerations of the role of individuals, separately or collectively, as they respond to or try to lead organizations.

We have analyzed the relationships between size and structure and between technology and structure. A good part of the literature discussed treats these as "either/or" phenomena: either size *or* technology alone causes particular structural forms. This is basically absurd. A more reasonable approach is that these factors interact and contribute to particular structural forms. Robert Dewar and Jerald Hage have tested this approach with a longitudinal analysis of the welfare organizations studied by Hage and Aiken.[62] They find that size is a good predictor of some aspects of structure, while technology works well with others. In addition, and perhaps equally importantly, they conclude that not even a combination of the size and technology considerations predicts structure all that well. There must therefore be additional intervening variables, one of which is the environment of the organization.

THE ENVIRONMENT

In later chapters the environment of organizations will be considered in detail; here our concern is simply to trace some of the implications of organizational environments for organizational structure. By environment we mean anything outside the organization that has an impact on it. Of major concern is the social environment, but obviously the physical environment of organizations is also important, particularly for those that utilize or affect the physical environment.

The Aston group has investigated structural differences and similarities of organizations in different societies and has found that certain aspects of structure are affected by different cultures while others are not.[63] In studies conducted in the United Kingdom, Canada, and the

[62] Robert Dewar and Jerald Hage, "Size, Technology, Complexity, and Structural Differentiation: Towards a Theoretical Synthesis," mimeographed paper, Graduate School of Management, Northwestern University, Evanston, Illinois. The interaction of size and technology is also noted by C. Frederick Eisele in "Organizational Size, Technology, and Frequency of Strikes," *Industrial and Labor Relations Review*, 27, No. 4 (July 1974), 560–71.

[63] David J. Hickson, C. R. Hinings, C. J. McMillan, and J. P. Schwitter, "The Culture-Free Context of Organization Structure: A Tri-National Comparison," *Sociology*, 8, No. 1 (January 1974), 59–80; and Charles J. McMillan, David J. Hickson, Christopher R. Hinings, and Rodney E. Schneck, "The Structure of Work Organizations Across Societies," *Academy of Management Journal*, 16, No. 4 (December 1973), 555–69.

United States, little difference was found in patterns of autonomy and specialization, but there was more reliance upon written documents in North America. In the United Kingdom, the greater emphasis on traditionalism apparently diminishes the need for written documents. Nevertheless, consistent patterns of relationships are found among size, technology, and structure. From these data it is hypothesized that organizations will in fact be different in different societies, but that the relationships among structural characteristics will be of the same patterns. Thus, for example, organizations in India may be less formalized than those in the United States, but large organizations in India will still be more formalized than smaller ones.

The multinational firm is apparently affected by the country of its origin.[64] Thus, a Japanese firm with operations in the United States would exhibit different structural characteristics than a Dutch firm with a similar operation. This would hold true even when all the employees of the different operations were American citizens.

The environments of organizations vary not only among different societies. Even within a given society conditions can render them "friendly" or "hostile."[65] Consider, for example, colleges and universities. During the early 1960s the environment of these organizations was friendly: money was pouring in from private and government sources; buildings were going up and research was encouraged; there was a general public confidence that it was by education that our society would be improved. In the 1970s the environment is hostile: the basic values of higher education are being questioned, with the liberal arts under severe attack; the research that undergirds every discipline is questioned in Congress and state legislatures; funds are cut. The petroleum crises created similar hostility toward automobile manufacturers and petroleum firms.

Pradip Khandwalla suggests that in a friendly environment, organizations will be structurally differentiated. The environment will be monitored by differentiated personnel who are then integrated by a series of mechanisms such as committees and *ad hoc* coordinating groups. If the environment turns hostile, the organization will "tighten up" by centralizing and standardizing its operations.

A similar conclusion is reached by Jeffrey Pfeffer and Huseyin Leblebici in their study of the effects of competition.[66] In highly com-

[64] Hans Schollhammer, "Organization Structures of Multinational Corporations," *Academy of Management Journal*, 14, No. 3 (September 1971), 345–65.

[65] Pradip N. Khandwalla, "Environment and its Impact on the Organization," *International Studies of Management and Organization*, 2, No. 3 (Fall 1972), 297–313.

[66] Jeffrey Pfeffer and Huseyin Leblebici, "The Effect of Competition on Some Dimensions of Organizational Structure," *Social Forces*, 52, No. 2 (December 1973), 268–79.

petitive situations, there is a greater demand for control and coordination. Reports are more frequent and there are more written communications and a greater specification of decision procedures. When competition is less intense, there are more frequent changes in product design, production processes, and number of products. Less competition provides some "slack" so that the organization can afford to do more than its routine competitive activities. Again it should be stressed that the varying degrees of competitive environments exist for all organizations and not just those in the business sector.

The argument thus far has been that organizational structure is *contingent* upon size, technology, and environment. The data in support of the argument are quite persuasive. But neither the argument nor the data conclusively explain organizational structure. To the argument that has been presented must be added the element of *choice*.

STRUCTURE AND CHOICE

Organizations do not automatically adjust to technological and environmental demands, nor do they automatically grow to a particular size. Organizational form is based on decisions. These decisions are made on the basis of strategic choices, discussed in an earlier chapter.[67] This approach has been elaborated by Raymond E. Miles, Charles C. Snow, and Jeffrey Pfeffer.[68] Noting that the size and technology approaches have yielded inconsistent results, they suggest that organizations are faced with environments differing in their rates of change and degree of uncertainty. They also note that specific parts of organizations are affected by specific environmental elements. The legal department of an organization has different environmental interactions than does the public relations department.

Decision makers in the dominant coalitions within organizations select those parts of the environment with which they will be concerned. This selection is done within a political framework in which membership in the dominant coalition can shift, as can the distribution of power within it. On the basis of selective perception of the environment, appropriate strategies can be selected for dealing with this environment. This decision making includes utilizing the appropriate technology for implementing the strategy. Technology is thus brought into the organization. The decisions also involve strategies for arranging roles and relationships to

[67] John Child, "Organizational Structure, Environment, and Performance: The Role of Strategic Choice," *Sociology*, 6, No. 1 (January 1972), 1–22.

[68] Raymond E. Miles, Charles C. Snow, and Jeffrey Pfeffer, "Organization-Environment: Concepts and Issues," *Industrial Relations*, 13, No. 3 (October 1974), 244–64.

control and coordinate the technologies being employed. This is done to ensure continuity of the organization, its survival and growth.[69] As will be seen in the later discussion of decision making, none of this necessarily occurs automatically and on totally rational bases.

To illustrate this process, a real-life situation can be used. The Twin Cities (Minneapolis–St. Paul) area has been considering the feasibility and desirability of constructing a domed stadium for its professional football and baseball teams to protect them and their fans from inclement weather. Suppose it is decided that the domed stadium is desirable and an organization is established to supervise such construction. After some internal squabbling to establish who has power within the organization, it is decided that a particular fund-raising technique will be used to build a particular form of stadium. Both of these are technologies; both require staffing of a particular size; both have to deal with a particular environment. Some of the environment is hostile to the idea of a stadium in the first place, while others are supportive. The fund-raising wing of the organization must deal with this. The construction wing must deal with a physical environment that is different from a more temperate climate, and must deal as well with its own social environment.

But although an organization's structure is not just an automatic response to size, technology, and environment, the types of response to size, technological, and environmental demands are limited in number. If we want to raise funds for a stadium, there are just a few ways to do it, as there are for producing television sets. The conclusion then must be that all four of the factors that have been discussed—size, technology, environment, and choice—are important and intertwined. Organizational theory has not developed to the point where these can be combined into a predictive mathematical formula. We do know, however, that large size, coupled with a routine technology, coupled with a hostile and competitive environment, coupled with a dominant coalition composed of traditional executives will yield a structure with an intense division of labor, high formalization, and high centralization. These are the structural elements that will be dealt with in the next chapters.

SUMMARY AND CONCLUSIONS

This chapter has defined organizational structure, noting that organizations actually have multiple structures because there is intraorganiza-

---

[69] For historical accounts of this process see Alfred Chandler, *Strategy and Structure: Chapters in the History of Industrial Enterprise* (Cambridge, Mass.: The Massachusetts Institute of Technology Press, 1962).

tional variation. We have examined evidence regarding the influences of size, technology, environment, and choice. Research regarding each has been presented and criticized, with the conclusion that the most intelligent approach combines these structural determinants into a comprehensive explanation, as was just done.

We are now ready to discuss the features of structure—complexity, formalization, and centralization.

5

complexity

The term "complex organizations" describes the subject matter of this entire book—and indeed is the title of several important works. In this chapter we will look carefully at the concept of complexity, noting what it is, and what are its sources and its consequences. From this examination it should become clear that the complexity of an organization has major effects on the behavior of its members, other structural conditions, processes within the organization, and relationships between the organization and its environment. The premise will again be that external conditions and internal processes are the dominant factors determining the form of an organization.

Like size, complexity is one of the first things that hits a person entering any organization beyond those of the simplest form: division of labor, job titles, multiple divisions, and hierarchical levels are usually immediately evident. Any familiarity with large corporations (and many small ones), the government, the military, or a school system verifies this. Organizations that seem very simple at first glance may exhibit interesting forms of complexity. Local voluntary organizations, such as the Rotary Club, labor union locals, and garden clubs usually have committees for programs, publicity, membership, community service, education, finance, and other matters, all with their attendant structure. These kinds of organization must make provisions for the control and coordination of activities just as their more complex counterparts must.

The issue is itself made more complex by the fact that individual parts of an organization can vary in their degree of complexity. In a study of the regional office of a major oil company, for example, it was found that there were six divisions, as shown on the organization chart, figure 5-1. The heads of the divisions had equal rank in the organization, and each was thought to be equally important to the overall success of the organization. When the divisions themselves were examined, it was found that they varied not only in size—from three to 100 members—but also in complexity. The largest division, distribution, had five sepa-

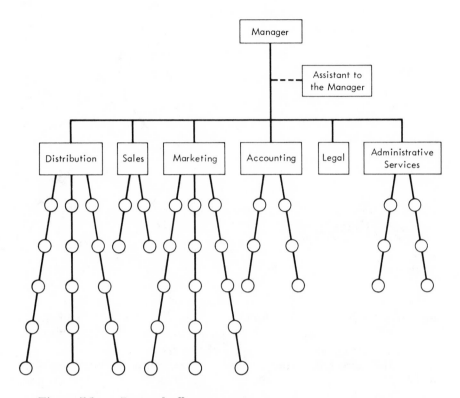

Figure 5-1   Regional office organization

rate hierarchical levels with three important subdivisions, each of which was further specialized by tasks performed by specific work groups. The smallest division, which performed legal services associated with land acquisition and other problems of service-station development, was composed of a lawyer and two secretaries.

Intraorganizational variations in complexity can also be seen in manufacturing firms with research and development departments. These departments are likely to be characterized by a shallower hierarchy than other divisions of the organization have. While there may be several levels above them, the research and development workers will be rather loosely supervised, with a wide span of control. In manufacturing departments, the span of control for each supervisor is shorter and the whole unit will look more like a pyramid. (See figure 5–2.)

These examples indicate the obvious—complexity is not a simple issue. The concept contains several components, which do not necessarily vary

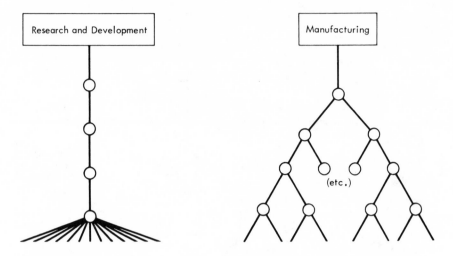

Figure 5-2   The shape of two departments in the same organization

together. At the same time, the concept itself conveys a meaning in organizational literature: complex organizations contain many subparts requiring coordination and control, and the more complex an organization is, the more serious these issues become. Since organizations vary widely in their degree of complexity, regardless of the specific component of complexity used, and since wide variations are found within specific organizations, the issue is important for the overall understanding of organizations.

COMPLEXITY AS A VARIABLE

Before we can make sense out of the various research studies on complexity, we must examine the components of the concept. The three elements of complexity most commonly identified are: horizontal differentiation; vertical, or hierarchical, differentiation; and spatial dispersion.

Horizontal Differentiation

Horizontal differentiation applies to the subdivision of the tasks performed by the organization among its members. Unfortunately for conceptual clarity, there are two basic ways in which such tasks can be broken down and assigned. The first way is to give highly trained specialists a rather comprehensive range of activities to perform, and the second is to minutely subdivide the tasks so that nonspecialists can perform them. The first approach is exemplified by the professional or craftsman in the organizational setting who is solely responsible for complete operations.[1] He is given the responsibility and the authority to carry out the task to its completion. The second form of horizontal differentiation is most plainly seen on the assembly line, where each worker performs only one or a few repetitive tasks. The nature of the task itself is important here, since it is the routine and uniform task that is most amenable to the second type of differentiation; nonroutine and quite varied tasks are more commonly subdivided according to the first type.

Several writers have developed specific definitions for these forms of horizontal complexity. Jerald Hage, in his "axiomatic" theory, defines complexity as the "specialization in an organization . . . measured by the number of occupational specialties and the length of training required by each. The greater the number of occupations and the longer the period of training required, the more complex the organization."[2] Hage's assumption is that the more training people have, the more they are differentiated from other people who might have similar amounts of training but in different specialties. This definition is almost identical in its implications to that of James Price, who states, "*Complexity* may be defined as the degree of knowledge required to produce the output of a system. The degree of complexity of an organization can be measured by the degree of education of its members. The higher the education, the higher the complexity."[3]

In some later research, Hage and Aiken develop this approach further:

We interpret complexity to mean at least three things: the number of occupational specialties, the professional activity, and the professional training. Organizations vary in the number of occupational specialties that they utilize in achieving their goals. This variable was measured by asking respondents to report their major duties; each respondent was then classified according to the type of occupational specialty, e.g., psychiatrist, rehabilitation counselor, teacher, nurse, social worker, and so on. The

[1] For a discussion of craft-organized work, see Arthur L. Stinchcombe, "Bureaucratic and Craft Administration of Production," *Administrative Science Quarterly*, 4, No. 2 (September 1959), 168–87. For a comprehensive discussion of the nature of professionally controlled work, see Howard M. Vollmer and Donald L. Mills, *Professionalization* (Englewood Cliffs, N.J.: Prentice-Hall, Inc., 1966); Richard H. Hall, *Occupations and the Social Structure*, 2nd ed. (Englewood Cliffs, N.J.: Prentice-Hall, Inc., 1975), Chapter 4.

[2] Jerald Hage, "An Axiomatic Theory of Organizations," *Administrative Science Quarterly*, 10, No. 3 (December 1965), 294.

[3] James L. Price, *Organizational Effectiveness: An Inventory of Propositions* (Homewood, Ill.: Richard D. Irwin, Inc., 1968), p. 26.

variable, degree of professional activity, reflects the number of professional associations in which the respondents were involved, the number of meetings attended, and the number of offices held or number of papers given at professional meetings. The amount of professional training was based on the amount of college training as well as other professional training.[4]

Hage and Aiken's research was carried out in health and welfare organizations, where the emphasis on professional backgrounds was very appropriate. While this emphasis is not universally applicable in all types of organizations, the point regarding extent of training and depth of experience would hold across organizations.

This form of horizontal differentiation introduces additional complexities into the organization, in that a high level of specialization requires coordination of the specialists. In many cases, personnel specifically designated as coordinating personnel have to be assigned to ensure that the various efforts do not work at cross-purposes and that the overall organizational tasks are accomplished.

A different approach to horizontal differentiation can be seen in the work of Peter Blau and Richard Schoenherr. Their definition is the "number of different positions and different subunits in the organization,"[5] and their emphasis is on the formal structure as defined by the organization.[6] An organization is more complex if it has more such positions and subunits. Organizations spread out horizontally as work is subdivided for task accomplishment. This definition is similar to the indicators of complexity used by Hall and his associates. They used the number of divisions within an organization and the number of specialties within the divisions as complexity indicators. Pugh and his associates approach the issue in a closely related way, although they use the term "specialization" in their discussion of this phenomenon.[7] They also intro-

[4] Jerald Hage and Michael Aiken, "Relationship of Centralization to Other Structural Properties," *Administrative Science Quarterly*, 12, No. 1 (June 1967), 79–80.

[5] Peter M. Blau and Richard A. Schoenherr, *The Structure of Organizations* (New York: Basic Books, Inc., Publishers, 1971), p. 16. The same approach is used by Blau and his associates throughout their research.

[6] We disregard for the present the common distinction between "formal" and "informal" aspects of organizational structure. While deviations from formal organizational arrangements are the rule rather than the exception, the fact is that the formal structure, as used by several of the studies to be discussed, is the framework within which informal patterns operate. A more extensive examination of this issue will be presented in the next section of the book.

[7] D. S. Pugh et al., "Dimensions of Organizational Structure," *Administrative Science Quarterly*, 13, No. 1 (June 1968), 72–74, 78–79.

duce the concept of "configuration" as an overall indicator of the "shape" of the organization. This latter concept contains the vertical as well as the horizontal factor of work subdivision by task.

These two approaches to horizontal differentiation appear to have very similar roots, since both are concerned with the division of labor within the organization. The critical difference between these forms of horizontal differentiation appears to be the scope of the ultimate tasks of the organization.[8] Organizations that attempt to carry out a wide variety of activities and that have clients or customers who require a variety of services would divide the labor into work performed by specialists.[9] The more minute division of labor would occur when the organization's tasks are not so diffuse, and when the organization has grown in size, since such a division of labor provides an economy of scale. These two forms of complexity are *not* alternative ways to organize for the same task. But the two forms *are* likely to occur within the same organization, since most organizations face uncertainty and must deal with the routine.

Vertical Differentiation

Vertical or hierarchical differentiation is a less complicated matter than horizontal differentiation. Research into this vertical dimension has used straightforward indicators of the depth of the hierarchy. Meyer uses the "proliferation of supervisory levels" as his measures of the depth of an organization.[10] Pugh et al. suggest that the vertical dimension can be measured by a "count of the number of job positions between the chief executive and the employees working on the output."[11] Hall et

[8] Robert Dewar and Jerald Hage, "Size, Technology, Complexity, and Structural Differentiation: Towards a Theoretical Synthesis," mimeographed paper, Graduate School of Management, Northwestern University, Evanston, Illinois, 1975.

[9] *Ibid.* Dewar and Hage label the use of specialists as "complexity" and the use of the minute division of labor as structural differentiation. William B. Tyler, "Measuring Organizational Specialization: The Concept of Role Variety," *Administrative Science Quarterly*, 18, No. 3 (September 1973), 383–92, approaches the issue in the same way, using the term "specialization" for the minute division of labor and "specialist" as it has been used here. There is no automatic relationship between the factors being discussed and the nature of specialization utilized. While organizations respond to functional or contingency demands, they are also political entities in which specialists may be added to particular operations because of the power of particular individuals and groups in the hierarchy. See John Child, "Parkinson's Progress: Accounting for the Number of Specialists in Organizations," *Administrative Science Quarterly*, 18, No. 3 (September 1973), 328–48.

[10] Marshall W. Meyer, "Two Authority Structures of Bureaucratic Organization," *Administrative Science Quarterly*, 13, No. 2 (September 1968), 216.

[11] Pugh et al., "Dimensions," p. 78.

al. used the "number of levels in the deepest single division" and the "mean number of levels for the organization as a whole" (total number of levels in all divisions/number of divisions) as their indicators.[12]

These direct indicators of vertical differentiation involve an important assumption that should be made explicit: authority is distributed in accordance with the level in the hierarchy; that is, the higher the level, the greater the authority. Although in the vast majority of cases this would be a valid assumption, the proliferation of levels can represent phenomena other than the distribution of authority. For example, in organizations that utilize professional personnel, arrangements may not have been made to allow advancement within the same job title. A physicist may be hired as a physicist, but if the organization's policies do not allow much of a salary range for that job title, the person in question may be "promoted" to a higher position without an actual change in his work. In this example, the organization would not be as deep as it appears. Many organizations facing this issue have removed salary restrictions for their professional personnel, allowing the person to retain his job title but providing a wider range of pay within a particular job title. Nevertheless, an essentially false hierarchy may be erroneously observed through the exclusive use of number of levels as defined by the organization.

Another, similar difficulty is the question of whether authority is actually distributed throughout the hierarchy. This issue will be taken up in detail in a later chapter, but it should be noted here that a relatively deep hierarchy concentrates power at the top of the organization, with those in intermediate positions having little to do other than routine administrative work. Both these exceptions to the rule (that authority is distributed according to the rank in the hierarchy) require an extremely detailed knowledge of the organization before these conclusions may be drawn. In the great majority of cases, however, the simple measures of vertical differentiation that have been used are realistic indicators of the distribution of authority.

Both horizontal and vertical differentiation present organizations with problems of control, communication, and coordination. Subunits along either axis (this would include both aspects of horizontal differentiation) are nuclei that are differentiated from adjacent units and the total organization according to horizontal or vertical factors. The greater the differentiation, the greater the potentiality for difficulties in control, coordination, and communication.

---

[12] Richard H. Hall et al., "Organizational Size, Complexity, and Formalization," *American Sociological Review*, 32, No. 6 (December 1967), 906.

Spatial Dispersion

The final element in complexity, spatial dispersion, can actually be a form of horizontal or vertical differentiation. That is, activities and personnel can be dispersed in space, according to either horizontal or vertical functions, by the separation of power centers or tasks. An example of the former case are field offices of sales or welfare organizations, in which the tasks performed by the various field offices are essentially identical (low complexity on the horizontal axis) and the power in the organization is differentiated between the central office and the field offices. An example of the latter case are local plants of a manufacturing concern, each of which is specialized by product and technology.

Spatial dispersion becomes a separate element in the complexity concept when it is realized that an organization can perform the same functions with the same division of labor and hierarchical arrangements in multiple locations. A business firm, for example, can have a complex set of sales procedures requiring highly specialized salesmen in the field. These salesmen can be dispersed from a central office or through regional or state or local offices, with essentially the same hierarchical arrangements. Complexity is thus increased with the development of spatially dispersed activities, even if the horizontal and vertical differentiation remains the same across the spatially separated units.

The spatial-dispersion concept is relatively simple to operationalize. In a study of labor union locals, Edna Raphael notes, "The spatial dispersion of members refers to the number of spatially separated places in which the members of a local union are employed. This . . . is a continuous quantitative variable. At one extreme of the continuum, organizations have memberships concentrated in one-plant settings. At the opposite end of the continuum, the members are so extremely dispersed spatially that they even rotate continuously among numerous shops, jobs, and employers within a geographical space of at least several square miles."[13] Hall, Haas, and Johnson used the following indicators in their study: (1) the degree to which physical facilities are spatially dispersed, (2) the location (distance from the organizational headquarters) of the spatially dispersed facilities, (3) the degree to which personnel are spatially dispersed, and (4) the location of spatially dispersed personnel.[14] These indicators are highly correlated.

---

[13] Edna Raphael, "The Anderson-Warkov Hypothesis in Local Unions: A Comparative Study," *American Sociological Review*, 32, No. 5 (October 1967), 770.

[14] Hall et al., "Organizational Size," p. 906.

VARIANCE OF COMPLEXITY ELEMENTS

The discussion thus far has suggested that the three major elements of complexity vary, often independently of each other. Before further discussing such independent variance, it should be stressed that these elements can obviously vary together. Organizations with little horizontal, vertical, or spatial complexity can easily be identified—the small business comes most readily to mind. The same phenomenon can occur, however, in large organizations. Michel Crozier's analysis of two separate government organizations in France graphically demonstrates this.[15] The first organization, a clerical agency, was characterized by a very simple division of labor: while tasks were highly routine and repetitious, there was little differentiation among them. Also, considering the size of the organization, there was a very shallow hierarchy. The organization was not complex on the horizontal and vertical axes.

The third axis of spatial dispersion is added when the French tobacco company (the "Industrial Monopoly") in Crozier's analysis is considered. Thirty spatially dispersed plants comprise the system. The plants are fairly large, with 350 to 400 employees on the average, but there are only six categories of workers in each plant. Production workers, who are paid equal wages throughout the system, comprise the bulk of the labor force, and there is little differentiation among their tasks. Maintenance workers are more specialized, with electricians, boilermakers, and metal workers in this group. The third group is the shop foremen, who hold supervisory positions in both plant and white-collar office operations. Even here, the tasks performed are quite similar. Administrative jobs, such as personnel, purchasing, or accounting, are few in number and minimally professionalized. There is one technical engineer per plant. The top position is that of the plant director, who usually has an assistant.

This relatively large dispersed organization is structurally very simple. The simplicity does not mean that it does not face severe problems—Crozier documents these in great detail—but that the problems are based on external and internal conditions that are not related to its structure. The imposition of civil service personnel regulations, the power of the maintenance personnel—who can actually control the output of the plants by the speed at which they maintain the equipment—and certain

[15] Michel Crozier, *The Bureaucratic Phenomenon* (Chicago: University of Chicago Press, 1964).

characteristics of the French society combine to make these organizations much less efficient and effective than they might be. It seems clear that increased complexity on the vertical and horizontal axes would do little to improve the performance of these plants. In both the tobacco monopoly and the clerical agency (which was also characterized by a poor performance record), the structural characteristics are based upon the tasks to be performed and the technology available, rather than being a simple function of size. These noncomplex organizations are massive systems designed to perform simple and unchanging tasks. It can be hypothesized that if the tasks and technology were altered to develop a more effective system, the organizations would become more complex.

In direct contrast to the simple organizations just described, the diversified industrial or government organization serves as an example of the organization that is complex on all three axes. Huge industrial concerns, such as Standard Oil of New Jersey or du Pont, are characterized by extreme complexity. The same would be true for operations of national, state, and some local governments, as well as such diverse organizations as the Catholic Church, the New York City school system, and the University of California.

These extreme cases serve as a reminder that organizations can be highly or minimally complex in all facets of the complexity concept. Other common-sense examples suggest that such covariance is not the necessary pattern. A college, for example, usually has a low degree of vertical differentiation and usually no spatial dispersion, but a high degree of horizontal differentiation. Most manufacturing plants would have a greater division of labor along the horizontal axis than those studied by Crozier, although the hierarchical levels may be the same. The offensive unit of a football team is highly specialized but essentially has only two ranks. High vertical differentiation with little horizontal differentiation is exemplified by the army batallion.

In Chapter 4 we considered the factors associated with different structural characteristics. These are the sources of the various forms of complexity that have been discussed. If we know why organizations are differentially complex, we should then be able to specify some of the consequences of this complexity.

THE CONSEQUENCES OF COMPLEXITY

The first point to be considered is that of spatial complexity, a topic that has been overly neglected in research. Anderson and Warkow, in their examination of the size of the administrative component of organizations discussed in the previous chapter, considered the spatial-dispersion factor. One of their major findings was that the "relative size of the administrative component *increases* as the number of places at which work is performed increases."[16]

This finding was not upheld in Raphael's study of labor union locals. In this case, spatial dispersion was associated with a decrease in the size of the administrative component. Raphael attributes the difference in findings to the fact that labor unions are voluntary associations, and the dispersed locals are semiautonomous from centralized control and operate on their own. She also points out that the dispersed locals tend to be less democratic than those that are centralized and have a larger administrative apparatus.[17] In the centralized setting, according to this analysis, there is a greater likelihood that intensive communication networks will develop thus enhancing the likelihood of democratic processes. The differences in the control mechanism of the voluntary association lead to a more oligarchic situation in the dispersed voluntary association, since a managerial clique can be formed containing elected leaders and selected members who perform many of the administrative functions. This lowers the size of the administrative component in the dispersed unions, but also decreases the opportunities for participation of the rank and file.

These findings reemphasize the fact that voluntary organizations are qualitatively different in many important attributes from nonvoluntary organizations. The differences in control and administrative mechanisms found by Raphael are only part of the picture. Such organizations obviously require a different form of attachment of members and consistent efforts to maintain member support.[18] These differences make generalizations comparing nonvoluntary to voluntary organizations extremely dangerous. It is fairly clear that they are not exact opposites in every characteristic, but the structure and processes in voluntary organizations clearly require careful analysis to determine where the two forms of organizations coincide and where they do not.

Another examination of spatial dispersion is contained in the research of Pugh et al. As in the case of size, they treat number of operating sites as a contextual variable rather than as an element of the organization's structure, but as was also the case with size, spatial dispersion can per-

[16] Theodore Anderson and Seymour Warkov, "Organizational Size and Functional Complexity," *American Sociological Review*, 26, No. 1 (February 1961), 27.

[17] Raphael, "Anderson–Warkov Hypothesis," pp. 773–76.

[18] See Amitai Etzioni, *A Comparative Analysis of Complex Organizations* (New York: The Free Press, 1961), pp. 40–67, for an extended discussion of this point.

haps more legitimately be treated as a structural characteristic. The research setting, it will be remembered, is the English Midlands, and the organizations themselves do not represent the entire spectrum, being concentrated in engineering and the metallurgical industries.[19] Nevertheless, the organizations did vary in dispersion, with service-oriented organizations having the greatest degree of dispersion.

The relationships with other structural characteristics further indicate the consequences of complexity in general. Spatial dispersion was inversely related to structuring of activities. Activities are structured when work roles are predefined; and in dispersed organizations, the workers have more discretion in how they carry on their day-to-day activities. Spatial dispersion was positively related to concentration of authority. Important organizational decisions were dispersed to multiple operating sites. Since the work is specialized and a taller hierarchy is found in such situations, the finding that authority is concentrated in these settings is consistent with the earlier findings. There was also a positive relationship between dispersion and line control of work flow, meaning, as was indicated earlier, that the actual work being performed is controlled by the workers in direct contact with the product, clients, or customers. When there is line control of work flow, there are centrally controlled personnel policies to ensure that the workers are selected for their ability to carry out the work, without a lot of variation among them. In the case of spatial dispersion, therefore, while the workers on the "line" do not have specific operating procedures spelled out for them and have a rather large degree of control over what they do on the job, the basic decisions regarding what they work on and who will be employed in the first place are retained by the organization. Dispersion is thus accompanied by the retention of certain kinds of control by the central organizations.[20]

An assumption throughout this discussion is that most organizations are complex in one of the various configurations discussed. Another assumption, verifiable from a variety of forms of evidence, is that *there is a strong tendency for organizations to become more complex as their own activities and the environment around them become more complex.* Since organizations grow in size, and since size and complexity are related, this is a moderately well-supported assumption. Organizations that survive become more complex.

Increased complexity leads to greater problems of coordination and control. Now let us examine these problems in more detail.

[19] D. S. Pugh et al., "The Context of Organization Structures," *Administrative Science Quarterly,* 14, No. 1 (March 1969), 104.

[20] *Ibid.,* pp. 108–12.

COORDINATION AND CONTROL

In their significant study, *Organization and Environment*, Lawrence and Lorsch examined the sources and consequences of complexity. Their approach to complexity is through the term *differentiation*,[21] by which they mean the division of organizations into parts to perform their activities (horizontal differentiation, in our terms), such as sales, production, or research. To this rather standard approach to differentiation, Lawrence and Lorsch add components that are implicit in the discussions of complexity presented here. They note that structural differentiation includes differences in attitude and behavior on the part of members of the differentiated departments. These include orientations toward the particular goals of the department, differing emphases on interpersonal skills, varied time perspectives, and the type and extent of formalization of the structure. Departments therefore vary not only in the specific tasks they perform, but also in the underlying behavior and outlooks of their members.

The data for the analysis of differentiation come from firms in three industries in the United States. The first set of industries was comprised of firms making and selling plastics in the form of powder, pellets, and sheets.

> Their products went to industrial customers of all sizes, from the large automobile, appliance, furniture, paint, textile, and paper companies to the smaller firms making toys, containers, and household items. The organizations studied emphasized specialty plastics tailored to specific uses rather than standardized commodity plastics. They all built their product-development work on the science of polymer chemistry. Production was continuous, with relatively few workers needed to monitor the automatic and semiautomatic processing equipment.[22]

These organizations were in a highly competitive market situation. According to the executives interviewed, the major competitive issue was the development of new and revised products and processes. The life cycle of any product was likely to be short, since competitors were

[21] Paul R. Lawrence and Jay W. Lorsch, *Organization and Environment: Managing Differentiation and Integration* (Cambridge: Harvard Graduate School of Business Administration, 1967). It should be noted that differentiation is not identical to complexity as used in this discussion. It is close enough, however, for comparability.
[22] *Ibid.*, p. 24.

all engaged in intensive research and could make even a very successful product quickly obsolete. The executives noted that "the most hazardous aspect of the industrial environment revolved around the relevant scientific knowledge."[23] These organizations were in a changing and "turbulent" environment, with both input—in the form of scientific knowledge —and the consumption of output—in the form of customer satisfaction from purchasing the product—highly uncertain. On the other hand, the production process itself was characterized by its certainty. Once the original technical specifications for a particular product were developed, the production process could proceed quite automatically, since the mix between such production variables as pressure, temperature, and chemical composition could be easily measured, and monitoring was part of the production process itself.

The six organizations studied within the plastics industry each had four basic functional departments—sales, production, applied research, and fundamental research—that differed in their own structures. The production departments were the most formalized, the fundamental research units the least. Sales department personnel were the most concerned with interpersonal relationships, and production departments were the least, with the two research units falling in between. The interesting dimension of the time perspective taken shows the departments falling into a predictable pattern—from shortest to longest time perspective, sales, production, applied research, and fundamental research.[24] The members of the various departments were also differentiated in terms of personal goals, with sale personnel concerned with customer problems and the marketplace; production personnel with cost reduction and efficiency; and research personnel concerned with scientific matters, as well as the more immediate practical issues of process improvement and modification. The scientific personnel were not as concerned with purely scientific matters as the authors had anticipated, but they did have clearly different goals from those of the members of other departments.

Differentiation in these organizations thus clearly involves more than sheer differentiation by task. The members of the departments were differentiated according to organizationally important behaviors and attitudes. Equally or perhaps more important for the general discussion is

23 *Ibid.*, p. 25.
24 The importance of the time perspective has been particularly stressed by Elliot Jaques in *Equitable Payment* (London: Heinemann Educational Books, Ltd., 1961). The differences between departments are important in the utilization of a "time-span of discretion" as a basis for payment, as formulated by Jaques. The same criterion should not be used across departments.

the fact that these differences in task, behavior, and attitude are directly related to the kind of environment that the various departments must work with in their short- and long-run activities. *A high degree of differentiation (complexity) is therefore related to a highly complex and differentiated environment.*[25] In this case the complexity refers to the competitive situation in which the organizations find themselves (this degree of competition is not limited to profit-making organizations) and to the rapidly changing and complicated technological world in which they must survive.

To provide contrasts for the plastics firms, Lawrence and Lorsch studied two other industries; the major factor in their selection was the rate of environmental change. The second chosen was the standardized container industry. The rate of sales increase in this industry was at about the level of the rate of population growth and the growth of the gross national product, so the organizations in the industry were approximately keeping even with the environment in these respects. More important for the purposes of their study, no significant new products had been introduced in two decades. The major competitive factors were "operational issues of maintaining customer service through prompt delivery and consistent product quality while minimizing operating costs."[26] While these are not easy or simple tasks to perform, they are stable; and the problems and prospects for the future are much more certain than in the plastics field.

The third set of organizations studied was in the packaged foods industry. In terms of environmental conditions, these organizations were intermediate between the plastics and container firms. While they engaged heavily in innovations, the rate of new-product introduction and the growth of sales were less than in the plastics industry, but more than in the container field.

When the differentiation within the organizations in these three industries was examined, the findings were as predicted—the plastics firms were the most differentiated, followed by the food firms, and then by the container firms. From this evidence and that presented earlier, the role of the environment in shaping an organization becomes obvious. The specific form an organization takes is dependent upon the environmental conditions it faces. Added to this, of course, are the considerations of size, traditions within a particular organization or set of organizations, and the idiosyncrasies of individual organizations. These

---

[25] This conclusion builds on and is supported by the work of Tom Burns and G. M. Stalker in *The Management of Innovation* (London: Tavistock Publications, 1961).

[26] Lawrence and Lorsch, *Organizations and Environment,* p. 86.

latter factors are "added on" after the environmental considerations, since the environment imposes the basic requirements for shaping the organization; the other considerations appear to be limited to variations on the central theme provided by the environment.

If this interpretation of the sources of complexity is taken as correct (and even if it is not), the major question remains: What does complexity do to an organization? Lawrence and Lorsch provide some important indications of the consequences in their further analysis of organizations in these three industries. They base their analysis on the concept of *integration*, which they define as "the quality of the state of collaboration that exists among departments that are required to achieve unity of effort by the demands of the environment."[27] The authors are also concerned with the effectiveness of the organizations. Here they use rather standard and appropriate market and economic measures. Organizations are more effective when they meet environmental pressures and when they allow their members to achieve their individual goals.

The results of the analysis of integration and effectiveness are in some ways surprising. In the plastics industry, the most effective organizations are those with the greatest degree of differentiation, and these also face the most severe integration problems. Their effectiveness in the face of high differentiation is explained by their successful conflict resolution. It is not the idea of successful conflict resolution that is surprising; it is the fact that the effective organizations were characterized by a high degree of conflict in the first place—that they were not totally harmonious, with all personnel working as members of one happy team. From the data discussed earlier, it is apparent that the differentiation in terms of departmental and individual attitudes and behavior would lead inevitably to conflict. In these organizations, such conflict contributes to effectiveness.

Conflict per se, of course, would be detrimental to the organization if it were not resolved. So another important contribution of this research is its analysis of conflict resolution. The authors do not suggest that there is one best form of such resolution. Rather, they provide evidence that conflict-resolution processes vary according to the specific conflict situations in a particular form of organization. In the case of the highly differentiated plastics organizations, integration is achieved by departments or individuals who are in a position, and have the knowledge available, to work with the departments involved in conflict situations. In this case, the position is relatively low in the managerial hierarchy rather than at the top. This lower position is necessary because of the specific knowl-

[27] *Ibid.*, p. 47.

edge required to deal with the departments and issues involved. The highly differentiated and effective organization thus anticipates conflict and establishes integrating (conflict-resolving) departments and individuals whose primary purpose is to work with the departments in (inherent) conflict. Another important consideration is that the integrating departments or individuals are equidistant between the conflicting departments in terms of their time, goal, interpersonal, and structural orientations. This middle position leads to effective resolution not through simple compromise, but rather through direct confrontations between the conflicting parties. Conflict resolution in this setting thus becomes a process whereby the parties thrash out their differences in the open with the assistance of integrators who understand both their positions.[28]

In the container corporations, with their lesser degree of differentiation, conflicts also arise, but not to the extent found in the plastics firms, owing to less differentiation. In the container industry, conflicts are resolved at the top of the organization,[29] because those at the top have greater knowledge, made possible by the stable environment and the lack of differentiation between organizational segments. Lacking differentiation, knowledge is not as specialized, and a top executive can have a good grasp of what is going on in the major divisions. Lawrence and Lorsch suggest that in this case, and in others like it, decentralization of influence would be harmful.[30] The food-processing firms generally fall between the plastics and the container firms in the extent of their differentiation and in the integration problems faced.

A major conclusion from this analysis is that *effectiveness is not achieved through following one organizational model*. While our concern here is with neither effectiveness nor organizational models, this conclusion is vitally important for understanding organizations. In other words, *there is no one best way to organize for the purpose of achieving the highly varied goals of organizations within a highly varied environment*. Particular combinations of goals and activities within particular kinds of environments do call for particular organizational structures if effectiveness is a major criterion for the organization. Organizational structure is thus not a random phenomenon, but is based on the factors that have been stressed throughout this analysis.

This conclusion is strengthened from consideration of Blau and

---

[28] *Ibid.*, pp. 54–83.
[29] Two organizations each were studied in the food and container industries.
[30] *Ibid.*, pp. 131–58.

Schoenherr's findings,[31] based on research into government finance and public personnel agencies. They also find that increased complexity engenders problems of communication and coordination. Personnel in the managerial hierarchy spend more time in dealing with these problems than in direct supervision in a highly complex organization. There is also pressure in complex organizations to add personnel to handle the increased control and coordination activities, increasing the proportion of the total personnel devoted to such activities.

This fact introduces an interesting paradox into the analysis of organizations. While large organizations can experience savings through economies of large size, the complexity that is related to large size creates cross-pressures to add managerial personnel for control, coordination, and conflict-reduction. Decisions to physically disperse, add divisions, or add hierarchical levels may be made in the interests of economy. At the same time, the economies realized may be counterbalanced by the added burdens of keeping the organization together. Complex organizations are thus complex in more ways than just their structure. The processes within such organizations are also complex. The techniques that are effective and efficient within a simple structure just may not be effective or efficient in a more complex case.

SOME ADDITIONAL CORRELATES OF COMPLEXITY

Complexity is related to additional characteristics of organizations. Hage and Aiken's analysis of program change in the 16 welfare organizations they studied illustrates this point well.[32] Program change in these agencies involves the adoption of new services and techniques—implicitly to increase the quality of the services rendered. Whether this is in fact the case is not specified, but it can be hypothesized that in a period of rapid change in the total social system and rapid developments in treatment technologies, program change would at least be related to efforts to upgrade the services performed.

The findings from this study suggest that complexity is related to the rate of program change. The more occupational specialties represented in an agency, the greater the likelihood of program change. However, the effect of this form of complexity is minimized when other organizational characteristics are examined. The function (or task) of the or-

[31] Blau and Schoenherr, *The Structure of Organizations,* pp. 311–29.

[32] Jerald Hage and Michael Aiken, "Program Change and Organizational Properties," *American Journal of Sociology,* 72, No. 5 (March 1967).

ganization, as defined by the amount of time a client spends with the agency (the more time the client spends with the agency, the more complete its service), is highly correlated with the number of occupational specialties. When organizational size and auspices are controlled, the relationship between the number of occupational specialties and rate of program change disappears. This is explained by the sequence of the development of these characteristics. The function, size, and auspices affect the number of occupational specialties found in an organization, and this is in turn related to the rate of program change. Since function is the strongest of the predictors, the line of reasoning presented previously is again confirmed. What an organization does affects its structure, in terms of both size and occupational specialization.

Evidence from the same study in regard to vertical differentiation suggests that when authority is concentrated at the top of the organization, the rate of program change decreases. Although Hage and Aiken do not have direct information on the number of hierarchical levels, the implication from their data is that a low number of levels is negatively associated with this form of change. In this case, the lower-level organizational members—professionals—are not used in the decision-making process and are thus underutilized. Another finding in the same study bears directly on this: the rate of participation in decision making is strongly and positively related to high rates of program change. The effective utilization of professional personnel involves their being allowed to enter the decision-making process through some power in the hierarchy. If they are without power, their contributions are minimized. These findings and the derived interpretations are consistent with the general literature on professionals in organizations.

Both vertical and horizontal differentiation are related to higher rates of program change. This finding suggests that when such forms of differentiation are present, much information will be flowing in the system —information that will contain conflicting ideas and proposals. Organizations that are complex in this way face the problem of integrating the diverse occupations and ideas deriving from the different organizational members. Later studies confirm that such conflict is present and must be dealt with by the organization. The proper method of handling such conflict is *not* by suppression; we have seen that this would represent the exact opposite of the effective utilization of highly trained personnel. We will see later that such conflicts actually work to the organization's advantage.

Aiken and Hage continued their investigation of these sixteen agencies three years later, following up some of the leads from the previous research. The dependent variable in the most recent study was organizational interdependence, as indicated by the number of joint programs in which the agencies participate. The findings from this analysis are not surprising in light of the earlier findings and discussion. *"Organizations with many joint programs are more complex organizations, that is they are more highly professionalized and have more diverse occupational structures."*[33] The interpretation given to these findings is that a decision to engage in joint programs leads to the importation of new specialties into the organization, since joint programs are likely to be highly specialized and the personnel in the agency would not have the skills necessary for participation.

These findings have interesting implications for organizations and for the society of which they are a part. Aiken and Hage state:

> Our assumptions help to explain the increasing frequency of organizational interdependency, especially that involving joint programs. As education level increases, the division of labor proceeds (stimulated by research and technology), and organizations become more complex. As they do, they also become more innovative. The search for resources needed to support such innovations requires interdependent relations with other organizations. At first, these interdependencies may be established with different goals and in areas that are more tangential to the organization. Over time, however, it may be that cooperation among organizations will multiply, involving interdependencies in more critical areas, and involve organizations having more similar goals. It is scarcity of resources that forces organizations to enter into more cooperative activities with other organizations, thus creating more integration of organizations into a community structure. The long-range consequence of this process will probably be a gradually heightened coordination in communities.[34]

If there is a tendency for organizations to become more complex because of internal and external pressures, the implication of these findings is that joint programs and other interorganizational relationships will continue to develop, probably at an increasing rate. In the long run this would lead to a society in which the web of interrelationships between organizations would become extremely intricate and the total society more organizationally "dense." This in turn implies a condition in which both individuals and the society as a whole are dependent upon fewer and more complex organizations. The nature of these organizations and their orientation toward the good of the few or of the many present the

---

[33] Michael Aiken and Jerald Hage, "Organizational Interdependence and Intra-organizational Structure," *American Sociological Review*, 33, No. 6 (December 1968), 920.

[34] *Ibid.*, pp. 928–29.

society with the dilemma of the source of control of the organizations. If this trend is realized, decisions regarding organizational futures become decisions about society.

The short-run implications of these findings would seem to be that the more complex an organization is, the more complex it will become, since the development of new programs and interorganizational relationships both lead to additional complexity. The Aiken–Hage approach to complexity has been organized around the utilization of professionals to accomplish and advance the tasks of the organizations studied. Since not all organizational members are professionalized, and since horizontal differentiation involves more than this variable, our focus will now shift to alternative modes of differentiation and their relationships with other variables.

Hage and Aiken's work on program change implies that how organizations change is related to their organizational characteristics. This implication is supported in later research by J. Victor Baldridge and Robert A. Burnham.[35] Their research compared the effects of structural characteristics (such as size and complexity), together with environmental conditions (changing or heterogeneous), with individual characteristics (age, attitudes, and education) in terms of their impact on organizational innovation. They found that the organizational characteristics were more strongly related to innovation in organizations. This does not negate the role of the individual, but suggests that factors such as complexity are crucial in understanding how and why processes such as innovation occur.

SUMMARY AND CONCLUSIONS

This chapter has dealt with a central variable in organizational analysis. The discussion has been based on research carried out in a wide variety of organizational settings. The emphasis has been on comparative research rather than on case studies, in the belief that while case studies can generate interesting hypotheses, firm conclusions can be drawn only from a broader test of the hypotheses derived. Despite the soundness of the research cited in the discussion, it is still premature to accept the results without reservations. Additional research in a wider variety of settings, including the vast array of voluntary organizations, is necessary before definite conclusions are warranted. The disparity between formal

[35] J. Victor Baldridge and Robert A. Burnham, "Organizational Innovation: Individual, Organizational, and Environmental Impacts," *Administrative Science Quarterly*, 20, No. 2 (June 1975), 165–76.

specifications of relationships and the manner in which they are actually carried out must be determined. In spite of these reservations and problems, this chapter has revealed several important points about complexity and, more important, about organizations.

Complexity takes several forms: horizontal differentiation—through an intense division of labor or through the performance of tasks by specialists; vertical differentiation; and spatial dispersion. It was emphasized that organizations can vary internally in the degree to which complexity on these various axes is present. In terms of structure, organizations with an intense subdivision of labor tend to have less vertical differentiation. Those with horizontal differentiation by specialists usually have rather tall hierarchies. These differences are largely attributable to the nature of the technology being employed in the organization.

Regardless of the form, high degrees of complexity introduce problems of coordination, control, and communication for the organization. The Lawrence and Lorsch research indicates that such problems are sources of conflict for the organization, but that such conflict is positively related to effectiveness if it is resolved in the appropriate manner. Indirectly, therefore, complexity is also related to effectiveness. This conclusion only holds, of course, when the technology and environment require complexity. In those cases where less internal differentiation is demanded, high levels of complexity would not contribute to organizational effectiveness.

The evidence presented strengthens the theme of the entire analysis. Environmental and technological factors, together with the related consideration of the nature of the personnel, traditions, decision making, and other internal conditions, determine the form of an organization at any particular point in time. As these factors change, the form of the organization will also change, as will its outcomes in terms of innovations or interactions with other organizations.

6

formalization

In this chapter formalization, alluded to several times in previous discussions, will be explicitly defined, with its antecedents and consequences spelled out. An additional dimension will be added to the discussion: the individual and his or her reactions to the degree of formalization in the organization. A person's behavior is vitally affected by the degree of such formalization, because individual discretion is inversely related to the amount of behavior that is preprogrammed by the organization.

No given degree of formalization is assumed to be good or bad. Instead, the more difficult position is taken: it depends. Contingencies and choice are again the major determinants of the degree of formalization. A critical contingency is the manner in which people in the organization are viewed by the organizational decision makers. If a set of people are viewed as having excellent judgment and self-control, formalization will be low; if they are viewed as incapable of making their own decisions and requiring a large number of rules to guide their behavior, formalization will be high. Other contingencies involve those already discussed, namely technological and environmental factors.

The introduction of the individual does not mean a shift away from the organizational level of analysis. Indeed, formalization has important consequences for the organization as a whole as well as for its subunits. As with individuals, these consequences are contingent upon the organization's is operating conditions.

THE NATURE OF FORMALIZATION

Some of the essence of formalization has already been discussed under the subject of the Weberian model of bureaucracy. The rules and procedures designed to handle contingencies faced by the organization are part of what is called formalization. The extent of rules and procedures varies. The simple matter of what time a person gets to work can differ widely among and within organizations in regard to the degree to which this act is formally specified. At the high end of the formalization continuum are organizations that specify that a person must be at his desk or work spot at 8 A.M. or he will be "docked" a half-hour's pay. Close to the other end there are no rules about being in the office or shop at a particular time, just as long as the work gets done. This is typified by many academic institutions.[1] The variation in the extent of such rules is not a matter of the professionalization of the labor force, as might be assumed. Many law firms, for example, require their members to register with their secretaries exactly where they will be going when they leave the office and how long they will be gone.

Maximal Formalization   Rules, therefore, can vary from highly stringent to extremely lax. These variations exist on the whole range of behaviors covered by organizational rules. The same kinds of variations exist in terms of procedures. A simple example of highly formalized procedures is the assembly line, where a piece of material is *always* passed in the same direction, with the same work being performed on it, or, in an office setting, where letters requesting a certain type of information are *always* processed in the same way, with the same type of information returned to the requester. The extreme examples of this, of course, are the computer-prepared responses to inquiries about such things as under- or overpayments of credit-card bills. This is one example of a highly formalized procedure in which the organization has been able to preprogram its responses to a wide variety of contingencies. Much of the frustration that people feel when they receive a computer printout rather than a personal letter is due to their feeling that their request was apparently just like everyone else's—that they are not unusual cases and therefore can be treated in a highly formalized way. The real frustration comes, of course, when it is in fact an unusual case and the computer procedures are inappropriate to the request. Despite the personal exasperation that this can develop, the fact remains that a large proportion of the communications that come into an organization can be handled by such formalized procedures.

Minimal Formalization   At the other end of the formalization-of-procedures continuum would be cases that are unique and for which no procedures have been developed. In these cases, members of the organization must use their own discretion in deciding what to do. At

---

[1] There may well be informal norms operative in this area that are quite strong. For example, I once worked in a situation where, for a period of time, the informal expectation was that Saturday mornings were to be spent at the office, even if this meant only a token appearance. For the moment, however, the informal aspect of rules, procedures, etc., will be ignored.

the extreme would come the cases Perrow has said call for intuition, and even perhaps inspiration, in solving—unique situations with no prepro-grammed answers.[2] In terms of our concern with organizational struc-tures, such uniqueness must be a regular part of the organization's (or subunit's) activities. That is, a unique situation becomes routine if it is repeated over time, and formalized procedures can then be developed to handle this once-unique situation. Thus, nonformalized organizations are those that deal constantly with new situations for which precedents do not exist—such as, for example, organizations engaging in frontier areas of scientific research of which the forthcoming results are not known. Organizations dealing with human problems, such as mental health clinics, would be in a similar situation.

At this point it should be noted that it usually doesn't matter whether the procedures or rules are formalized in writing. Unwritten norms and standards can frequently be just as binding as written ones.[3] Neverthe-less, most research utilizes the written system as the basis for assessment and analysis.

Jerald Hage makes essentially the same point when he states:

> Organizations learn from past experiences and employ rules as a repository of that experience. Some organizations carefully codify each job, describing the specific details, and then ensure conformity to the job prescription. Other organizations have loosely defined jobs and do not carefully control work behavior. *Formalization,* or standardization, is measured by the proportion of codified jobs and the range of variation that is tolerated within the rules defining the jobs. The higher the proportion of codified jobs and the less the range of variation allowed, the more formalized the organization.[4]

In their later research, Hage and Aiken follow essentially the same definition of formalization:

> Formalization represents the use of rules in an organization. Job codification is a measure of how many rules define what the occupants of positions are to do, while rule observation is a measure of whether or not

[2] Charles Perrow, "A Framework for the Comparative Analysis of Organizations," *American Sociological Review*, 32, No. 2 (April 1967), 196.

[3] See Jerald Hage and Michael Aiken, *Social Change in Complex Organizations* (New York: Random House, Inc., 1970), pp. 22–23.

[4] Jerald Hage, "An Axiomatic Theory of Organizations," *Administrative Science Quarterly*, 10, No. 3 (December 1965), 295.

the rules are employed. In other words, the variable of job codification represents the degree to which the job descriptions are specified, and the variable, rule observation, refers to the degree to which job occupants are supervised in conforming to the standards established by job codification. Job codification represents the degree of work standardization while rule observation is a measure of the latitude of behavior that is tolerated from standards.[5]

These variables are operationalized by asking the members of organizations to respond to a series of questions bearing directly on these issues. Measures of their perceptions of their own organization are thus used to determine the extent to which the organizations are formalized.

A similar definitional perspective is found in the work of Pugh et al. They define formalization as "the extent to which rules, procedures, instructions, and communications are written."[6] They also include "standardization" (the extent to which "there are rules or definitions that purport to cover all circumstances and that apply invariably"[7]) as one of their basic dimensions of organizational structure. These variables are operationalized by using official records and documents from the organization to determine such matters as the number of procedures of various kinds and the proportion of employees who have handbooks describing their tasks. An analysis of the data from the English firms studied reveals that standardization and formalization combine with specialization when the component scales are factor-analyzed. The authors call this factor the "structuring of activities."[8] They note that this brings the issue of role specificity to the forefront as an important organizational consideration. In highly formalized, standardized, and specialized situations, the behavior of the role occupant is highly specified, leaving him few options that he can exercise in carrying out his job.[9]

The similarities between these definitions point up the general consensus about the meaning of formalization. Even when quite different measures of this variable are used in research, the same meaning is utilized, an all too rare occurrence in organizational analysis. The methodological differences deserve some comment at this point. Formalization has been approached from two basic perspectives. The utili-

[5] Jerald Hage and Michael Aiken, "Relationship of Centralization to Other Structural Properties," *Administrative Science Quarterly*, 12, No. 1 (June 1967), 79.

[6] D. S. Pugh et al., "Dimensions of Organizational Structure," *Administrative Science Quarterly*, 13, No. 1 (June 1968), 75.

[7] *Ibid.*, p. 74.

[8] *Ibid.*, p. 84.

[9] *Ibid.*, p. 86.

zation of members' perceptions, as exemplified by the Hage and Aiken work, relies upon the average or median score on responses to a question or set of questions to determine the degree of formalization for the organization (or subunit) as a whole.[10] The alternative approach, as followed by Pugh et al., is the utilization of official records and information from key informants about the organization. This also yields a formalization score for the organization. Unfortunately, despite the similar conceptualizations, these methods apparently yield somewhat different results.

There are several possible reasons for these differences. In the perceptual approach, members of the organizations may not be giving their actual perceptions, possibly because of some fear of reprisal by the organization even though the researchers assure the anonymity of the respondent. While this undoubtedly occurs in some cases, it does not seem to be a major factor; other research using the same approach has demonstrated that the scores from the perceptual scales are quite valid when other indicators are used as validity checks.[11] A much more likely explanation is that perceptions of organizations do in fact differ from the officially described patterns. The many valuable studies that have shown the existence of "informal" procedures and work-group structures in organizations suggest that what actually goes on in an organization can differ markedly from what is officially described and prescribed.

Scores on perceptual scales may thus represent an accurate portrayal of an organization's degree of formalization or other structural features. This would imply that the use of official records or statements is of no use. This is not the case. The official system sets the parameters for any deviance that does occur. A prescribed degree of formalization is the starting point from which actual behavior begins. As a general rule, organizations that are more formalized on paper are more formalized in practice. Both methods can be used in ranking a set of organizations on their degree of formalization, even though the exact scores for each organization are not the same. The ideal method, of course, would be to measure rates of behavior to determine any aspect of organizational life; but the costs involved would be so tremendous that little more than a case study would be possible. The more economical measures described are used in order to obtain data that, although somewhat less accurate, do allow comparisons across organizations.

---

[10] The questionnaire items used are taken from scales developed by Richard Hall. The indices are found in Hage and Aiken, "Relationship of Centralization," p. 79.

[11] See Richard H. Hall, "The Concept of Bureaucracy," *American Journal of Sociology*, 69, No. 1 (July 1963), 32–40.

Another interesting point here is that deviations from the officially prescribed patterns are undoubtedly not random. That is, in some organizations, the deviance will be more pronounced and widespread than in others. Although the factors associated with these varying patterns of deviance in organizations are yet to be determined, the cruciality of the norms and the strength with which they are enforced appear to be decisive here. The extent to which the members *believe* in the norms would also be important. Policies are carried out by individuals. At the same time, the establishment of procedures and policies by an organization essentially sets its course for future activities. The organization and its members perform in accordance with the established policies.

FORMALIZATION AND OTHER ORGANIZATIONAL PROPERTIES

Centralization of Power

Power is an important component in any social system. As we shall see in detail in the next chapter, the distribution of power has major consequences for the performance of an organization and the behavior of its members. In their study of social welfare agencies, Hage and Aiken found that formalization was rather weakly associated with a centralized decision-making system.[12] Organizations in which the decisions were made by only a few people at the top relied on rules and close supervision as a means of ensuring consistent performance by the workers. These organizations were also characterized by a less professionalized staff. Thus, the presence of a well-trained staff is related to a reduced need for extensive rules and policies.

This interpretation is supported in Blau's analysis of public personnel agencies. In organizations with highly formalized personnel procedures and rigid conformity to these procedures, Blau found a decentralization of authority.[13] At first glance this is contradictory, since the evidence seems to say that formalization and decentralization are related. A closer examination reveals strong compatibility with the Hage and Aiken findings. In this case, adherence to merit-based personnel procedures ensures the presence of highly qualified personnel at the local (decentralized) level. These people are then entrusted with more power than are personnel with more questionable qualifications. Formalization in

[12] Hage and Aiken, "Relationship of Centralization," pp. 80–90.
[13] Peter M. Blau, "Decentralization in Bureaucracies," in Mayer N. Zald, ed., *Power in Organizations* (Nashville, Tenn.: Vanderbilt University Press, 1970), p. 160.

one area of operations is thus associated with flexibility in another. On this point Blau states:

> Rigidity in some respects may breed flexibility in others. Not all aspects of bureaucratization are concomitant. The bureaucratic elaboration of formalized personnel procedures and rigid conformity with these personnel standards do not necessarily occur together, and neither aspect of bureaucratization of procedures gives rise to a more rigid authority structure, at least not in employment security agencies. Indeed, both strict conformity with civil service standards and the elaboration of these formalized standards have the opposite effect of fostering decentralization, which permits greater flexibility.[14]

This rather simple set of findings reinforces a notion expressed earlier —complex organizations are complex. Formalization in one area brings pressures to bear to decrease formalization in another area. Organizations are thus constantly in conflict, not only between individuals or subunits, but also between and within the processes and structures that make up the organization.

It is important to note that the research of Hage and Aiken and of Blau deals with relatively professionalized work forces. One of the hallmarks of professionalization is the ability and willingness to make decisions based upon professional training and experience. It is not surprising to find lower levels of formalization in such situations. When the work force under consideration does not or is assumed not to have this decision-making capacity, the implications of the Blau findings have to be reexamined. In that case, formalized personnel procedures would probably be associated with a more centralized decision-making system, with the formalization level probably more consistent in all phases of the operation. It must be noted that the organization retains control over the individual in both cases. By selecting highly qualified individuals, it assures itself that the individuals will act according to organizational demands.[15]

Program Change

Further research by Hage and Aiken into the rate of program change in the agencies reveals that formalization is also related to the num-

---

[14] *Ibid.*

[15] See Peter M. Blau and Richard A. Schoenherr, *The Structure of Organizations* (New York: Basic Books, 1971), pp. 347–67.

ber of new programs added in the organizations.[16] In this case, formalization is negatively associated with the adoption of new programs. The reduction of individual initiative in the more formalized setting is suggested as the major reason for this relationship. In organizations that establish highly specific routines for the members to follow, there is likely to be little time, support, or reward for involvement in new ideas and new programs.

In their analysis of organizational interdependence, Aiken and Hage found that formalization was not very important in explaining the number of joint programs in which the agencies under investigation were engaged.[17] Apparently, factors other than formalization come to be important for this type of linkage. This is somewhat inconsistent with the idea expressed earlier that formalization would tend to impede the innovativeness that joint programs would seem to require. Aiken and Hage suggest that the development of joint programs has increased suddenly, so that organizational procedures might be in a state of flux. They also believe that the diversity of occupations (complexity) is by far the dominant influence here, actually overriding other considerations.

Technology

In their continuing research in these 16 agencies, Hage and Aiken then looked at the relationship between technology and facets of organizational structure. They follow the suggestions of Perrow and Litwak and divide the organizations into "routine" and "nonroutine" categories on the basis of scores derived from members' responses to a series of questions.[18] Even though these are all social agencies, there is a marked difference in the degree of routineness.

> The highest on routineness is a family agency in which the case-workers use a standard client interview that takes less than fifteen minutes. The purpose of the interview is to ascertain the eligibility of clients for county, federal, or state medical aid. An interviewee said: ". . . somewhat routine—even though each patient is individual, the type of thing you do with them is the same. . . ." The organization at the other extreme is an

---

[16] Jerald Hage and Michael Aiken, "Program Change and Organizational Properties," *American Journal of Sociology*, 72, No. 5 (March 1967), 511–17.

[17] Michael Aiken and Jerald Hage, "Organizational Interdependence and Intraorganizational Structure," *American Sociological Review*, 33, No. 6 (December 1968), 925–26.

[18] See Perrow, "A Framework," and Eugene Litwak, "Models of Bureaucracy Which Permit Conflict," *American Journal of Sociology*, 67, No. 2 (September 1961), 177–84.

elite psychiatric family agency in which each member is an experienced therapist and allowed to work with no supervision at all.[19]

The relationship between routinization and formalization is in the expected direction. *"Organizations with routine work are more likely to have greater formalization of organizational roles."*[20] (Italics in original.) Since these organizations tend to be on the nonroutine end of an overall continuum of routineness, the findings are even more striking: had organizations more toward the routine end of the continuum been included, the differences observed would probably have been greater. These findings, of course, strengthen the general argument that has been made throughout this book.

Hage and Aiken's research, one of the most thorough and systematic pieces of ongoing research available in the literature, is based on data from a limited number of organizations of relatively similar characteristics. The limitations inherent in using this type of data base are difficult to avoid, given the intrinsic difficulties in organizational research. But despite these limitations, their findings are generally consistent with those of Pugh's research team, which proceeded independently and with very different measures.

It will be remembered that the Pugh research was carried out on a sample of English work organizations. These researchers were interested in obtaining "hard" indicators of the organizations and the contexts in which they operated. Their major indicator of technology was *work flow integration.*

> Among organizations scoring high, with very integrated, automated, and rather rigid technologies, were an automobile factory, a food manufacturer, and a swimming baths department. Among those scoring low, with diverse, nonautomated, flexible technologies, were retail stores, an education department, and a building firm.[21]

While they contain more diversity than those in the Aiken and Hage study, these organizations are clustered toward the routine end of the routine–nonroutine continuum. As would be expected from the previous

---

[19] Jerald Hage and Michael Aiken, "Routine Technology, Social Structure and Organizational Tools," *Administrative Science Quarterly,* 14, No. 3 (September 1969), 369.

[20] *Ibid.,* p. 371.

[21] D. S. Pugh et al., "The Context of Organizational Structures," *Administrative Science Quarterly,* 14, No. 1 (March 1969), 103.

discussion, technology emerges as an important predictor of the degree to which activities are structured in these organizations. It is not as closely associated with structuring as is the size factor, but as Chapter 4 pointed out, size is misleading as a predictor in these circumstances.

In a later examination of the same data, Hickson et al. subdivide the technology concept into three components.[22] "Operations technology," the techniques used in work flow activities, ranging from automated equipment to pens and pencils, includes the ideas of the degree of automation of equipment, the rigidity of the sequence of operations, and the specificity of the evaluation of the operations. The second component, "materials technology," concerns the materials processed in the work flow. Perrow has pointed out the importance of the perceived uniformity and stability of the materials, and Rushing has shown that the "hardness" of materials makes an important difference in the division of labor in organizations.[23] The third component, "knowledge technology," refers to the characteristics of the knowledge used in the work flow. Perrow's approach is again used, with the primary indicators the number of exceptional cases encountered and the degree of logical analysis used in solving problems.

This appears to be a useful set of distinctions for the technology concept. Unfortunately, the British researchers have data on only the operations technology phase. Nevertheless, their findings and interpretations are vital additions to the understanding of what leads to important organizational structural characteristics. The primary conclusion from this analysis is that technology is *not* the major "cause" of structure. Using only the operations-technology component, the finding remains that size predominates as a predictor of structure. The authors conclude:

> . . . *variables of operations technology will be related only to those structural variables that are centered on the workflow.* The smaller the organization, the wider the structural effects of technology; the larger the organization, the more such effects are confined to particular variables, and size and dependence and similar factors make the greater overall impact. In the smaller organizations, everyone is closer to the "shop-floor," and structural responses to the problems of size (for example) have not begun to show. In larger organizations, managers and administrators are buffered

22 D. J. Hickson, D. S. Pugh, and Diana C. Pheysey, "Operations Technology and Organization Structure: An Empirical Reappraisal," *Administrative Science Quarterly,* 14, No. 3 (September 1969), 378–97.

23 William A. Rushing, "Hardness of Material as Related to Division of Labor in Manufacturing Industries," *Administrative Science Quarterly,* 13, No. 2 (September 1968), 229–45.

from the technology itself by the specialist departments, standards procedures, and formalized paperwork that size brings with it.[24]

These conclusions seem extremely reasonable, given all the arguments that have preceded these findings. While the role of technology is discounted from the evidence at hand, it appears quite logical that the material and knowledge phases of the technological concept would come into play among those organizational units "buffered" from the operations technology. A knowledge of an organization's size, types of technology, and other such factors will thus permit a prediction of the type of organizational structure it will have.

Tradition

One additional component should be added to these considerations. Organizations emerge in different historical eras, face varying contingencies, and develop different traditions. These differences in turn influence how such factors as size and technology affect the degree of formalization and other such characteristics. For example, if for some reason—such as the belief system of an important early top executive—an organization became highly formalized in its codification of job descriptions in writing, it would probably continue to be more formalized over time than other factors would predict.

Organizations cannot be viewed as solely subject to the pressures of size, technology, environment, and so on. They develop characteristics that are embedded in the formal and informal systems of the organization. These traditional factors have largely been ignored by organizational analysts, perhaps because they are so difficult to codify. At the common-sense level, they are important and deserve more attention than they have received.

We have seen from the total discussion that formalization is related to several important organizational characteristics. By its very nature, formalization is central to the life of and in organizations. The specification of rules, procedures, penalties, and so on, predetermines much of what goes on in an organization. Indeed, formalization is a major defining characteristic of organizations, since behavior is not random and is directed by some degree of formalization toward a goal.

We have examined the relationships between formalization and other organizational properties. The focus will now shift to the individual in the organization. Like formalization, individuals, too, must be treated as

[24] Hickson et al., "Operations Technology," p. 395.

variables, since they bring different abilities and habits and other behaviors with them into the organization and develop their own styles of behavior once they are in. While our focus here will be on the individual, the consequences for the organization will also be noted.

FORMALIZATION AND THE INDIVIDUAL

Members

An extreme example of formalization can be found in Crozier's analysis of the two French organizations.[25] He notes, "Impersonal rules delimit, in great detail, all the functions of every individual within the organization. They prescribe the behavior to be followed in all possible events. Equally impersonal rules determine who shall be chosen for each job and the career patterns that can be followed."[26] This extremely high degree of formalization, plus several other characteristics of the organizations, create a "vicious circle" in which the workers follow the rules for the sake of the rules themselves, since this is the basis on which they are evaluated. The rules become more important than the goals they were designed to help accomplish. The organization becomes very rigid and has difficulties dealing with customers and other aspects of the environment. Since the rules prescribe the kinds of decisions to be made, those in decision-making positions tend to create more rules when situations arise for which there are no precedents. Rules become security for the employees. There is no drive for greater autonomy, since that would be threatening. There is a strong desire to build safeguards through increased rigidity. The personnel in such a system become decreasingly free to operate on their own initiative, and, in fact, seek to reduce the amount of freedom to which they are subject. To one who values individual freedom, this is a tragedy. It would be presumptuous to say that it is such for the individuals involved, even though the argument could be made that the long-run consequences for them and for the total social system may indeed be tragic from several moral and ethical perspectives. For the organization, the consequences are clear: it becomes maladaptive to changes of any sort.

The personal and organizational dysfunctions were recognized over 30 years ago in Robert Merton's seminal discussion of the "bureaucratic personality." Merton notes that a trained incapacity can develop in the

---

[25] Michel Crozier, *The Bureaucratic Phenomenon* (Chicago: University of Chicago Press, 1964).

[26] *Ibid.*, pp. 187–88.

kind of situation under discussion. Actions and decisions based on past training and experience may be very inappropriate under different conditions. Merton suggests that the process whereby these conditions develop is part of the system itself.

> The bureaucrat's official life is planned for him in terms of a graded career, through the organization devices of promotion by seniority, pensions, incremental salaries, etc., all of which are designed to provide incentives for disciplined action and conformity to the official regulations. The official is tacitly expected to and largely does adapt his thoughts, feelings, and actions to the prospect of this career. But *these very devices* which increase the probability of conformance also lead to an over-concern with strict adherence to regulations which induces timidity, conservatism, and technicism. Displacement of sentiments from goals onto means is fostered by the tremendous symbolic significance of the means (rules) [italics in original].[27]

Nonmembers

This strict and even excessive adherence to the rules can also have negative consequences for persons not in the organization itself. Clients who have regular contact with the organization, such as welfare recipients or students in registration lines at colleges and universities, are constantly dismayed and angered by the impersonal and rule-bound treatment they all too often receive. The individual feels like a number, or a "hole in an IBM card."

Reactions to Formalization

This rather dismal view of life in a highly formalized organization is extended by Victor Thompson's description of "bureaupathic" and "bureautic" behavior. Thompson suggests that the kinds of behavior discussed by Merton are caused by feelings of insecurity. Bureaupathic behavior "starts with a need on the part of the person in an authority position to control those subordinate to himself."[28] Superordinates themselves, except at the very top of the organization, are subordinate to someone else, and so this control can tend to be the too-rigid adherence to rules that has been discussed, since this protects the individual from

---

[27] Robert K. Merton, "Bureaucratic Structure and Personality," in Merton, *Social Theory and Social Structure*, rev. ed. (New York: The Free Press, 1957), pp. 200–201.

[28] Victor Thompson, *Modern Organizations* (New York: Alfred A. Knopf, Inc., 1961), p. 154.

making possibly erroneous decisions and actions on his own. According to Thompson, the most significant source of insecurity in modern organization is

> . . . the growing gap between the rights of authority (to review, to veto, to affirm) and the specialized ability or skill required to solve most organizational problems. The intellectual, problem-solving content of executive offices is being increasingly diverted to specialists, leaving hierarchical rights (and duties) as the principal components of executive posts. Persons in hierarchical positions are therefore increasingly dependent upon subordinate and nonsubordinate specialists for the achievement of organizational (or unit) goals. The superior tends to be caught between the two horns of a dilemma. He must satisfy the nonexplicit and nonoperational demands of a superior through the agency of specialized subordinates and nonsubordinates whose skills he only dimly understands. And yet, to be counted a success he must accept this dilemma and live with its increasing viciousness throughout his life. He must live with increasing insecurity and anxiety.[29]

Thompson suggests that these pressures lead to a "drift" toward the introduction of more and more rules to protect the incumbents of offices, exaggerated aloofness, resistance to change, and an overinsistence on the rights of office. These reactions are organizationally and personally damaging.

The second form of behavior—bureautic—is also personally and organizationally dysfunctional. This type of reaction involves striking out at the system, personalizing every encounter, and taking every rule as one designed to lead to one's own personal frustration.

> The bureautic employee is not likely to get into the hierarchy, and so may come to be regarded as a failure. Because of his inability to enter intelligently into abstract, complex, cooperative relationships, he tends to be pushed to one side, unless he has some unusual skill that the organization badly needs. He is often regarded as "queer." All of these facts add to his bitterness and increase his suspiciousness. He projects his failures onto the organization and the impersonal "others" who are his enemies. He feels he is surrounded by stupidity and maliciousness. He feels powerless and alienated from the system.[30]

[29] *Ibid.*, pp. 156–57.
[30] *Ibid.*, p. 176.

While some would argue with the psychological mechanisms that Thompson uses in his development of these reactions to the organization, the reactions themselves do exist.

From the discussion thus far, it seems that life in an organization almost inevitably leads to some form of personal and organizational malfunctioning. But these negative reactions are not inevitable and universal. There are critics of the total system who suggest that it is too corrupt and corrupting and should be abolished. A more reasoned approach is to ask under what circumstances and with what consequences such conditions exist.

Some clues to the answers can be found in the literature on professionals in organizations. There is strong interest in this topic since increasing numbers of professionals of all sorts are working in organizations, and many occupations are attempting to professionalize. Analyses of the relationships between professionals and their employing organizations formerly proceeded from the premise that there are built-in strains between professional and organizational principles and values.[31] Recent research has looked at this relationship more closely, attempting to discover the conditions under which strain is felt, since it assumes that there can be situations in which the professional is able to carry out his work with a minimum amount of interference from the organization, while the organization is able to integrate the work of the professionals for its own benefit.

This approach is followed in George Miller's analysis of the degree of alienation experienced by scientists and engineers employed in a large corporation in the aerospace industry.[32] These professionals reported that they felt more alienation when their supervisor used directive, rather than participative or laissez-faire, supervisory practices, and less alienation in situations in which they themselves had some control over the decisions affecting their work. The same general pattern was found in regard to other incentives that the organization provided professionals. There was less alienation when the scientists and engineers had some part in deciding the nature of their own research efforts, when the company provided opportunities and a climate for the pursuit of their own professional careers, and when the company encouraged

[31] See, for example, William Kornhauser, *Scientists in Industry* (Berkeley: University of California Press, 1963); and Peter M. Blau and W. Richard Scott, *Formal Organizations* (San Francisco: Chandler Publishing Co., 1962).

[32] George A. Miller, "Professionals in Bureaucracy, Alienation Among Industrial Scientists and Engineers," *American Sociological Review*, 32, No. 5 (October 1967), 755–68.

purely professional activities, such as the publication of papers or pursuit of additional training.

Miller also found that the length of professional training was associated with the extent of alienation felt. The more training a person has, the more he is likely to feel alienation under those conditions that produce it for the group of professionals as a whole. That is, for a Ph.D. scientist, the absence of encouragement of professional activities is more likely to produce alienation than it is for an M.A. scientist.[33] Utilizing the idea of intraorganizational variations in structure, Miller examined the extent of alienation felt by the professionals when the specific work location was controlled. Some of the professionals worked in a basic-research laboratory in the company, but most were employed in research and development in one of the major production units. As might be expected, the personnel in the basic-research laboratory experienced much less alienation than those in the production-oriented unit.

The organizational structure in which these professionals worked was related to their degree of alienation from work. Professionals were chosen to be examined because they bring to the organization a set of externally (professionally) derived standards by which they can guide their own behavior. The presence of organizational guidelines (formalization) is thus a duplication and probably perceived as less valid than are the norms of the profession involved. *For professionals, therefore, the greater the degree of formalization in the organization, the greater the likelihood of alienation from work.*

This point is supported further when two additional research reports are considered. Part of the research of Aiken and Hage has been concerned with the degree of alienation felt by the professionals in the 16 social welfare agencies they examined.[34] They, too, were concerned with alienation from work—although their measurement of this variable was quite different from that used by Miller—but they also looked at alienation from expressive relations. This was measured by responses to questions asking the degree of satisfaction felt about superiors and coworkers. The less satisfaction felt, the more the individual is alienated from expressive relations.

As would be expected from the direction of this discussion, the greater the degree of job codification of the organization, the more alienated

---

[33] Some differences were also found between the scientists and engineers, but this is not of importance in the present discussion.

[34] Michael Aiken and Jerald Hage, "Organizational Alienation: A Comparative Analysis," *American Sociological Review*, 31, No. 4 (August 1966), 497–507.

were the workers, in both areas of alienation. Alienation was much more strongly felt in terms of the job itself. "This means that there is great dissatisfaction with work in those organizations in which jobs are rigidly structured; rigidity may lead to strong feelings of work dissatisfaction but does not appear to have such a deleterious impact on social relations in the organization."[35] Strict enforcement of rules was strongly related to both forms of alienation; social relations are also disturbed when rules are strictly enforced. It was also found that both forms of alienation were high when authority in the organizations was centralized and the members had little opportunity to participate in decision making. Again, it must be stressed that these findings hold for the psychiatrists, social workers, and rehabilitation counselors included in this study.

A different approach was taken in my analysis of the relationships between professionalization and bureaucratization.[36] Bureaucratization is a broader concept than formalization, but it contains many of the same implications, as indicated in earlier discussions of the topic. I attempted to demonstrate that professionalization, like formalization, is a continuous variable, with some occupations being more professionalized than others. The study included physicians, nurses, accountants, teachers, lawyers, social workers, stockbrokers, librarians, engineers, personnel managers, and advertising account executives. After the occupations were ranked according to their attitudes toward several professional values, the average scores for each occupation were matched with the scores on bureaucratization measures for the organizational units in which these people worked. The results of the rank-order correlational analysis are shown in Table 6-1.

These results indicate that in general, bureaucratization is inversely related to professionalization. This is consistent with the argument in this section. Examined more closely, these findings reveal some interesting patterns. There is a relatively weak inverse relationship between the hierarchy-of-authority dimension and the professional attitudes. The presence of a relatively rigid hierarchy may not adversely affect the work of professionals if the hierarchy is recognized as legitimate. This is similar to the findings of Blau, who suggests that the presence of a hierarchy may facilitate communications from the professionals to the top of the organization. If the hierarchy of authority is legitimate and does facilitate communications, it apparently does not matter whether or not decisions are made in a prestructured way—and particularly if the work of the professionals can be carried out without extensive interference by the organization.

[35] *Ibid.*, p. 504.

[36] Richard H. Hall, "Professionalization and Bureaucratization," *American Sociological Review*, 33, No. 1 (February 1968), 92–104.

TABLE 6-1	RANK-ORDER CORRELATION COEFFICIENTS BETWEEN PROFESSIONALISM SCALES AND BUREAUCRACY SCALES				
	Professional Organization Reference	Belief in Service to Public	Belief in Self- Regulation	Sense of Calling to Field	Feeling of Autonomy
Hierarchy of Authority	—.029	—.262	—.149	.148	—.767**
Division of Labor	—.236	—.260	—.234	—.115	—.575**
Rules	—.144	—.121	—.107	.113	—.554
Procedures	—.360**	—.212	—.096	.000	—.603**
Impersonality	—.256	—.099	—.018	—.343*	—.489**
Technical Competence	.593**	.332*	.420**	.440**	.121

$* = p < .05.$
$** = p < .01.$
Source: Richard H. Hall, "Professionalization and Bureaucratization," American Sociological Review, 33, No. 1 (February 1968), 102.

A stronger negative relationship is found on the division-of-labor dimension. This means that the presence of professionals impedes minute specialization of tasks within the organization. A weaker relationship is found on the presence-of-rules dimension. The kinds of rules the organizations develop in these cases apparently do not interfere with the work of the professional. There is a stronger negative relationship on the procedural-specifications dimension. As more procedures are specified by the organization, the burden on the professionals apparently is stronger. In this case, the professionals are likely to want to utilize procedures that they themselves develop on the job or through their professional training. The inverse relationship between degree of professionalization and the organizational emphasis on impersonality is indicative of the fact that the professional personnel are inclined to deal face-to-face with fellow professionals and develop strong colleague ties. These strong ties are the exact opposite of organizationally desired impersonality, which implies an absence of affective relationships within the organization. The strong positive relationship between the professional variables and the organizations' utilization of technical competence as the basis for their personnel procedures is not surprising. The professions themselves verbalize and practice the idea that a person should be judged by his performance and other rational criteria. This is clearly compatible with organizational usage of the same idea.

Viewing these findings from another perspective, the strong negative relationships between the "feeling of autonomy" professional variable and the first five bureaucratic dimensions is an important indicator of the relationship between bureaucratization and professionalization. This finding indicates that ". . . increased bureaucratization threatens professional autonomy. It is in these relationships that a potential source of conflict between the professional and the organization can be found. The strong drive for autonomy on the part of a professional may come into direct conflict with organizationally based job requirements. At the same time, the organization may be threatened by strong professional desires on the part of at least some of its members."[37]

Formalization and Professionalization

All the studies that have been discussed have concluded that professionalization and formalization are incompatible. The more professionalized the work force, the more likely that formalization will lead to conflict and alienation. A major implication of these findings is that *formalization and professionalization are actually designed to do the same thing—organize and regularize the behavior of the members of the organization*. Formalization is a process in which the organization sets the rules and procedures and the means of ensuring that they are followed. Professionalization, on the other hand, is a nonorganizationally based means of doing the same thing. From the organization's point of view, either technique would be appropriate, as long as the work gets done.

It is exactly at this point that the organization faces a major internal dilemma. If it allows too little freedom for its members, they are likely to feel oppressed, alienated, and "bureaucratic," and to engage in rule following for its own sake. If, on the other hand, it allows more freedom, behavior is apt to become erratic and organizationally irrelevant. A basic factor here appears to be the kind of guidelines for behavior that the individual himself brings to the organization. The more work standards he brings with him, the less the need for organizationally based standards.

It is difficult, of course, for the organization to know what kind of

[37] *Ibid.*, pp. 102–3.

standards a person brings with him. Even the use of a relatively common criterion, such as membership in a recognized profession, is not a perfect predictor, since not all members of a profession act in accordance with its standards. And when the organization moves into other personnel areas, away from the professions or established crafts, the availability of such external criteria may disappear. Because even well-developed external criteria such as professionalization may at times be organizationally irrelevant, the organization has to develop its own system of rules and procedures to accomplish what it is attempting to do.

A basic problem here is that the organization may have uncertain and inaccurate knowledge about its personnel. It may, for example, assume that its female workers are interested only in finding a husband and getting married, and may thereby rigidly structure the positions involved. This could make the work so unenjoyable that marriage would look like an attractive alternative to the women involved.

Here one point should be mentioned that is obvious but often ignored. There is nothing inherently more moral or excellent in professional or craft standards than in organizational norms. Many analyses of the relationships between professionals and their employing organizations seem to imply that the professional standards are somehow better than those of the organizations. Unless there are available specific criteria of what the organization and the professionals are trying to accomplish, such an assumption is unwarranted.

Before moving to additional implications of formalization for the individual and the organization, we must draw another conclusion from the analysis of professionals in organizations. The emphasis in much of the research in this area is on conflict between the professional and his employing organization. Evidence from the Hall research suggests that such conflict is not inevitable and should not be assumed without demonstration. This research found, for example, that the legal departments of large organizations are not necessarily more bureaucratized than law firms of comparable size. The lawyer working in the trust department of a bank may actually be working in an organizational environment similar, and perhaps even identical, to the one he would find in a law firm. This suggests that it is very possible to find organizational structures that are compatible with the degree of professionalization of their members.

The finding that legal or other professional departments in organizations may not be more bureaucratized or formalized than autonomous law firms raises another issue. The legal department of a bank is clearly less formalized than the division in charge of handling, sorting, and verifying checks. As is true of complexity, degrees of formalization vary within the organization. This can be most easily seen between departments, but it also occurs between levels in the organization. In general, the higher the level, the less the formalization.[38]

At the beginning of this chapter it was noted that formalization involves assumptions about the nature of the men and women in organizations. Without delving very far into the realm of psychology, it should be noted that the evidence is unclear in regard to exactly what people are like in their interactions with organizations. Some writers, such as Chris Argyris, believe that people move toward "adulthood," in which they seek autonomy, independence, control over their world and to develop their abilities to the utmost.[39] Others are not so sure.[40] Some people may simply not have any desire for autonomy or for self-actualization of any sort. While this is deplorable on humanistic grounds, it is nevertheless a fact. Thus, while some people are highly frustrated in a highly formalized setting, others would not be. By the same token, a low degree of formalization would be a satisfying condition to some, but not to others. A convenient way to deal with this issue is through the idea of *role* as it has been used in the organizational literature.

FORMALIZATION AND ROLES

Robert Kahn et al. have provided the most widely used and systematic framework for the understanding of the phenomena under discussion. It was developed in their work on the factors associated with role stress. The framework is illustrated in figure 6-1. The authors begin their discussion of this model by noting:[41]

> To a considerable extent, the role expectations held by the members of a role set—the prescriptions and proscriptions associated with a particular position—are determined by the broader organizational context. The

---

[38] See Richard H. Hall, "Intraorganizational Structural Variation: An Application of the Bureaucratic Model," *Administrative Science Quarterly*, 7, No. 3 (December 1962), 295–308; and John Child, "Strategies of Control and Organizational Behavior," *Administrative Science Quarterly*, 18, No. 1 (March 1973), 1–17.

[39] Chris Argyris, "Personality and Organization Theory Revisited," *Administrative Science Quarterly*, 18, No. 2 (June 1973), 141–67.

[40] See Jay Lorsch and John Morse, *Organizations and Their Members* (New York: Harper and Row, 1974), and E. Lauck Parke and Curt Tausky, "The Mythology of Job Enrichment: Self-Actualization Revisited," *Personnel*, 52, No. 5 (September–October 1975), 12–21.

[41] Robert L. Kahn, Donald M. Wolfe, Robert P. Quinn, J. Diedrick Snoek, and Robert A. Rosenthal, *Organizational Stress: Studies in Role Conflict and Ambiguity,* Copyright © 1964 John Wiley & Sons, Inc. Reprinted by permission of John Wiley & Sons, Inc.

organizational structure, the functional specialization and division of labor, and the formal reward system dictate the major content of a given office. What the occupant of that office is supposed to do, with and for whom, is given by these and other properties of the organization itself. Although other human beings are doing the "supposing" and the rewarding, the structural properties of organizations are sufficiently stable so that they can be treated as independent of the particular persons in the role set. For such properties as size, number of echelons, and rate of growth, the justifiable abstraction of organizational properties from individual behavior is even more obvious.

The organizational circle (A) in Figure [6-1], then represents a set of variables. Some of them characterize the organization as a whole: for example, its size, number of ranks or status levels, the products it produces, or its financial base. Other variables in this set are ecological, in that they represent the relation of a certain position or person to the organization; for example, his rank, his responsibilities for certain services in the division of labor, or the number and positions of others who are directly concerned with his performance.

Arrow 3 asserts a causal relationship between various organizational variables and the role expectations and pressures which are held about and exerted toward a particular position. For example, a person in a liaison position linking two departments is likely to be subjected to many conflicting role pressures because his role set includes persons in two separate units, each having its own goals, objectives, and norms. In general, the organizational conditions surrounding and defining the positions of one's role senders will determine in part their organizational experience, their expectations, and the pressures they impose.

[The personality circle (B)] is used broadly to refer to all those factors that describe a person's propensities to behave in certain ways, his motives and values, his sensitivities and fears, his habits, and the like. . . . [The interpersonal relations circle (C) refers to] the more or less stable patterns of interaction between a person and his role senders and to their orientations toward each other. These patterns of relationships may be characterized along several dimensions, some of them stemming from the formal structure of the organization, others from informal interaction and the sharing of common experiences. The following dimensions are seen as particularly important in the present context: (1) *power* or ability to influence; (2) *affective bonds,* such as respect, trust in the cooperativeness and benevolence of the other, and attraction or liking; (3) *dependence* of one on the other; and (4) the style of *communication* between the focal person and his associates.

As Figure [6-1] indicates, interpersonal relations (Circle C) fulfill some functions parallel to those described in connection with personality factors. The kind of pressure exerted by role senders upon the focal person

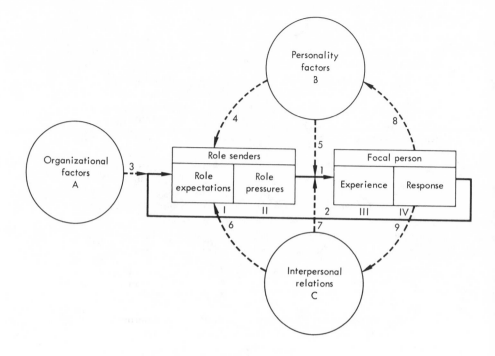

Figure 6-1   A theoretical model of factors involved in adjustment to role conflict and ambiguity

Source: Robert L. Kahn et al., Organizational Stress: Studies in Role Conflict and Ambiguity, *Copyright © 1964 John Wiley & Sons, Inc. Reprinted by permission of John Wiley & Sons, Inc.*

depends to some degree upon the nature of relations between them (Arrow 6). Role senders who are superior in the formal hierarchy will present their demands in a different manner from subordinates or peers. Pressures will also be interpreted differently depending on the relationship between focal person and role senders (Arrow 7). For example, pressures from relatively powerful associates arouse more tension than similar pressures from others. Finally, the nature of a person's behavioral reactions to a given experience may be affected by interpersonal relations in the situation. For example, such coping responses as overt aggression may be virtually ruled out when the pressures are exerted by a hierarchical superior.[42]

[42] *Ibid.,* pp. 31–33.

Sources of Role Conflict and Ambiguity

An important consideration, implied in this model but not made sufficiently clear, is that the input into behavior from the three major sources (organizational, personality, and interpersonal) is not constant and equal. In a highly formalized organization, for example, the organizational factor is designed to and usually does outweigh the other factors. In the less formalized situation, personality and interpersonal factors would be more dominant.

This model and the research from which it emerged assume that the "mix" between these factors is not always perfect. One kind of improper mix occurs when there are too many role messages being sent to an individual, with role conflict resulting. Incompatible expectations may be sent to a person: on the one hand, by the organization in terms of formal requirements of his job; on the other, from members of his role set, who attempt through interpersonal means to make him behave in accordance with their own desires, which may be different from the organizationally demanded behaviors. In some cases, the organizational demands themselves may be in conflict, as when a "supervisor requests a man to acquire material which is unavailable through normal channels and at the same time prohibits violations of normal channels."[43]

When a person is asked to perform a series of tasks that are incompatible with one another, he is experiencing "role overload." It is impossible for the person to complete all his assigned tasks at one time. "He is likely to experience overload as a conflict of priorities; he must decide which pressures to comply with and which to hold off. If it is impossible to deny any of the pressures, he may be taxed beyond the limit of his ability."[44] This conclusion is verified by Stephen Sales' analysis of organizational factors associated with coronary disease.[45] He finds that it is among personnel in overloaded positions that the risk of coronary problems is the highest. Dissatisfaction with one's work is also related to coronary problems, but this is not our concern here. Role overload and role conflict result from the combination of organizational, interpersonal, and personal demands that are in excess of capacity and ask competing behaviors on the part of the individual.

Essentially the opposite condition is present when *role ambiguity*

---

[43] *Ibid.*, p. 20.

[44] *Ibid.*

[45] Stephen M. Sales, "Organizational Role as a Risk Factor in Coronary Disease," *Administrative Science Quarterly*, 14, No. 3 (September 1969), 325–37.

occurs—that is, when insufficient information is sent to a person on how he is to perform his role. As in the case of conflict, the effects of ambiguity on the individual can be severe. He may not know what he is to do and may undergo stress because of this uncertainty. The absence of information can be based in any of the three sources of behavior.

Formalization and Role Behavior

This discussion of role behavior has been designed to indicate the interplay between organizational and other factors in determining the behavior of individuals in organizations. From the discussion, it should be clear that the degree of formalization of the expectations about how a particular role is to be played is an important component of how the role is played and how the individual reacts to his situation in the organization. In respect to improving performance of individuals within the organization, increasing their morale, and improving the overall performance of the organization, the proper mix between formalization and the personal and interpersonal characteristics has to be achieved. Since personnel vary, it is impossible to come up with a single prescription of how to do this. What is required, apparently, is sufficient flexibility on the part of the organization to enable it to adapt to developments in its personnel. If it adds highly trained people in a research and development section, for example, it should not expect to impose the same structure on these personnel that it does on another section of the organization.[46] Similarly, if the personnel in any section of the organization for one reason or another are able to provide more personal guidelines for their behavior than they initially could, the organization should be able to relax its own set of rules and procedures. Since most people do in fact learn, it would follow that this relaxation should be a rather normal and expected kind of phenomenon.

The role concept is a useful device for understanding the interplay among personal, interpersonal, and organizational factors as they impinge upon the behavior of organizational members. One author, David Hickson, maintains that role theory may be the key to understanding the various perspectives on organizations. According to Hickson, "Theory has converged upon the specificity (or precision) of role prescription and its obverse, the range of legitimate discretion."[47] This convergence takes

---

[46] The importance of not imposing a rigid structure on people who are to be innovative is strongly made by Victor Thompson in "Bureaucracy and Innovation," *Administrative Science Quarterly*, 10, No. 1 (June 1965), 1–20.

[47] David J. Hickson, "A Convergence in Organizational Theory," *Administrative Science Quarterly*, 11, No. 2 (September 1966), 225.

the form of criticism and advocacy of alternative ways of specifying role behavior. The formalization or specificity continuum extends from situations where "prescription is in general terms and goes no further than outlining the boundaries of legitimate discretion to roles where all but a fraction of role behavior is minutely described. Somewhere near the latter extreme comes the semi-skilled assembly-line operator, as well as particular activities in the performance of some roles, for example the first violin player while on stage."[48]

Hickson lists, among others, most of the authors we discussed in the section on perspectives on organizations, in terms of how they think roles ought to be prescribed by the organization. He then notes that the concentration on the degree of role specification, while useful as a means of structuring various organizational theorists and a useful exercise in its own right, *may have led to a situation in which other important questions are ignored.* He states:

> Grouping writers by the variables they have associated with role specificity draws attention to other ranges of variables, where little or nothing has been done; for example, small-group formation in organizations, and small-group processes from sociometric choice to tension-release mechanisms. It could be asked whether there are more groups per organization if specificity is lower: Are they smaller? Are they more cohesive? Do they show more tension? And so on. Nor have possible relationships been tested with personality traits, attitudes, or ways of thinking. For example, does not organizational innovation presuppose individual creativity? If so, then the low specificity associated with innovation must also be related to creativity. But, in addition, it is hypothesized that low specificity is related to anxiety and power conflict. Drawing these several hypotheses together, if innovation is associated with low specificity, then the underlying individual creativity must not only survive conditions of anxiety and power conflict but even derive stimulation from them. Can this be tested in the field in organizations?[49]

This last question is still to be answered. Hickson is correct in noting that a premature sense of closure can be felt if organizational theorists look only at the role concept. It is an extremely useful tool, however, for examining the interface between the individual and the organization. The attention paid to specificity or formalization is also not unwarranted, since it is so crucial to the understanding of organizations.

---

[48] *Ibid.*
[49] *Ibid.,* pp. 234–35.

THE IMPORTANCE OF FORMALIZATION

Formalization is the organizational technique of prescribing how, when, and by whom tasks are to be performed. This specification can be rigid or loose. The pattern it takes depends on several factors. The task being performed, the knowledge base from which task performance emerges, and the nature of the personnel have all been shown to be related to the degree of formalization. Lawrence and Lorsch's research has indicated that an optimal mix between the degree of formalization and these other factors is important for organizational effectiveness. This research also partially answers Hickson's query regarding the place of conflict in the innovative process, since in this case conflict was inherent and beneficial in the organizations involved in the innovative process. All these considerations suggest that formalization cannot be viewed as an evil or a good, but rather as an element of organizational structure that varies, as it should, from situation to situation and over time within any one situation.

Like other facets of organizational structure, formalization is subject to and dependent upon changing conditions. These changes can come from outside the organization in terms of environmental and technological shifts. They can also come from within the organization as the nature of the organization's members changes and the relationships between the parts of the organization are altered. Despite the dynamic nature of structure, it must be reemphasized that it is from structure and as a reaction to structure that the processes within organizations occur. The structure, including size, complexity, and formalization, is a "given" at any point in time.

SUMMARY AND CONCLUSIONS

This chapter began with the premise that an organization's degree of formalization significantly affects how the organization and its members perform. While none of the studies discussed attributed causal primacy to structural factors, it is clear from the analysis that structural characteristics have important relationships with other major organizational features, such as rate of change, the distribution of power within the organization, and relationships with the environment. We have also seen that the degree of formalization has important consequences for the individual. He can overreact, becoming a slave to the rules or fighting them for the sake of fighting. The individual can be dulled by an over-specification of how he is to perform in the organization. At the same time, if inappropriately guided by the organization by either too much or too little specification, the behavior of individuals can have extremely negative consequences for the organization.

The entire discussion has been guided by evidence suggesting strongly that organizational structure is formed by influences from outside and inside the organization. A major external influence is certainly the technological environment in which the organization operates. This would include the material, operations, and knowledge facets of the technology concept. While technology appears to be the key environmental variable, others would include relationships with other such general environmental factors.

Internally, the role of the professional was stressed, largely owing to the amount of evidence that has been amassed regarding the professional in the organization. Since they probably constitute the most conspicuous occupational group in organizations—with the possible exception of some of the crafts, which, for the purposes of this discussion, would have similar characteristics—and since more and more occupations are attempting to professionalize and more and more professionals are working in organizations, it is understandable that the work of professionals would be so highly emphasized.

Although the evidence discussed comes largely from the realm of the professions, the major point made was that the individual brings guidelines for his own behavior with him. It is the degree of congruence between these individual guidelines and those that the organization needs for the fulfillment of its tasks that is critical in determining the appropriate degree of formalization. These personal guidelines can obviously vary in terms of their strength, saliency, and content within any occupational grouping in the organization. Whether a person is a professional or not, his amount of previous training and experience is probably a major factor in determining how self-guiding he can be.

Another obviously important source of the degree of formalization is the decision-making process within organizations. People in decision-making positions determine whether or not the organization should "tighten up" its procedures. They also develop images about the people in the organization as being capable or incapable of self-direction.

Formalization is necessary in organizations. The degree of formalization is the variable that should be kept under constant scrutiny as an important practical matter. For the organizational analyst, the degree of formalization is a major variable for understanding both the organization and the performance and thoughts of its members.

An extremely useful tool for bridging the organizational and individual levels of analysis is the role concept. Roles contain individual, interpersonal, and organizational components as they are enacted. As Hickson has demonstrated, role specification has been a major focus for many of the students of organizations. While, as he suggests, it might be useful to move beyond this point, the role concept would appear to be of continued utility in understanding behavior in organizations.

7

centralization

Power (the development and maintenance of which will be discussed in the next chapter) always shows patterns of distribution. In the present chapter we will be concerned with this distribution of power, or, more specifically, with centralization. Probably the major defining character-istic of centralization is that power distributions are *determined in advance* by the organization. For instance, at the University of Minnesota there is a very centralized decision-making process in regard to whether an academic department will get additional faculty positions. However, the decision as to who should be hired to fill a vacancy is almost totally decentralized. Each department can decide the area of specialty it wishes to build and the background of the individual sought to fill it. Only "rubber-stamp" approval is required from the university administration (assuming that affirmative action and other federal or state criteria are employed).

Another example of variation in the degree of centralization can be seen in the use of credit cards. In some department stores, every pur-chase, no matter how small, that is charged must be checked through the store's computer. (The credit card number is punched into a mini-terminal and an instantaneous reading of the customer's current credit status is flashed back.) In other stores, the sales clerks can use their own discretion on purchases up to a certain amount of value. These discre-tionary decisions are undoubtedly based on how the customer is dressed, if he or she is known to the clerk, and so on. In each example, the organizational units or individuals are given different degrees of auton-omy in their actions. Centralization thus can refer to either individuals or units, such as divisions or departments, within the organization. It also, obviously, refers to *levels* within organizations, as when it is speci-fied that only people of a particular rank have the right to make certain kinds of decisions.

WHAT IS CENTRALIZED OR DECENTRALIZED?

Of the several aspects of centralization, the most obvious is the right to make decisions. This can be very specifically spelled out in terms of who or what has the right to make which kinds of decisions and when. If most decision making occurs at the top, the organization is centralized. The matter is not that simple, however, since the organization can have predetermined policies regarding even these decisions. Table 7-1 illustrates the intermixing of decision-making rights and organizational policies.

TABLE 7-1 FORMS OF CENTRALIZATION		
	POLICIES, PROCEDURES, AND RULES	
Level for Referring Decisions not *Covered by Policies*	*Few Policies/Broadly Defined*	*Many Policies/ Narrowly Defined*
TOP—Headquarters personnel	11 *Autocracy*/Highly Centralized. Few decisions are made by lower level personnel, and these are governed by broad policies. Most decisions must be referred to higher level management.	12 *Bureaucracy* / Centralized. Decisions are made by operating personnel within the framework of restrictive policies, procedures, and rules; problems not covered must be referred to higher levels for decisions or policy clarification.
BOTTOM— Operating personnel	21 *Collegial*/Highly Decentralized. Most decisions are made at lower levels without policy restrictions; other decisions made at lower levels within the framework of policies.	22 *Bureaucracy* / Decentralized. Most decisions are made at lower levels within the framework of the policies; personnel have discretion on problems *not* covered by policies.

Source: Arlyn L. Melcher, Structure and Process of Organizations: A Systems Approach *(Englewood Cliffs, N.J.: Prentice-Hall, Inc., 1975), p. 150.*

In the table it can be seen that in the "bureaucracy/centralized" cell (No. 12), operating personnel can make decisions, but they are limited by the policies of the organization. However, because the extent to which situations are covered by policies can vary widely, centralization is not a simple matter of who makes decisions. If personnel at lower levels in the organization are making many decisions, but the decisions are "programmed" by organizational policies, a high degree of centralization remains.

Another element of centralization is how activities are evaluated.[1] The evaluation process involves the determination of whether work was done properly, well, or promptly. If evaluation is carried out by people at the top of the organization, there is centralization, regardless of the level at which decisions are made. A situation in which there is centralized evaluation would probably—but not necessarily always—also be one in which policies are centralized.

Like formalization, the degree of centralization of an organization indicates its view of its personnel. In a highly centralized situation the personnel are not trusted to make decisions or evaluate themselves. Less centralized situations indicate a greater willingness to permit the personnel to carry out their activities in a more autonomous way.

It is not just the organization's definition of the qualities of its personnel that determines centralization, however. Research evidence strongly indicates that the familiar factors of size, technology, environment, and, of course, choice are also critical matters.

SIZE

Research evidence in regard to the relationships between size and centralization is paradoxical. From their study of state employment security offices, Blau and Schoenherr conclude that "the large size of an agency produces conflicting pressures on top management, as it heightens the importance of managerial decisions, which discourages delegating them, and simultaneously expands the volume of managerial responsibilities, which exerts pressure to delegate some of them."[2] The net result of increasing size is increased delegation or decentralization. The risk of delegation is lessened if personnel have expert qualifications. A

---

[1] Sanford M. Dornbusch and W. Richard Scott, *Evaluation and the Exercise of Authority* (San Francisco: Jossey-Bass Publishers, 1975), p. 82.

[2] Peter M. Blau and Richard A. Schoenherr, *The Structure of Organizations* (New York: Basic Books, 1971), p. 130.

centralized policy in regard to employee qualifications thus appears to contribute to delegated power.

One problem with this line of reasoning (a variation of the chicken–egg debate) should be noted: it is impossible to determine if increased size leads to pressures to delegate and thus to utilize experts, *or* if the hiring of experts leads to pressures to delegate, with size not really being a factor. The question cannot be answered with the kinds of data now available, but probably a combination of the two types of answer is most appropriate.

Blau's further research on colleges and universities revealed basically the same findings.[3] Large universities were more decentralized than smaller ones. Academic institutions and government agencies show a major difference in the qualifications of their personnel. In the government agencies, qualified personnel were utilized to carry out the organization's policies; in the academic organizations, the highly qualified personnel were able to gain power for themselves and to exercise a great deal of power over educational policies. In this case, size is clearly in interaction with a technological factor in its contribution to decentralization.

In a study using the Aston data and their measures on a second set of data, Roger Mansfield reaches conclusions essentially the same as those of the Blau research.[4] Mansfield found that increasing size is related to the increasing use of rules. This leads to the decentralization of decision making but not to loss of control for the organization. In smaller organizations, specialists report directly to the top of the organization, while in larger ones, problems are handled at a decentralized level, but under the guidance of organizationally based rules.

It is only common sense that it is impossible to control large organization from the top: because much more is happening than an individual or set of individuals can comprehend, there is inevitable delegation. As in the case of other structural characteristics, however, size is not the only answer.

---

[3] Peter M. Blau, *The Organization of Academic Work* (New York: John Wiley & Sons, 1973). This point is also recognized in the work of Edward A. Holdaway, John F. Newberry, David J. Hickson, and R. Peter Heron, "Dimensions of Organizations in Complex Societies: The Educational Sector," *Administrative Science Quarterly*, 20, No. 1 (March 1975), 37–58. They point out that different forms of control and hierarchy are possible in different sets of organizations.

[4] Roger Mansfield, "Bureaucracy and Centralization: An Examination of Organizational Structure," *Administrative Science Quarterly*, 18, No. 4 (December 1973), 77–88. See also John Child, "Organizational Structure and Strategies of Control: A Replication of the Aston Study," *Administrative Science Quarterly*, 17, No. 2 (June 1972), 163–77.

TECHNOLOGY

The technological factor has already been implied in the discussion. Some work is delegated, with the control remaining at the top of the organization by the use of rules governing the work. Other work is delegated to specialists who make their own decisions at lower levels in the organizations. Work that is delegated with controls is *routine* in terms of its technology.[5] In a bank, for example, each teller can handle thousands of dollars if the transactions are routine in the form of a series of small cash deposits and withdrawals. But if an individual presents a check for $2000 and asks for cash, it is a different matter. In this case, handling thousands of dollars is not delegated, but rather the decision moves back up the organization.

Dornbusch and Scott contribute to the analysis of technology and centralization[6] by noting that organizations deal with a variety of tasks that vary in their clarity, predictability, and efficacy. These are rather familiar distinctions in the literature on technology, with the possible exception of efficacy, which refers to "the means which have been developed for achieving desired outcomes."[7] Dornbusch and Scott point out that the variety of tasks performed in an organization means in essence that it has multiple technologies and thus must structure itself differently according to the task. This is in keeping with our earlier comments on intraorganizational structural variations. These variations are linked to these different tasks with their varied technologies.

Dornbusch and Scott utilize the concepts of "directive," guidance by rules, and "delegation," the actual decentralization of power to lower-level personnel. They conclude:

> Generally, in the interests of organizational effectiveness and efficiency, we would expect tasks which are high on clarity, predictability, and efficacy to be allocated by directive, tasks low on these three dimensions we would expect to be allocated by delegation. In its simplest terms, the argument is that, given high clarity as to the objectives to be obtained, high predictability of the resistance to be encountered, and established procedures for successfully handling this resistance, it is efficient to develop standardized, routine procedures which performers are directed to

[5] John Child, "Strategies of Control and Organizational Behavior," *Administrative Science Quarterly*, 18, No. 1 (March 1973), 1–17.
[6] Dornbusch and Scott, *Evaluation and the Exercise of Authority*.
[7] *Ibid.,* p. 82.

follow. High clarity contributes specific success criteria for use in designing sequences of activities. When the resistance confronted is predictable, it is possible to specify in advance the appropriate task activities to perform. When highly efficacious sequences of activities have been developed, performers will be expected to follow these set routines.[8]

These ideas were proven to be accurate by tests in a diverse set of organizations. It is thus critical to know what the task is before assuming a given degree of centralization will be found or before making a decision in regard to the appropriate degree of decentralization. The complex task will be delegated to a specialist, who uses his or her knowledge in handling the issue. As Blau's work suggests, organizations retain control through their hiring of specialists, but the control is not as tight as that which derives from organizational directives.

Another aspect of technology adds some slight confusion to the discussion. Participative management, which means that subordinates are consulted in regard to decisions that affect them,[9] was analyzed by James Taylor, who found that it was more likely to be successful in situations involving advanced technology.[10] Advanced technology here refers specifically to that concentrated at the work-flow level; thus, participative management is most effective in the more automated kinds of situations. Participative management can occur in situations that are otherwise highly centralized if the final authority is still retained by the superior in the situation.

Hage and Aiken's work has shown that participation in decision making—a different aspect of centralization—is related to the absence of rules, thus suggesting that centralization by rules and centralization by nonparticipative decision making tend to operate together.[11] Hage and Aiken's work, it should be remembered, is based on reports from organizational members themselves rather than on official records such as the Aston and Blau researches use. In this instance, the findings in regard

[8] *Ibid.*, pp. 82–83. This approach is congruent with Hage and Aiken's findings in "Routine Technology, Social Structure, and Organizational Goals," *Administrative Science Quarterly*, 14, No. 3 (September 1969), 366–77.

[9] For a discussion of participation, see Melcher, *Structure and Process of Organizations*, Chapter 14.

[10] James C. Taylor, "Some Effects of Technology in Organizational Change," *Human Relations*, 24, No. 2 (April 1971), 105–23. These findings are similar to those of Woodward, *Industrial Organization: Theory and Practice*.

[11] Jerald Hage and Michael Aiken, "Relationship of Centralization to Other Structural Properties," *Administrative Science Quarterly*, 12, No. 1 (June 1967), 72–92. See also Jerald Hage, *Communication and Organizational Control: Cybernetics in Health and Welfare Settings* (New York: John Wiley & Sons, 1974).

to centralization appear to be equivalent. In routine situations, rules govern the actions of the organizational members and there is likely to be little in the way of delegation of power through participation. In less routine situations, the opposite would be true.

Two cautions should be attached to these conclusions. First, participation in decision making *may not* mean that power is delegated. As suggested above, if the final decision still rests in the hands of the superiors in the organization, little power is actually delegated and participation is advisory at most. Although participation *may* help in the implementation of a decision, unless it contributes to the actual decision, there is no decentralization or delegation of power.

The second caution regards a phenomenon hardly touched upon by sociologists and other organizational researchers: budgetary controls, such as internal audits. Such controls have the potentiality of retaining a great deal of control at the top of the organization. Very few studies of centralization utilize this component of the distribution of power.[12] None of the studies of centralization considered so far have included budgetary considerations in their measurements or analyses. It would certainly appear that budgetary matters could be centralized in different ways than the allocation of tasks and other forms of power.

ENVIRONMENTAL FACTORS

The relationships among size, technology, and centralization have not been straightforward. The same is true in the case of environmental conditions. Research in this area has come to rather contradictory conclusions, although the contradictions can probably be resolved.

The contradiction is based largely on how much competition an organization faces in the environment. From their study of 30 business firms in India, Anant R. Negandhi and Bernard C. Reimann suggest that competitive market conditions make decentralization more important for organizational success than in less competitive situations.[13] This study was a successful replication of the Lawrence and Lorsch contingency

[12] Exceptions are Geert H. Hofstede, "Budget Control and the Autonomy of Organizational Units" (Zagreb, Yugoslavia: Proceedings of the First International Sociological Conference on Participation and Self-Management, 1972), 2, pp. 109–13; and William G. Ouchi and Mary Ann Maguire, "Organizational Control: Two Functions," *Administrative Science Quarterly*, 20, No. 4 (December 1975), 559–69.

[13] Anant R. Negandhi and Bernard C. Reimann, "A Contingency Theory of Organization Re-examined in the Context of a Developing Country," *Academy of Management Journal*, 15, No. 2 (June 1972), 137–46.

theory previously discussed. Further analysis of their data indicated that the degree of dependence on other organizations was actually more strongly associated with decentralization than were the factors of size, technology, and market competitiveness.[14] Negandhi and Reimann indicate, as has been done in the present analysis, that the perceptions of the organizational decision makers are a critical mediating variable between the organization and the environment.[15] It is they who make the strategic choices about the environment and about how the organization will respond to it. In this set of findings, the competitiveness of the environment affects the degree of decentralization.

A very different conclusion is reached in a study of 38 small manufacturing firms in the United States.[16] In this study it was found that a more competitive environment led to a greater demand for control and coordination. There was a greater frequency of reporting, more emphasis on written communications, and a greater specification of decision-making procedures—in short, a much greater degree of centralization. It was also found that in less competitive environments there were more changes in product design, production processes, and number of products.

The contradictory findings seem to offer few conclusions about the effects of competition on centralization. A good part of the difficulty may lie in the fact that the more general characteristics of the organizational environments were not specified. For example, in an expanding economy in which the competing organizations are all gaining, decentralization may occur. If the economy is one of scarcity, in which one organization's gain is the others' loss, the tightening up and centralization that Pfeffer and Leblebici found would occur.[17]

If it is critical that the organization's environment be monitored, as for market or technological changes, decentralization would be most appropriate. If, on the other hand, the environment is stable and the organization is essentially insulated from change, centralization would be more workable.

[14] Negandhi and Reimann, "Correlates of Decentralization: Closed and Open System Perspectives," *Academy of Management Journal*, 16, No. 4 (December 1973), 570–82.

[15] Negandhi and Reimann, "Task Environment, Decentralization, and Organizational Effectiveness," *Human Relations*, 26, No. 2 (April 1973), 203–14.

[16] Jeffrey Pfeffer and Huseyin Leblebici, "The Effect of Competition on Some Dimensions of Organizational Structure," *Social Forces*, 52, No. 2 (December 1973), 268–79.

[17] Pradip N. Khandwalla, "Environment and Its Impact on the Organization," *International Studies of Management and Organization*, 2, No. 3 (Fall 1972), 297–313, suggests this approach, using the concepts of hostile and nonhostile environments.

Since centralization deals with power, the basic variable of politics, a brief look should be given to the manner in which the centralization of organizations is related to more general political processes. General political conditions are part of the environment of organizations, but organizations also help shape this environment.

CENTRALIZATION AND GENERAL POLITICAL CONSIDERATIONS

The overriding importance of organizations for the social order is underscored by considering some examples of their use for political purposes. Organizations can be shaped to be part of the process of political change and development. As was discussed earlier, China is using its organizations as a means of continuing political indoctrination and involvement.[18] Yugoslavian socialism has developed a program of "self-management" in which the workers in an enterprise elect a workers' council that in turn elects the management of the enterprise. This is not participative management of the sort discussed above, but rather management by participation. Enterprises in the Israeli kibbutz system (composed of *small* organizations) have a socialist ideology that is promoted by a system of rotation of all people through all positions.

These ideological purposes are not always met. In Yugoslavia, participation is lower and alienation is higher than the ideology indicates or political leaders desire.[19] In Israel, nonkibbutz organizations are more like their Western counterparts than they are like the kibbutz.

A major study of differing patterns of centralization in five countries has been conducted by Arnold Tannenbaum et al.[20] This research was carried out in manufacturing plants in Austria, Italy, Israel, Yugoslavia, and the United States. Austria and Italy are basically capitalist, like the United States, and Israeli kibbutzim and the Yugoslav economy are socialist. Israel and the United States contained the plants that were most successful—as defined by the standards used in the country in question, but including such universal factors as efficiency and morale.

---

[18] Martin King Whyte, "Bureaucracy and Modernization in China: The Maoist Critique," *American Sociological Review*, 38, No. 2 (April 1973), 149–63.

[19] For a discussion of some of the problems which have been faced in Yugoslavia, see Veljko Rus, "The Limits of Organized Participation," Proceedings of the First International Conference on Participation and Self-Management, Vol. 2, Zagreb, 1972, pp. 165–88.

[20] Arnold S. Tannenbaum, Bogdan Kavčič, Menachem Rosner, Mino Vianello, and George Wieser, *Hierarchy in Organizations* (San Francisco: Jossey-Bass Publishers, 1974).

The kibbutz plants are highly decentralized, with the effects of hierarchy virtually eliminated. In the United States, hierarchy is present, but its effects are mitigated by several factors. There is a limited potential for upward worker mobility in the American plants, but it is greater than in the Italian plants. There is also greater participativeness in the American plants. Workers are consulted and treated more as equals, even though they are not equal in power, and the rewards are higher.

Nevertheless, in the American plants there is no attempt to reduce inequality. This is a political stance, even though it may be unrecognized as such. The tendency toward participativeness in the American plants is viewed by some as manipulation. For example, the Tannenbaum researchers conclude:

> A position to which some of us subscribe, for example, argues that the approach to hierarchy described above supports techniques of "human relations" that maintain rather than eliminate substantial gradients of power and reward. It therefore covers over and diverts attention from the exploitation and injustice suffered by workers. Workers in the American plants, for example, do not *feel* as alienated as workers elsewhere but in fact they *are* powerless with respect to basic policy issues. Because of "human relations" a discrepancy exists between the subjective and objective experience of alienation. The Italian workers are more realistic and better adjusted in this sense. Jobs are frustrating to them, opportunities for self fulfillment or for achievement are sparse, and workers feel dissatisfied and poorly motivated. Italian workers *know* they are without power and quite realistically, they *feel* alienated. This realism is a symptom of good adjustment, not bad, although in terms of our conventional measures the Italian worker looks poorly adjusted. American workers, on the other hand, appear well adjusted and they report high levels of opportunity and satisfaction. Some actually feel a sense of responsibility in their plant—at least more than do workers in other places. But this is only because the "human relations" approach is so effective in its manipulation. The approach no doubt works in mitigating some of the psychological effects of hierarchy, but it does so without making any basic changes in hierarchy and, in the view of some of us, it is therefore subject to question from a moral standpoint.[21]

This Marxist approach gets at the very heart of the political issue involved in centralization. Management by participation, as in the case of Israel and Yugoslavia, is a direct attempt to alter traditional power arrangements within a society. The Chinese approach, which is not partici-

---

[21] *Ibid.*, p. 220.

pative but rather is designed to strengthen the power of the current regime, emphasizes political indoctrination and loyalty. It is highly centralized. The American approach, which increasingly features participation of some degree in decision making, does not attempt to redistribute power. It does, however, minimize the perceptible effects of power differences. Those of the Tannenbaum et al. researchers who judge this as immoral and misleading miss an important consideration. Even if it is agreed that workers are exploited to even a small degree, the end result remains in question: What is the more likely—a situation such as that in Italy, where the exploitation is definitely felt, or a situation such as that in the United States, where it is more moderately felt? It could be, for example, that at some time in the future, American workers, having experienced at least symbolic participation, would press very hard for actual participation. Those who had never experienced participation might not necessarily want to move in this direction.

This whole discussion is made somewhat moot by two considerations. First, participation schemes in Israel, Yugoslavia, and elsewhere are typically most successful in situations of relatively simple technology and in organizations that are relatively small and not complex. It is very questionable whether participative management would work in situations of technological sophistication or in large organizations of high complexity. Rank and file workers would be unable to comprehend all of the operations of such organizations, and probably would not desire to do so. They would yield to technical experts and those trained for management of large-scale organizations. This, of course, is basically what happens now in the United States and elsewhere.

The final consideration, developed by the Dutch sociologist Cornelius Lammers,[22] is that participative management involves taking *part* in decision making, while both management by participation and self-management involve workers taking *over* organizational management. The former is a functional form of decentralization that leads to greater efficiency and effectiveness, while the latter two forms are structural decentralization that lead to power equalization. Both forms of democratization are unlikely to occur together.

True power equalization in organizations is extremely unlikely. The very nature of organizations requires some form of hierarchy once organizations move beyond very small size, simple technologies, and low levels of complexity. As in the wider society, power differences are ubiquitous. The effects of such power differences can be minimized by

[22] Cornelius J. Lammers, "Self-Management and Participation: Two Concepts of Democratization in Organizations" *Organization and Administrative Sciences*, 5, No. 4 (Winter 1975), 35–53.

TABLE 7-2   CONSEQUENCES OF CENTRALIZATION ON ORGANIZATIONAL
              PROCESSES

| Organizational Processes | CONSEQUENCES | |
	Advantages	Disadvantages
Coordination	Greater coordination through central direction and uniform policies	Uniform policies apply regardless of the degree to which local conditions vary
Decision making: perspective	Company as a whole is considered in decisions when made by top management and staff personnel and where lower level managers make decisions within the parameters of policy statements issued by headquarters	The company perspective is likely to ignore the special features/problems of divisions, departments, and work units
Decision making: speed	In emergencies, central staff and management can mobilize the information and make decisive decisions without delay	The normal decision process results in delays; flow of information up and flow of orders/policies down take time; central personnel are often overloaded so decisions are further delayed

Source: Arlyn L. Melcher, Structure and Process of Organizations: A Systems
Approach (Englewood Cliffs, N.J.: Prentice-Hall, Inc., 1975), p. 157.

making them less abrasive through participative schemes, or actual
changes of the decision-making process can be attempted in terms of
who has power. Nevertheless, power distributions will remain.

THE CONSEQUENCES OF CENTRALIZATION

The centralization in organizations says a great deal about the society
in which they are found. A society in which the majority of organizations
are highly centralized is one in which the workers have little say about
their work. The same would probably be true in terms of their partici-

pation in the society. The degree of centralization of organizations also is an indication of what the organization assumes about its members: high centralization implies an assumption that the members need tight control, of whatever form; low formalization suggests that the members can govern themselves. In both cases, it should be remembered, the control is in behalf of the organization.[23] Professionals and other expert personnel in organizations do not work in behalf of their professions. Their expertise is in behalf of the organization.

A major consequence of varying degrees of centralization is for the organization itself. As shown in Table 7-2, the consequences of a high degree of centralization can be positive or negative for the organization, depending on the situation. Once again, the appropriate degree or form of organizational structure depends on the situation at hand. Thus a major problem is that it is not always possible to adjust the degree of centralization to fit a changing situation.

SUMMARY AND CONCLUSIONS

Centralization is the power distribution in an organization that is determined in advance by the organization. Like the other structural properties that have been examined, it is related to the factors of size, technology, environment, and choices made within the organization. Forms of centralization have important implications for both individuals and the wider society.

Like all structural characteristics, centralization is a given condition of organizations at any point in time. This does not mean that it never changes in degree. Indeed, the most severe power struggles in organizations can involve the issue of centralization. Strikes and rebellions have to do with power.

Organizations change, sometimes slowly and sometimes dramatically. Whenever they change, a new structure is formed. This new structure serves as the basis for both organizational actions and actions in response to the organization. Organizational change results from structure and leads to structure. In the chapters that follow, we will consider successively the processes of power, conflict, leadership, decision making and communications.

[23] Blau and Schoenherr, *The Structure of Organizations*, Chapter 9.

THREE

organizational processes

The analysis now shifts from examining *what* an organization is like structurally to *why* it is that way. The subjects of this section—power, conflict, leadership, decision making, communications and change—are all related to structure, both resulting from it and leading to it. These processes are important for more than structural analysis. Each is a critical component for understanding organizations. Leadership, for example, has been so talked about, written about, researched—and occasionally practiced—that many people believe that it is the key to organizational success or failure. We will examine leadership in conjunction with the rest of what we know about organizations to see just how important it really is. The same approach to the other topics will be taken. We will see how they operate in organizations and what the impact of their operation is.

The concern of this section is with issues that are important to members of any organization. For example, what individual(s) or group has power in an organization and why? The answer is more complex than the simple matter of rank in a hierarchy. The use of power has products more complex than simple compliance. Are power differences based on interpersonal relationships, or are there some power differences between organizational units as well? We know that conflict occurs within organizations, but we are less sure about its implications. Is conflict ever good for an organization? Decisions are constantly being made in organizations, but is there any hope that they are rational? Furthermore, for whom are they rational? Is the answer to almost every organizational problem more and better communications? What leads to change and innovation in organizations?

195

Questions like these will occupy our attention for the next several chapters. The answers will not be perfectly clear. The issues are complex and often contradictory. Furthermore, the study of process is more difficult than the study of structure, so that research in the area is both less plentiful and less rigorous. It is rather hard, for example, to study organizational conflict, since the participants are quite unlikely to want a sociologist intruding into the heat of conflict with an 18-page questionnaire or other data-collection instrument. Furthermore, much of the writing in the area is in the form of advocacy or in terms of how to be a better leader, communicator, or conflict resolver. The concern will continue to be the organization, with less interest in the individuals involved. As will be seen, however, individual variations have a tremendous effect on processes in the organization.

8

power and conflict

In organizations, power is the whole basis of patterns of centralization, and conflict is a major contributor to change. Every social relationship can be viewed as involving power, and with conflict either manifest or latent in every situation. When a superior asks a subordinate to do something or a professor asks a student to read something, it is a power act. The interests of the parties involved may be in conflict. Power and conflict are related, but not perfectly correlated: Conflict *may* result from the exertion of power, but it is not an inevitable result. In fact, probably most power acts are rather willingly complied with, with conflict being the exception rather than the rule.

As noted earlier, while there is extensive writing about these topics, they have not been the subject of as much empirical research as the structural aspects of organizations have. We will thus have to rely on information that is less complete and make our interpretations on a more tentative basis than in the earlier discussion.

THE NATURE OF POWER IN ORGANIZATIONS

Power can usually be rather simply defined. Most of the many treatises dealing with the concept are in general agreement that it has to do with relationships between two or more actors in which the behavior of one is affected by the other. The political scientist Robert Dahl defines power thus: "A has power over B to the extent that he can get B to do something B would not otherwise do."[1] This simple definition contains

---

[1] Robert Dahl, "The Concept of Power," *Behavioral Science*, 2 (July 1957), 202–3. For other general discussions of power, see Robert Bierstedt, "An Analysis of Social Power," *American Sociological Review*, 15, No. 6 (December 1950), 730–38; Peter M. Blau, *Exchange and Power in Social Life* (New York: John Wiley & Sons, Inc., 1967); Abraham Kaplan, "Power in Perspective," in Robert L. Kahn and Elise

the essence of the power concept. It also implies an important point that is often neglected: the power variable is a relational one; power is meaningless unless it is exercised. A person or group cannot have power in isolation; it has to be in relationship to some other person or collectivity.

Power Relationships

The relational aspect of power is specifically developed in Richard Emerson's comments on the importance of dependency relationships in the total power constellation. He suggests that power resides *"implicitly in the other's dependency"*[2]; in other words, that the parties in a power relationship are tied to each other by mutual dependency.

> Social relations commonly entail *ties of mutual dependence* between the parties. A *depends* upon B if he aspires to goals or gratifications whose achievement is facilitated by appropriate actions on B's part. By virtue of mutual dependency, it is more or less imperative to each party that he be able to control or influence the other's conduct. At the same time, these ties of mutual dependence imply that each party is in a position, to some degree, to grant or deny, facilitate or hinder, the other's gratification. Thus, it would appear that the power to control or influence the other resides in control over the things he values, which may range all the way from oil resources to ego-support, depending on the relation in question.[3]

Dependency is particularly easy to see in organizations, which by their very nature require interdependence of personnel and subunits. The existence of power relationships is also generally easy to see. Gary Wamsley notes that in highly bureaucratized organizations, ". . . power or authority would tend to be hierarchic: each level would have just that amount of power necessary to carry out its responsibilities; ascendant levels in the hierarchy would have increasing power based on broader knowledge about the organization and/or greater task expertise. . . ."[4]

Boulding, eds., *Power and Conflict in Organizations* (New York: Basic Books, Inc., Publishers, 1964), pp. 11–32; and Max Weber, *The Theory of Social and Economic Organizations,* trans. A. M. Henderson and Talcott Parsons (New York: The Free Press, 1947), pp. 152–93.

[2] Richard M. Emerson, "Power Dependence Relations," *American Sociological Review,* 27, No. 1 (February 1962), 32.

[3] *Ibid.*

[4] Gary L. Wamsley, "Power and the Crisis of the Universities," in Mayer N. Zald, ed., *Power in Organizations* (Nashville, Tenn.: Vanderbilt University Press, 1970), p. 53.

The design of these types of organizations rests largely on the power variable, with the intent of ensuring that each level in the organization has sufficient power. When an issue arises that is out of the purview of an office at a particular level, it is passed up the organization until it reaches the level where the decision can appropriately be made. Of course, few organizations approximate this ideal type, because the power arrangements are affected by informal patterns worked out over time and by personal differences in the exercise of the power available in an office. Nevertheless, in many organizations, power relationships are tightly prescribed and followed, and they are highly visible to all who enter the organization.

While in such settings power is very easily seen and experienced, in others it is more obscure. In some situations it is extremely hard to isolate. Rue Bucher tells the following anecdote as an example of this:

> According to the students' statements, the dean asserted that "nobody in
> the university has the authority to negotiate with the students. . . ."
> "Obviously somebody in the university makes policy decisions," the
> statement said, "and until an official body comes forward, we consider the
> present situation a refusal to negotiate our demands."[5]

In the situation described, neither the students nor the university administration in question could locate an office or individual who had the power to negotiate with students. The students' perception that this constitutes a refusal to negotiate is only partially accurate. This type of matter had not arisen before, and there was undoubtedly no established way to handle such situations because the power relationship was yet to be determined. Wamsley notes that in such situations, power is "variable; situationally or issue specific; surrounded by checks and balances; an interdependent relationship, often employing negotiation and persuasion and often found in changing coalitions."[6]

Power is as much a fact of university life as of corporate life, even if it takes a different form and is expressed in different ways. In campus situations such as student–administration confrontations, issues and relationships are being explored that had not really been part of the pre-existing power system. (It is interesting that it is usually the administration that is involved in such confrontations, when the issues the students are most concerned about generally have their origins in faculty actions or inactions.) Because more power is thus introduced into the system as

[5] Rue Bucher, "Social Process and Power in a Medical School," in Zald, ed., *Power in Organizations*, p. 3.

[6] Wamsley, "Power and the Crisis," p. 53.

arrangements are made to handle such incidents in the future, we see that there is no fixed amount of power (zero-sum game) in the system for all time; the amount of power can contract or expand.

In the discussion of the relative clarity of power relationships in organizations it is implicit that power must be viewed as more than merely interpersonal. The subunits in an organization also have varying amounts of power. Perrow, for example, in a study of industrial firms, found that the sales departments were overwhelmingly regarded as the most powerful units in the organizations involved.[7] The members of the other departments regarded them that way and apparently behaved accordingly. Ignoring interdepartmental power relationships by looking only at interpersonal power obscures an important facet of organizational power.

Two additional aspects of power should be noted. First, power is an act:[8] it is something that is used or exercised. Too frequently the act of power is ignored in analyses of power, which tend to focus on the results of a power act. These results can be of several forms, including compliance or conflict, but the exertion of power is what is of interest to us here. The second point is that the recipient of power is crucial in determining if a power act has occurred. If the recipient interprets an act as a power act, he or she will respond on that basis, whether or not the power wielder intended to utilize power.

Types of Power

The discussion thus far has treated power as a unitary concept, but there is a long history of distinguishing *types* of power. Probably the best-known and most widely used classification system is Weber's.[9] Weber makes a basic distinction between power and *authority*. Power involves force or coercion and would not be an important factor as an internal process in organizations except in cases such as slave-labor camps, some prisons, some schools, and so on. Authority, on the other hand, is a form of power that does not imply force. Rather, it involves a "suspension of judgment" on the part of its recipients. Directives or orders are followed because it is believed that they ought to be followed. Compliance is voluntary. This requires a common value system among

---

[7] Charles Perrow, "Departmental Power and Perspective in Industrial Firms," in Zald, *Power in Organizations,* pp. 59–89.

[8] Burton P. Halpert and Richard H. Hall, "Power and Conflict: Separable or Inseparable," mimeographed paper, Lawrence: University of Kansas, 1976.

[9] Max Weber, *Theory of Social and Economic Organization* (New York: The Free Press, 1947), pp. 324–28.

organizational members, as Scott notes, and this condition is usually met.[10]

It is useful at this point to distinguish between authority and persuasion or personal influence. Authority involves an acceptance of the power system as one enters the organization, while persuasion or influence are power situations in which the decision is made, consciously or unconsciously, at the particular moment the power appeal is sent from the power holder. When a persuader becomes institutionalized, in the sense of being always accepted and thus legitimated by the recipient, this becomes authority.

Many current social controversies revolve around the authority issue. When members of a system do not accept the values of the system, as in the case of the radical movement, authority as expressed by the police, courts, or organizational rules becomes nonlegitimate for the people involved. A whole new frame of reference is brought into play, as are other forms of power, such as coercion and persuasion. The fact that such situations are noteworthy is indirect evidence of the overwhelming dominance of authority as the form of power in organizations.

Weber further distinguishes between types of authority, developing his well-known typology of traditional, charismatic, and legal authority.[11] *Legal authority* is the type of most power relationships in modern organizations; it is based on a belief in the right of those in higher offices to have power over subordinates. *Charismatic authority* stems from devotion to a particular power holder and is based on his personal characteristics. This type is certainly found in modern organizations, to which it can be either a threat or a benefit. If a person in an authority position can extend his legal powers through the exercise of charismatic authority, he has more power over his subordinates than that prescribed by the organization. If the performance of the subordinates is enhanced (assuming for the moment that their performance enhancement is also beneficial to the actors themselves), such an addition is beneficial. If, on the other hand, charismatic authority is present in persons outside the formal authority system, distortions in that system will be evident. As we will see later, it is unlikely that a person with legal authority will be able to extend his power through the exercise of charisma. The third form, *traditional authority,* is based on belief in the established traditional order and is best exemplified by operating monarchies. Vestiges of this form can be found in organizations in which the founder or a dominant figure is still present, when terms such as "the old man wants it that way" are verbalized and the wishes of the "old man" are followed.

10 W. Richard Scott, "Theory of Organizations," in Robert E. L. Faris, ed., *Handbook of Modern Sociology* (Chicago: Paul McNally and Co., 1964), p. 497.

11 Weber, *Theory of Social and Economic Organization,* p. 328.

Dornbusch and Scott have added an important contribution to our understanding of authority.[12] They found that control in organizations was based on the process of evaluation. The individual who evaluates one's work has authority. Control through evaluation is most effective when the individuals being evaluated believe the evaluations are important, central to their work, and capable of being influenced by their own efforts. If the evaluations are believed to be soundly based, they will be more controlled by the evaluation process. Dornbusch and Scott also note that authority is granted from above as well as from below. In a multilevel hierarchy, people in a position to evaluate others are legitimated from subordinates and also from their own superiors.

Power Bases

Since Weber's time, there have been several attempts to classify the power concept into still more useful categories. One of the approaches that has attracted a good deal of attention is that of John French and Bertram Raven.[13] Their concern is primarily with the bases of interpersonal power, but their conclusions can easily be extended to the organizational level. Their typology is based on the nature of the relationship between the power holder and the power recipient. *Reward* power, or "power whose basis is the ability to reward," is limited to those situations in which the reward is meaningful for the power recipient. The second power basis is *coercive* power, based on the recipient's perceptions of the ability of the power holder to distribute punishments. French and Raven note that the same social relationship could be viewed as one of reward power in one instance and coercive power in a second. If a worker obeys a foreman's order through fear of punishment, it is coercive power; if another worker obeys in anticipation of a future reward, it is reward power.

The third form of power is very close to the implication of the Weberian distinction between power and authority. This type is called *legitimate* power. The recipient acknowledges that the power holder has the right to influence him and he has an obligation to follow the directions of the influence. *Referent* power is present when a power recipient identifies with a power holder and tries to behave like him. In this case, the power holder may be unaware that he is in fact a power

---

[12] Sanford M. Dornbusch and W. Richard Scott, *Evaluation and the Exercise of Authority* (San Francisco: Jossey-Bass Publishers, 1975).

[13] John R. P. French and Bertram Raven, "The Bases of Social Power," in Dorwin Cartwright and Alvin Zander, eds., *Group Dynamics*, 3rd ed. (New York: Harper & Row, Publishers, 1968), pp. 259–69.

holder. The final form, *expert* power, is based on the special knowledge attributed to the power holder by the recipient. The power recipient behaves in a particular way because he believes that the information possessed by the holder is relevant and that he himself does not have that sort of information available. The simplest example here, of course, is in the professional–client relationship, when the client follows the "doctor's orders."

All these forms of power are found in organizations. All are also, or can be, part of the legitimate authority system, except for referent power. The ability to reward or coerce is often viewed as legitimate, even though at times coercion is distasteful. The presence of staff experts in almost all organizations is in essence a recognition of the legitimacy of expert power. Thus, while French and Raven distinguish legitimate power from the other bases, all the bases with the exception of referent power are legitimate within the organizational framework.

Distinguishing between the forms of power is an empty exercise unless it means something for the organization and its participants. In the next section, some of these consequences will be identified.

SOME CONSEQUENCES OF POWER RELATIONSHIPS

Compliance and Involvement

Using a typology of power quite similar to French and Raven's, Etzioni has attempted to develop both a typology and an analytical scheme for organizational analysis built around the power variable.[14] Etzioni identifies three forms of power: coercive, remunerative, and normative. Normative power "rests on the allocation and manipulation of symbolic rewards and deprivations through employment of leaders, manipulation of mass media, allocation of esteem and prestige symbols, administration of ritual, and influence over the distribution of 'acceptance' and 'positive response.'"[15] This form of power is quite close to French and Raven's referent power, and the other two categories proposed by Etzioni are almost identical to coercive and reward power in the French and Raven discussion. Expert and legitimate power are omitted; Etzioni suggests that legitimate authority is based on one of the three power bases, anyway, and that legitimate authority has been overused in organizational analyses. This is an oversimplification, but the

[14] Amitai Etzioni, *A Comparative Analysis of Complex Organizations,* rev. ed. (New York: The Free Press, 1975).
[15] *Ibid.,* p. 5.

formulation itself is useful for our purposes, since it indicates the range of consequences that can be linked to the different forms of power.

Etzioni links the three forms of power to the kinds of involvement that the lower participants in organizations have with the organization. By lower participants he means those who are subject to the power in the organization. In using the simple dichotomy of elites or organizational representatives and lower participants, Etzioni glosses over the important fact that most people in most organizations are both power holders and power recipients, since they are between the very top and the very bottom of the organization. The lower participants in an organization that uses coercive power are characterized as having an *alienative* involvement with the organization, an intensely negative orientation, most easily seen among "inmates in prisons, prisoners of war, people in concentration camps, enlisted men in basic training, [where] all tend to be alienated from their respective organizations."[16]

In organizations using remunerative power, the involvement is neither positive nor negative and is generally of low intensity. "*Calculative* orientations are predominant in relationships of merchants who have continuous business contacts. Attitudes of (and toward) permanent customers are often predominantly calculative, as are relationships among entrepreneurs in modern (rational) capitalism. Inmates in prisons who have established contact with prison authorities, such as 'rats' and 'peddlers,' often have predominantly calculative attitudes toward those in power."[17] This same form of involvement would characterize many workers in production and clerical positions, if their work is viewed as a means to ends that are found outside the work situation; and it would also be characteristic of the guards in the prison setting, where alienation is found among the inmates.

Moral involvement characterizes those in organizations utilizing normative power. This is a high-intensity form of involvement and can be seen in the behavior of a "parishioner in his church, the devoted member in his party, and the loyal follower [in following] his leader. . . ."[18] Etzioni notes that moral involvement can take two forms. Pure moral commitments are based on an internalization of norms and in identification with the authority of the organization. Social commitment, on the other hand, is based on a sensitivity to pressures from members of the individual's primary group. In the latter case, the person has not internalized the norms to any great extent, but rather goes along with the beliefs and behaviors of people who are significant to him.

[16] *Ibid.*, p. 10.
[17] *Ibid.*
[18] *Ibid.*

The forms of power and kinds of involvement form the basis for the organizational typology. Etzioni recognizes the presence of mixed types, containing more than one form of power and involvement. In primary and secondary schools, for example, coercion is a secondary pattern to the normative power that is more often utilized. Coercion largely disappears in higher education. Therapeutic mental hospitals similarly use coercion as a supplemental process. Professional organizations, such as law firms, universities, and research organizations, utilize normative compliance patterns, with utilitarian compliance a close second. Newspapers are an interesting combination, also, in that the production side of the operation is characteristically utilitarian, while the editorial side is predominantly normative. The same pattern would characterize other parts of the mass media. Labor unions are a heterogeneous category, with all forms of power being represented. Most are utilitarian–normative, according to Etzioni. These combinations and difficulties in placement weaken this formulation as a typological effort; but the correlates of these compliance patterns that Etzioni identifies are important for our uses here.

The first set of correlates is concerned with goals and effectiveness. There are three major types of goals: *"order, economic,* and *culture."* The typical form of compliance structure for each type of goal is as would be expected: coercive, utilitarian, and normative. The same pattern holds for effectiveness, which is enhanced if organizations can move toward congruent compliance systems.

A second major concern is with the manner in which power is distributed in organizations. Etzioni notes that both instrumental and expressive leaders are found in most organizations and that the way these forms of leadership interact is highly dependent on the basic power system. In coercive organizations, inmates develop a separate social system in which expressive leadership predominates, although instrumental factors are present in the case of persons who engage in merchandising, "escape-engineering," and so on. In normative organizations, where few boundaries exist between upper and lower participants, there is a tight integration between the levels in the organization. In utilitarian organizations, expressive and instrumental leaderships are usually separated, with the instrumental leader's orders generally followed without too much dissension. Forms of leadership are related to organizational effectiveness, according to Etzioni.

In normative organizations it is functional for the expressive elite to subordinate the instrumental one; this seems indeed to be the case in the Jesuit order, the Episcopalian church, and in some labor unions, but not in other normative organizations, particularly egalitarian churches. In utilitarian organizations, high productivity is associated with subordination of the expressive elite by the instrumental elite, and cooperation between the two. In coercive organizations the antagonism between organizational and informal elites makes for an unstable relationship instead of a clear pattern of subordination.[19]

Etzioni then examines the kind of integration of members found in the three forms of organizations. Consensus is highest in normative organizations, lowest in coercive, and intermediate in utilitarian. Communications in the three types of organizations are also quite different. There are many blockages to communications between ranks in coercive organizations, few in normative, with the utilitarian organizations again holding an intermediate position. There is a high rate of horizontal expressive communication in coercive organizations and egalitarian normative organizations, while in hierarchical normative organizations there is a high rate of downward expressive communications. In utilitarian organizations, there is a high rate of downward and upward instrumental communications. The socialization of members is carried out primarily by fellow inmates in coercive systems, particularly in the expressive sphere. Normative organizations are heavily involved in the socialization process, since they rely tremendously on the commitment of their members. Utilitarian organizations need not engage in as much direct socialization, since they rely on outside agencies for a supply of trained personnel.[20]

Attention is then focused on the relationships between these compliance patterns and the environment of each organization. Coercive organizations have few activities outside the organization itself, while normative organizations are much more likely to be involved in a series of activities in the wider environment. Utilitarian systems, unless they bring in normative patterns, are likely to be rather narrow in their activities in the wider environment.[21]

Conformity

Donald Warren has utilized the French–Raven power typology in his analysis of how schoolteachers conform to organizational controls.[22] Warren is concerned with behavioral as opposed to attitudinal conformity as the dependent variable in the power relationship. Behavioral

---

[19] *Ibid.*, p. 126.

[20] *Ibid.*, pp. 127–50.

[21] *Ibid.*, pp. 151–74.

[22] Donald I. Warren, "Power, Visibility, and Conformity in Formal Organizations," *American Sociological Review*, 33, No. 6 (December 1968), 951–70.

conformity is compliance "in overt behavior, but without internalization of norms."[23] Attitudinal conformity involves both compliance and internalization. Warren also deals with the visibility of the power recipients. He suggests that those recipients who are subject to coercive and reward power must be highly visible, since their performance must be constantly under surveillance by the power holder. On the other hand, referent and expert power recipients can be much less visible, since they share the same social goals as the power holder. In these latter power forms, the recipients are motivated to conform and there is less need for direct surveillance.

Warren finds that in most of the schools studied, more than one form of power was used. The combinations of power forms confirm what would be normally expected. Expert and referent power tend to be found together and are closely related, while coercive and legitimate have a minimal relationship. Coercive power was the type found alone most often, while referent and expert power were most often combined with one of the other forms. These combinations are important from a theoretical standpoint; they suggest that in these cases, power is not something that is available in a social system in a fixed amount (zero-sum game). Power is a variable within the system, as to both type and amount.

The findings in regard to conformity are particularly interesting. Table 8-1 indicates the types of conformity associated with the different power bases. The differences between behavioral conformity and attitudinal conformity are particularly striking, because the form of power that is successful in one form of conformity tends to be very unsuccessful in the other. The contribution of referent power to conformity is "particularly decisive in achieving social control, regardless of its combination with other power bases."[24] The most important conclusions to be reached from these data, according to Warren, are that "effective social control is the result of diverse processes of individual conformity, and that there are systematic linkages of those processes to different bases of social power."[25]

Warren then adds the professionalism of the teachers to his analysis. He finds that in highly professionalized settings, coercive power is weak, whereas it is a stronger base in less professionalized settings. The addition of the professional variable weakens the impact of reward power, which apparently is not a major basis for control in these school settings.

[23] *Ibid.*, p. 954.
[24] *Ibid.*, p. 961.
[25] *Ibid.*, p. 962.

| Figure 8-1 | RANK-ORDER CORRELATIONS BETWEEN SOCIAL POWER BASES AND TYPES OF CONFORMITY: 18 SCHOOL AVERAGES |

Type of Conformity	Coercive Power	Reward Power	Expert Power	Legiti- mate Power	Referent Power	All Bases
Total						
Conformity	+.337*	+.362*	+.255	+.368	+.753*	+.703*
Behavioral						
Conformity	+.661*	+.335*	−.147	+.015	+.136	+.488*
Attitudinal						
Conformity	+.151	+.306	+.395*	+.509*	+.718*	+.654*
Attitude						
Socialization	+.113	+.256	+.015	+.216	+.636	+.480

* Significant at .05 level.
In total conformity, teachers use approach preferred by the principal.
Behavioral conformity represents teacher use of approach preferred by the principal but would prefer another approach.
Attitudinal conformity represents teacher use of approach preferred by the principal which is also preferred by teacher.
Attitude socialization represents a shift in teacher attitude closer to the principal's approach.
Source: Donald I. Warren, "Power, Visibility, and Conformity in Formal Organizations," American Sociological Review, 33, No. 6 (December 1968), 961.

Legitimate, expert, and referent power are all linked to professionalism, with legitimate power having the strongest association. The control system in a highly professionalized school, then, appears to be most effective when these three forms of power are utilized. Control would tend to be ineffective when coercive or reward power is the major basis used. This is consistent with most of the discussions of professionals in organizations.

The findings in regard to the forms of power and of behavioral and attitudinal conformity, and in regard to the role of professionalism, have some important implications. The major one is that the form of power used will vary in its effectiveness according to the type of conformity sought and the kinds of personnel over which the power is wielded. Since not all personnel are professional and since attitudinal conformity is at times both unnecessary and almost impossible to achieve, coercive and reward power cannot be viewed as inherently dysfunctional. On the other hand, since attitudinal conformity can reduce the need for surveillance and hence the costs (behavioral and financial) of power, the other forms of power can in some cases be viewed as being more effective in a wide variety of organizational situations.

Any one of the forms of power discussed can also be viewed as a socially negative or positive process. There is a rather constant implication (not necessarily implied by Warren) that referent, legitimate, and expert power are somehow better and more democratic than coercive or reward power. It should be clear that power holders or power systems can be viewed as legitimate, expert, or referent for reasons that in the long or short run are organizationally or societally dysfunctional or disastrous. This latter point, of course, is almost impossible to document while the system is in operation. At the same time, it is important not to assume the inherent goodness of any of the power forms discussed.

Perceptions of Authority

A related approach has been taken by Robert Peabody in his analysis of perceptions of organizational authority.[26] Peabody distinguishes four forms of authority. Authority of *position* is similar to a combination of French and Raven's coercive and reward power bases, since it involves the right to hire and fire, promote or demote, and distribute rewards. Peabody's definition of *legitimacy* is essentially the same as French and Raven's, while his terms *competence* and *person* are almost identical with expert and referent power. Peabody examined the perceptions of authority among members of a social welfare agency, a police department, and an elementary school. His interview data provide some insights into the way power recipients view those in a position of authority.

Some comments reflecting legitimate authority were:

"Authority to me is something you are bound to obey. It's something that I respect."

"A lot of authority is in the manual—it's the law."[27]

References to the authority of position have a slightly different flavor:

"The person with the rank has the final say. Whether you agree with him or not, you go along with him."

[26] Robert L. Peabody, "Perceptions of Organizational Authority: A Comparative Analysis," *Administrative Science Quarterly*, 6, No. 4 (March 1962), 463–82.
[27] *Ibid.*, p. 476.

"Authority is mostly our supervisor and grade-II supervisor."[28]

A quite different frame of reference is evident when authority is seen to be based on competence. Here the respondents are talking about their own authority rather than that of their superiors, but the point is made clear:

> "I have the final word in licensing. There is no written law as to what a good foster home or what a bad foster home is, except as we have defined it in our experience and knowledge. We have the authority to deny the license entirely. And it's based on this knowledge and experience rather than the manual."

> "Well, my authority is completely within my classroom, and I'm given a great deal of authority there. And I'm appreciative of this. I'm given a complete reign. I can use my own philosophy, mainly because it's the philosophy of the district. With a good teacher, *that's O.K. With a bad teacher it's not* [italics added]."[29]

Authority of the person can be easily seen in the next comment:

> "Authority is based on someone to lead . . . so a person in authority would have to be a leader. He would have to have the ability to command and other traits of leadership. . . ."[30]

Although this form of data is not the strongest in the world, the findings from this study are interesting in that they show how authority patterns form configurations in the organizations studied. In the police department, authority of position was emphasized, as might be expected from the ever-present reminders of official rankings, such as uniforms and quasi-military behaviors. A rather surprising finding is that authority of person also proved to be extremely important in this setting. Human-relations skills were constantly noted here as being important, more so than for the social workers and teachers in the study. Peabody attributes this finding to the fact that particular kinds of people are attracted to the kind of work that policemen do, although he does not specify what kinds of people these are. Another interpretation offered by Peabody

---

28 *Ibid.*, p. 478.
29 *Ibid.*
30 *Ibid.*, p. 479

is that skill in interpersonal relations is emphasized as a basis for authority in the absence of clear criteria of technical competence. He suggests that as "younger, career-oriented police officers with college training in police administration replace older, 'small-town cops,' the importance attached to authority of competence in this police department will probably increase."[31] Whether this does in fact happen, of course, still remains to be seen.

The social workers also exhibited a rather surprising pattern. They overwhelmingly emphasized authority of position. According to Peabody, this is a function of this particular organization. Very few members had had graduate training in social work, so that the overall competence level was relatively low; and the organization was headed by a matriarchal figure. The teachers, on the other hand, 75 percent of whom had had some graduate training, emphasized authority of competence over the other forms.

The Peabody and Warren studies emphasize two important points. The first is that the nature of the personnel—in this case, their degree of professionalization—is strongly related to the form of power utilized in the organization. One would predict that when inappropriate forms are used, the likelihood of disruptive conflict would be increased. Although the professionalization variable was used in these two studies and indeed seems to be a crucial factor in many organizations, other components of the characteristics of the power recipients besides professionalization would surely be important in regard to the kinds of power that can most effectively be used.

The second point is that in both studies multiple power forms were present and utilized. Organizational power apparently involves more than a simple utilization of one or the other of the forms of power that have been discussed. Power forms tend to exist in combination in the kinds of organizations studied. In both studies, of course, it is to the organization's advantage to obtain more than sheer behavioral conformity, since it would be extremely beneficial if the members of the organization also had attitudes corresponding to their behavior. Power through legitimacy, coercion, or position must apparently be supplemented by factors such as competence or human-relations skills.

It would be erroneous to generalize from these two studies about all organizations and all power relationships. There are many situations, for example, in which more than one form of power is found, but *not* within the same person or position. Etzioni has pursued this issue in

<hr>

[31] *Ibid.*, p. 480.

his analysis of patterns of dual leadership in organizations.[32] He took his lead from laboratory studies that found that in task-oriented groups, expressive (or socioemotional) leaders emerge who rank high in interpersonal dealings, in addition to instrumental (or task) leaders who rank high in stressing task performance; Etzioni suggests that these two forms of leadership are seldom combined in one person. Although there are undoubtedly a few "great men" who successfully carry out both forms of leadership, in most situations these roles are separated. From this analysis, Etzioni notes that the familiar distinction between the formal and informal leaders receives strong empirical support from the laboratory studies. More important, the instrumental leader is the one appointed by the organization, except where the organization itself is primarily expressively oriented, while the expressive leader emerges in the course of social interaction among work groups.

From this point, Etzioni goes on to apply his familiar distinctions between organizations, suggesting that in socializing and other expressive organizations, the organization is dependent upon expressive leadership; in segregating organizations, such as prisons, expressive leadership is not required; and in producing organizations, expressive leadership is of secondary importance. This argument is consistent with Etzioni's distinctions, mentioned earlier, between forms of power. What is important here is the application of these ideas to the power relationships under discussion. Etzioni suggests that in coercive or segregating organizations, attempts at utilizing expressive leadership—such as in rehabilitation of prisoners—are likely to fail, given the predominance of instrumental power sources. The few rehabilitation personnel scattered over a large number of prisons have their power dissipated against the force of the existing power structure.

A more important consideration in terms of the preceding discussion is the fact that a first-line supervisor in a producing organization is unlikely to be able to play both the expressive and the instrumental role. He is appointed to his position as an instrumental leader. From the evidence available, informal or expressive leaders emerge in such situations. If the supervisor is exposed to and expected to exercise human-relations skills, he is probably doomed to failure, according to Etzioni. If he attempts to engage in expressive leadership, he will be confronting a preexisting expressive leader. At some point in time he will have to choose between expressive and instrumental activities, as when his own superiors want to see production increased or some other instrumental task accomplished. If he attempts to implement the instru-

[32] Amitai Etzioni, "Dual Leadership in Complex Organizations," *American Sociological Review*, 30, No. 5 (October 1965), 688–98.

mental directive, his role as an expressive leader is severely threatened, since he can no longer be "one of the boys."

While the Warren and Peabody studies identified multiple power patterns within the same organizations, the power relationships analyzed were general rather than situation-specific. If Etzioni is correct, multiple forms of power that are incompatible are unlikely to be successfully used over time. For example, a holder of expert power may sometimes also serve as a referent, whereas reward and referent power would appear to be incompatible. In the kinds of organizations studied, it is conceivable that the power patterns described involved more than the one-to-one power relationship among the individuals involved. The types of organizations studied—schools, police departments, and social welfare agencies —can probably be characterized as organizations with multiple power relationships, and thus the findings are not surprising. It would be extremely useful to have information on the relative strength of the identified power bases linked to specific situations, so that a clearer picture of the nature of power in organizations would be available.

Our study of power in the form of authority has not yet taken into account the potential of participation by power recipients in the power relationship. In the last chapter, the impact of participation on centralization was discussed. Here we are concerned with the simple question of the extent to which participation in decision making affects the power of the individuals in power positions. There appears to be very little effect—although participation can sometimes increase the power of the power holder. Rosner et al. found that greater worker participation did not reduce the influence of the manager.[33] Workers felt that they had more personal influence, trust, and responsibility, but the actual influence of the manager was unaffected. In a related study, Mulder and Wilke found that participation actually increases the power of the power holder.[34] This occurs when neither the power holders nor recipients have expertise in the issue at hand. If the power recipients gain in expertise before the participation, their power relative to that of the power holder will increase.

Power and Communications

So far, we have focused principally on the manner in which individuals are controlled within various power systems. But power systems

[33] M. Rosner, B. Kavčič, A. S. Tannenbaum, M. Vianello, and G. Weiser, "Worker Participation and Influence in Five Countries," *Industrial Relations*, 12, No. 2 (May 1973), 200–212.

[34] Mauk Mulder and Henke Wilke, "Participation and Power Equalization," *Organizational Behavior and Human Performance*, 5, No. 5 (September 1970), 430–48.

involve more than the control of individuals. A study by Joseph Julian indicates that the communication system within an organization is also affected by the power arrangements.[35] Using data from five hospitals, Julian found that the hospital power systems differed largely according to the nature of the hospitals. In voluntary general hospitals, the power system tended to be normative, while in a tuberculosis sanatorium and a veteran's hospital, coercive patterns were a more evident part of the power relationship. Julian obtained his information about the power relationships from the patients in the hospitals. Obviously, patients are only one of several groups in hospitals subject to the power system. The "semi-professional" staff (including nurses and technicians) and the non-professional staff (orderlies and kitchen help) also are subject to the established power system. Data are not available to determine if the power relationships with patients are the same as those with the paid staff. They are probably not exactly equivalent, especially since remuneration enters the picture with regard to the staff personnel. This indicates again the probability that multiple power relationships characterize most organizations. This would particularly be the case when the organization contains such members as clients or students.

Julian supplies some insights into the nature of normative and coercive power as applied through sanctions on the patients. Normative sanctions include "explaining the situation to the patients again in more detail," and "asking relatives or friends to talk to the patient." The explanations and talks are designed to make the patient comply with the hospital's (doctor's) wishes. Coercive sanctions include "putting a patient under sedation to keep him quiet and restricting the patient's activity. . . ."[36]

When the communication patterns between hospital staff members and the patients are analyzed, it is found that there are more communication blockages under the more coercive system. These communication blockages are actually functional for the organizations. Julian states:

> Within the framework of this study, normative–coercive hospitals, which control and block patient activities to a greater extent than normative hospitals, restrict communication for coordinative purposes. In a more general way, normative–coercive organizations have more communication blocks because they are more effective for realizing the goal of control or coordination.[37]

[35] Joseph Julian, "Compliance Patterns and Communication Blocks in Complex Organizations," *American Sociological Research,* 31, No. 3 (June 1966), 382–89.
[36] *Ibid.,* p. 385.
[37] *Ibid.,* p. 386.

Another important finding of the Julian study is that the hospitals varied not only in the *type* of control utilized but also in the *amount*. In the largest general hospital more coercive sanctions were employed than in the other general hospitals,[38] and the overall amount of control exercised was also higher. At any point in time, the amount of power is undoubtedly fixed, but over time and across organizations the amount varies.

In our discussion thus far, we have been concerned with the power relationships between upper and lower participants in organizations—the vertical dimension of power. As indicated earlier, these relationships can occur at any point in the vertical structure of an organization. That is, vertical power can be found between a president and the vice-presidents of a university, as well as between faculty and students. Much of this relationship involves the way in which a superior interacts with his subordinates. The behavior and attitudes of both parties in a vertical relationship have been a primary focus of studies of "leadership" or management "styles," and will be dealt with in the next chapter.

HORIZONTAL POWER RELATIONSHIPS

The vertical dimension is only one part of power relationships in organizations. But power relationships between individuals and units horizontal to each other are a less systematically studied component of total power systems. Interdepartmental, staff–line, and professional–organizational relationships are all familiar loci of the horizontal dimension.

Before we look at some of the research in this area, an apparent contradiction must be clarified. The term "horizontal power relationships" seems to represent an inconceivable situation. If the parties in the relationship have exactly equal amounts of power, then as soon as one gains power at the expense of the other, a vertical element is introduced. But the concern here is with relationships among units and persons who have positions relative to each other that are basically lateral. In these lateral relationships, the power variable can become a major part of the total relationship. It is conceivable that power will not enter the relationship if the parties have no reason to attempt to influence each other's behavior. However, the power variable would almost inevitably enter such relationships when issues such as budgetary allocations, out-

---

[38] One of the other general hospitals was a university hospital. This makes it somewhat different from the typical general hospital, but for the purposes here it can be grouped with general hospitals.

put quotas, priorities for personnel, and other such matters come into the picture.

Staff-Line Relationships

Horizontal or lateral power relationships have been carefully analyzed by Melville Dalton.[39] Perhaps his best-known contribution is the analysis of staff–line conflict. (The staff is roughly equivalent to what has been called the supportive or administrative component in earlier discussions, while the line in this case is engaged in the production-output activities of the organization.) Dalton found that these personnel were in rather constant conflict in several areas. The staff personnel tend to be younger, have more formal education, be more concerned with proper dress and manners, and be more theoretically oriented than the line managers in the organizations studied. This is a basis for conflict, but it is also part of the power relationship. The power aspect, aside from its importance in actual conflict situations, comes in when the staff attempts to get some of its ideas implemented (expert power).

Power is also exerted in terms of the personal ambitions of the people involved. Dalton assumes that both sets of managers seek income, promotions, power in the organization, and so on. In the organizations studied, the line personnel held the power in controlling the promotion process; but at the same time, they feared that the staff might come up with ideas that would put the line's modes of operations under serious scrutiny as being outmoded or unimaginative. In this instance we have an example of two different forms of power as a part of one power relationship. The outcome is a series of conflicts between line and staff that, viewed from outside the organization, are costly to it. There is a fairly high turnover among staff personnel, who apparently feel that they are not getting anywhere in the organization. The staff resents the line, and vice versa.

In order to accomplish anything, the staff must secure some cooperation from the line. This requires giving in to the line by moderating proposals, overlooking practices that do not correspond to rigid technical standards, and in general playing a rather subservient role in dealing with the line. If this is not done, the staff's suggestions would probably go unheeded. This in turn would make their output zero for the time period, and their general relevance for the organization would then be questioned.[40] This, of course, is not a unique situation. The exact extent

[39] Melville Dalton, *Men Who Manage* (New York: John Wiley & Sons, Inc., 1959), pp. 71–109.

[40] *Ibid.*, pp. 104–10.

of such conflicts and conditions under which they occur are unfortunately not clear, since Dalton had a small sample, composed only of manufacturing organizations. But that this sort of phenomenon is a major component of traditional manufacturing firms, and that variations of the patterns described are found in every organization, seem to be generally accepted.

Professional–Organizational Relationships

The analysis of staff–line relationships has been largely replaced in recent years by a concern with professional–organizational relationships. These are usually expressed in terms of conflict. The power components of this type of relationship are similar in many ways to the staff–line conflicts discussed by Dalton. A major difference would appear to be that the organizational members with whom the professionals interact, while not professionals in the traditional sense, are usually not poorly educated people who have come up through the ranks. The modern executive is also well educated and is likely to show the same kinds of interest in general social values as the professional.[41]

It is commonly noted in discussions of professionals in organizations that the "reward" power system for them is more complicated than for other organization members.[42] Professionals typically desire the same kinds of rewards as other people, in terms of money and other extrinsic factors, but they are also likely to want recognition from fellow professionals as good lawyers, scientists, or whatever. In addition, evaluation of their work, which is difficult for someone not in that profession, is likely to be made by just such personnel. This is true in many cases even if the evaluator, in an administrative position, is a member of the same profession. For example, a research scientist in an organization is likely to be under the supervision of another scientist who has been promoted to research administration. The very fact that the latter is now working in administration prevents him or her from keeping up with developments in that scientific discipline; since they occur rapidly it is difficult even for the practicing scientist to keep abreast of what is occurring.

Since the organization must in some way control all its members, the issue becomes very difficult with respect to the professional. If it tries

[41] See Renato Tagiuri, "Value Orientations and the Relationship of Managers and Scientists," *Administrative Science Quarterly*, 10, No. 1 (June 1965), 39–51.

[42] For extended discussions of these points see William Kornhauser, *Scientists in Industry* (Berkeley: University of California Press, 1963); *Administrative Science Quarterly*, 10, No. 1 (June 1965), entire issue; and Howard M. Vollmer and Donald L. Mills, eds., *Professionalization* (Englewood Cliffs, N.J.: Prentice-Hall, Inc., 1966), Chapter 8.

to exert legitimate control through the hierarchy, the professional is apt to resist it. If it turns over the control of the professional to other professionals, the organization not only loses control, but is uncertain as to whether the professionals involved are contributing to the organization exactly what the organization thinks they should. This dilemma is frequently resolved by allowing the professionals to control themselves, with a fellow professional (for example, the research administrator) held accountable for the work of that unit as a collectivity. This allows the professional to work in a situation of less direct scrutiny but provides the organization with a system of accountability.

The reward system in these situations is also frequently altered. Instead of promoting professionals by moving them higher in the administrative system, organizations are developing "dual ladders" for their promotion system, whereby professionals can advance either by being promoted in the traditional way or by staying in their professional unit and with their work, but at increasingly higher salaries.[43] Additional rewards for professionals can come through publication and participation in the affairs of their profession. Organizations can also provide these kinds of incentives. As the professional becomes better known in the field, his or her own power increases. At the same time, the organization continues to have power over him, by providing the reward system as a whole.

This discussion has involved ways in which the power issue may be resolved. But obviously, in many cases the issues are not resolved and professionals are in conflict with the rest of the organization. They may feel that the organization is intruding into their work through unnecessary rules and regulations, or that their contributions are receiving insufficient attention and reward. The members of the organization in contact with the professionals, on the other hand, may view them as hopelessly impractical and out of touch with what is really important for the organization. These lateral power relationships will probably increase, because professionals and professionalizing occupations are becoming increasingly important to organizations of every variety.

Another form of lateral power relationship that would often involve professionals is in the area of expertise. Since there is no one universal organizational or societal truth system, experts can take differing views on what is good, rational, legal, or effective for the organization. When the perspectives of accountants, lawyers, research scientists, management consultants, and executives are combined, it is extremely unlikely that

---

[43] For a criticism of this technique, see Chris Argyris, "On the Effectiveness of Research and Development Organizations," *American Scientist*, 56, No. 4 (1969), 344–55.

a common viewpoint will emerge even after serious discussions. As the level of training and expertise increases in organizations, such differences will probably increase, also, and the power of expertise may well become a greater source of conflict for organizations.

Cliques   A different view of lateral power relationships is provided by Dalton, in his analysis of the formation and interaction of cliques in industrial organizations.[44] Dalton shows that personal self-interest can take the form of clique formation across organizational lines. Cliques can form vertically as well as horizontally, of course. In either case, coalitions are formed for the purpose of gaining something for the members involved. "Horizontal defensive" cliques, for example, develop when members of an organization at the same level band together in the face of real or imagined threats to their security by automation or reorganization. The "horizontal aggressive" clique is formed to accomplish a purpose—perhaps to halt the expansion of a staff or professional department that is seen as usurping some of the power of the clique's members. Dalton's analysis shows that organizations are constantly filled with interpersonal power situations as events and conditions shift over time. These power relationships need not, and in fact usually do not, follow the established organizational hierarchical or horizontal system.

Dalton's analysis tends to lead one to view organizations as a "bewildering mosaic of swiftly changing and conflicting cliques, which cut across departmental and traditional loyalties. . . ."[45] While this view is warranted as a check on an overformalistic view of organizations, it is an overreaction. Cliques would not form if there were not a common base for interaction or if there were not already interaction among members. Rather than being random, clique formation obviously begins from the established organizational order and then becomes variations from that order. The fact that these cliques can form vertically or horizontally and represent personal and subunit interests reflects the constant interplay of the power variables within the organization.

Uncertainty and Dependency

Crozier's analysis of the French organizations gives another view of power along the horizontal dimension. Departments in the tobacco firms were in a constant power struggle, with the maintenance men holding the most power because of their knowledge in repairing the equipment necessary to the production process. Production workers and their super-

---

[44] Dalton, *Men Who Manage*, pp. 57–65.

[45] Nicos P. Mouzelis, *Organization and Bureaucracy* (Chicago: Aldine Publishing Company, 1968), p. 159.

visors were essentially helpless unless the maintenance personnel performed their work. This, of course, gave the maintenance men a great deal of power in the organization. Crozier states:

> With machine stoppages, a general uncertainty about what will happen next develops in a world totally dominated by the value of security. It is not surprising, therefore, that the behavior of the maintenance man—the man who alone can handle the situation, and who by preventing these unpleasant consequences gives workers the necessary security—has a tremendous importance for production workers, and that they try to please him and he to influence them.[46]

In analyzing this situation, Nicos Mouzelis notes:

> The strategy consists in the manipulation of rules as means of enhancing group prerogatives and independence from every direct and arbitrary interference from those higher up. But as rules can never regulate everything and eliminate all arbitrariness, areas of uncertainty always emerge which constitute the focal structural points around which collective conflicts become acute and instances of direct dominance and subordination re-emerge. In such cases the group which by its position in the occupational structure can control the unregulated area has a great strategic advantage which is naturally used in order to improve its power position and ensure a greater share of the organizational rewards.[47]

This is a vivid example of the dependence relationship inherent in a power situation. If it were not for the essential expertise of the maintenance men in this situation, the production workers would not be so dependent. Although the Crozier study is perhaps an extreme case, it does illustrate how lateral relationships can become built around the power of the parties involved.

Additional insights into this kind of power relationship are provided by Perrow, in a study directly concerned with the power of different departments in organizations.[48] Using data from twelve industrial firms based on answers to the question, "Which group has the most power?" Perrow found that the firms were overwhelmingly dominated by their sales departments. This domination is shown in figure 8-1. Although

[46] Michel Crozier, *The Bureaucratic Phenomenon* (Chicago: University of Chicago Press, 1964), p. 109.
[47] Mouzelis, *Organisation and Bureaucracy*, p. 160.
[48] Perrow, "Departmental Power."

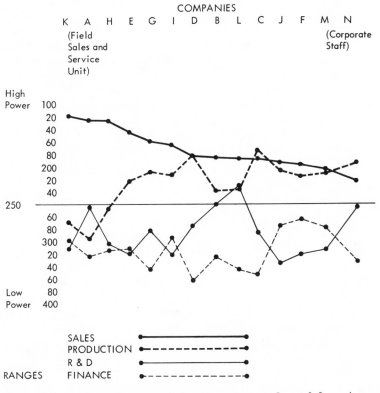

Figure 8-1   Overall power of departments in industrial firms (means of departmental means)

Source: Charles Perrow, "Departmental Power and Perspective in Industrial Firms," in Mayer N. Zald, ed., Power in Organizations *(Nashville, Tenn.: Vanderbilt University Press, 1970), p. 64.*

he does not have direct evidence, Perrow believes that this would be the case in most industrial firms in the United States.

Since manufacturing firms must sell their products, and since customers (institutional or individual) "determine the cost, quality, and type of goods that will be produced and distributed,"[49] the customer determines organizational success. While all departments in the organization contribute to customer satisfaction, it is sales that has the most direct contact with this important group:

[49] *Ibid.*, p. 65.

. . . sales is the main gate between the organization and the customer. As gatekeeper, it determines how important will be prompt delivery, quality, product-improvement, or new products, and the cost at which goods can be sold. Sales determines the relative importance of these variables for the other groups and indicates the values which these variables will take. It has the ability, in addition, of changing the values of these variables, since it sets pricing (and in most firms adjusts it temporarily to meet changes in opportunity and competition), determines which markets will be utilized, the services that will be provided, and the changes in products that must be made. As the link between the customer and producer, it absorbs most of the uncertainty about the diffuse and changing environment of customers.[50]

Perrow then generalizes that the most critical function in an organization tends to have the most power, linking his analysis to Crozier's. He notes that in the one firm that was production-dominated, the production department was able to get control of the computer and inventory and purchasing. It was in a position to tell the sales department that could or could not be done under existing conditions. These same functions could be handled in the finance department, as was the case in another firm, with finance passing the information along to sales, thus giving sales power over production. The combination of critical function and dependence gives sales its power position in these organizations.[51]

A PERSPECTIVE ON POWER IN ORGANIZATIONS

The discussion thus far has been largely descriptive, dealing with various studies of vertical and horizontal power relationships. In this section, we will try to bring some of these considerations together in an overview of power in organizations.

Amount of Power

The first point to be made here is a quantitative one, concerning the amount of power in an organization. This would appear to be a rather simple issue, since someone in a management position has a specified

[50] *Ibid.*

[51] These findings are similar, except in terms of who holds the power, to those of Paul R. Lawrence and Jay W. Lorsch, *Organization and Environment: Managing Differentiation and Integration* (Cambridge: Harvard Graduate School of Business Administration, 1967).

amount of power over a person beneath him. The matter is not that simple, however, when multiple bases of power are present. C. J. Lammers deals with this issue when he states, "To sum up, managers and managed in organizations at the same time come to influence each other more effectively and thereby generate joint power as the outcome of a better command by the organization over its technological, economic, and human resources in the service of certain objectives."[52] Lammers assumes that the members are seeking the same basic goals. This joint influence is actually a condition of more power in the organization than was the case before mutual influence entered the picture. If the French and Raven classification of power bases is utilized, it is obvious that the amount of power in an organization, as well as in a single interpersonal situation, is a variable. The amount of power in an organization changes over time.[53]

In summarizing a series of studies on the amount of power in organizations, Arnold Tannenbaum notes that the expansion of power

. . . may occur under either of two classes of conditions. The first is that of an external expansion of power into the organization's environment. The second concerns a number of internal conditions that subsume: (1) structural conditions expediting interaction and influence among members, and (2) motivational conditions implying increased interest by members in exercising control and a greater amenability by members to being controlled. These conditions may sometimes be related. For example, extending control by the organization into its environment may bring more decisions within the purview of the organization that are subject to the control of its members, thus increasing the possibility of a greater total amount of control. At the same time such increased opportunities to exercise control within the organization may increase the members' involvement in and identification with the organization and hence increase their interest in exercising control and their amenability to being controlled. Members, then, as possible control agents, engage in more frequent influence attempts, and as possible objects of control, provide new opportunities to one another to exercise control. Thus external developments may affect social and psychological processes within the organization conducive to a high level of internal control, just as conditions of a high level of involvement by members and of a high level of control within the

[52] C. J. Lammers, "Power and Participation in Decision Making," *American Journal of Sociology*, 73, No. 2 (September 1967), 204.

[53] Although most discussions deal with increases in the amount of power in a system, it is entirely plausible that the amount could also decrease.

organization may contribute to the strength of the organization and hence
to its power in the environment. . . .[54]

This view that the amount of power varies in organizations has to be
approached with some caution. First, the amount does not vary dramatically from situation to situation. Factors leading to an increase or
decrease would typically not be rapid or sudden in their impact—with
the exception of something like a disaster, in which case the amount of
power in the organization could change very dramatically. Generally,
however, changes in the amount of power will be gradual. A second
caution is that at any one point in time the amount of power in an organization is fixed—a zero-sum game. If one person or group gains in
power, another loses. Power acts are carried out within a fixed-amount
framework. It is the framework that is altered over time.

Distribution of Power

When the focus is shifted from the amount of power to the reasons
why power is distributed as it is, several points stand out. The ability
to cope with uncertainty leads to power differentials.[55] Coping with uncertainty means that an organizational unit is able to deal with some
issue of concern to the organization. If the concern is financial, for example, the unit able to attract resources will gain in power.[56] In the
perspective of the Aston group, coping with uncertainty is coupled with
both the centrality of the organizational unit to the total organization
and its nonsubstitutability. Units that cope well with uncertainty and
are irreplaceable and central to the work flow of the organization will
have increased power.

An empirical examination of this theoretical approach revealed that
this process did in fact operate, but with a minor modification.[57] The

[54] Arnold S. Tannenbaum, *Control in Organizations* (New York: McGraw-Hill
Book Company, 1968), pp. 14–15.

[55] D. J. Hickson, C. R. Hinings, C. A. Lee, R. E. Schneck, and J. M. Pennings,
"A Strategic Contingencies" Theory of Intraorganizational Power, *Administrative
Science Quarterly,* 16, No. 2 (June 1971), 216–29. Dennis J. Palumbo, "Power and
Role Specificity in Organizational Theory," *Public Administration Review,* 29, No. 3
(May/June 1969), 237–48, found the same uncertainty in relation to individual
power.

[56] Gerald R. Salancik and Jeffrey Pfeffer, "The Bases and Use of Power in Organizational Decision Making: The Case of a University" *Administrative Science
Quarterly,* 19, No. 4 (December 1974), 453–73.

[57] C. R. Hinings, D. J. Hickson, J. M. Pennings, and R. E. Schneck, "Structural
Conditions of Intraorganizational Power," *Administrative Science Quarterly,* 17, No. 1
(March 1974), 22–44.

modification is the fact that some organizational units are delegated important tasks in the first place. They can increase their power by effective coping. In other instances, power can be developed in situations in which organizational units enter new and important areas of uncertainty, cope well, and develop more power.

This approach implies that power is constantly shifting within the organization, as units gain and lose power according to how well they cope with uncertainty. While this is true, in that power struggles are an important component of any situation, too great a reliance on an imagery of constantly shifting power would be a mistake. Once an organizational unit obtained power, it would try very hard to maintain that power relationship. In their study of a university, Pfeffer and Salancik found that the more powerful units received more resources—the rich get richer and the poor get poorer.[58]

As Robert Michels reminds us, power has a self-perpetuating aspect.[59] Thus, those in power in an organization tend to remain in power. They have resources, and the power recipients do not. The very fact that legitimacy is such an important consideration in organizational power arrangements sets the stage for the perpetuation of existing power distributions.

Most of the discussion of power in organizations has been concerned with the manner in which an individual or unit is able to control the behavior of others in the organization. The emphasis has been on the idea that power is not a static phenomenon, even with the same personnel involved. But the issue becomes more complicated if problems of succession of personnel at all levels are considered. Studies by Alvin Gouldner, Robert Guest, and Oscar Grusky have indicated that changes in the top management can have important repercussions for the total organization, particularly when the new leader tries to utilize a different power basis than did his predecessor.[60] The turnover of personnel also contributes to the instability of power relationships.

The distribution of power in organizations has ramifications beyond those already discussed. The distribution of resources within an organiza-

[58] Jeffrey Pfeffer and Gerald R. Salancik, "Organizational Decision Making as a Political Process: The Case of a University Budget" *Administrative Science Quarterly,* 19, No. 2 (June 1974), 135–51.

[59] Robert Michels, *Political Parties* (New York: Thomas Y. Crowell Company, 1962).

[60] Alvin Gouldner, *Patterns of Industrial Bureaucracy* (New York: The Free Press, 1954); Robert Guest, "Managerial Succession in Complex Organizations," *American Journal of Sociology,* 68, No. 1 (July 1962), 47–54; and Oscar Grusky, "Corporate Size, Bureaucratization, and Managerial Succession," *American Journal of Sociology,* 67, No. 3 (November 1961), 355–59.

tion, including rewards, budget items, and personnel, is affected by the power system.[61] Since the allocation system is affected by the existing power system, it tends to perpetuate the existing system. Zald points out that the accounting and information systems within organizations are important agents of power; they determine the emphasis given to particular kinds of activities and the information that is available to various members of the organization. Zald also notes that the nature of the incentive system within the organization is an important power consideration, since it provides the basis, both in nature and extent, on which rewards are distributed.

External Factors

The focus of our discussion has been primarily on factors internal to the organization. Zald points out that external considerations also play an important role in the power system of the organization.[62] Here factors such as associations of similar organizations (trade associations or baseball leagues), relationships with suppliers and users of the organization's output, regulatory agencies, and other indirectly involved parties affect the amount and distribution of power within the organization. An example of this is provided by Richard Peterson, who notes that the National Labor Relations Board, after its establishment in the 1930s, facilitated the growth in power of labor unions. At the same time, the increasing complexity of labor laws and regulations led to the development of specialists in labor relations, and these personnel also gained in power in the organization, largely as a consequence of these external factors.[63] External economic conditions also affect the power system in organizations as markets for labor and outputs shift, the source of "raw materials" is altered, and the nature of the organization's clientele varies.

POWER IN VOLUNTARY ORGANIZATIONS

This analysis appears to be applicable to all organizations. But before we conclude this section, a brief consideration of power in voluntary or-

[61] See Mayer N. Zald, "Political Economy: A Framework for Comparative Analysis," and Louis R. Pondy, "Toward a Theory of Internal Resource Allocation," in Zald, ed., *Power in Organizations,* pp. 221–61, 270–311.

[62] Zald, "Political Economy," pp. 229–36.

[63] Richard A. Peterson, "Some Consequences of Differentiation," in Zald, ed., *Power in Organizations,* p. 146.

ganizations is in order. Voluntary organizations have all the characteristics of other organizations in regard to the nature and importance of power as an internal process. They are somewhat different, however, because of the apparent need for membership participation in order for the organization to remain viable. Most analyses point to the cruciality of the democratic process for voluntary organizations, since this form of power determination tends to assure continued participation. John Craig and Edward Gross suggest that in addition voluntary organizations must remain permeable to new ideas and interests if democracy is to be maintained.[64] This permeability assures continued participation by maintaining membership interest in issues that are new and around which power can cluster, thus preventing the tendency toward oligarchy. Maintaining membership involvement is crucial for such organization. From most of the evidence, it is apparent that this involves distributing some form of power among all the organizational participants, regardless of the power form and other considerations.

LOWER PARTICIPANTS

We have focused on vertical and horizontal components of power relationships in organizations. Before attempting to bring together the findings of the studies examined and developing an overview of power, a final form of the power relationship should be examined. This type is rare in organizations, but anyone who has had any contact with an organization has confronted it from time to time. The power of "lower participants" in organizations can be a source of both frustration and wonder; secretaries are capable of causing extreme frustration and embarrassment, among other things, for their bosses, and hospital attendants can in some cases make physicians dependent upon them.[65]

David Mechanic has identified some of the sources of power of lower participants.[66] As we shall see, these are not too different from the general sources of power that have been discussed in the earlier sections. What is different is that the lower members of organizations are able to amass the resources that a purely structural analysis would suggest

[64] John G. Craig and Edward Gross, "The Forum Theory of Organizational Democracy: Structural Guarantees as Time Related Variables," *American Sociological Review*, 35, No. 1 (February 1970), 19–33.

[65] Thomas J. Scheff, "Control over Policy by Attendants in a Mental Hospital," *Journal of Health and Human Behavior*, 2 (1961), 93–105.

[66] David Mechanic, "Sources of Power of Lower Participants in Complex Organizations," *Administrative Science Quarterly*, 7, No. 3 (December 1962), 349–64.

should not be theirs. The first source of power is expertise coupled with the difficulty of replacing the person in question. The maintenance men in Crozier's study had this form of power over the managers in the tobacco industry. Another example is a person in a clerical position who gains power by being the only one in an organization who knows how to perform a particular operation. This person thus becomes indispensable, with all work having to go through his hands. In some cases, patterns of personal likes and dislikes can "make or break" another person in the organization who ostensibly has a higher position; for example, requests for information can be conveniently "lost."

A second source of power is the amount of effort and interest expressed on the job. Mechanic notes the example of university departmental secretaries who can have "power to make decisions about the purchase and allocation of supplies, the allocation of their services, the scheduling of classes, and, at times, the disposition of student complaints. Such control may in some instances lead to sanctions against a professor by polite reluctance to furnish supplies, ignoring his preferences for the scheduling of classes, and giving others preference in the allocation of services."[67] Removal of this power from secretaries itself involves the expenditure of time and effort. A departmental chairman is unlikely to come down hard on a trusted secretary, whereas he might with younger or disfavored faculty.

Several other factors are associated with lower participants' power. One is the attractiveness of the individual involved; personal or physical attractiveness can lead to relationships that are outside the organization's (or individual's) intent. Physical location and position within an organization can make one person more critical than another; a major information processor can have strong control over those who are dependent on him for accurate information. Coalitions among lower participants can also increase their power. Rules themselves can provide a source of power, in that strict adherence to a highly formalized rules system can hold up operations in the organization. A supervisor cannot really criticize his subordinates if they point out to him that they are following the letter of the law.

THE CONSEQUENCES OF POWER

The discussion thus far has alluded to the consequences of the exertion of power. The dominant consequence is to some observers the least

[67] *Ibid.*, p. 359.

interesting: people or units comply. This is most typically the case when power is well legitimated. Compliance, and even willing compliance, is extremely frequent. People come to work on time, do what their bosses desire, and produce their goods or deliver their services. Organizational units generally also comply or obey.

This is not the only response, however. As Blau has pointed out, the power recipient can withdraw from the situation or attempt to circumvent or go around the power holder.[68] Another possible response is conflict with the power holder. It is to conflict that we now turn.

CONFLICT IN ORGANIZATIONS

Many of the major forms of conflict within organizations are already well known to anyone concerned with organizations or the society in general. Labor–management conflict is a prominent part of our social heritage, as well as of organizational life. The existence of professional– organizational and staff–line conflicts has already been amply discussed. Many of the power relationships described in the previous section are also conflict situations.

In this section, the bases, forms, and consequences of conflict in organizations will be analyzed. (The analysis will focus on conflict *within* organizations; conflict between organizations, and between organizations and the wider society, will be handled in the last section of the book.) The focus will be on the analysis rather than on providing detailed examples. Most such examples are well known, and can be extrapolated from the discussions of power. As in the case of power, relatively few empirical studies of conflict are more than ex post facto case studies.

Conflict in organizations involves more than simple interpersonal conflict. (Not that interpersonal conflict is necessarily simple, given the complexities of the human personality, but for our purposes it is only part of the picture.) The psychologist Nevitt Sanford makes this point in a historical perspective when he states, "Twenty years ago, it seemed easy to account for organizational conflict by blaming the problem behavior of individuals. But the simple formula, 'trouble is due to trouble-makers,' is unfortunately inadequate in the light of our present knowledge of the social process."[69] The inadequacy of the individualized approach to con-

---

[68] Peter M. Blau, *Exchange and Power in Social Life* (New York: John Wiley & Sons, 1964), pp. 118–19.

[69] R. Nevitt Sanford, "Individual Conflict and Organizational Interaction," in Kahn and Boulding, eds., *Power and Conflict in Organizations*, p. 95.

flict is based on the fact that organizational considerations and the very nature of organizations themselves contribute to conflict situations.

Bases of Conflict

Another psychologist, Daniel Katz, has identified three organizational bases of conflict. The first is "functional conflict induced by various subsystems within the organizations."[70] This form of conflict involves the fact that:

> Every subsystem of an organization with its distinctive functions develops its own norms and values and is characterized by its own dynamics. People in the maintenance subsystem have the problem of maintaining the role system and preserving the character of the organization through selection of appropriate personnel, indoctrinating and training them, devising checks for ensuring standard role performance, and so on. These people face *inward* in the organization and are concerned with maintaining the *status quo*. People in the procurement and disposal subsystems, however, face *outward* on the world and develop a different psychological orientation. These differing orientations are one built-in source of conflict. Put in another way, the systems of maintenance, production, and adaptive development each develop their own distinctive norms and frames of reference which contain their own elements of potential conflict.[71]

Although the focus is on the psychological states of the members of the organizations, the point is important, since different subunits in organizations perform tasks that come into conflict because they are basically incompatible.

The second source of conflict is the fact that units have similar functions. Conflict here can take the form of "hostile rivalry or good-natured competition. . . ."[72] Such competition can be beneficial, but it can also be destructive. The final form of organizationally based conflict is "hierarchical conflict stemming from interest-group struggles over the organizational rewards of status, prestige, and monetary reward."[73] Since less than total satisfaction with the reward structure is common, and since subgroups develop their own communication systems and norms, it is normal that lower-level personnel "try to improve their lot by joining

[70] Daniel Katz, "Approaches to Managing Conflict," in Kahn and Boulding, *Power and Conflict*, p. 105.
[71] *Ibid.*, pp. 105–6.
[72] *Ibid.*, p. 106.
[73] *Ibid.*

forces as an interest group against the more privileged members of the organization."[74] Although one typically thinks of blue-collar workers and unions in this regard, the process would operate with white-collar workers and subgroups in the management hierarchy.

Stephen Robbins approaches the bases of conflict in a different manner.[75] He suggests that conflict can result from imperfect communications in which communications can be distorted, semantic difficulties can exist, knowledge contains intrinsic ambiguities, and communications channels can be imperfectly used. Structural conditions also lead to conflict; large size, the heterogeneity of the staff, styles of supervision, the extent of participation, the reward system, and the form of power used are among such conditions. Robbins also notes that personal-behavior variables are important in the areas of personality dimensions and interactions, role satisfactions, and individual goals. In addition, conflict can emerge from differences between total occupational groups, such as different professions or groups with different power in the organization as in labor–management conflict.[76] Furthermore, just as we cannot assume that the organization will always act rationally, there can be no assumption that individuals will not "depart from rational, reality-based behavior in their individual struggles against one another or in their participation in group struggles."[77]

These bases of conflict are an inherent element of organizations and thus conflict itself must be viewed as inherent. At the same time, the fact that these antecedents or bases of conflict are present does not mean that conflict will take place. Before conflict can ensue, the parties involved must perceive that they are in a position to interfere with the other party.[78] A decision must be made to engage in conflict. Whether the decision is based on rational calculation or fervid emotion, or is individual or collective, it does *not* occur automatically.

[74] *Ibid.*

[75] Stephen P. Robbins, *Managing Organizational Conflict: A Nontraditional Approach* (Englewood Cliffs, N.J.: Prentice-Hall, Inc., 1974).

[76] See Ralf Dahrendorf, *Class and Class Conflict in Industrial Society* (London: Routledge and Kegan Paul, 1959); Jerald Hage and Michael Aiken, *Social Change in Complex Organizations* (New York: Random House, 1970); and David Silverman, *The Theory of Organizations* (New York: Basic Books, 1971).

[77] Katz, "Approaches to Managing Conflict," pp. 106–7.

[78] See Thomas A. Kochan, George P. Huber, and L. L. Cummings, "Determinants of Intraorganizational Conflict in Collective Bargaining in the Public Sector," *Administrative Science Quarterly*, 20, No. 1 (March 1975), 10–23; and Stuart M. Schmidt and Thomas A. Kochan, "Conflict: Toward Conceptual Clarity," *Administrative Science Quarterly*, 17, No. 3 (September 1972), 371–81.

The Conflict Situation

We have been looking at the bases of conflict situations and the parties engaged in them. A more complete view adds to these components the conflict process itself and the aftermath. Kenneth Boulding has provided a framework for a composite view of the total conflict situation.[79] He suggests that there are four components in the process. First are the parties involved. Conflict must involve at least two parties—individuals, groups, or organizations. Hypothetically, therefore, there can be nine types of conflict—person–person, person–group, and so on. Boulding suggests that there is a tendency toward symmetry in these relationships, in that person– or group–organizational conflict tends to move toward organizational–organizational conflict. This is based on the power differentials that are likely to exist between these different levels in the organization.

As the next component in his framework, Boulding identifies the "field of conflict," defined as "the whole set of relevant possible states of the social system. (Any state of the social system which either of the parties to a conflict considers relevant is, of course, a relevant state.)"[80] What Boulding is referring to here are the alternative conditions toward which a conflict could move. If the parties in a conflict have a particular power relationship with one another, with one having more power than the other, the field of conflict involves a continuation of the present state, plus all the alternative conditions. These alternatives include both parties' gaining or losing power or one's gaining at the expense of the other. This concept is indicative of the process nature of conflict, in that the parties in the situation will seldom retain the same position in relation to one another after the conflict is resolved or continued. The field of conflict includes the directions of the movement as the process occurs.

The third component is the dynamics of the conflict situation. That is, each party in a conflict will adjust its own position to one that it feels is congruent with that of its opponent. If one of the parties becomes more militant, the other will probably do the same. This assumes of course that the power available to the two parties is at least moderately comparable. A nonorganizational example of the dynamics can be found in international relations, where nations will intensify their own conflict efforts in anticipation of or reaction to their opponents' moves. This can escalate into all-out war and eventual total destruction, or can stabilize at some point along the way. The same phenomenon occurs in organizations, with

[79] Kenneth E. Boulding, "A Pure Theory of Conflict Applied to Organizations," in Kahn and Boulding, *Power and Conflict*, pp. 136–45.

[80] *Ibid.*, p. 138.

the equivalent of all-out war in the case of labor–management conflicts that end in the dissolution of the company involved. The dynamic nature of conflict can be seen in the fact that there is an increase and decrease in the intensity of a conflict during its course. While the field of conflict may remain the same, the energies devoted to it vary over time.

The final element in the Boulding model is the "management, control, or resolution of conflict."[81] The terms used suggest that conflict situations are generally not discrete situations with a clear beginning and end.[82] They obviously emerge out of preexisting situations and do not end forever with a strike settlement or lowering of the intensity of the conflict. Boulding notes that organizations attempt to prevent conflict from becoming "pathological" and thus destructive of the parties involved and the larger system. One form of conflict resolution is a unilateral move; according to Boulding, a good deal of conflict is resolved through the relatively simple mechanism of the "peaceableness" of one of the participants. While it relates primarily to interpersonal conflict, this idea can be utilized in the organizational setting. Peaceableness simply involves one of the parties' backing off from the conflict. The other party reacts to this in most cases by also backing off, even if he would prefer to continue, and the conflict is at least temporarily resolved. This kind of resolution is seen in labor–management disputes when one of the parties finally decides to concede on some points that were formerly "nonnegotiable."

Reliance upon peaceableness is potentially dangerous, however, because the parties just may not exhibit this kind of behavior. For the peaceable party itself, this strategy is hazardous if the opponent is operating pathologically or irrationally to any degree. For this reason, organizations develop mechanisms to resolve or control conflict. One technique here is to placate the parties involved by offering them both some form of "side payment" as an inducement to stop the conflict—for example, in professional–organizational conflict the professionals may be given concessions in the form of relaxing some organizational rules they feel to be excessively burdensome.

Unfortunately, research in this area has not indicated what are the reactions of the rest of the organization to conflicts with professional units. It is possible that such conflicts are resolved simply by concessions to the professionals, and a realistic view would suggest that something has to be done for the other members of the organization also, since they often resent the greater freedom given to the professionals. Even though

---

[81] *Ibid.*, p. 142.

[82] In Robbins, *Managing Organizational Conflict*, much of the argument is that management in organizations ought to stimulate conflict as a means of achieving organizational change. He presents a series of suggestions for conflict resolution.

the professionals are sometimes physically separated from the rest of the organization in an attempt to minimize comparisons and distinctions between the groups involved, it would seem that increasing benefits for the professional group would lead to a demand from the nonprofessionals for comparable concessions. These could could take the form of increases in the rewards offered or greater likelihood of moving up in the organizational hierarchy.

Conflicts in organizations can also be resolved through the offices of a third party. The third party might be a larger organization that simply orders the conflict behavior to cease under the threat of penalties (as when the government prohibits strikes and lockouts in a labor dispute that threatens the national interest) or might be a mediator. Since intraorganizational conflict takes place within a larger context, the organization can simply prohibit the conflicting behavior. This does not resolve the issues involved, but it reduces the intensity of the conflict behavior. Mediation can do the same, and can even lead to a complete resolution of the conflict by presenting new methods of solution that might not have occurred to the parties involved, or by presenting a solution that would not be acceptable unless it were presented by a third party.

The resolution of a conflict leads to a stage that Louis Pondy calls the aftermath.[83] This is a useful concept because conflict resolution does not lead to a condition of total settlement. If the basic issues are not resolved, the potentiality for future, and perhaps more serious, conflicts is part of the aftermath. If the conflict resolution leads to more open communications and cooperation among the participants, this, too, is part of the aftermath.[84] Since an organization does not operate in a vacuum, any successful conflict resolution in which the former combatants are now close allies is not guaranteed to last forever. Changes in the environment and altered conditions in the organization can lead to new conflict situations among the same parties or with others.

Conflict is not inherently good or bad for the participants, the organi-

---

[83] Louis R. Pondy, "Organizational Conflict: Concepts and Models," *Administrative Science Quarterly*, 12, No. 2 (September 1967), 304. See also Louis Pondy, "Variations of Organizational Conflict," *Administrative Science Quarterly*, 14, No. 4 (December 1969), 499–505, for an additional categorization of the forms of conflict. This entire issue of *Administrative Science Quarterly* is devoted to organizational conflict of various types.

[84] Much of the thought on the consequences of conflict has been crystallized in the works of Lewis Coser. See Lewis A. Coser, *The Functions of Social Conflict* (New York: The Free Press, 1956), and *Continuities in the Study of Social Conflict* (New York: The Free Press, 1967). Coser notes that despite the attention paid to conflict in recent years, there has been little in the way of empirical research to show for all the attention (*Continuities*, pp. 7–8).

zation, or the wider society. *Power and conflict are major shapers of the state of an organization. A given organizational state sets the stage for the continuing power and conflict processes, thus continually reshaping the organization.*

SUMMARY AND CONCLUSIONS

This chapter has attempted to identify and trace the consequences of power and conflict in organizations. Common sense suggests that these are important to the operations of any organization and that the lives and behavior of organizational members are vitally affected by their relative power positions. The discussion concluded that power is a reciprocal relational phenomenon between the parties involved, and that each party is dependent on the other. The power relationships can be rigidly specified in advance or can develop as the relationship itself develops. This point reemphasizes the close connection between organizational structure and processes, since it is the structure that sets the original limits on the relationship.

Although power relationships are typically thought to be interpersonal, power differentials between organizational units are also important. Inter-unit power relationships usually take place along the lateral or horizontal axis in the organization. Vertical or hierarchical arrangements by definition involve a power component. Also on the vertical dimension, but not in an organizationally planned way, are the power bases developed by lower participants that allow them to exert power over those farther up the organizational hierarchy.

In addition to this directional aspect of power, we discussed the forms of power inside and outside organizations. There is agreement that power in organizations does not take just one form—legitimate authority—and that extraorganizational considerations are important in power relationships. The empirical research reviewed provided additional insights into these relationships. From the outset it became apparent that most power relationships involve the use of more than one form of power. Because individuals and organizational units develop relationships over time, additional elements will almost surely be added to prestructured power arrangements.

The nature of the power system used in the organization has important consequences for the manner in which individuals attach themselves to the organization and for the more general issue of organizational effectiveness. If inappropriate power forms are used, the organization is likely to be less effective than it might otherwise be. Studies of power in organizations reiterate the dominant theme of this book—that organizational structure and processes are in constant and reciprocal interaction. Power relationships develop out of and then alter existing structural arrangements.

In a broader look at power, it was emphasized that power is not a fixed sum in organizations. The amount of power in the system can increase or decrease. Although a power system is often established by the organization, the considerations discussed above regarding multiple forms of power and the reciprocity involved in the power relationship make a general growth in power almost inevitable.

It was also pointed out in this section that the power variable is vital in determining internal resource allocations. This fact leads to the conclusion that power relationships in organizations tend to be stable, since the original allocation of resources will be an important determinant of future power relationships. The fact that external considerations affect the power distribution and relationships within an organization is a reaffirmation of the general systems approach that has been taken throughout. Organizational structure and processes are in interaction with the environment and organizational outputs affect the environment, which then in turn becomes a potentially altered form of input.

The discussion of conflict in organizations was somewhat truncated because of the close relationship between this process and power, power being an important, even decisive, element in conflict. The identification of the various forms, stages, conditions, and consequences of conflict point up its endemic nature in organizations. To view organizations as entities in which conflict upsets the equilibrium is to misunderstand reality. Conflict is part of the normal state of an organization. The consequences of conflict are also normal, in that they are both organizationally and individually positive and negative.

In the next chapter, an issue related to power will be discussed. Leadership involves one or more of the forms of power discussed, since it can be exerted from a position of legitimate authority or expertise, or can develop as a form of referent power. We will analyze alternative forms of leadership and their consequences for the organization.

9

leadership and decision making

Probably more has been written and spoken about leadership than about any other topic considered in this book. Whether the organization be the local school district, a labor union, an athletic team, or the nation, there seems to be a constant assumption that new leadership will turn it, the organization, around. In every election at every level of government, the call for leadership goes out. Anyone who follows sports is aware of the air of expectation surrounding the appointment of a new coach or manager. A new school superintendent or university president is selected by a blue-ribbon committee with extensive inputs from all of the parties likely to be involved. Elections in labor unions and other voluntary organizations always contain the assumption that continuation of the old or the election of the new leaders will make an important difference in the continuing operation of the organization. In short, leadership would seem to be *the* crucial thing to understand about organizations.

The view presented in this chapter is exactly the opposite. In the research and theory to be examined it will be found that leadership is heavily constrained by many of the factors discussed in previous chapters—organizational structure, power coalitions, and environmental conditions. It will also be argued that for most organizations in most circumstances changing leadership is little more than a cosmetic treatment. The same basic approach will be taken in discussing constraints on the decision-making process. These constraints limit the practical usefulness of formal sophisticated decision-making models.

LEADERSHIP

Why is leadership the subject of such belief and sentiment? Leadership seems to be an extremely easy solution to whatever problems are ailing an organization. Looking to new leadership can mask such issues as inappropriate structural arrangements, power distributions that block effective actions, lack of resources, archaic procedures, and other, more basic organizational problems.

With all this, one might wonder. Then why study leadership, and why have there been so many studies in the past? The fact is that in certain situations leadership is important, even critical. The situations, however, are much more infrequent and much more constrained than most treatises on leadership consider.

What is leadership? Leadership is a special form of power, closely related to the "referent" form discussed in the previous chapter, since it involves, in Etzioni's words, "the ability, based on the personal qualities of the leader, to elicit the followers' voluntary compliance in a broad range of matters. Leadership is distinguished from the concept of power in that it entails influence, i.e., change of preferences, while power implies only that subjects' preferences are held in abeyance."[1]

For our purposes, Etzioni's general definition, if not the specific distinction made, is extremely useful. That followers do in fact alter their preferences to coincide with those of the leader is an important consideration. The followers *want* to go along with the wishes of the leader. Alvin Gouldner takes essentially the same position when he states that the leader is "any individual whose behavior stimulates patterning of the behavior in some group."[2] The leader therefore is an influence on what the members of the group do and think.

Functions of Leadership

The differences between leadership and power are still insufficiently developed, however, since leadership can occur in any group at any level within the organization. Phillip Selznick provides the needed distinction when he notes that leadership involves *critical* decisions. It is more than group maintenance.[3] According to Selznick, the critical tasks of leadership fall into four categories. The first involves the definition of the institutional (organizational) mission and role. This is obviously vital in a rapidly changing world and must be viewed as a dynamic process. The second task is the "institutional embodiment of purpose," which involves building the policy into the structure or deciding upon the means to achieve the ends desired. The third task is to defend the organization's

---

[1] See Amitai Etzioni, "Dual Leadership in Complex Organizations," *American Sociological Review*, 30, No. 5 (October 1965), 690–91.

[2] Alvin Gouldner, in Alvin Gouldner, ed., *Studies in Leadership* (New York: Harper & Row, Publishers, 1950), p. 17.

[3] Phillip Selznick, *Leadership in Administration* (New York: Harper & Row, Publishers, 1957), p. 29.

integrity. Here, values and public relations intermix; the leader represents his organization to the public and to its own members as he tries to persuade them to follow his decisions. The final task is the ordering of internal conflict.[4]

Here again, as Selznick points out, these functions can operate at all organizational levels. The position taken here is that *leadership can occur in any group or organizational situation.* For our purposes, however, most important for the organization is the leadership (or lack of leadership, in some cases) that occurs at the top of the organization, where the tasks of the leader have real impact on the organization. It is here that our attention will be primarily focused.

One further set of distinctions should be made before we proceed with an analysis of leadership. Studies carried out in small-group laboratories have consistently found that leadership is actually a differentiated process, with *task* or *instrumental* activities rather clearly separated from *socioemotional* or *expressive* activities.[5] Drawing on the work of Robert Bales and his associates, Etzioni develops a "dual leadership" approach to organizations, suggesting that in most cases leadership rests in the hands of more than one person, and that the demands of the two forms may conflict. Organizational demands will determine which form will be successful, with socioemotional more effective in normative organizations and task in instrumental organizations. Etzioni concludes that, at least for first-line supervisors, attempts to improve socioemotional leadership qualities are doomed to failure, since these efforts will run headlong into the existing socioemotional leader, who has risen to his position in the interactions of the work group. This type of interpretation, of course, is counter to the ideas and ideals of the "human-relations" school of management, which stresses the utility of socioemotional interactions in the leadership process. There appears to be growing agreement that the use of human relations in leadership positions is no guarantee that any form of behavioral change by members of the organization will take place.[6]

[4] *Ibid.*, pp. 62–63. These functions are essentially the same as those identified in Ralph Stogdill's monumental review of research on leadership, *Handbook of Leadership: A Survey of Theory and Research* (New York: The Free Press, 1974). Stogdill has reviewed some 3000 studies of leadership.

[5] See for example, Robert F. Bales, "The Equilibrium Problem in Small Groups," in Talcott Parsons, Robert F. Bales, and Edward A. Shils, eds., *Working Papers in the Theory of Action* (New York: The Free Press, 1953), pp. 111–61; and Robert F. Bales and Phillip E. Slater, "Role Differentiation in Small Decision Making Groups," in Talcott Parsons and Robert F. Bales, eds., *Family Socialization and Interaction Processes* (New York: The Free Press, 1955), pp. 259–306.

[6] Charles Perrow, *Complex Organizations: A Critical Essay* (Glenview, Ill.: Scott, Foresman and Co., 1972), pp. 111–12.

The use of human relations skills has also been the subject of criticism in terms of the manner in which subordinates are actually manipulated without their knowing it, as was noted in the last chapter. The type of behavior that will lead to behavioral change is contingent upon the situation, as will be seen below.

It is critical to note that leadership at the top of an organization is vastly different from leadership at the first-line supervisory level. Because most studies of leadership have been carried out with first-line people, a good part of the development of leadership theory is confused.

Components of Leadership

Every organization has an individual or set of individuals at the top decision-making level who can exercise power simply by giving orders and making decisions. This is simple power of position and does not involve leadership as we will approach it here. Our view of leadership involves what a person does above and beyond the basic requirements of his position. *It is the persuasion of individuals and innovativeness in ideas and decision making that differentiates leadership from the sheer possession of power.* A mechanical reliance on organizational position would bring about a situation in which the characteristics of the individuals filling top positions would make no difference whatsoever. The organization would be totally constrained by precedent and its own structure.

The ideas expressed thus far have implied strongly that individual characteristics are crucial for the leadership role. Although this appears to be the case, extreme care must be taken to put it in the proper perspective. There is a very real danger in assuming that because individual characteristics are crucial for the leadership function, there is a set of *traits* that leaders possess. The literature regarding leadership took this approach at one time, with a major goal of the research being identification of the key leadership traits. This approach didn't get very far, for two reasons. The basic one was that common leadership traits could not be identified. No set of characteristics is possessed by leaders and not by followers. This realization led to the second contributing factor in the downfall of the trait approach. Attention increasingly turned to the *situation* in which leadership was exhibited.[7]

The situational approach takes the position that the set of conditions of the moment—the situation—defines by whom and in what manner leadership will be expressed. In one situation, one individual will emerge as the leader; in another situation, another individual. This approach has

[7] For a discussion of this point see Gouldner, *Studies in Leadership,* and Stogdill, *Handbook of Leadership.*

largely dominated the sociological approach to leadership, especially in small-group studies, but in recent years it has come under fire for its inattention to the characteristics of those who rise into leadership positions. The emergent position is that while different situations demand different forms of leadership and thus generally different individuals, particular skills and behaviors will be called for in each different situation. This is a blending of the trait and situational approaches and appears to avoid the serious pitfalls of each.

This combination approach is used by Edwin Hollander and James Julian. They reject the trait and situational approaches per se, noting that both tell us something about leadership, but not the whole story. To the ideas that have already been stated, they add the important element of interaction between leader and followers.[8] The leader *influences* his followers in the interaction process, and their reactions, of course, have an impact on his own behavior.

From the perspective taken here, organizational leadership is a combination of factors. The most obvious is the high *position* in the organization. This gives the leader his power base and leads followers to the expectations that he has a legitimate right to that position and that he will in fact engage in the leadership process by shaping their own thoughts and actions and performing the leadership functions for the organization as a whole.[9] These expectations can be seen even in periods of dissidence within the organization, when there is leadership succession and the followers express the hope that the new person will provide what the old one did not.

In addition to the position held, the leadership role demands that the *individual behave in such a way that the expectations of the followers are fulfilled.* Here the interrelationships between the characteristics of the individual and the position filled become crucial. Rather than suggesting that there is one set of leadership "traits," the evidence indicates that the particular characteristics giving rise to leadership behavior vary with the situation. According to Stogdill,

> Individuals who continue to rise in the hierarchy tend to identify
> themselves with top leadership and with the organization. Job satisfaction

[8] Edwin P. Hollander and James W. Julian, "Contemporary Trends in the Analysis of Leadership Processes," *Psychological Bulletin*, 71, No. 5 (May 1969), 387–97.

[9] This is consistent with Cartwright's approach, which suggests that a distinction should be made between the power of a position (power) and the power of a person (leadership). For our purposes, the person must have the position at the top of the organization before he can exercise the type of leadership under discussion. See Dorwin Cartwright, "Influence, Leadership and Control," in James G. March, ed., *Handbook of Organizations* (Chicago: Rand McNally & Co., 1965), pp. 4–5.

tends to increase as level in the organization increases. High-level leaders tend to value job challenge and autonomy, while lower level leaders tend to value security and stability. Followers value the leader who has influence with his superiors, is identified with the organization, and demonstrates effectiveness in working for their welfare and comfort. Studies of leadership behavior indicate that leaders described high in both initiating structure (letting followers know what to expect) and consideration (looking out for the welfare of followers) tend to promote high degrees of follower satisfaction and, in some cases, group performance. Persuasiveness emerges as the most pervasive characteristic when leader behavior is described in terms of a wide variety of items. Other behavioral items highly weighted on a general factor are concerned with the reconciliation of conflicting demands, structuring expectations, retention of the leadership role, consideration of follower welfare, and pressure for goal attainment.[10]

An individual would be able to "transfer" into another leadership role only if the situation and the followers were comparable to the previous leadership situation. The approach allows a rapprochement between the emphasis on individual traits and the emphasis on the situation.

Now let us move to the central issue: What do leaders do for or to an organization, and how do they do it?

THE IMPACT OF LEADERSHIP ON THE ORGANIZATION

There is little direct evidence regarding the effect that top leaders have on organizations, simply because there has been very little research on top organizational leadership. Organizational researchers have not gotten access to top business and government leaders. Nor have they been concerned with the role of leadership in terms of its broad organizational consequences. In order to study leadership, we will extrapolate from the large number of studies of supervision and the smaller number of studies of top leadership succession.

Studies of leadership in organizations are confusing, if not downright chaotic, even to those who are well versed in the literature.[11] A major factor in the confusion, aside from the ideological biases evident in some investigations, is the large number of dependent variables used in leadership analyses. If variations in the amount or style of leadership are taken as the independent variable, then a whole series of variables has been

[10] Stogdill, *Handbook of Leadership*, p. 412.
[11] Cartwright, "Influence, Leadership and Control," p. 3.

treated as the dependent ones. These run the gamut from hard measures of productivity to the more elusive factors of morale and satisfaction.

Leadership Styles

Research regarding leadership has come to focus around two contrasting styles or approaches to the leadership role. These are the authoritarian (task) and supportive (socioemotional) approaches. The biases alluded to earlier are evident and understandable when these two terms are brought into the discussion (who would want to support authoritarianism?). The supportive leader is "characterized by . . . employee oriented, democratic behavior, uses general supervision, and is considerate of his subordinates."[12] The authoritarian leader, on the other hand, is much more likely to rely on the power of his position and to be more punishment-centered. A very evident problem for the discussion here is that the authoritarian form actually may not be leadership in the way we have defined it.

The supportive leader utilizes socioemotional appeals to his subordinates. This involves:

Consideration for Subordinates. The leader considers the needs and preferences of his subordinates, whom he treats with dignity and kindness, and is not punitive in his dealings with them. Such a leader is frequently referred to as "employee-centered" as opposite to "work-centered" or "task-centered."

Consultative Decision Making. The leader asks his subordinates for their opinions before he makes decisions. Such a leader is consultative, participative, or democratic (as opposed to unilateral, autocratic, or arbitrary) in his decision making.

General Supervision. The leader supervises in a general rather than a close manner, delegates authority to his subordinates, and permits them freedom to exercise discretion in their work rather than imposing tight controls and close (frequently overbearing) supervision.[13]

In their excellent review of the research in the leadership area, Filley and House find that supportive leadership, as opposed to autocratic leadership, is quite consistently related to several indicators of subordinate satisfaction and productivity:

[12] Alan C. Filley and Robert P. House, *Managerial Processes and Organizational Behavior* (Glenview, Ill.: Scott, Foresman and Company, 1969), p. 399.
[13] *Ibid.*, pp. 399–400.

1. There is less intragroup stress and more cooperation.
2. Turnover and grievance rates are lower.
3. The leader himself is viewed as more desirable.
4. There is frequently greater productivity.

The evidence here is confounded, unfortunately, by the possibility that the workers themselves may contribute to their greater satisfaction and productivity by their own attitudes and behavior, independent of that of the leader. They might just be high-producing, positively oriented employees who "do not require close, autocratic supervision, and therefore it is possible for the supervisor of such employees to be more human-relations oriented."[14] Despite this possibility, the weight of the evidence is that supportive leadership does lead to more positive attitudinal responses, particularly on the part of subordinates.

The productivity issue is not as clear as the attitudinal one. While some evidence does suggest that greater productivity is associated with supportive supervision, other studies report no difference, or that there is actually more output when autocratic styles are used.[15] An obvious question here is, What does the organization want? If satisfied employees are desired, then the supportive approach has clearly been shown to be more effective. Short-run output gains, on the other hand, may be more easily achieved under an autocratic system. There is also evidence to suggest that when workers expect to be supervised in an autocratic style, supportive supervision can be counterproductive and satisfaction-threatening.

In summarizing these leadership studies, Filley and House conclude that supportive leadership behavior is most effective when:

1. Decisions are not routine in nature
2. The information required for effective decision making cannot be standardized or centralized
3. Decisions need not be made rapidly, allowing time to involve subordinates in a participative decision-making process

and when subordinates:

4. Feel a strong need for independence
5. Regard their participation in decision making as legitimate

[14] *Ibid.*, p. 402.

[15] See Robert Dubin, "Supervision and Productivity: Empirical Findings and Theoretical Considerations,' in Robert Dubin, George Homans, Floyd Mann, and Delbert Miller, *Leadership and Productivity* (San Francisco: Chandler Publishing Co., 1965).

6. See themselves as able to contribute to the decision-making process
7. Are confident of their ability to work without the reassurance of close supervision.[16]

This particular kind of organization is similar to some that have already been described in the section on organizational structure: the less formalized organizations that must rely on the inputs of their own members if they are to be effective. Their technology is such that there is a constant search for new ideas and solutions to problems. The obvious corollary of the findings in regard to the kind of organization in which supportive leadership styles are likely to be effective is that in the opposite kind of organization, such forms of leadership are *least* likely to be effective. That is, in organizations in which decisions are routine, information is standardized, and so on, effective leadership is more likely to take the autocratic form, because inputs from the individual members of the organization are not so important and there is not the same need for time spent in the decision-making process. In addition, it can be postulated that there are organizational members who either are threatened by the decision-making process or have no wish to participate in it, and for whom the provision of ready-made answers in the form of formal procedures or decisions made for them is a satisfying or at least non-threatening situation.

These interpretations are strongly buttressed by the findings emerging from Fred Fiedler's continuing studies of the leadership process.[17] Fiedler finds that in stable, structured situations, a more strict, autocratic form of leadership is most likely to be successful, while in a situation of change, external threat, and ambiguity, the more lenient, participative form of supervision would work better. Of course, in some organizations conditions will change in one direction or another, suggesting that an effective leader in one situation may not be such in another. Thus, another contingency approach is evident.

Factors Affecting Leadership Impact

Several aspects of the research discussed thus far ought to be made distinct before the present analysis proceeds. As indicated earlier, most of the studies have been performed with personnel from relatively lower

[16] Filley and House, *Managerial Processes*, pp. 404–5.
[17] Fred E. Fiedler, *A Theory of Leadership Effectiveness* (New York: McGraw-Hill Book Company, 1967) and "The Effects of Leadership Training and Experience: A Contingency Model Explanation," *Administrative Science Quarterly*, 17, No. 4 (December 1972), 453–70.

echelons in the organization. Regardless of the level within the organization, it is clear that the situation being faced and the personnel being led are important determinants as to which form of leadership is likely to be most effective. It can be argued that it would be good, from an individual or societal perspective, if all personnel were self-motivating and desirous of participating in the decision making, and that the organization as a whole would be healthier if it were constantly innovating and engaging in continual interactions with its environment; but the facts suggest that neither condition necessarily exists in practice. This then leads to the conclusion that a revamping of leadership styles in organizations is no panacea to be applied to all organizations and all members therein.

The important aspect of the research for our purposes is the demonstrated fact that leadership at this level does make a difference in terms of objective performance indicators and the attitudes of the personnel involved. The question is not one of style but of impact. If production can be increased or the acceptance of a new mode of organization quickened, leadership does come to be an important process. The extrapolation from this conclusion to top leadership is relatively easy, if unsupported by existing research. The range of behavior affected by first- or second-line supervisors is actually quite small. If the jump is made to the range of behavior that can be affected by those at the top of the organization, the potential for a real impact of leadership can be readily seen. Even in terms of performance and attitudes, the high-level subordinates of high administrators can be affected, and their performance in turn has an impact right down the organization.

An additional point is that leadership and the total managerial function are apparently vitally affected by one of the major considerations throughout this analysis—the technology of the organization involved. The previously discussed research of Joan Woodward and of Lawrence and Lorsch lends support for this conclusion, as does the research of Elmer Burack.[18] These findings systematically document the interplay between the organization's structure, as affected by the technology, and the management structure. Technological factors set limits on the amount and kinds of variations that can be introduced into the system, thus limiting certain aspects of what a leader can do.

Now that we have formed some conclusions about the impact of leadership at both top and lower levels, let us examine the available evidence concerning changes in personnel at the top of the organization.

[18] Elmer H. Burack, "Industrial Management in Advanced Production Systems: Some Theoretical Concepts and Preliminary Findings," *American Sociological Quarterly*, 12, No. 3 (December 1967), 479–500.

Leadership Succession

Analyses of managerial succession have been largely limited to case studies, with the exception of some concern about organizational size and the rate of managerial succession. These latter studies will be discussed later; for the moment, we shall look at some of the implications from the case studies.

Probably the best known of these is Alvin Gouldner's *Patterns of Industrial Bureaucracy,*[19] an analysis of a gypsum plant and mine that underwent a major and dramatic change in top personnel. The former manager had engaged in loose, almost indulgent practices in regard to rule observance and other standards. The parent organization, concerned about the production record of the plant, replaced the old manager with a new man who had the specific mandate of increasing production. The new man knew he would be judged by his record of production, so his alternatives were to continue the established pattern—a procedure that probably would not have worked in any event, since he did not have the personal ties of his predecessor—or to enforce the already-existing rules of conduct and performance. He chose the latter course, and as a result the total system became "punishment-centered." This lead to a severe increase in internal tension and stress.

This example is in direct contrast to a case described by Robert Guest.[20] Guest's study was made from observations in a large automobile factory. He states:

> Both studies [his and Gouldner's] examine the process by which organizational tensions are exacerbated or reduced following the succession of a new leader at the top of the hierarchy. Succession in Gouldner's case resulted in a sharp increase in tension and stress and, by inference, a lowering of overall performance. The succession of a new manager had the opposite results in the present case. Plant Y, as we chose to call it, was one of six identical plants of a large corporation. At one period in time the plant was poorest in virtually all indexes of performance—direct and indirect labor costs, quality of output, absenteeism and turnover, ability to meet schedule changes, labor grievances and in several other measures. Interpersonal relationships were marked by sharp antagonisms within and between all levels.

> Three years later, following the succession of a new manager, and with no changes in the formal organizational structure, in the product, in the

[19] Alvin Gouldner, *Patterns of Industrial Bureaucracy* (New York: The Free Press, 1954).

[20] Robert H. Guest, "Managerial Succession in Complex Organizations," *American Journal of Sociology,* 67, No. 1 (July 1962), 47–54.

personnel, or in its basic technology, not only was there a substantial reduction of interpersonal conflict, but Plant Y became the outstanding performer among all of the plants.[21]

The dramatic differences between these two cases might lead one to some sort of "great-man" theory of leadership, with Gouldner's successor a nongreat man and Guest's the opposite. Guest correctly rejects this approach and instead attributes the differences to the actions each man took when confronted with an existing social structure. A major aspect of this social structure was the expectations of higher management in the organizations involved. While both new managers were expected to improve the situation, the new man at the gypsum plant felt that he was expected to get rid of the personnel who were not performing properly. He felt that he was—and probably actually was—under more severe pressure to turn the organization around in a short period of time.

There were some other important differences in the organizations. The tradition in the gypsum plant was that the new top man came from "inside," and in this case he did not. In addition, the former manager had been active in the community surrounding the plant. The successor thus came into a situation in which there were negative feelings from the outset. The former manager also had a cadre of subordinates tied to him through personal loyalty. The successor had little recourse but to use the more formal bureaucratic mechanisms of control. At the automobile factory, on the other hand, the total social setting was different. The factory was in a large metropolitan area in which the previous managers had not become involved. The history of top management succession was one of relatively rapid turnover (three to five years), with the new men coming from outside the plant itself. Thus, unlike the gypsum plant personnel, the auto plant personnel were used to the kind of succession they experienced.

Another, more subtle difference that Gouldner describes is the fact that in the gypsum plant, the indulgency pattern and the developed social structure among the personnel were such that there was no orientation toward cutting costs and improving productivity. The previous system was a comfortable one in which rewards, both intrinsic and extrinsic, came without such an orientation.

The predecessor at the auto plant had attempted to use his formal powers in increasing productivity. Like his successor, he was under great pressure to improve the operation, but he chose to attempt this by close and punitive supervision. The successor decided to move in a different path by using more informal contacts with his subordinates and bringing

[21] *Ibid.,* p. 47.

them into the decision-making process. Also, this man worked through the existing organizational hierarchy, whereas the new man at the gypsum plant, after some failures with the established subordinates, brought in some of his own men, thus setting up a formal hierarchy that was in a sense superimposed on the existing social structure.

Rational choice from a range of possible alternative courses of action is probably uncharacteristic of most decisions that are made; but alternative approaches to problems can still be selected, whether unconsciously, by default, or by some form of conscious decision making. In the first case under discussion, the gypsum plant manager chose to try to raise the organization's performance by enforcing rules to the letter of the law—dismissing men, for example, for offenses that had previously been largely ignored. The auto plant man, on the other hand, "relegated rule enforcement to a second level of importance."[22]

Guest moves beyond his data and draws a conclusion from the comparison between his and Gouldner's cases. He suggests that the success of the auto plant manager was due in large part to gaining the consent of the governed, or democratization of the leadership process. Gouldner, in a comment regarding Guest's research, notes that the total situations in which the successions occurred were different. The gypsum plant event occurred during a period of recession, with labor relatively plentiful, but with the pressures for improvement probably more intense.[23] The implication here is that when the total situation is viewed, it is incorrect to conclude that one or another approach to the leadership process is always the corect one, even though in both of these cases the autocratic approach was less successful.

From the evidence presented in these two studies, it should be clear that top management has the potential for really drastic impacts on the organization, although it cannot yet be stated what proportion of the variance of organizational performance can be accounted for by this leadership role. Indeed, it would appear that this would vary according to the situation, since the range of alternatives even formally allowed would vary widely. Nevertheless, leadership can be seen as having a major impact on what happens to and within the organization.

Some indications of the factors associated with leadership's potentiality for major impact emerge from additional studies of managerial succession. There have been several attempts to specify the relationship between organizational size and the rate of succession. Oscar Grusky examined the largest and smallest deciles of the 500 largest companies in

---

[22] *Ibid.,* p. 52.
[23] Alvin Gouldner, "Comment," *American Journal of Sociology,* 67, No. 1 (July 1962), 54–56.

the United States (in terms of sales volume), and Louis Kriesberg looked at state and local mental health agencies and public health departments.[24] Both came to the conclusion that size and rate of succession are related. That is, the larger the organization, the higher the rate of succession. Gerald Gordon and Selwyn Becker, noting some contradictions between these findings and some others, reexamined the Grusky data and supplemented it with additional information from a sample of the next 500 largest business organizations.[25] They found an inverse relationship between size and rate of succession, with the smaller companies having a slightly higher turnover rate among top management. In commenting on this finding, Kriesberg notes that the rate of succession is undoubtedly affected by more than the size factor, with the typical career lines within the organization a major consideration. If the organization builds in the expectation of rapid executive turnover, this will obviously increase the rate.

An additional important factor noted by Kriesberg is the likelihood of interindustry differences.[26] An industry-by-industry analysis would be more definitive than a simple lumping together of all organizations. In keeping with the general theme of this analysis, an adequate typology of organizations should allow some prediction of the kinds of organizations in which succession rates will be high. Without such a typology, the technology factor, implied by Kriesberg, would appear to be important. *What the organization does and the environment in which it works have an impact on how rapidly top leadership changes are made and the extent to which such leadership can actually affect the organization.*

But one point in regard to organizational size is clear: other things being equal, the larger the organization, the less the impact of succession would be. Large organizations are apt to be more complex and formalized, and thus more resistant to change. It would therefore be likely that top leadership would be unable to "turn the organization around" in either direction in a short period of time, unless it were a totally autocratic system. Referring back to the discussion of rationality in organizations, it would appear that the impact of top leadership on the organization

[24] Oscar Grusky, "Corporate Size, Bureaucratization, and Managerial Succession," *American Journal of Sociology,* 69, No. 3 (November 1961), 261–69; and Louis Kriesberg, "Careers, Organizational Size, and Succession," *American Journal of Sociology,* 68, No. 3 (November 1962), 355–59.

[25] Gerald Gordon and Selwyn Becker, "Organizational Size and Managerial Succession: A Re-examination," *American Journal of Sociology,* 70, No. 2 (September 1964), 215–22.

[26] Louis Kriesberg, "Reply," *American Journal of Sociology,* 70, No. 2 (September 1964), p. 223.

would be a matter of rather small differences when compared with past administrations. This assumes, of course, that the past or present groups do not operate on the basis of total irrationality.

An indication of the extent of the difference that leadership can make on the organization can be found in some rather offbeat research regarding major league baseball managers. Baseball managers stand in an unusual organizational position. In relation to the total baseball organization, their role is similar to that of the foreman; but in relation to the playing team only, their role is similar to that of the top executive. Baseball teams are convenient units for analysis, since they "ideally, were identical in official goals, size, and authority structure."[27] Grusky was concerned with the relationship between managerial succession and organizational effectiveness. Here again, baseball teams are ideal because effectiveness is reflected directly in the won–lost statistics; how you play the game is not a crucial variable in professional sports.

The findings from the analysis were that the teams with the poorest records had the highest rates of succession. In interpreting these findings, Grusky rejects the common-sense notion built around succession as the dependent variable—that low effectiveness leads to a vote of confidence from the owner, then a firing. Instead, he develops a more complicated analysis, which is in keeping with the previous discussion.

If a team is ineffective, clientele support and profitability decline. Accordingly, strong external pressures for managerial change are set in motion and, concomitantly, the magnitude of managerial role strain increases. A managerial change may be viewed in some quarters as attractive in that it can function to demonstrate publicly that the owners are taking concrete action to remedy an undesirable situation. The public nature of team performance and the close identification of community pride with team behavior combine to establish a strong basis for clientele control over the functioning of the team. These external influences tend to increase the felt discrepancy between managerial responsibility and actual authority. Since the rewards of popularity are controlled externally, individual rather than team performance may be encouraged. Similarly, the availability of objective performance standards decreases managerial control and thereby contributes to role strain. The greater the managerial role strain, the higher the rates of succession. Moreover, the higher the rates of succession, the stronger the expectations of replacement when team performance declines. Frequent managerial change can produce important dysfunctional consequences within the team by affecting style of supervision and disturbing the informal network of interpersonal

[27] Oscar Grusky, "Managerial Succession and Organizational Effectiveness," *American Journal of Sociology*, 69, No. 1 (July 1963), 21.

relationships. New policies and new personnel create the necessity for restructuring primary relationships. The resulting low primary-group stability produces low morale and may thereby contribute to team ineffectiveness. Declining clientele support may encourage a greater decline in team morale and performance. The consequent continued drop in profitability induces pressures for further managerial changes. Such changes, in turn, produce additional disruptive effects on the organization, and the vicious circle continues.[28]

This rather complicated explanation is challenged by William Gamson and Norman Scotch. Based on a different approach to baseball teams' won–lost records, Gamson and Scotch advance a "ritual scapegoating no-way casualty theory."[29] This theory essentially suggests that the manager doesn't make any difference.

> In the long run, the policies of the general manager and other front-office personnel are far more important. While judicious trades are helpful (here the field manager may be consulted but does not have the main responsibility), the production of talent through a well-organized scouting and farm system is the most important long-run determinant. The field manager, who is concerned with day-to-day tactical decisions, has minimal responsibility for such management functions.[30]

Gamson and Scotch note that the players are a critical factor, suggesting that at one point in baseball history, regardless of who was manager, "the Yankees would have done as well and the Mets would have (or more accurately, could have) done no worse."[31] When the team is doing poorly, the firing of the field manager is ritual scapegoating. "It is a convenient, anxiety-reducing act which the participants of the ceremony regard as a way of improving performance, even though (as some participants may themselves admit in less stressful moments) real improvements can come only through long-range organizational decisions."[32] Gamson and Scotch add that there does seem to be at least a short-run improvement in team performance in cases where the manager is changed in midseason. They suggest that this might be attributable to the ritual itself.

Grusky, in a reply to the Gamson-Scotch criticism, further analyzes

---

[28] *Ibid.,* p. 30.

[29] William Gamson and Norman Scotch, "Scapegoating in Baseball," *American Journal of Sociology,* 70, No. 1 (July 1964), 70.

[30] *Ibid.*

[31] *Ibid.*

[32] *Ibid.,* pp. 70–71.

the data regarding midseason changes. Adding the variable of whether the new manager came from inside or outside the organization, he finds that the inside manager is more successful. He takes this as partial evidence that his more complicated theory is more reasonable, since the inside man is likely to be aware of the interpersonal arrangements and the performance of his predecessor and thus more likely not to make the same mistakes again.[33]

This may seem at first glance a lot of words spilled over a relatively minor matter in the larger scheme of things, but the points that these authors are addressing are very relevant for the present analysis. While Gamson and Scotch follow the line of reasoning taken here, that those at the very top of the organization have a greater impact than those further down the hierarchy, Grusky's argument that external and internal pressures for success affect performance is directly in line with the evidence presented by Gouldner and Guest. The kinds of personnel available are modified by the social system of which they are a part. It is within this framework that leadership behavior takes place. Although the important question of just how much leadership behavior actually contributes to the organization is left unanswered, the baseball studies do suggest that both positive and negative results ensue with managerial succession. Few cases of neutral effects are found in the analyses.

A final research finding on rates of executive succession should be noted. In an analyis of a business firm and a military installation, Grusky came to the conclusion that rapid rates of succession are associated with limitations on executive control.[34] In the military, which is characterized by a high degree of formalization, thereby limiting the discretion of any one individual, there is an intentional high turnover among all ranks.

The implication here is that in organizations with relatively loose structures and where the leadership is expected to have a great deal to do with what goes on in the organization, leadership behavior will have a large impact. Since most organizations are in fact relatively highly structured, either in terms of the formal system or the more informal interpersonal system, there are finite limits on what the leader can accomplish. Succession in the United States presidency, which is accompanied by pomp, circumstance, and other lavish ceremonies, tends *not* to make as much difference as the partisan supporters of the new incumbent would hope. Indeed, there is evidence that the total system serves to

[33] Oscar Grusky, "Reply," *American Journal of Sociology*, 70, No. 1 (July 1964), 72–76.

[34] Oscar Grusky, "The Effects of Succession: A Comparative Study of Military and Business Organization," in Oscar Grusky and George A. Miller, eds., *The Sociology of Organizations* (New York: The Free Press, 1970), pp. 439–54.

frustrate the implementation of new policies. The suggestion has been made, for example, that each new administration of the United States government be allowed to replace civil servants with their own appointees (assuming that the appointees can qualify by civil service criteria), so that program implementation can be achieved.[35]

The argument thus far has been that organizational structural conditions affect how much impact leadership can have. There are several other important considerations. As noted above, Grusky believes that whether the successor is an insider or outsider (to the organization) makes a difference, suggesting that, for baseball teams at least, the insider is more successful. In terms of overall change in the organization, however, it appears that the person brought in from the outside will be more able to institute greater changes. Donald Helmich and Warren Brown suggest that the outsider is able to replace subordinates with selected lieutenants of his or her own choice.[36] The constellation of immediate personnel around the outsider can be changed more easily than the insider's could be. The decision to move to an insider or outsider is not always available, of course. Political considerations within an organization, its financial situation, and a dearth of outsiders may force an organization to go with insiders, thus limiting the amount of change possible. (In many cases, of course, change is not necessary or seen as desirable, so that the question of insider versus outsider is not a critical one.)

Any person coming into a top leadership position is, in a very real sense, a captive of the organization. John Kenneth Galbraith, for example, has noted that for many substantive decisions involving pricing, investment, merchandising, and new products, the chief executive of an organization is actually the "victim" or "captive" of the organization.[37] He notes, however, that the chief executive does have powers of appointment to critical positions and can initiate studies that later bring about major changes.

Another set of constraints on what the top leadership of an organization can do consists of the external *environment* of the organization. This is dramatically seen in an analysis of 167 major U.S. corporations by Lieberson and O'Connor.[38] They were concerned with the sales, earnings,

[35] See the *Washington Star*, July 16, 1970, p. 2.

[36] Donald L. Helmich and Warren B. Brown, "Successor Type and Organizational Change in the Corporate Enterprise," *Administrative Science Quarterly*, 17, No. 3 (September 1972), 371–81.

[37] John Kenneth Galbraith, "The U.S. Economy is not a Free Market Economy," *Forbes*, 113 (May 16, 1974), 99.

[38] Stanley Lieberson and James F. O'Connor, "Leadership and Organizational Performance: A Study of Large Corporations," *American Sociological Review*, 37, No. 2 (April 1972), 117–30.

and profit margins of these corporations over a 20-year period. Their ingenious research considered the issue of executive succession in terms of its impact on these performance criteria. The effects of succession were also lagged over one-, two-, and three-year periods to permit the maximum impact of leadership change to demonstrate itself. They also considered the economic behavior of the industry (e.g., steel versus air transportation), the position of the corporation within the industry, and the state of the economy as a whole. Their findings are startling to those who really believe in leadership: ". . . all three performance variables are affected by forces beyond a leader's immediate control. . . ."[39]

For sales and net earnings, the general economic conditions, the industry, and the corporation's position within it were more important than leadership. Leadership was important for profit margins, but still heavily constrained by the environmental conditions.

Lieberson and O'Connor do not claim that leadership is unimportant; nor is the claim made here. Leadership is clearly important in changing organizational directions, developing new activities, considering mergers or acquisitions, and setting long-run policies and objectives. At the same time, from all of the evidence that has been presented, it must be realized that the organizational and environmental constraints drastically limit the likelihood of major change on the basis of leadership alone. The implications of such findings are crucial for organizational analysis and for understanding a total society. In established organizations or nations, the impact of leadership is heavily constrained, and leadership change (whether to a new organizational or national leader) will not make too much of a difference. For the *new* organization or nation, leadership is obviously more important. Leadership is also critically important in times of organizational crisis.

This discussion of leadership has ignored an important consideration—the motivations of the leaders. Two generations ago, Adolph Berle and Gardiner Means had argued that corporate executives have become technical managers, separated from the concerns of capitalist owners.[40] More recently, Maurice Zeitlin et al. and others have argued that corporate leadership is the modern capitalist class with phenomenal power and

---

[39] *Ibid.*, p. 124. Marshall Meyer has argued that the major research issue in terms of the environmental impact on leadership is to determine when organizations respond to the environment and when they do not: "Leadership and Organizational Structure," *American Journal of Sociology*, 81, No. 3 (November 1975), 514–42.

[40] Adolph A. Berle and Gardiner C. Means, *The Modern Corporation and Private Property* (New York: The Macmillan Company, 1932).

wealth in their organizations and in society as a whole.[41] Organizational decisions are made on the basis of continued acquisition of power and wealth. But for the analysis of organizations it does not matter if the top leaders are interested in their own wealth and power or are simply technocratic managers, since their organizational roles and impacts would not differ. However, the question of the organization's impact on the society remains a major one, since what is good for an organization may not be good for society. This is true whether or not the organizations are corporations, school systems, or churches.

LEADERSHIP IN THE VOLUNTARY ORGANIZATION

The discussion thus far has concerned the work organization, in which the leader is appointed on the basis of criteria set up in advance. The situation is somewhat different in the voluntary organization, in which the leader is elected to office. Without getting into the questions of what kinds of persons are likely to be elected and how they perform their duties, some interesting issues should be mentioned. It has long been noted that in voluntary organizations there is a tendency toward oligarchy, in that the group in power wants to stay there and will endeavor to ensure its continuation in office.[42] In looking at union leadership, Arnold Tannenbaum notes that leaders have higher incomes than the rank and file they represent. In fact, they are more likely to live like their adversaries in management than like their own union members.

> In addition to its clear financial superiority, the leader's job places him in a world of variety, excitement, and broadened horizons which is qualitatively richer and psychologically more stimulating than his old job in the plant. There are also many tensions and frustrations in the leadership role, and long hours are often required. But these are part of the deep involvement which leaders have in their work. By and large, a return to the worker role would represent an intolerable loss to most leaders.[43]

[41] Maurice Zeitlin, Lynda Ann Ewen, and Richard Earl Ratcliff, "New Princes for Old? The Large Corporations and the Capitalist Class in Chile," *American Journal of Sociology*, 80, No. 1 (July 1974), 87–123. See also Michael Patrick Allen, "Management Control in the Large Corporation: Comment on Zeitlin," *American Journal of Sociology*, 81, No. 4 (January 1976), 885–94, and Zeitlin, "On Class Theory of the Large Corporation: Response to Allen," same issue, 894–903.

[42] The classic statement of this position is found in Robert Michels, *Political Parties* (New York: Thomas Y. Crowell Company, 1962).

[43] Arnold S. Tannenbaum, "Unions," in March, ed., *Handbook of Organizations*, p. 752.

This personal desire to stay in the leadership position is coupled with several other factors that can lead to oligarchy. The leaders may be able to develop a monopoly on the kinds of skills required for leadership, such as verbal ability, persuasive techniques, and so on. They obtain political power within the organization through patronage and other favors. Given their position, it is relatively easy to groom their successors. Since the nature of unions involves a time cycle in regard to contract negotiations, the leaders can provide the membership with continual reminders of what they have achieved and what they are going to try to achieve the next time. The skills developed in this phase of the union's operation are unlikely to be part of the rank and file's repertoire.

The tendency toward oligarchy is apparently found in most voluntary organizations where there is a wide gap between members and leaders in the rewards (intrinsic and extrinsic) received. Where the gap is not so great, there is a greater tendency toward democracy. Lipset, Trow, and Coleman's analysis of the International Typographical Union demonstrates this point.[44] This union is one in which the members enjoy relatively high pay and a strong sense of community with their fellow members and leaders alike, and it is quite democratic.

Voluntary organizations can also be differentiated from work organizations on the basis of the strong likelihood of a form of "dual leadership." Analyses of political parties have indicated the existence of both public and associational leadership. The public leaders are those who run for and hold public office, while the associational leaders operate behind the scenes. An exception would be the British parliamentary system, where the two forms of leadership tend to coincide.[45] While unofficial power arrangements certainly exist in work organizations, they appear to be more fully developed in the voluntary organization, since the latter is characterized by much looser structural arrangements. And this looser structuring would appear to be related to another important consideration: in voluntary organizations, the leader is more likely to have a strong impact than in more structured organizations, because there are more possibilities for variation in the voluntary setting.

DECISION MAKING

One of the most critical activities of leaders is to engage in the decision-making process. Their decisions are made about the major functions that

[44] Seymour Martin Lipset, Martin A. Trow, and James S. Coleman, *Union Democracy* (New York: The Free Press, 1956).

[45] See Joseph A. Schlesinger, "Political Party Organization," in March, ed., *Handbook of Organizations*, pp. 766–68.

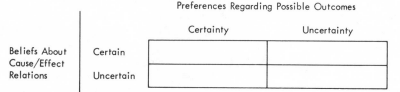

Figure 9-1   Decision processes

Source: James D. Thompson, Organizations in Action *(New York: McGraw-Hill Book Co., 1967), p. 134.*

leadership is expected to perform—setting goals, deciding upon the means to the end, defending the organization from attacks from the outside, and resolving internal conflict.

Of course, almost every position in an organization involves some decision making. Such a simple matter as the size of paper to insert in a typewriter involves a judgment. It also involves a clear set of alternatives and a clear set of outcomes, together with what are probably already-established preferences for the outcome of this decision-making process. This is not the kind of decision we are concerned with here; it is a tactical decision, which adds little or nothing to the organization. What we are concerned with are strategic decisions that affect the fate of the enterprise. It should be made clear, however, that even strategic decisions can be made by people who are not identified as organizational leaders. As was discussed in Chapter 8, lower participants can be very important in deciding what sort of information gets to people in leadership roles. Decision making is thus distinct from leadership.

Variables and Constraints

A useful approach to the kinds of decisions that have strategic importance for the organization is provided by James Thompson. Thompson notes that "decision issues always involve two major dimensions: (1) beliefs about cause/effect relationships and (2) preferences regarding possible outcomes."[46] These basic variables in the decision-making process can operate at the conscious or the unconscious level. As an aid in understanding the process, Thompson suggests that each variable can be (artificially) dichotomized as indicated in figure 9-1.

[46] James D. Thompson, *Organizations in Action* (New York: McGraw-Hill Book Company, 1967), p. 134.

In the cell with certainty on both variables, a "computational" strategy can be used. In this case the decision is obvious and can be performed by a computer with great simplicity. An example here would be simple inventorying, in which, when the supply of a particular item reaches a particular level, it is automatically reordered. Obviously, this is in no way a strategic situation and will not be of concern to us here. The other cells present more problems and are thus more crucial for the organization.

When outcome preferences are clear, but cause/effect relationships are uncertain, we will refer to the *judgmental strategy* for decision making. Where the situation is reversed and there is certainty regarding cause/effect but uncertainty regarding outcome preferences, the issue can be regarded as calling for a *compromise strategy* for decision making. Finally, where there is uncertainty on both dimensions, we will speak of the *inspirational strategy* for decision making, if indeed any decision is forthcoming.[47]

The obvious critical factor in this framework is information. The amount and kind of information determine the certainty in the decision-making process. The implication is that the more certain the knowledge, the easier and better the decision making. Unfortunately, information does not flow automatically into an organization. Whatever is happening inside or outside an organization is subject to the perceptions and interpretations of the decision makers.[48] Miles, Snow, and Pfeffer suggest that decision makers can take four stances in their perceptions.[49] They can be "domain defenders," who attempt to allow little change to occur; "reluctant reactors," who simply react to pressures; "anxious analyzers," who perceive change but wait for competing organizations to develop responses and then adapt to them; or "enthusiastic prospectors," who perceive opportunities for change and want to create change and to experiment. These different perceptual bases are developed through the individual decision maker's experiences in the organization. Thus, the same external or internal conditions can be viewed differently, depending upon who is doing the perceiving.

Examples are easy to observe. Many organizational decision makers

[47] *Ibid.*, pp. 134–35. The similarity of this approach to Perrow's should be evident.

[48] Robert B. Duncan, "Characteristics of Organizational Environments and Perceived Environmental Uncertainty," *Administrative Science Quarterly*, 17, No. 3 (September 1972), 313–27.

[49] Raymond E. Miles, Charles C. Snow, and Jeffrey Pfeffer, "Organization–Environment: Concepts and Issues," *Industrial Relations*, 13, No. 3 (October 1974), 244–64.

are now dealing with the fact that women employees are no longer satisfied to work in just clerical positions or accept unequal pay for equal work. This can be viewed enthusiastically as an opportunity to bring more and more qualified personnel into the organization or as a threat to the domain of the "old boys," to be defended by ignoring the demands of women.

Information does not move automatically to those in decision-making positions. It is part of the communications process within organizations. As will be seen in the next chapter, the communications process itself is almost guaranteed to withhold, expand, or distort information. In addition, organizations scan different environments in different fashions. For example, although they usually use as much information as they can from outside the organization, they apparently cease to do this when they develop bases in other countries, as multinational corporations have.[50] In these cases, the information-scanning process turns inside the organization, with the potential that much will be missed on the outside.

Although information is a critical component of decision making, equally important are beliefs about cause and effect. In some areas of knowledge, certainty about cause and effect is quite well developed, while in others the knowledge is probabilistic at best. Since all organizations are social units interacting with society, any involvement of humans in either the cause or the effect part of the equation introduces an element of uncertainty. Complete knowledge is undoubtedly rare in the kinds of decisions with which we are concerned. In discussing the effects of the incompleteness of knowledge and information, Thompson notes that in organizations working at the frontiers of new knowledge—as in the aerospace industry, medical research, and so on—even though all the variables that are known to be relevant are controlled as far as possible, the presence of imperfections and gaps in knowledge lead to the use of the judgmental strategy. Knowledge about cause and effect is further weakened when some elements of the process are beyond the organization's control. Welfare programs, for example, are affected by the people being served and the wider community that supports or rejects the total program. Still another situation in which the cause-and-effect relationship becomes unclear is when the organization is in competition with another organization over which it cannot exercise control. In this case the judgmental strategy is also used, since the organization cannot decide for sure exactly what will happen as a result of its own efforts.

In addition to changes in the nature of the cause/effect knowledge

[50] Warren J. Keegan, "Multinational Scanning: A Study of the Information Sources Utilized by Headquarters Executives in Multinational Companies," *Administrative Science Quarterly*, 19, No. 3 (September 1974), 411–21.

system that occur as new knowledge becomes available—as in the case of new medical discoveries that alter the approach of hospitals to their patients—another important component of the system should be specified. The nature of cause and effect is actually really certain in only a few cases. Cause-and-effect "knowledge" is vitally affected by the belief or truth system that is prevalent in the organization. The importance of this can be seen clearly in the case of welfare systems that have two major alternative truth systems, which can lead to different interpretations of the same knowledge inputs. The organizations can believe, on the one hand, that those on some form of welfare assistance are in that condition through their own fault; or on the other hand, that the condition exists because of societal imperfections. While there would seldom be a complete acceptance of either extreme position, the dominant truth system would serve as the mechanism by which information coming into the system is interpreted on a cause-and-effect basis, leading to different kinds of decisions being made. Similar examples can be noted concerning the strategies adopted in regard to supervisory practices, international relations, and most other organizational decisions. From the cause/effect standpoint, then, while information is a key factor, interpretation of it remains a variable that, while usually constant in most organizations, still affects the outcomes of the decisions that are made. The adoption of a different truth system could lead to entirely different decisions, based on the same information.

The outcome-preference side of the Thompson paradigm contains even more ambiguities for the organization than the cause/effect side. The discussion of goals and rationality in organizations is central here, since it is the decisions that are made about goals that become the outcome preferences. In the operations of an organization, the decisions that are made are obviously among several possible outcomes for the organization. Here the same concerns about knowledge and truth systems are extremely important, since they will help determine exactly what the leadership in the organization will decide in regard to a particular issue.

Outcome preferences are also affected by several other factors. Thompson notes that when human beings are the objects of the organizations' efforts, conflicting desired outcomes can be derived from the subjects themselves. Here again the example of welfare clients can be used. Similarly, in a prison "with therapeutic objectives, some compromise seems inevitable, for conflicting outcome preferences of prisoners force the prison to add custody as an outcome preference."[51] The organization may also be constrained in its choices among outcome preferences by short-

[51] Thompson, *Organization in Action*, p. 137.

ages of inputs. If a university would like to develop a national reputation in some field, its preferred outcome may have to be modified if it is unable to secure the kinds of faculty and students to assist it in this endeavor. The case would be similar in the production process if the materials needed were in short or low-quality supply.

Rationality

To these constraints, which are outside the control of the organization and the decision makers, must be added the individual constraint of the limited amount of rationality available in the decision-making process. As Simon has so ably pointed out, decisions are made on the basis of "bounded rationality."[52] The reasons for the limits on rationality are linked to the inability of the system as a whole to provide maximum or even adequate information for decision making, and the inability of the decision maker to intellectually handle even the inadequate information that is available. Leaving the issue of information aside for the moment, it is clear that the more important a decision is for the organization, the greater the number of factors contributing to the condition of the organization at the moment that the decision has to be made, and the more far-reaching the consequences of the decision. The intellectual ability to handle these multitudinous factors is just not available among current and past organizational leaders to the degree that they and those affected by the decisions would desire.

This line of reasoning is extended by Cohen, March, and Olsen in their "garbage can" model of decision making,[53] by which it essentially is argued that organizations have a repertoire of responses to problems (located in the garbage can). If a proposed solution to a problem appears to be satisfactory or be appropriate, it is applied to the problem. Interestingly, this model also suggests that the garbage can also contains the problems. What this means is that organizational decision makers do not perceive that something is occurring about which a decision has to be made until the problem matches one that they have already had some experience with. Another element of decision making that we will touch upon briefly is participation in the process itself. As we have seen previ-

---

[52] Herbert A. Simon, *Models of Men, Social and Rational* (New York: John Wiley & Sons, Inc., 1957). See also Perrow, *Complex Organizations*, pp. 146–50, for a further discussion of Simon.

[53] Michael D. Cohen, James G. March, and Johan P. Olsen, "A Garbage Can Model of Organizational Choice," *Administrative Science Quarterly*, 17, No. 1 (March 1972), 1–25. See also Charles E. Lindblom, "The Science of Muddling Through," *Public Administration Review*, 19, No. 2 (Spring 1959), 79–88.

ously, participation by subordinates has mixed consequences for the organization and the participants. The same is true of decision making. Alutto and Belasco indicate that greater participation can be dysfunctional if the participants already feel satisfied or even saturated with their role in decision making.[54] If they feel deprived, bringing them into the decision-making process will increase their involvement in and acceptance of the decision that is made. A useful insight on participation in decision making is provided by Frank Heller:[55] if a decision is important for the organization, a nonparticipative style is likely to be used; if the decisions are important for the subordinates in terms of their own work, a more participative approach would be taken. If the organizational decision makers believe that the subordinates have something to contribute to the decision or its implementation, then participation is more likely. Again, this is done on the basis of limited or bounded rationality.

The entire decision-making process can be viewed as a dialectical process.[56] The "thesis" is the condition in which the organization grows over time in a relatively stable environment. The organization attempts to limit its risks and decisions are made in a discrete sequence. Unanticipated, sudden changes in the environment provide the impetus for the "antithesis," in which the previous operations no longer work. Older modes of decision making are inappropriate. New decision-making modes, however rational, are established, forming the new "synthesis." This in turn becomes standardized and the sequence is repeated.

It would be possible to list at length organizational decisions that have been spectacular successes and failures. On the failure side, one need only look at the Edsel, the Vietnam war, or Watergate and its cover-up. On the success side, we could examine the Mustang, other wars, or the election of President Nixon after Watergate (a temporary success, to be sure). The same organizations make successful and unsuccessful decisions. Organizational leaders do attempt to be rational, as they define it. Their sources of information, their belief systems, environmental constraints, organizational constraints, their own intelligence, and luck all contribute to the success or failure of a particular decision. Decision makers dip into their garbage cans or repertoires of decisions that have been successful in

[54] Joseph Alutto and James A. Belasco, "A Typology for Participation in Organizational Decision Making," *Administrative Science Quarterly*, 17, No. 1 (March 1972), 117–25.

[55] Frank A. Heller, "Leadership Decision Making and Contingency Theory," *Industrial Relations*, 12 (May 1973), 183–99.

[56] Ernest E. Alexander, "Decision Making and Organizational Adaptation: A Proposed Model," paper delivered at Eighth World Congress of Sociology, Toronto, 1974.

the past. The success and impact of the decisions are determined by the same set of constraints that surrounds the leadership role. Thus, decision-making, like leadership, must be viewed as being *contingent* upon the internal and external constraints on all aspects of organizations.

SUMMARY AND CONCLUSIONS

In this chapter, the attempt was made to place a human factor, leadership behavior, within the larger framework of analysis. We began with the empirical conclusion that leadership behavior affects followers. To this was added the idea that since our concern was with top organizational leadership, the impact on the followers and the organization should therefore be greater. Since there is not as much information about this form of individual input into the organization as is desirable, the topic had to be approached somewhat indirectly.

It was first noted that the current conceptualization of leadership involves a combination of factors. *The position in the organization itself, the specific situations confronted, the characteristics of the individuals involved, and the nature of the relationships with subordinates all affect leadership behavior and the impact of that behavior.* Since all of these except the position itself are variables, it is exceedingly difficult to develop single standards or prescriptions for leadership. From the many studies of leadership effectiveness at lower levels in the organization, the conclusion was reached that there is no one style of leadership that is successful at all times. The total situation must be viewed if leadership is to be understood.

The important question of whether or not leadership makes any kind of difference in the organization was of necessity also approached indirectly. Since it has been found that leadership behavior affects both behavior and attitudes at lower levels in the organizations, the extrapolation was made that it is important at the top. The studies of top management succession led to the same conclusion, tempered by the many other factors that also determine what happens to the organization. It is unfortunate that we do not know exactly in what ways and under what conditions such impacts occur. From the perspective of the total analysis, it is clear that top leadership is important for the organization as a whole. But we cannot specify how much more or less important, or under what conditions it is of importance when compared with some of the other factors considered, such as the existing organizational structure, informally derived power relationships, pressures from the environment, relations with other organizations, and so on. We can state, however, that it *is* important, and hope that future research will begin to assess the relative strengths of these factors under various conditions.

Since a large element of the leadership process involves making critical decisions, the nature of decision making was then considered. The importance of information and the nature of the belief systems of those involved was stressed. The complexity of the conditions under which decisions are made and the difficulties in predicting outcomes were also discussed. Like the rest of organizational life, decision making takes place in a situation of many cross- and conflicting pressures, so that a movement in one direction is likely to trigger countermovements in others. At the same time, it is critical for the organization as new contingencies are continually faced.

Since information is central to decision making, and since communications allow information to flow, we will now examine this process in organizations.

10

communications and organizational change

Each of us can perceive or interpret the same communications differently. Consider, for example, the array of different answers to any one essay question on an examination. Communications are more than an individual matter, however. What we perceive and interpret or send as a message is affected by our own background, including our position in an organization. A piece of information has a very different meaning to me as chairman of the Department of Sociology at the University of Minnesota than it would if I were a new assistant professor in psychology or industrial relations. In this chapter, those factors that affect the sending, perception, and interpretation of communications will be examined.

Throughout the analysis, the emphasis on strategic choice and contingency approaches has meant that organizations do or should change according to the internal and external conditions that are faced. In this chapter we will examine the change process more directly. We will also look at some techniques that have been suggested to increase the effectiveness of organizational change. It should not be forgotten, however, that organizations are remarkably stable. Structures tend to persist. The critical process of power tends to be conservative. That is, the people or units in power tend to remain in power, thus resisting change. As we all know, of course, changes do occur and it is this fact that will be examined here.

THE IMPORTANCE OF COMMUNICATIONS

Organizational structures, with their varying sizes, technological sophistication, and degrees of complexity and formalization, are designed to be or evolve into information-handling systems. The very establishment of an organizational structure is a sign that communications are supposed to follow a particular path. The fact that the officially designated structure is not the operative one indicates only that communications do not

266

always follow the neatly prescribed lines. Power, leadership, and decision making rely upon the communication process either explicitly or implicitly, since these processes would be meaningless in the absence of information.

Organizational analysts have ascribed varying degrees of importance to the communication process. Chester Barnard, for example, states, "In an exhaustive theory of organization, communication would occupy a central place, because the structure, extensiveness, and scope of the organization are almost entirely determined by communication techniques."[1] This approach essentially places communication as the cause of all else that happens in the organization—a rather extreme view that is balanced by others that hardly mention communication at all.[2] The most reasonable approach is one that views communication as varying in centrality according to *where* one is looking in an organization and *what kind* of organization is being studied.

Katz and Kahn note the varying importance of communication when they say:

> When one walks from a factory to the adjoining head-house or office, the contrast is conspicuous. One goes from noise to quiet, from heavy electrical cables and steam pipes to slim telephone lines, from a machine-dominated to a people-dominated environment. One goes, in short, from a sector of the organization in which energic exchange is primary and information exchange secondary, to a sector where the priorities are reversed. The closer one gets to the organizational center of control and decision making, the more pronounced is the emphasis on information exchange.[3]

These intraorganizational differences are important. Equally vital are interorganizational differences. Harold Wilensky suggests that four fac-

---

[1] Chester I. Barnard, *The Functions of the Executive* (Cambridge, Mass.: Harvard University Press, 1938), p. 91.

[2] For example, Alan C. Filley and Robert J. House, *Managerial Processes and Organizational Behavior* (Glenview, Ill.: Scott, Foresman and Company, 1969), and Paul R. Lawrence and Jay W. Lorsch, *Organization and Environment: Managing Differentiation and Integration* (Cambridge: Harvard Graduate School of Business Administration, 1967), contain no direct references to communications; while Amitai Etzioni, in *A Comparative Analysis of Complex Organizations* (New York: The Free Press, 1961), and *Modern Organizations* (Englewood Cliffs, N.J.: Prentice-Hall, 1964), gives very little attention to the topic.

[3] Daniel Katz and Robert L. Kahn, *The Social Psychology of Organizations* (New York: John Wiley & Sons, Inc., 1966), p. 223.

tors determine the importance of communications or intelligence for the organization:

> (1) the degree of conflict or competition with the external environment —typically related to the extent of involvement with and dependence on government; (2) the degree of dependence on internal support and unity; (3) the degree to which internal operations and external environment are believed to be rationalized, that is, characterized by predictable uniformities and therefore subject to planned influence; and affecting all of these, (4) the size and structure of the organization, its heterogeneity of membership and diversity of goals, its centrality of authority.[4]

Communication is most important, therefore, in organizations and organizational segments that must deal with uncertainty, that are complex, and that have a technology that does not permit easy routinization. Both external and internal characteristics affect the centrality of communication. The more an organization is people- and idea-oriented, the more important communication becomes. Even in a highly mechanized system, of course, communications underlie the development and use of machines. Workers are instructed on usage, orders are delivered, and so on. At the same time, the routineness of such operations leads to a lack of variability in the communication process. Once procedures are set, few additional communications are required. While communications occur rather continuously in such settings, their organizational importance is limited unless they lead to severe distortions in the operations. The same point can be made in regard to many persons in the communication process itself. The long-distance telephone operator is vital to modern organizations as they attempt to communicate rapidly over wide geographical areas. What is desired of the operator, however, is unvarying performance; the operator's ideas and personality are irrelevant to the communication process. The current phasing out of the operator is indicative of the actual unimportance of this role. The important people—and machines—are those that can, as a matter of design or fact, provide an input into the communications system.

The process of communication is by definition a relational one; one

---

[4] Harold L. Wilensky, *Organizational Intelligence: Knowledge and Policy in Government and Industry* (New York: Basic Books, Inc., Publishers, 1967), p. 10. Wilensky's study is very useful as an analysis of the needs of organizations for information from their environment. The focus in this chapter is on communication as an *internal* process. As Wilensky clearly demonstrates, communications are equally important in environmental transactions.

party is the sender and the other the receiver at a particular point in time. (As we will see in more detail later, the relational aspect of communication affects the process). The social relations occurring in the communication process involve the sender and receiver and their reciprocal effects on each other as they are communicating. If a sender is intimidated by his receiver during the process of sending a message, the message itself and the interpretation of it will be affected. Intimidation is just one of a myriad of factors with the potential for interrupting the simple sender–receiver relationship. Status differences, different perceptual models, sex appeal, and so on, can enter the picture and lead to distortions of what is being sent and received.

These sources of distortion and their consequences will occupy a good deal of attention in the subsequent discussion. Ignorance of the potentiality for distortion has been responsible for the failure of many organizational attempts to improve operations simply by utilizing more communications. Katz and Kahn point out that once the importance of communications was recognized, many organizations jumped on a communications bandwagon, believing that if sufficient communications were available to all members of the organization, everyone would know and understand what was going on and most organizational problems would disappear.[5] Unfortunately, organizational life, like that in the outside world, is not that simple, and mere reliance on more communications cannot bring about major, positive changes in the organization itself.

Before we turn to a more comprehensive examination of communications problems and their consequences in organizations, a simple view of optimal communications should be presented.[6] The view is simple because it is directly in line with the earlier comments regarding effectiveness and decision making.

Communications in organizations should provide accurate information with the appropriate emotional overtones to all members who need the communications content. This assumes that neither too much nor too little information is in the system and that it is clear from the outset who can utilize what is available. It should be evident that this is an impossible condition to achieve in a complex organization.

In the sections that follow, the factors leading to this impossibility will be examined, from those that are apparently inherent (through learning) in any social grouping to those that are peculiarly organizational.

---

[5] Katz and Kahn, *Social Psychology*, p. 225.

[6] For a discussion of the limitations of a totally rationalistic approach to organizational communications, see Wilensky, *Organizational Intelligence*, pp. x–xi.

THE BASES OF COMMUNICATIONS SYSTEMS

Communications in organizations take many forms. Some are totally interpersonal, others concern matters internal to the organization, while still others are concerned with linkages between organizations and their environments. Tables 10-1 and 10-2 indicate the parameters of these forms of communications and some of the major variables to be considered for each form.

The focus of the present discussion will be primarily on communications within the organization. In the following chapters, the external communications will be considered. The discussion will generally follow

TABLE 10-1	COMMUNICATION CONTEXT, TYPES OF COMMUNICATION, AND PRIMARY INFLUENCES ON INFORMATION TRANSMISSION

Context for communication	Type of communication (Level-of-analysis)	Primary influences on information transmission
Independent of the organization	a. Interpersonal	a. Cognitive phenomena, and social roles and norms
Within the organization	a. Interpersonal	a. Organizational roles and norms plus applicable social norms
	b. Inter-unit	b. Inter-departmental relations, aggregate effects of information exchanged
External to the individual organization	a. Inter-organizational	a. Relations among organizations
	b. Organizational-environmental	b. Environmental components

Source: Karlene H. Roberts, Charles A. O'Reilly III, Gene E. Bretton, and Lyman W. Porter, "Organizational Theory and Organizational Communications: A Communications Failure?" Human Relations, 27, No. 4 (May 1974), 515.

the categorization of variables presented in Figures 10-1 and 10-2. We will be concerned with horizontal communications to a greater extent than is suggested in these figures.

INDIVIDUAL FACTORS

Since communication involves something being sent to a receiver, what the receiver does with or to the communicated message is perhaps the most vital part of the whole system. Therefore the perceptual process becomes a key element in our understanding of communications in organizations.

The perceptual process is subject to many factors, which may lead to important differences in the way any two people perceive the same person or message. Sheldon Zalkind and Timothy Costello have summarized much of the literature on perception in the organizational setting and have noted that even physical objects can be perceived differently.[7] The perceiver may respond to cues he or she is not aware of, be influenced by emotional factors, use irrelevant cues, weigh evidence in an unbalanced way, or fail to identify all the factors on which his or her judgments are based. People's personal needs, values, and interests enter the perceptual process. Most communications take place in interaction with others, and how one person perceives the "other" in the interaction process vitally affects how a person will perceive the communication, since other people are more emotion-inducing than physical objects. For example, research has shown that one person's interactions, and thus perceptions, are affected by even the expectations of what the other person will look like.

These factors are common to all perceptual situations. For the analysis of perceptions in organizations, they must be taken as basic conditions in the communication process. So it is obvious that perfect perception, that is, perception uniform across all information recipients, is impossible in any social situation. The addition of organizational factors makes the whole situation just that much more complex.

Communications in organizations are basically transactions between individuals. Even when written or broadcast form is used, the communicator is identified as an individual. The impression that the communication receiver has of the communicator is crucial to how the communication

[7] Sheldon Zalkind and Timothy W. Costello, "Perceptions: Some Recent Research and Implications for Administration," *Administrative Science Quarterly*, 7, No. 2 (September 1962), 218–35. See also Wilensky, *Organizational Intelligence,* for an additional discussion.

TABLE 10-2 COMMUNICATION, INDIVIDUAL, ORGANIZATIONAL, AND ENVIRONMENTAL VARIABLES RELATED WITHIN EACH LEVEL OF ANALYSIS

Context (1)	Level of Analysis (2)	VARIABLES			
		Communication (3)	Individual (4)	Organizational (5)	Environmental (6)
Independent of the organization	Interpersonal	Message characteristics Feedback Information overload Source credibility Information processing Nonverbal	Personality variables Perceptions Needs Social roles and norms Social goals Attitudes		Culture Spatial arrangements
Within the organization	Interpersonal	Message characteristics Feedback Overload Information processing Source credibility Modality choice Gatekeeping Distortion Speed Directionality Coding Network alignment Activity level Accuracy	Organizational rules, norms, goals Status-authority Influence Expectations Mobility Satisfaction	Hierarchy —number of levels —line/staff Size —total organization —subunit Structure —tall-flat —centralized/decentralized Performance criteria Reward structure Technology/work flow Formalization	

Inter-unit	Aggregate effects of information by organizational members on the above variables	Liaison roles
		Interdepartmental relations
		Departmental status
		Work group relations
Inter-organizational	Aggregated information Processing Sensing mechanism Uncertainty absorption —rules —cycles	Inter-organizational relations —dependency —status and influence Climate —satisfaction —leadership style Structure Hierarchy Technology Performance criteria Organizational maturity
Organizational-environmental		
External to the organization		Rate of change —technology —market Perceived equivocality of the environment

Source: Karlene Roberts et al., "Organizational Theory and Organizational Communications," pp. 516–17.

is interpreted. Impressions in these instances are not created *de novo;* the receiver utilizes his or her own learned response set to the individual and the situation. The individual's motives and values enter the situation. In addition, the setting or surroundings of the act of communication affect the impression. A neat, orderly, and luxuriously furnished office contributes to a reaction different from the one given by an office that looks as though a tornado just struck a paper mill. Since the perceptual process itself requires putting ideas and people into categories, the interaction between communicators is also subject to "instant categorization"; that is, you cannot understand another person unless he is placed in some relevant part of your learned perceptual repertoire. Zalkind and Costello point out that this is often done on the basis of a very limited amount of evidence[8]—or even wrong evidence, as when the receiver notes cues that are wrong or irrelevant to the situation in question.

The role that the individual plays in the organization affects how communications are perceived or sent. In almost all organizations, people can be superordinates in one situation and subordinates in another. The assistant superintendent of a school system is superordinate to a set of principals, but subordinate to the superintendent and the school board. Communications behavior differs according to the particular role being played.[9] If the individual is in a role in which he or she is or has been, or feels, discriminated against, communications are affected. Athanassiades found that women who had suffered discrimination in their roles had a lower feeling of autonomy than others in the same role.[10] This in turn was related to distortions in the information which they communicated upward in the organization.

All these factors are further complicated by the well-known phenomenon of stereotyping. This predisposition to judge can occur before any interaction at all has taken place. It can involve labels such as "labor" or "management" or any other such group membership. The characteristics of the individual involved are thus assumed to be like those of the group of which he is a member—and in probably the vast majority of cases, the characteristics attributed to the group as a whole are also great distortions of the actual world. In the sense being used here, stereotyping involves the imposition of negative characteristics on the members of the com-

---

[8] Zalkind and Costello, "Perceptions," p. 221.

[9] L. Wesley Wager, "Organizational 'Linking-Pins': Hierarchical Status and Communicative Roles in Interlevel Conferences," *Human Relations,* 25, No. 4 (September 1972), 307–26.

[10] John C. Athanassiades, "An Investigation of Some Communication Patterns of Female Subordinates in Hierarchical Organizations," *Human Relations,* 27, No. 2 (March 1974), 195–209.

munications system. The reverse situation—attributing socially approved characteristics—can also occur, of course, with an equally strong potential for damage to the communication process.

Other factors that enter the communication process in somewhat the same manner are the use of the "halo effect," or the use of only one or a few indicators to generalize about a total situation; "projection," or a person's assuming that the other member of a communications system has the same characteristics as his or her own; and "perceptual defense," or altering inconsistent information to put it in line with the conceptual framework already developed. All the factors that have been mentioned here are taken note of in the general literature on perception and must be assumed to be present in any communications systems. They are not peculiar to organizations.

The literature has also indicated that the characteristics of the perceived person affect what is perceived. Zalkind and Costello cite four conclusions from research regarding the perceiver.

1. Knowing oneself makes it easier to see others accurately.
2. One's own characteristics affect the characteristics that are likely to be seen in others.
3. The person who is self-accepting is more likely to be able to see favorable aspects of other people.
4. Accuracy in perceiving others is not a single skill.[11]

These findings are linked back to the more general considerations—tendencies to stereotype, project, and so on. It is when the characteristics of the perceived are brought into the discussion that organizational conditions become important. Factors such as status differences and departmental memberships affect how a person is perceived. The person may be labeled a sales manager (accurately or not) by a production worker, and the entire communications system is affected until additional information is permitted into the system. The situation in which the communication takes place also has a major impact on what is perceived. This is particularly vital in organizations, since in most cases the situation is easily labeled and identified by the physical location.

ORGANIZATIONAL FACTORS

These rather general conclusions from the literature on perception are directly relevant for the understanding of communications in an organiza-

[11] *Ibid.*, pp. 227–29.

tion. All the factors discussed are part of the general characteristics of communications. In the organization, two additional major components of the communications system must be examined: vertical and horizontal considerations greatly affect the communication process.

Vertical Communications

Patterns of vertical communications have received a good deal of attention, primarily because they are seen as vital in organizational operations. From the lengthy discussions of organizational structure, power, and leadership it should be evident that the vertical element is a crucial organizational fact of life. Since communications are also crucial, the vertical element intersects in a most important way. Vertical communications in organizations involve both downward and upward flows.

Downward Communications   Katz and Kahn identify five elements of downward communications.[12] The first is the simple and common *job instruction*, in which a subordinate is told what to do either through direct orders, training sessions, job descriptions, or other such mechanisms. The intent of such instructions is to ensure reliable job performance. The more complex and uncertain the task, the more generalized such instructions. As a rule, the more highly trained the subordinates, the less specific such instructions are, because it is assumed that they will bring with them an internalized knowledge of how to do the job, along with other job-related knowledge and attitudes.

The second element is more subtle and less often stressed. It involves the *rationale* for the task and its relationships to the rest of the organization. It is here that different philosophies of life affect how much this sort of information is communicated. If the philosophy is to keep the organizational members dumb and happy, little such information will be communicated. The organization may feel either that the subordinates are unable to comprehend the information or that they would misuse it by introducing variations into their performance based on their own best judgment of how the task should be accomplished. Aside from the philosophy-of-life issue, this is a delicate matter. All organizations, even those most interested in the human qualities of their members, have hidden agendas of some sort at some point in time. If the total rationale for all actions were known to all members, the potential for chaos would be high, since not all members would be able to understand and accept the information at the cognitive or emotional levels. This danger of too much communication is matched by opposite danger of the too little, which also

---

[12] Katz and Kahn, *Social Psychology*, pp. 239–42.

has a strong potential for organizational malfunctioning. If the members are given too little information, and do not and cannot know how their work is related to any larger whole, there is a strong possibility of alienation from the work and the organization. Obviously, the selection of the best path between these extremes is important in the establishment of communications.

The third element of downward communications is *information* regarding procedures and practices within the organization. This is similar to the first element, in that it is relatively straightforward and noncontroversial. Here again, whether or not this is linked to the second element is problematic.

Feedback to the individual regarding his performance is the fourth part of the communications system. This is almost by definition a sticky issue, particularly when the feedback has a negative tone to it. If the superior has attempted at all to utilize socioemotional ties to his or her subordinates, the issue becomes even more difficult. And it becomes almost impossible when the work roles are so thoroughly set in advance by the organization that the worker has no discretion on the job at all. In these cases, only a totally conscious deviation would result in feedback. In the absence of deviation, there will probably be no feedback other than the paycheck and other routine rewards. Where discretion is part of the picture, the problem of assessment deepens, because feedback is more difficult to accomplish if there are no clear criteria on which to base it. Despite these evident problems, feedback is a consistent part of downward communications.

The final element of this type of communication involves *ideology*. The organization attempts to indoctrinate subordinates into accepting and believing in the organization's (or subunit's) goals. The intent here, of course, is to get the personnel emotionally involved in their work and add this to the motivational system.

In relation to the first-line supervisor–worker relationship, these elements seem simple; they become more complex when the focus is shifted to a top executive–vice-president situation. While the same elements are present, the kinds of information and range of ideas covered are likely to be much greater in the latter example. Talcott Parsons provides a way of understanding these differences when he categorizes organizations by institutional, managerial, and technical levels.[13] The institutional level is concerned with relating the organization to its external world by ensuring that the organization continues to receive support from its constituency

---

[13] Talcott Parsons, *Structure and Process in Modern Society* (New York: The Free Press, 1960), pp. 63–69.

and other organizations in contact. Common examples here are boards of directors or trustees whose primary function is often to maintain this sort of support. It has been suggested that the college or university president has had a predominantly institutional role in recent history. Fund raising and legislative relationships occupied a great deal of his or her time. As student and faculty dissidence grew, the college president was put into the position of attempting to solve internal problems while at the same time playing the institutional role. The incompatibility of these demands can be readily observed through the exceedingly high turnover rate in this position.

The managerial level deals with the internal administration of the organization. Once strategic decisions are made, they must be administered, and the managerial level is concerned with how the organization will carry out these decisions. The technical level is involved with the translation of this information into specific job descriptions and direction.

The existence of these three levels requires that communications be translated as they cross levels. While it can be assumed that all levels speak the same language and indeed that each may understand completely what the others are doing, the fact remains that the tasks are different and the content and intent of communications are also different.

Dysfunctions of Hierarchy   The very presence of hierarchies in organizations introduces still more complications into the communications than those already discussed. The form of interaction itself is apparently affected by level in the hierarchy. Merlin Brinkerhoff has found that at higher levels in organizations, communications tend to take the form of staff conferences, while at the first-line supervisor level, the communications are more often in the form of spontaneous communicative contacts.[14] Even when new contingencies were faced by the higher levels, the spontaneous form did not occur. This does not mean that the spontaneous form is necessarily more appropriate, but rather that there is an apparent use of established protocol even in the face of new situations.

Information content is also related to hierarchy. O'Reilly and Roberts found that favorable information is passed upward, while unfavorable information, as well as more complete, more important information, tends to be passed laterally, rather than up or down the hierarchy.[15] They also

[14] Merlin B. Brinkerhoff, "Hierarchical Status, Contingencies, and the Administrative Staff Conference," *Administrative Science Quarterly*, 17, No. 3 (September 1972), 395–407.

[15] Charles A. O'Reilly III and Karlene H. Roberts, "Information Filtration in Organizations: Three Experiments," *Organizational Behavior and Human Performance*, 11, No. 2 (April 1974), 253–65.

suggest that trust between superior and subordinate lessens the impact of hierarchy.

Blau and Scott have pointed out several specific dysfunctions of hierarchy for the communications process.[16] In the first place, such differences inhibit communications. Citing experimental and field evidence, Blau and Scott note the common tendency for people at the same status level to interact more with one another than with those at different levels. There is a tendency for those in lower status positions to look up to and direct friendship overtures toward those in higher status positions. This increases the flow of socioemotional communications upward, but at the same time leaves those at the bottom of the hierarchy in the position of receiving little of this type of input. This situation is further complicated by the fact that those in higher status positions also direct such communications upward rather than reciprocating to their subordinates, thus reducing the amount of satisfaction derived for all parties.

A second dysfunctional consequence is the fact that approval is sought from superiors rather than peers in such situations. Nonperformance criteria enter the communications system, in that respect from peers, which can be earned on the basis of performance, can become secondary to approval-gaining devices that may not be central to the tasks at hand. The plethora of terms ranging from "apple-polishing" to more profane expressions is indicative of this.

The third dysfunction identified by Blau and Scott has to do with the error-correcting function of normal social interaction. It is commonly found that interaction among peers tends to sort out errors and at least enter a common denominator through the interaction process. This is much less likely to happen in downward communication. The subordinate is unlikely to tell the superior that he or she thinks an order or an explanation is wrong, for fear of his or her own status. Criticism of one's superior is not the most popular of communications in organizations.

Another aspect of the hierarchical pattern that can present problems in organizations is the very nature of the hierarchy itself. If the superior is chosen on the basis of ability, it is likely that he or she is more able than the subordinates. If this is the case and the ability takes the form of intellectual superiority, a communications gap can exist because of the different levels of thought on which the superior and subordinates operate. The same type of situation occurs when the subordinates are all experts and the superior becomes a generalist because of his or her administrative duties. Examples here can be found within organizations

[16] Peter M. Blau and W. Richard Scott, *Formal Organizations* (San Francisco: Chandler Publishing Co., 1962), pp. 121–24.

employing professionals. When the superior communicates downward, it must be as a nonexpert, and this lack of expertise may limit his or her credibility to the subordinates.

These problems associated with downward communication in organizations are compounded by the previously discussed factors affecting perception. Since rank in an organization is a structural fact, it carries with it a strong tendency for stereotyping. The very terms "management," "worker," "enlisted man," and so on, are indicative of the value loadings associated with rank. As will be seen shortly, these status differences do have their positive side; but the negative connotations attached to many of the stereotypes, and the likelihood that communications will be distorted because of real or assumed differences between statuses, builds in difficulties for organizational communications.

In keeping with the earlier discussion in which it was noted that complex organizations contain characteristics that work in opposition to each other, there are also beneficial aspects to hierarchical patterns for the communication process. The studies of Blau and his associates, cited earlier, are a case in point.[17] It will be recalled that in organizations with highly trained or professionalized personnel, these studies found that a tall hierarchy was associated with effectiveness. The explanation was that the hierarchy provided a continuous source of error detection and correction. The presence of experts in an organization also increases the extent of horizontal communications.[18] These can take the form of scheduled or unscheduled committee meetings or more spontaneous interactions. Communications are a vital source of coordination when organizations are staffed with a diverse set of personnel with different forms of expertise.[19] If a tall hierarchy is found in an organization with a low level of differentiation in terms of expertise, it is apparently due to the need for extensive downward communications.[20] When a hierarchy is composed of people of equal or higher ability than the subordinates, their function in this regard is clear. They can make suggestions and offer alternatives that might not be apparent to subordinates. This assumes, of

[17] Peter M. Blau, Wolf V. Heydebrand, and Robert E. Stauffer, "The Structure of Small Bureaucracies," *American Sociological Review*, 31, No. 2 (April 1966), 179–91; and Blau, "The Hierarchy of Authority in Organizations," *American Journal of Sociology*, 73, No. 4 (January 1968), 453–67.

[18] Jerald Hage, Michael Aiken, and Cora Bagley Marrett, "Organizational Structure and Communications," *American Sociological Review*, 36, No. 5 (October 1971), 860–71.

[19] John Brewer, "Flow of Communication, Expert Qualifications, and Organizational Authority Structure," *American Sociological Review*, 36, No. 3 (June 1971), 475–84.

[20] *Ibid.*

course, that some of the more dysfunctional elements of hierarchical arrangements are minimized. Furthermore, unless one assumes that people always rise to a level just above that of their competence, the superiors may in fact be superior.[21] That is, they may actually have more ability than their subordinates. If this is recognized and legitimated by the subordinates, some of the hierarchical problems are again minimized.

The most obvious contribution of a hierarchy is coordination. If one accepts the common model of communications spreading out in more detail as they move down the hierarchy, then the role of the hierarchy becomes clear. It is up to the superior to decide who gets what kind of communications and when. He or she becomes the distribution and filtering center. Given the vast amount of information that is potentially available for the total organization, this role is crucial. In a later section, we will discuss the nature of hierarchical arrangements and how they can be optimally utilized. For the moment, it is sufficient to note that status differences are obviously important for and endemic to downward communications.

Upward Communications   Contrary to the law of gravity, communications in organizations must also go up, even when nothing is going down. According to Katz and Kahn, "Communication up the line takes many forms. It can be reduced, however, to what the person says (1) about himself, his performance, and his problems, (2) about others and their problems, (3) about organizational practices and policies, and (4) about what needs to be done and how it can be done."[22] The content of these messages can obviously range from the most personal gripe to the most high-minded suggestion for the improvement of the organization and the world; and they can have positive or negative consequences, from a promotion or bonus to dismissal. (A case in point is that of a civilian official in the U.S. Department of Defense who attempted to rectify excessively costly procurement procedures and lost his job.) The most obvious problems in upward communications is again the fact of hierarchy. The tendencies we noted regarding downward communications can be equally impediments to upward communications.

The situation is even more complex, in some ways, because the person communicating upward can realistically feel threats either to himself or to his work group if certain kinds of information are made available to the superiors in the system. A person is unlikely to pass information up if it will be harmful to himself or his peers. Thus, the amount and kind of information that is likely to be passed upward is affected by the

---

[21] See Laurence J. Peter and Raymond Hull, *The Peter Principle* (New York: William Morrow & Co., Inc., 1969).

[22] Katz and Kahn, *Social Psychology*, p. 245.

fact of hierarchy. Anyone who has been in any kind of organization knows that discussions with the boss, chairman, president, foreman, or other superior are, at least initially, filled with something approaching terror, regardless of the source of the superior's power in the organization.

Another facet of upward communications is important: whereas communications downward become more detailed and specific, those going up the hierarchy must become condensed and summarized. Indeed, a major function of those in the middle of a hierarchy is the filtering and editing of information. Only crucial pieces of information are supposed to reach the top. This can be seen in clear relief at the national level, where the president of the United States receives capsule accounts of the huge number of issues with which he is concerned. Regardless of the party in power, the filtering and editing process is vital in the hierarchy, since the basis on which things are "edited out" can have enormous repercussions by the time the information reaches the top. Here as well as in downward communications, the perceptual limitations we noted earlier are in operation, so there is a very real potential for distorted communications and, more important, for decisions different from those that would have been made if a different editing process were in force.[23]

Communications in Flat Hierarchies   The discussion thus far has been built around the typical hierarchical arrangements, with multiple levels in a step-by-step progression up the line. When organizations are flatter, different considerations enter the picture. In the first place, more nonfiltered communications come to the superior in the system. Hypothetically, at least, all persons in a flat structure have equal access to the superior. On the basis of experimental evidence, Carzo and Yanouzas found that while communications took somewhat more time in a taller structure, conflict resolution and coordination were slower in the flat structure.[24] In the flat structure also, the superior must be able to communicate with all his subordinates, so he must be able to understand what they are doing. Since the flat structure is more likely to be found when the subordinates are experts of one kind or another, this is quite unlikely in practice. In these cases, then, upward communications are inhibited by the strong potential for inability to communicate.

Communications with "Outsiders"   An additional form of vertical communications is too frequently omitted in the organizational literature.

---

[23] Wilensky, in *Organizational Intelligence,* is particularly insightful in his historical analysis of intelligence errors and how they affect national policies. For a dramatic account of the same phenomenon in relation to the Vietnam war, see David Halberstam, *The Best and the Brightest* (New York: Random House, 1972).

[24] Rocco Carzo, Jr., and John N. Yanouzas, "Effects of Flat and Tall Organizational Structures," *Administrative Science Quarterly,* 14, No. 2 (June 1969), 178–91.

Organizations deal with customers and clients. These groups do not necessarily form a vertical relationship, to be sure, since the relationship can actually be in any direction—up, down, or sideways. In the case of clients, the direction is usually downward, in that the client, as a welfare recipient, patient, or student, is typically viewed in this light. Customers can be courted (upward), expected (horizontal), or merely accepted (downward). These are not fixed relationships, as we can see from the recent revolts by students, welfare recipients, and even consumers. Nevertheless, in most cases the direction seems to be downward.

The nature of the communications to these "outsiders" is affected by their relationships with the organization, in terms of the power they hold vis-à-vis the organization. Joseph Julian has shown that the structure of the organization itself also makes a difference in the communications system to clients.[25] Using data from a set of hospitals, Julian related the nature of the compliance patterns in the hospital to the communications system. The hospitals were categorized according to the Etzioni formulation into normative (general hospital) and normative-coercive (sanatorium and veteran's hospital) types. Julian found more communications blockages in the more coercive hospitals; these blockages were used as a means of client control. In the normative hospitals, on the other hand, more open communications were related to greater effectiveness. Here the appeal was to the patients' beliefs that what the hospital was doing for them was the correct thing. The nature of the relationship to the clients in this case was related to the openness of the communications system.

In a somewhat related study, William Rosengren found that in mental hospitals that move to the "therapeutic milieu" approach, the hierarchical tendencies are minimized and the patient becomes much more a part of the communications system.[26] As organizations dealing with clients redefine their relationships with the clients, such alterations in the communications system are inevitable. As clients and paraprofessionals are brought more and more into the decision-making process, previously existing hierarchical arrangements interfere with effective communications.

At this point, a major dilemma must be noted. The introduction of clients and paraprofessionals into the communications system of a welfare, medical, or school system increases the range of inputs into the

[25] Joseph Julian, "Compliance Patterns and Communication Blocks," American Sociological Review, 31, No. 3 (June 1966), 382–89.

[26] William Rosengren, "Communication, Organization, and Conduct," Administrative Science Quarterly, 9, No. 1 (June 1964), 70–90.

communication and decision-making processes. The helps correct some of the misconceptions and blocked perceptions that can characterize the way in which some professionals and some organizations deal with clients. At the same time, however, if the nonprofessionals for one reason or another begin to dominate the communications and decision-making systems, then the very reason for the presence of the professionals is nullified. This is part of the constant interplay between expertise and the desire for participation. It is a major consideration in understanding the problems associated with vertical communications in organizations.

Horizontal Communications

Communications in organizations go in more directions than up and down. Despite the obvious fact of horizontal communications, organizational analysts for a long time have concentrated more on the vertical aspect. According to Richard Simpson, the major reason for this skewed perspective has been that the classical writers on organizations themselves focused on the vertical, leading to this type of focus by their successors.[27] But whatever the reason, the horizontal component has received less attention, even though a greater proportion of the communications in an organization appear to be of this type. Simpson's study of a textile factory indicates that the lower the level in the hierarchy, the greater the proportion of horizontal communications. This is not surprising; if for no other reason, in most organizations there are simply more people at each descending level. This fact and the already-noted tendency for communications to be affected by hierarchical differences make it natural for people to communicate with those at about the same level in the organization. And those at the same level are more apt to share common characteristics, making communication even more likely.

It is important to distinguish between communications *within* an organizational subunit and those *between* subunits. In later sections, the latter will be examined more closely. For the moment our attention will be turned to communications within subunits.

This type of communication is "critical for effective system functioning."[28] In most cases, it is impossible for an organization to work out in advance every conceivable facet of every task assigned throughout the organization. At some point there will have to be coordination and discussion among a set of peers as the work proceeds. The interplay between individuals is vital in the coordination process, since the supervisor and

---

[27] Richard L. Simpson, "Vertical and Horizontal Communication in Formal Organizations," *Administrative Science Quarterly*, 4, No. 2 (September 1969), 188–96.
[28] Katz and Kahn, *Social Psychology*, p. 243.

the organization cannot anticipate every possible contingency. This is a rather sterile analysis, of course, since people desire—and the communications process contains—much more than task-related information.[29] The long history of research in industrial psychology and sociology has indicated the importance of peer interactions in at least partially meeting the socioemotional desires of the participants. The fact that the socioemotional side is brought into the leadership role (or at least the attempt is made) indicates the recognition of its importance. In peer interactions there is the greatest likelihood of such experiences in the organization. Katz and Kahn state:

> The mutual understanding of colleagues is one reason for the power of the peer group. Experimental findings are clear and convincing about the importance of socio-emotional support for people in both organized and unorganized groups. Psychological forces always push people toward communication with peers: people in the same boat share the same problems. *Hence, if there are no problems of task coordination left to a group of peers, the content of their communication can take forms which are irrelevant to or destructive of organizational functioning* [italics in original].[30]

The implication here is clear. It is probably beneficial to leave some task-oriented communications to work groups at every level of the organization so that the potentially counterproductive communications do not arise to fill the void. This implication must be modified, however, by a reference back to the general model that is being followed here. It will be remembered that organizational, interpersonal, and individual factors are all part of the way people behave in organizations. If the organizational arrangements are such that horizontal communications are next to impossible, then there is little likelihood of any communication. Work in extremely noisy circumstances or in isolated work locales would preclude much interaction. (These situations, of course, contain their own problems for the individual and the organization.) On the other side of the coin, too much coordination and communications responsibility left to those who, through lack of training or ability, are unable to come to a reasonable joint decision about some matter would also be individually and organizationally disruptive.

While it is relatively easy, in abstract terms, to describe the optimal

---

[29] For a discussion of this, see Dean Champion, *The Sociology of Organizations* (New York: McGraw-Hill Book Company, 1975), pp. 180–94.

[30] Katz and Kahn, *Social Psychology,* p. 244.

mix between vertical and horizontal communications in the sense that they are being described here, another element to communication among peers should be noted. Since the communications among peers tend to be based on common understandings, and since continued communications build up the solidarity of the group, work groups develop a collective response to the world around them. This is true for communications on the vertical axis as well as for other aspects of the work situation. This collective response is likely to be accompanied by a collective perception of communications passed to or through the work group. This collective perception can be a collective distortion. It is clear that work groups (as well as any other cohesive collectivity) can perceive communications in a totally different light from what was intended. A relatively simple communiqué, such as the fact that there is some likelihood of reorganization, can be interpreted to mean that an entire work force will be eliminated. While this type of response can occur individually, the nature of peer relationships also makes it possible as a collective phenomenon.

Interaction among peers is only one form of horizontal communication. The other major form, obviously vital for the overall coordination of the operations, occurs between members of organizational subunits. While the former has been the subject of some attention, the research concerning the latter has been minimal. The principal reason seems to be that such communications are not supposed to occur. In almost every conceivable form of organization, they are supposed to go through the hierarchy until they reach the "appropriate" office, at the point where the hierarchies of the two units involved come together. That is, the communications are designed to flow through the office that is above the two departments involved, so that the hierarchy is familiar with the intent and content of the communications. In a simple example, problems between production and sales are supposed to be coordinated through either the office or the individual in charge of both activities.

Obviously, such a procedure occurs in only a minority of such lateral communications. There is a great deal more face-to-face and memo-to-memo communication throughout the ranks of the subunits involved. A major reason for this form of deviation is that it would totally clog the communications system if all information regarding subunit interaction had to flow all the way up one of the subunits and then all the way back down another. The clogging of the system would result in either painfully slow communications or none at all.

Therefore, the parties involved generally communicate directly with each other. This saves time and can often mean a very reasonable solution worked out at a lower level with good cooperation. However, it may mean also that those further up the hierarchy are unaware of what has happened, and this can be harmful in the long run. A solution to this problem is to record and pass along the information about what has been done; but this too may be neglected, and even if it is not neglected it may not be noticed.

While the emphasis in this discussion has been on coordination between subunits, it should be clear that much of the communication of this sort is actually based on conflict. The earlier discussions of the relationships between professionals and their employing organizations can be brought in at this point. When professionals or experts make up divisions of an organization, their areas of expertise are likely to lead them to different conclusions about the same matter.[31] For example, in a petroleum company it is quite conceivable that the geological, engineering, legal, and public relations divisions could all come to different conclusions about the desirability of starting new oil-well drilling in various locations. Each would be correct in its own area of expertise, and the coordination of top officials would obviously be required when a final decision had to be made. During the period of planning or development, however, communications between these divisions would probably be characterized as nonproductive, since each of the specialists involved would be talking his own language, one that is unfamiliar to those not in the same profession. From the evidence at hand, each division would also be correct in its assessments of the situation and would view the other divisions as not understanding the "true" meanings of the situation.

This type of communications problem is not limited to professionalized divisions. Whenever a subunit has an area of expertise, it will move beyond other divisions in its conceptualization of a problem. Communications between such subunits inevitably contain elements of conflict. The conflict will be greater if the units involved invest values in their understanding and conceptualizations. Horizontal communications across organizational lines thus contain both the seeds and the flower of conflict. Such conflict by definition will contribute to distortion of communications in one form or another. At the same time, passing each message up the line to eliminate such distortion through coordination at the top has the dangers of diluting the message in attempts to avoid conflict, and of taking so much time that the message can become meaningless. Here again, the endemic complexities of an organization preclude a totally rational operation.

Communications Networks   Before turning to a more systematic examination of the consequences of all these communications problems in organizations, a final bit of evidence should be noted regarding the

---

[31] See Jerald Hage, *Communications and Organizational Control* (New York: John Wiley & Sons, Inc., 1974), pp. 101–24.

manner in which communications evolve. The communication process can be studied in laboratory situations; among organizational character- istics, it is perhaps the most amenable to such experimentation. There has been a long history (Bavelas, Leavitt, etc.) of attempting to isolate the communications system that is most efficient under a variety of cir- cumstances.[32] These laboratory studies are applicable to both the ver- tical and horizontal aspects of communications, since the manner in which the communications tasks are coordinated is the major focus. Three primary communications networks between members of work groups have been studied. The "wheel" pattern is one in which persons at the periphery of the wheel all send their communications to the hub. This is an imposed hierarchy, since those at the periphery cannot send messages to each other; it is the task of the hub to do the coordinating. The "circle" pattern permits each member of the group to talk to those on either side, with no priorities. The "all-channel" system allows every- one to communicate with everyone else.

Using success in arriving at a correct solution as the criterion of ef- ficiency, repeated investigations have found the wheel pattern to be superior. The other patterns can become equally efficient if they develop a hierarchy over time, but this of course *takes* time, and meanwhile efficiency is reduced. Katz and Kahn and Blau and Scott note that the more complex the task, the more time is required for the communica- tions network to become structured.[33] The importance of these findings for our purposes is that whether the communications are vertical or hori- zontal, hierarchical patterns emerge. In the vertical situation, the hier- archy is already there, although the formal hierarchy can be modified through the power considerations of expertise or personal attraction. In the horizontal situation, a hierarchy will emerge. In addition, it must be noted that the task being performed, based on the technology involved, will in part determine where the coordination will occur. It is not a ran- dom phenomenon, nor is it necessarily one based on formal position. There is another critical aspect of this for our overall analysis: most organizations have a preestablished *structure*, and it is this that is critical to the success of the communications that take place within it.

---

[32] See, for example, Alex Bavelas, "Communication Patterns in Task Oriented Groups," *Journal of the Acoustic Society of America*, No. 22 (1950), 725–30; and Harold J. Leavitt, "Some Effects of Certain Communications Patterns on Group Per- formance," *Journal of Abnormal and Social Psychology*, 46, No. 1 (January 1951), 38–50.

[33] Katz and Kahn, *Social Psychology*, pp. 237–38; and Blau and Scott, *Formal Organizations*, pp. 126–27.

Now let us examine in more detail the consequences of the communications patterns we have discussed.

COMMUNICATIONS PROBLEMS

From all that has been said above, it should be clear that communications in organizations are not perfect. The basic consequence of existing communications systems is that messages are transformed or altered as they pass through the system. The fact that they are transformed means that the ultimate recipient of the message receives something different from what was originally sent, thus destroying the intent of the communication process.

Omission

Guetzkow suggests that there are two major forms of transformation —omission and distortion.[34] Omission involves the "deletion of aspects of messages," and it occurs because the recipient may not be able to grasp the entire content of the message and only receives or passes on what he or she is able to grasp. Communications overload, which will be discussed in more detail later, can also lead to the omission of materials as some messages are not handled because of the overload. Omission may be intentional, as when certain classes of information are deleted from the information passed through particular segments of the organization. Omission is most evident in upward communications, since more messages are generated by the larger number of people lower in the hierarchy. As the communications are filtered on the way up, the omissions occur. As was indicated earlier, when omissions are intentional, it is vital to know the criteria for decisions to omit some kinds of information and not others. It should be noted that omission can occur simply as a removal of details, with the heart of the message still transmitted upward. This is the ideal, of course, but is not usually achieved, since part of the content of the message is usually omitted also.

Distortion

Distortion refers to altered meanings of messages as they pass through the organization. From the earlier discussion of perceptions, it is clear

[34] Harold Guetzkow, "Communications in Organizations," in James G. March, ed., *Handbook of Organizations* (Chicago: Rand McNally & Co., 1965), p. 551. This article contains an excellent bibliography.

that people are selective, intentionally or unintentionally, about what they receive as messages. Guetzkow states:

> . . . because different persons man different points of initiation and reception of messages, there is much assimilation of meanings to the contexts within which transmission occurs. Frames of reference at a multitude of nodes differ because of variety in personal and occupational background, as well as because of difference in viewpoint induced by the communicator's position in the organization.[35]

Distortion is as likely to occur in horizontal communications as in vertical, given the differences between organizational units in objectives and values. Selective omission and distortion, or "coding" in Katz and Kahn's terms, are not unique properties of organizations. They occur in all communications systems, from the family to the total society. They are crucial for organizations, however, since organizations depend upon accurate communications as a basis for approaching rationality.

Overload

A communications problem that is perhaps more characteristic of organizations than other social entities is communications overload. Overload, of course, leads to omission and contributes to distortion. It also leads to other coping and adjustment mechanisms on the part of the organization. Katz and Kahn note that there are adaptive and maladaptive adjustments to the overload situation.[36] Omission and distortion are maladaptive. They are also normal.

Another device used when overload occurs is queuing. This technique lines up the messages by time of receipt or some other such criterion. Queuing can have positive or negative consequences. If the wrong priority system is used, less important messages may be acted upon before those that are really crucial reach the recipient. At the same time, queuing does allow the recipient to act on the messages as they come in without putting him in a state of inaction because of total overload. An example of this is an anecdote from a disaster following a major earthquake. Organizations dealing with the earthquake were besieged with messages. Those to which the victims could come and plead for help on a face-to-face basis, crowding into an office and all talking at once, quickly brought the organizations involved to a halt. The overload was

---

[35] *Ibid.*, p. 555.
[36] Katz and Kahn, *Social Psychology*, pp. 231–35.

so great that the communications could not be filtered in any way. Another organization received its messages by telephone, a device providing an arbitrary queuing mechanism based on an operating phone and the luck of finding an open line. This organization was able to keep functioning, because the messages came in one at a time. In a queuing situation, of course, there are no real criteria concerning which messages get through and which do not, other than time phasing and luck in getting a phone line.

A useful modification of queuing is the filtering process previously mentioned, which involves setting priorities for messages. The critical factor here is the nature of the priorities.

All the communications problems discussed derive from the fact that communications in organizations require interpretation. If there is a case of extreme overload, the interpretive process becomes inundated with so much material that it becomes inoperative. The other situations involve predispositions to interpret in particular ways, or structured pre-interpretations into categories and priorities set in advance.

Possible Solutions

With all the problems, potential and real, in the communication process, it is obvious that a "perfect" communications system is unlikely. But although perfection, like rationality, will not be achieved, organizations do have mechanisms by which they attempt to keep the communications system as clear as they can. Downs suggests several devices that are available to reduce the distortions and other complications in the communication process.[37] Redundancy, or the duplication of reports for verification, while adding to the flow of paper and other communications media in an organization, allows more people to see or hear a particular piece of information and respond to it. This is a correction device. Several means are suggested to bring redundancy about, including the use of information sources external to the situation—such as reports that are generated outside the organization itself—thus ensuring that reporting units and individuals coordinate their communications. This coordination can lead to collusion and thus more distortion, but it can be controlled through other monitoring devices.

Downs also suggests that communications recipients should be aware of the biases of the message senders and develop their own counterbiases as a protection device—a process that, of course, can be carried too far and be overdone, but that is the "grain of salt" that is part of all com-

---

[37] Anthony Downs, *Inside Bureaucracy* (Boston: Little, Brown and Company, 1967), pp. 118–20.

munications. But there is no guarantee that the recipient knows what the sender's biases are. Another method Downs advises is that in vertical communications the superior should often bypass intermediate subordinates and go directly to the source of the communications. While this can help eliminate some distortion, it can also lower morale in those bypassed.

Downs' final suggestion involves the development of distortion-proof messages, by using "predesignated definitions and easily quantifiable information."[38] All organizations use this approach but it becomes dangerous as soon as the communications begin to deal with areas about which there are uncertainties. As we discussed in detail in Chapter 3, overquantification can be a real danger, and the same is true of present categories that do not fit new or emerging situations. Nevertheless, for many routine events such a communications device is highly rational.

Jerald Hage has suggested that adding communications or coordination and control specialists is another possible answer to communications problems.[39] These would facilitate feedback in the communications process and also enhance the socialization of organization members. Hage also suggests that communications with the external environment are crucial and that the "boundary-spanning" role is crucial to the overall communications viability of the organization. These external relations are the subject of the final two chapters of this book, but it should be obvious that communications must extend outside the organization as well as within.

The nature, problems, and suggested solutions of communications all point to the centrality of this process for much of what happens in an organization. But it is evident that the communications system is vitally affected by other structural and process factors. Communications do not exist outside the total organizational framework. They cannot be over- or underemphasized. More and more accurate communications do not lead inevitably to greater effectiveness for the organization. The key to the communication process in organizations is to ensure that the correct people get the correct information (in amount and quality) at the correct time. All these factors can be anticipated somewhat in advance. If organizations, their members, and their environments were all in a steady state, the communications tasks would be easier. Since obviously they are not, the communication process must be viewed as a dynamic one, with new actors, new media, and new definitions constantly entering the scene.

[38] *Ibid.*, pp. 126–27.
[39] Jerald Hage, *Communication and Organizational Control*, p. 241.

ORGANIZATIONAL CHANGE

Since the communications process is one which is dynamic and subject to change as new actors, media, and definitions are introduced, we can begin to analyze organizational change. Information contained in the communications process frequently leads to organizational change. At times change is virtually forced on an organization, while at other times change is openly embraced and sought. Changed laws regarding equal employment opportunities for women and minority group members have forced many organizations to drastically alter their hiring practices. At the same time, many of the same organizations eagerly seek out new technological or managerial approaches to their internal and external problems. In this section we will examine the factors that are associated with an organization's capability (or lack thereof) for change. We will also critically examine some currently practiced strategies for organizational change.

ORGANIZATIONAL CHANGE CAPABILITY

Changes within an organization are not random; change occurs in relation to the past and present conditions of the organization. Zaltman, Duncan, and Holbek suggest that there are three forms of innovation or change that can take place in organizations.[40] The first is the *programmed* innovation that is planned through product or service research and development. *Nonprogrammed* innovations occur when there is "slack" in the organization in the form of more resources available than are presently needed. These are then used for innovative purposes. They are nonprogrammed because the organization cannot really anticipate when such extra resources will be available. Innovation is *distressed* when it is forced on the organization through failure and the perceived need to do something about it. Innovations can develop within the organization or be imposed upon it by government agencies or other forces in the environment.

As will be seen in the following chapters, these contacts with the environment are of critical importance.

---

[40] Gerald Zaltman, Robert Duncan, and Jonny Holbek, *Innovations and Organizations* (New York: Wiley Interscience, 1973), p. 10.

The characteristics of the innovation itself are of critical importance in determining whether or not it will be adapted. Zaltman, Duncan, and Holbek note that the following characteristics of an innovation make them more or less attractive and thus more or less likely to be utilized by an organization:

1. Cost. Cost factors involve two elements, the economic and the social. Economic costs include the initial cost of adapting an innovation or new program and the continuing costs of keeping it in operation. Social costs involve changed status arrangements within the organization as individuals and groups gain or lose power because of the new developments. Either type of cost is likely to be viewed as exorbitant by opponents and minimized by proponents of a proposed change.
2. Return on Investment. It is obvious that innovations will be selected which will yield high returns on investments. The situation is much more difficult, when an innovation or technological policy is in the non-business sector.
3. Efficiency. The more efficient innovation will be selected over a less efficient status quo situation or alternative innovation.
4. Risk and Uncertainty. The less the risk and uncertainty, the greater the likelihood of adapting an innovation.
5. Communicability. The clarity of the results is associated with likelihood of innovation.
6. Compatibility. The more compatible the innovation is with the existing system, the more likely it is to be adapted. This, of course, implies that organizations are likely to be conservative in their innovations or technological policies, since what is compatible is unlikely to be radical.
7. Complexity. More complex innovations are less likely to be adapted. Again, this is a strain toward conservativism.
8. Scientific Status. If an innovation is perceived to have sound scientific status, it is more likely to be adapted.
9. Perceived Relative Advantage. The greater the advantage, the more likely that adaption will occur.
10. Point of Origin. Innovations are more likely to be adopted if they originate within the organization. This is based at least partially on the perceived credibility of the source of the innovation.
11. Terminality. This involves the timing of the innovation. In some cases, an innovation is only worthwhile if it is adopted at a particular time or in a particular sequence in the organization's operations.
12. Status Quo Ante. This factor refers to the question of whether or not the decision to innovate is reversible. Can there be a return to the previous state of the organization, or is the decision irreversible? Related to this is the question of whether or not the innovation or technological policy is divisible. Can a little bit at a time be tried, or does a total package have to be adopted?

13. Commitment. This involves behaviors and attitudes toward the innovation. Participation in the decision to innovate tends to raise the commitment of organizational members toward the innovation. A higher level of commitment is associated with more successful innovation.

14. Interpersonal Relations. If an innovation or technological policy is likely to be disruptive to interpersonal relationships, it is less likely to be adopted.

15. Publicness versus Privateness. If an innovation is likely to affect a large part of the public, it will typically involve a larger decision making body than an innovation that is limited to a private party. The larger decision making body will tend to impede adoption.

16. Gatekeepers. This refers to the issue of whether or not an innovation must pass through several steps of approval or only one or two. The more the gatekeepers, the more likely that an innovation will be turned down.

17. Susceptibility to Successive Modification. If an innovation itself can be modified as conditions or the technology itself changes, it stands more chances of adoption. This is related to the idea of reversibility, since the organization is not "locked" into a path that might begin to move away from the original objective.

18. Gateway Capacity. The adoption of one innovation or the development of a technological policy is likely to lead to the capacity to involve the organization in additional such actions.

19. Gateway Innovations. This refers to the fact that some innovations, even small changes in an organization's structure, can have the effect of paving the way for additional innovations.[41]

The characteristics of the innovation interact with the characteristics of the innovating organization. Hage and Aiken have found that the following organizational characteristics are related to high levels of innovation:

1. High complexity in terms of professional training of organizational members.
2. High decentralization of power.
3. Low formalization.
4. Low stratification in terms of differential distribution of rewards (if high stratification is present, those with high rewards are likely to resist change).
5. A low emphasis on volume (as opposed to quality) of production.

[41] Gerald Zaltman, Robert Duncan, and Jonny Holbek, *Innovations and Organizations,* 2nd ed., pp. 33–45. Copyright © 1973 by John Wiley & Sons, Inc. Reprinted by permission of John Wiley & Sons, Inc.

6. A low emphasis on efficiency in terms of cost of production or service.

7. A high level of job satisfaction on the part of organizational members.[42]

Victor Baldridge and Warren Burnham have argued that these organizational characteristics are more important to the innovation process than are the attitudes of the members of the organization.[43] Hage and Dewar maintain the opposite, that the values of the elites in organizations are more important than structural characteristics.[44] Undoubtedly, the interaction of elite values and structural characteristics is what leads to high or low rates of change. For example, a complex organization that has a leader who is committed to change is much more likely to change than a noncomplex one that is headed by a person dead set against change. Other combinations of elite values and structural characteristics would yield different rates of change.

The role of elite values can perhaps be seen more forcefully if the process of change and innovation is viewed as a political process within the organization. Ronald Corwin studied the Teacher Corps, a federal program of the 1960s, and the manner in which the program was implemented by colleges and universities that were to train its members.[45] The Teacher Corps, as an innovation, was affected by the "political economy" of the colleges and universities involved.[46] That is, the economic conditions and the internal politics of the organizations affected how the innovation was adapted. Organizations are characterized by power struggles. The outcome of these struggles, along with the structure of the organization, determines whether or not a particular change will be made.

Change in organizations will occur if the ruling elites desire it, the structure is appropriate, and the innovation itself is compatible with the

[42] Jerald Hage and Michael Aiken, *Social Change in Complex Organizations.* (New York: Random House, 1970), pp. 30–61. See also Zaltman et al., *Innovations and Organizations.*

[43] J. Victor Baldridge and Warren R. Burnham, "Organizational Development and Change in Organizational Performance," *Administrative Science Quarterly,* 20, No. 2 (June 1975), 191–206.

[44] Jerald Hage and Robert Dewar, "Elite Values Versus Organizational Structure in Predicting Innovation," *Administrative Science Quarterly,* 18, No. 3 (September 1973), 279–90.

[45] Ronald G. Corwin, *Reform and Organizational Survival: The Teacher Corps as an Instrument of Educational Change* (New York: John Wiley & Sons, Inc., 1973), pp. 358–60.

[46] The political economy approach has been most fully developed by Mayer Zald, *Organizational Change: The Political Economy of the YMCA* (Chicago: University of Chicago Press, 1970) and *Power in Organizations* (Nashville, Tennessee: Vanderbilt University Press, 1968).

current state of the organization. Zaltman, Duncan, and Holbek add another dimension to the analysis of change. They agree with Hage and Aiken about the structural characteristics that are related to the adaptation of an innovation, but suggest in addition that for an innovation or change to be implemented, the organizational structure itself must change. Successful implementation requires less complexity and more formalization and centralization.[47] In essence, the organization has to "enforce" the change that it has decided to adapt. Once again, the form of the organization is contingent upon the task at hand.

Organizations obviously vary in the degree and rate of change. Internal and external factors and the nature of the change itself affect how an organization acts over time. Organizational change is also related to the extent to which the organization actively seeks to change itself. Several organizational change strategies currently being practiced will now be briefly discussed.

ORGANIZATIONAL CHANGE STRATEGIES

Organizations have adapted several change strategies as they attempt to deal with various exigencies. Our focus will be on organizational change, and not on such individual change strategies as sensitivity training, encounter therapy, or other such techniques designed to alter the behavior of individuals in organizations. The individualized techniques are largely unsuccessful, since the individuals involved always go back to the original situation, where neither fellow workers nor the organization itself has changed.[48] The organizational change strategies to be discussed are management by objectives (MBO), planning-programming-budgeting systems (PPBS), and organizational development (OD).

Management by Objectives

Management by objectives is an approach designed both to specify organizational objectives and to increase the motivation of organization members in pursuit of them.[49] It is also a technique for assessing the accomplishments of organizational units according to how well the objectives are met. The basic component of MBO is that the managers of

---

[47] Zaltman, Duncan, and Holbek, *Innovations and Organizations*, pp. 134–54.

[48] Champion, *The Sociology of Organizations*, Chapters 10 and 11.

[49] See Peter F. Drucker, *The Practice of Management* (New York: Harper & Row, 1973); and George S. Odione, *Management by Objectives* (New York: Pitman Publishing Corporation, 1965).

an organization come together to develop a list of major goals, determine responsibilities for achieving these goals, and develop guidelines for the assessment of goal attainment. MBO is basically an attempt to improve the rationality in an organization and also the commitment to task performance.

MBO works best when objectives are easily quantified. When the goals are qualitative, MBO has the potential of leading the organization down the garden path of excessive quantification. MBO also suffers from being part of the management system only. It typically does not involve workers below the managerial level. This can hinder its success, especially if the objectives sought and the speed with which they are to be accomplished is at variance with the desires of the workers. At times it is also difficult, even with a quantified goal, to determine exactly how much an organizational unit has accomplished.

MBO can increase the rationality in organizations. Like all other organizational decisions, MBO is limited by the problems with decision making and communications already presented. It is probably best viewed as an incremental step that is particularly applicable for organizations with readily quantifiable objectives.

Planning-Programming-Budgeting Systems

PPBS developed within the federal government and has spread into almost all areas of public organizations. It involves an approach to programming and budgeting in organizations that is very different from past approaches. PPBS utilizes program accounting—classifying past, present, and predicted expenditures by specific agency programs—in addition to traditional accounting approaches. It also uses multiyear costing, a technique to project costs beyond the specific budget year. Detailed descriptions of activities are required, including objectives, targets, choices made, alternatives considered, outputs, and effectiveness. This involves much greater specificity than in the past. Zero-base budgeting is another new aspect of PPBS. In this approach, budgets are prepared without reference to the previous years' budgets. The attempt is to prevent agency personnel and budgeting officials from simply assuming that programs ought to be continued because they were budgeted in the past. The final aspect of PPBS is cost-effectiveness or benefit–cost analysis. Cost-effectiveness seeks to find the best of a number of alternative ways to yield the desired level of output. Benefit–cost analysis is an attempt to rank spending proposals or to put them on a yes–no decision basis.[50]

---

[50] Leonard Merewitz and Stephen H. Sosnick, *The Budget's New Clothes* (Chicago: Markham, 1971), pp. 273–75.

PPBS is obviously an attempt to bring rationality into the process of budgetary decision making. In so doing it has created a vast mountain of paper, since each phase of PPBS requires its own set of reports and exhibits. In addition to this, not every government program can really be reduced to the cost-effectiveness sort of thinking. Ida Hoos maintains that this approach to government policy is actually reactionary, since approaches that are not amenable to PPBS are arbitrarily not even considered.[51] The cost-effectiveness of a food stamp program can definitely be determined, but the differential value of food for different portions of the population, such as the aged or the handicapped, cannot be put into the PPBS framework. Merewitz and Sosnick point out that agencies seek to survive, and thus, even with this form of budgetary control, under- and overestimates of costs and benefits creep into the picture.[52]

PPBS does force organizations to specify in greater detail exactly what it is they are trying to do. This may well be advantageous, if it is possible at some point to decide that certain programs are no longer quantitatively or qualitatively worth the investment. PPBS is not the answer, however, for all decision making within government organizations.

Organizational Development

"Organizational development refers to a long-range effort to improve an organization's problem-solving capabilities and its ability to cope with changes in its external environment with the help of external or internal behavior-scientist consultants or change agents, as they are sometimes called."[53] OD is primarily aimed at the management levels of organizations with the specific intent of improving interpersonal skills and relationships. Unlike more limited attempts to make individuals more sensitive to the needs of others and themselves, OD utilizes a total organizational perspective. It attempts to work through repeated feedback of problems and prospects to key groups in the organization. It works from the perceptions of the problems by key groups in the organization. The emphasis in OD is on units within organizations rather than on individuals, with the objective being units whose members relate to and understand each other and the objectives of their unit and the total organization.

[51] Ida R. Hoos, *Systems Analysis in Public Policy: A Critique* (Berkeley: University of California Press, 1972), p. 242.

[52] Merewitz and Sosnick, p. 278.

[53] Wendell French, "Organization Development: Objectives, Assumptions and Strategies," *California Management Review,* 12, No. 2 (Winter 1969), 23. See also Jong S. Jun and William B. Storm, *Tomorrow's Organizations: Challenges and Strategies* (Glenview, Ill.: Scott, Foresman and Company, 1969).

OD can be successful within important limits, which are of two kinds. First, any organization exists in a set of constraints. Just as top leadership is constrained by the state of the economy and other social conditions and by the organization's relative position in regard to other similar organizations, so also organizational development efforts can be totally thwarted by conditions beyond the control of organizational members or change agents. If the organization is going broke, OD won't help. The second problem is a direct follow-up of the analysis presented throughout this book. OD will be effective only if the organization's structure is appropriate for the contingencies it is facing. It will also be unsuccessful if power struggles at the top or in the middle of the organization pit groups against each other over organizational goals or procedures. OD assumes that all in the organization want to work for the benefit of the organization. This is a powerful assumption.

SUMMARY AND CONCLUSIONS

We have concluded our analysis of organizational processes by focusing on communications and change. Both processes are vitally affected by the structure of the organization, and both also respond to external demands. In addition, of course, the actors, with all of their abilities and imperfections, enter these processes. People in organizational roles transmit and receive communications and decide on the direction of change.

It should be abundantly clear that perfect communications systems are impossible. So too is an organization that responds perfectly to needs for change, whether simply as a response or on the basis of one of the change strategies discussed.

Throughout the discussion in this and previous chapters, we have alluded to factors external to the organization or its environment. It is to these matters that the analysis finally turns.

FOUR

organizations and society

Structure and process have been the primary topics of our analysis thus far. Throughout the analysis we have seen that factors outside the organization play a major role in what happens within the organization. In the next chapter, such topics as political forces, economic conditions, and technological change will be examined specifically, as will the relationships between organizations and how they affect an individual organization. The final chapter will turn the issue around by looking at the ways in which organizations affect their environment.

Our interest in organizational analysis must be broad enough to ask the questions, "*What does society do to organizations?*" and, "*What do organizations do to society?*" No complete answers to these questions are available. Partial answers and polemics have filled, and will probably continue to fill, the library shelves as well as the minds of decision makers for organizations and for society. The polemics do very little good, except in those few cases where they turn our interests to new, hitherto ignored directions. The partial answers reflect the severe limitations of the evidence recorded. Because the topics of this section have been minimally researched, our knowledge is spotty.

When we move from the abstract to the substance of these relationships, we can see how important these topics really are: wars, pollution, conspiracies, social movements, national development, inflation, political pressures, revolutions, and social-control systems are just a few of the topics that make up this subject. Wars are a special form of interorganizational relationship; inflation has an impact on all organizations; the developing nation must rely on organizations; and so on. While it certainly does not provide all the answers, organizational analysis does give us some important insights into why things happen as they do.

Such analyses should provide more, however. We don't know, for example, the extent to which a television network is affected by direct attacks from politicians, or which would make a bigger difference—adverse judgments passed against it by the Federal Communications Commission, or a sudden lag in advertising revenues. We also don't know the extent to which the interorganizational network that has been called the military–industrial complex is actually such a complex and how it really affects the total social system. We do hope, however, that analysis will provide partial answers, and that future research will tell us more than we have learned in the past.

11

the environment and the organization

Anyone who has read thus far already knows the conclusion of this chapter: the environment of organizations is a critical factor in understanding what goes on in and about an organization. Said in another way, no organization is an island unto itself.

The purpose of the present chapter is to specify the nature of organizational environments and the ways in which they impinge upon organizations. Some writers have argued that environmental factors are becoming more important for organizations as the environment becomes more *turbulent*, with accelerating rates and new directions of change.[1] The truth is probably that environments have always been critical, but that they are now receiving greatly increased attention from organizational analysts. Certainly Max Weber's classical analysis of the rise of capitalist organizations suggests that environmental conditions were no less important in the period following the Protestant Reformation.[2]

To approach the topic somewhat systematically, let us divide environmental conditions into two categories. The first contains those *general* conditions that must be of concern to all organizations—the economy, demographic changes, and so on. While particular organizations must respond to these facets of these conditions that are most relevant to them, the conditions themselves are the same for all. The second category contains *specific* environmental influences on the organization, such as other organizations with which it interacts or particular individuals who are crucial to it. In the case of specific environmental factors, the interaction is direct, whereas the general environment is not a concrete entity in

[1] Shirley Terreberry, "The Evolution of Organizational Environments," *Administrative Science Quarterly*, 12, No. 4 (March 1968), 590–613. The term "turbulence" is taken from F. E. Emery and E. L. Trist, "The Causal Texture of Organizational Environments," *Human Relations*, 18, No. 1 (February 1965), 24.

[2] Max Weber, *The Protestant Ethic and the Spirit of Capitalism* (London: George Allen and Unwin, 1930).

interaction, but rather comprises conditions that must be grappled with.[3]

The importance of the various environmental conditions varies over time; a condition that is important at one period may become insignificant at another. All the factors to be discussed have the potential of being critical. At present we do not have the research evidence to permit specification of the circumstances under which one is more important than the others; therefore, most of the discussion to follow will have to be taken as suggestive rather than definitive, and for the same reason many of the examples will be somewhat hypothetical.

THE GENERAL ENVIRONMENT

Technological Conditions

Probably the easiest place to begin the discussion of the general environment is with *technology*. Since this topic and the research surrounding it have already been the subject of much attention, it can set the stage for the less systematically researched topics that follow.

It will be remembered, following the works of Perrow, Lawrence and Lorsch, and others, that organizations operating in an uncertain and dynamic technological environment exhibit structures and internal processes different from those operating in a rather certain and unchanging technological situation.[4] While we need not at this point review the direction of the relationships and the supporting evidence, it is important to recognize that the organization responds to this aspect of its environment. In fact, in the business firms Lawrence and Lorsch studied, special organizational divisions were established (research and development) to keep the organization current. In other organizations, departments such as industrial engineering, management analysis, and so on, are so designated.

Beyond their empirical evidence that technology is salient in the

---

[3] This is a modification of William Dill's notion of "task environment," which refers to those elements in the environment that are relevant or potentially relevant for the organization. Our approach further specifies the nature of the relevant environment. See Dill, "Environment as an Influence on Managerial Autonomy," *Administrative Science Quarterly*, 2, No. 4 (March 1958), 409–43.

[4] Paul R. Lawrence and Jay W. Lorsch, *Organizations and Environment: Managing Differentiation and Integration* (Cambridge: Harvard Graduate School of Business Administration, 1967); Charles Perrow, "A Framework for the Comparative Analysis of Complex Organizations," *American Sociological Review*, 32, No. 2 (April 1967); and Joan Woodward, *Industrial Organizations* (London: Oxford University Press, 1962). For an extension of the technological environment approach, see Ray Jurkovich, "A Core Typology of Organizational Environments," *Administrative Science Quarterly*, 19, No. 3 (September 1974), 380–94.

operation of organizations, these findings have implications vital to our understanding of organizational–environmental transactions. In the first place, technology and other environmental characteristics are something "out there." The organization does not exist in a vacuum. A technological development in any sphere of activity will eventually get to the organizations related to it. New ideas come into circulation and become part of the environment as soon as they cease being the private property of any one individual or organization. Since the sciences have a norm of distributing knowledge, scientific developments become part of the public domain as a matter of course. A development that can be patented is a different matter, but if it is thought to be significant, other organizations will seek to copy it or further extend the previous development. In either case, an organization must keep up with such developments in any activity crucial to its continued success.

More subtle forms of the technological environment are found outside the hard sciences and engineering. In management and administration, new ideas are introduced through research, serendipity, or practice. One need mention only the organizational change strategies discussed in the previous chapter as an indication of the changing technologies and styles available to the administration of organizations. In service-oriented organizations such as schools, social-work agencies, and hospitals, the same types of technological shifts can be seen. Through one mechanism or another, the organization in any sphere of activity is made aware of technological developments that are or can be part of its own activities. An important mechanism appears to be the introduction of new personnel or clients who have had contact with alternative technologies and advocate their use in the organization in question. This, of course, can be a source of conflict in the organization, as can the technology-development and monitoring departments.

Organizations do not respond to technological change through absorption. Instead, the organization's political process operates through the advocacy of change or stability. Organizations of every kind contain their own internal "radicals" and "reactionaries," in terms of their responses to technological and other environmental conditions. Since the rate of technological and other environmental changes is not constant for all organizations, the degree to which they must develop response mechanisms varies. For all, however, technology remains an important consideration.

Legal Conditions

An environmental consideration often overlooked but potentially critical is the *legal conditions* that are part of the organization's surroundings.[5] Most organizations that operate outside the law respond to the legal system by their attempts to evade the law and remain underground. Organizations such as voluntary associations with a strictly local base may be relatively unaffected by legal considerations until laws are passed that affect their operations, or until they become developed to the point that they must register with one or another government agency. Airlines, for instance, must comply with safety, rate, alcoholic beverage, and a host of other laws and regulations. Since almost all organizations are affected directly or indirectly by the legal system, this fact must be introduced into the analysis. (For the moment, we will ignore the fact that regulated industries appear to have a great deal of control over their respective regulatory agencies.)

Many, probably most, organizations must live with federal, state, and local laws as constants in their environments. At the very least, they set many of the operating conditions of many organizations, ranging from specific prohibitions of certain kinds of behavior to regulations requiring reporting of income and staffing at periodic times of the year. The importance of laws is shown by the staffs of legal and other experts who form an important part of many organizations and who are specifically charged with interpreting and protecting the organizations' positions.

While the body of laws as a constant is an interesting analytical point, the dynamic aspect of the legal system points up the importance of laws for organizations. When a new law is passed or an interpretation modified, organizations must make some important changes if the law has relevance for them. Here again, relatively mundane matters such as tax and employment regulations are important. More striking are the cases of major shifts that affect organizations in the public and private sectors. For example, U.S. Supreme Court decisions regarding school desegregation have had tremendous impacts on the school organizations involved. The recent concern with the environment has resulted in laws and regulations concerning pollution that have affected many organizations as they utilize their resources in fighting or complying with the new statutes. Laws are thus important external constraints on organizations.

Political Conditions

Laws are not passed without pressures for their enactment. The *political situation* that brings about new laws also has its effects on organizations. To use the pollution example again, the political pressures brought by various conservation groups concerned about potential pollution has contributed in part to a real shortage of electrical power. The

---

[5] This is a component of Etzioni's discussion in Amitai Etzioni, *Modern Organizations* (Englewood Cliffs, N.J.: Prentice-Hall, Inc., 1964), pp. 110–11.

strong political pressures to reduce military and aerospace spending have led to crises of one sort or another for organizations in those areas. Police departments are buffeted back and forth between support for "law and order" and condemnation of "police brutality." School systems have drastically altered parts or all of their curricula in the face of threats from groups concerned with such topics as sex education or left-wing text-books. Some organizations are directly affected by the political process, because their hierarchy can be drastically changed by election results. All government units face this possibility after every election, as top officials are changed at the discretion of a new administration.

Organizations in the private sector are less directly affected than public ones, but they must still be attuned to the political climate. Since lobbying for legislation that will be favorable in terms of tax advantages or international trade agreements is an accepted part of the legislative and administrative system of the United States, organizations must devote resources to the lobbying process. The widespread illegal corporate contributions to domestic and foreign political parties and individuals is further evidence of the importance of the political factor for organizations. "Institutional advertising" is designed to generate some form of public support for the organization involved, as exemplified by the large amounts of money spent by oil companies during petroleum crises. This evidence points up the importance of the political process in the wider society for the organizations contained in it.

Economic Conditions

A societal condition that is more obvious, but again strangely neglected by most sociologists, is the state of the *economy* in which the organization is operating. To most businessmen, this is *the* crucial variable. In universities and in government work, experience also shows the importance of economic conditions when budgets are being prepared, defended, and appropriated in nonindustrial areas. Changing economic conditions serve as important constraints on any organization. Much of the earlier discussion of organizational size was based on the assumption that an organization has the economic capability to increase in size. In periods of economic growth, organizations, in general, also grow—and vice versa.

The economy is important for organizations in more than its relationship to gross size. Changing economic conditions do not affect all parts of an organization equally. In periods of economic distress, an organization is likely to cut back or eliminate those programs it feels are least important to its overall goals. Economic affluence permits government agencies to engage in a wider range of programs. Klatzky found that state employment agencies in wealthier states provided unemployment insurance to a greater proportion of the unemployed than did the agencies in the poorer states.[6] Since these agencies were paying out more, they also received a disproportionately larger share of federal funds than their less affluent peers in other states. The rich agencies get rich as the poor agencies get poor. This might well change if there is a movement to an economy of no growth, in which abundance is replaced by scarcity. Economic shifts of this sort will have a clear impact on organizational behavior and values.[7]

Changing economic conditions are, in fact, excellent indicators of the operative goals of organizations. The fact that organizational programs vary according to the economic conditions that are confronted contributes to a paradox for most organizations. Since total rationality is not an assumption of this analysis, it can be safely assumed that an organization cannot be sure of exactly what contribution each of its parts makes to the whole. For example, research and development can be viewed as one of the luxuries that should go when an organization faces some hard times. But by concentrating on the production and distribution of what R&D has done in the past, the organization may miss the development of a new product that would be of great long-run benefit. People in health-related research sponsored by the federal government have claimed that cutbacks in these activities have come at a time when crucial breakthroughs are about to be made. Here again, the decision is made on the economic ground that other activities are of greater importance. Tragic (and sometimes humorous) examples such as these could be given for probably every kind of organization. Periods of economic difficulty do force organizations to evaluate their priorities and trim off excess fat, if any is found. As in the case of the communication process, the criteria by which the evaluations are accomplished are the key variables.

Economic conditions surrounding organizations improve and decline, with the organizations responding to the situation. In their responses in any situation, the important factor of competition is present. Economic competition can be most easily seen in business organizations, where success is measured in the competitive marketplace. While the competition is not "pure," it is still an evident part of both the operative and value systems in a private-enterprise economy. What is less evident, but equally real, is economic competition among and within organizations outside the business sphere. From repeated experiences in government agencies at several levels, it is clear that competition is fierce during budget season.[8]

[6] Sheila R. Klatzky, "Organizational Inequality: The Case of the Public Employment Agency," *American Journal of Sociology*, 76, No. 3 (November 1970), 474–91.

[7] William G. Scott, "Organization Theory: A Reassessment," *Academy of Management Journal*, 17, No. 2 (June 1974), 242–54.

[8] See Aaron Wildavsky, *The Politics of the Budgetary Process* (Boston: Little, Brown and Company, 1964).

Government agencies are all competing for part of the tax revenues, which constitute a finite "pot." Organizations that rely on contributions from members, such as churches, are also affected by the general economic conditions, since the contributors have more or less income available. An interesting research question is the extent to which the severity of economic competition varies among organizations in all sectors of society. It seems almost equal, regardless of the organization's major emphases.

Demographic Conditions

Demography is another factor. The number of people served and their age and sex distributions make a great deal of difference to all organizations. As a general rule, an organization can predict its probable "market" for the future from information in census data, but population shifts are less predictable and make the organization more vulnerable. In a society where race, religion, and ethnicity are important considerations, shifts in these aspects of the demographic condition must also be considered. The most striking examples of the importance of demographic change come from organizations located in the central cities of growing metropolitan areas. Businesses, schools, and police departments have different clientele from what they once had, even though the organizations themselves might not reflect this. At least in the short run, it is the urban poor and minority-group members who suffer the consequences. The organizations themselves, however, eventually undergo transitions (usually painful) as they begin to realize that their clientele has become different and that they themselves must change.

Ecological Conditions

Related to the demographic scene is the general *ecological situation* surrounding an organization. The number of organizations with which it has contacts and relationships and the environment in which it is located are components of the organization's social ecological system. In an urban area, an organization is much more likely to have contacts with a myriad of other organizations than is one in a rural area. Since the density of other organizations around any particular organization varies widely, the potential for relationships also varies.

Shifting from social ecology to the physical environment, the relationships between organizations and ecological conditions become more evident because of the recent concerns about the total ecological system. It is increasingly clear that organizations have effects on the environment, as is abundantly demonstrated by the various organizations that pollute and the others that fight pollution. These topics are part of the concern of the next chapter.

A more subtle point is that the environment affects organizations. Factors such as climate and geography set limits on how they allocate resources. Transportation and communication costs rise if an organization is distant from its market or client. Even such mundane items as heating and cooling expenses must be considered limits on an organization. Although these factors are generally constants, since only in unusual circumstances are there significant changes, these conditions cannot be ignored in a total organizational analysis involving comparisons between organizations.

Cultural Conditions

The environmental conditions discussed thus far are fairly easily measured in terms of "hard" indicators of the degree to which they are present or absent. A more difficult task is to determine the extent to which they actually affect the organizations in a social system. For the present it has to be assumed that they make a difference, even though we cannot specify which is more important than the others in particular situations. Other conditions in the external environment that are vitally important are more difficult to measure. The first of these is the *culture* surrounding an organization. The experiences of organizations that attempt to establish new operating units across national boundaries or in different regions of the United States provide common-sense examples of the importance of cultural differences. Unless the values and behaviors of the indigenous population are understood and appreciated, such projects are likely to fail.

Research in this area, while oriented in a different direction, leads to the same conclusion: the culture of the system surrounding an organization has a major impact on the way the organization operates. Evidence for this conclusion comes from many studies conducted in various parts of the world. Notable among these are Crozier's analysis of two French bureaucracies and James Abegglen's study of Japanese factories.[9] Both confirm the point that the culture permeates the organizational boundaries through the expectations and actions of the personnel. Norms and behaviors that work in one setting are likely to be ineffective or even counterproductive in another. An understanding of a different culture is a prerequisite for any move by an organization into new areas.

[9] Michel Crozier, *The Bureaucratic Phenomenon* (Chicago: University of Chicago Press, 1964); and James C. Abegglen, *The Japanese Factory* (New York: The Free Press, 1958). Even within a single country, strong cultural differences affect the programs of similar organizations in different states or regions. See Richard L. Sutton, "Culture Context and Change-Agent Organizations," *Administrative Science Quarterly*, 19, No. 4 (December 1974), 547–62.

While the influence of the culture is now an accepted fact, it is not clear whether culture overrides other factors in determining how an organization is shaped and operates. There is evidence suggesting that organizations at an equivalent technological level—for example, at the same degree of automation of production—are quite similar in most respects, as was indicated in the chapter on structure. The basic problem is to sort out the influences of these various environmental factors as they impinge on the organization. Unfortunately, not enough is yet known for such fine distinctions to be made. The various factors discussed so far probably interrelate in their organizational effects in a rather complex interaction pattern. For example, it appears that the more routine and standardized the technology, the less the impact of cultural factors. The production of children's toy automobiles is probably carried out in similar organizations in Hong Kong, London, Japan, Switzerland, or Tonka, Minnesota. When one moves to less routinized technological operations, such as local government, the administration of justice, or highway construction, the impact of culture is likely to be higher.

The complexity of the issue can be seen when it is realized that we are dealing with only two of the variables we have discussed in these examples. If the other factors are added, the picture is much more difficult to comprehend. As research proceeds and some quantitative measures of the variables discussed become available, the complex interactions will be more understandable.

In its impact on organizations, culture is not a constant, even in a single setting. Values and norms change as events occur that affect the population involved. If they involve conditions relevant to the organization, these shifts are significant for it. Newspaper editorials, letters to the editor, and other colorations of reports in the mass media indicate how values can change in regard to particular organizations or types of organizations. These value shifts may precede or accompany political shifts, which would have a more direct kind of impact. Changes in consumer tastes represent another way that cultural conditions can affect organizations. Examples of this are easily found; a dramatic one is that of the contrasting experiences with the Edsel and Mustang cars by the Ford Motor Company.

We have suggested several features of the environment that are crucial for organizations. Howard Aldrich has dissected the environment in another way.[10] He suggests seven dimensions or continua along which the environment may vary:

[10] Howard Aldrich, "An Organization-Environment Perspective on Cooperation and Conflict in the Manpower Training System," in Anant R. Negandhi, ed., *Interorganization Theory* (Kent, Ohio: Kent State University Press, 1975).

1. Its *stability or instability* in terms of the degree of turnover of elements in the environment.
2. Its *homogeneity or heterogeneity* in terms of the degree of similarity among the population to be dealt with, both individual and organizational.
3. Its *concentration or dispersion* in terms of the degree to which the population dealt with is distributed across the range of the domain of the organization.
4. Its *environmental capacity* in terms of the level of resources available to the organization.
5. Its *domain consensus* in terms of the degree to which the organization's claim to its domain is disputed or recognized by other organizations.
6. Its *turbulence or placidness* in terms of the extent to which the environment is disturbed or changed by other external activities.
7. Its *mutability or immutability* in terms of the extent to which the environment is open to change or manipulation by the organization.[11]

Most of Aldrich's dimensions can be combined with those already discussed. Political conditions could be approached in terms of their degrees of stability, environmental capacity, domain consensus, turbulence, and mutability. Similar analyses or measurements could be done with technological, economic, and the other content areas of the environment. Such an approach might well be useful as an analytical or research strategy.

THE PERCEPTION OF THE ENVIRONMENT

We have been proceeding as though the environment is something "out there" beyond the organization, which anyone in the organization can readily spot and identify. It would be handy if this were the case, but it is not.

People have different positions in organizations. Some people are "gate keepers," who are designated to admit certain information about the environment that is relevant to the organization.[12] Their own perceptions are influenced by their position within the organization. Of course, the very definition of where the organization stops and the environment begins is open to question. Starbuck has pointed out that different positions are at an organization's boundaries, depending on what the activity at

[11] *Ibid.*, pp. 57–61.
[12] Saad Z. Nagi, "Gate-Keeping Decisions in Service Organizations: When Validity Fails," *Human Organization*, 33, No. 1 (Spring 1974), 47–58.

the moment is.[13] At times it can be the switchboard operator, while at other times it is the president or chief officer.

According to Starbuck, an organization *selects* those aspects of the environment with which it is going to deal.[14] Its selection process is affected by that of other organizations with which it is in contact. In this manner, organizations go about constructing or inventing their environments. This construction continues according to how the environment is perceived. The perception of the environment is of critical importance.[15] Just as the perceptions of individuals are shaped by their experiences, so, too, are organizations. Starbuck maintains that organizations are even *more* relativistic than individuals because of their constant comparisons with and sharing personnel among other comparable organizations.[16] From their perceptions regarding the environment, organizations develop a set of strategies for dealing with it. Starbuck's work strongly suggests that the organizational strategies are vitally affected by the selection and perception process.

THE IMPACT OF THE ENVIRONMENT ON THE ORGANIZATION

What do all of these environmental factors, however selected and perceived, do to organizations? There are several answers. In the first place, organizations vary in their vulnerability to environmental pressures.[17] The more dependent an organization is on its environment, the more vulnerable it is. An organization with strong financial resources is

[13] William H. Starbuck, "Organizations and Their Environments," in Marvin D. Dunnette, ed., *Handbook of Industrial and Organizational Psychology* (Chicago: Rand McNally & Co., 1976), pp. 1071–75.

[14] *Ibid.*, pp. 1078–80. See also Marshall W. Meyer, "Organizational Domains," *American Sociological Review*, 40, No. 5 (October 1975), 599–615. Meyer finds that the scope of the domain claimed or selected by organizations has an impact on its operations. Narrow domain claims are associated with stability and broad and inconsistent claims with loss of functions. Broad claims coupled with technological capacity and newness lead to domain expansion. Domain claims seldom contract.

[15] See Starbuck, "Organizations and their Environments," pp. 1080–81; Raymond E. Miles, Charles C. Snow, and Jeffrey Pfeffer, "Organization-Environment: Concepts and Issues," *Industrial Relations*, 13, No. 3 (October 1974), 244–64; and Robert B. Duncan, "Characteristics of Organizational Environments and Perceived Environmental Uncertainty," *Administrative Science Quarterly*, 17, No. 3 (September 1973), 313–27.

[16] Starbuck, "Organizations and Their Environments," pp. 1080–81.

[17] David Jacobs, "Dependency and Vulnerability: An Exchange Approach to the Control of Organizations," *Administrative Science Quarterly*, 19, No. 1 (March 1974), 45–59.

less vulnerable to economic fluctuations than is one with no reserves. In the mid-1970s petroleum and munitions manufacturers were highly dependent and vulnerable to political shifts in their sources of raw materials and their markets. These firms attempt to manipulate their environment through stabilizing the political conditions.

When an organization is vulnerable, it reacts to the environment. Several studies have shown that strong environmental pressures are related to increased formalization and a general "tightening" of the organization.[18] It is odd that the environmental pressures do this, since in many ways a looser organization is more adaptive to the environment and is more likely to develop innovations that might be beneficial over the long run. Organizations that are vulnerable to the environment, of course, face a greater risk of failure if an innovation happens not to be successful.

There are more measures of environmental impact than vulnerability alone. To focus only on this feature logically leads to a Darwinian conclusion that a natural selection process would occur, with only the fittest surviving.[19] But every organization is dependent on its environment to some degree. Each adapts internal strategies to deal with the perceived pressures. Contingency theory strongly suggests that there is no single best way to cope with environmental pressures. The specific stance that an organization takes derives from choices that are made within it. This decision-making process is a political one in the sense that different particular options are supported by different factions within the decision-making structure. The option finally selected is a consequence of the power of individuals and groups that support it. That environmental pressures often tighten the organization may be a consequence of the fact that this is the option that powerful segments of organizations have traditionally taken. It may not be the one most useful for the organization, of course.

Among the strategies that organizations develop for dealing with their environments, a critical one is to attempt to shape the environment itself. Hirsch has shown that the typical pharmaceutical manufacturing firm has

[18] See John Henry Freeman, "Environment, Technology, and the Administrative Intensity of Manufacturing Organizations," *American Sociological Review*, 38, No. 6 (December 1973), 750–63; Pradip N. Khandwalla, "Environment and Its Impact On the Organization," *International Studies of Management and Organization*, 2, No. 3 (Fall 1972), 297–313; Jean Boddewyn, "External Affairs: A Corporate Function in Search of Conceptualization and Theory," *Organization and Administrative Sciences*, 5, No. 1 (Spring 1974), 67–106; and Jeffrey Pfeffer and Huseyin Leblebici, "The Effect of Competition on Some Dimensions of Organizational Structure," *Social Forces*, 52, No. 2 (December 1973), 268–79.

[19] Howard E. Aldrich and Jeffrey Pfeffer, "Environments of Organizations," *The Annual Review of Sociology*, Vol. II, 1976.

been more successful than the typical firm in the phonograph record industry largely because the pharmaceutical firms have been able to control relevant aspects of their environments.[20] The pharmaceutical firms could exert control over pricing and distribution, patent and copyright laws, and external opinion-leaders. This control of the environment was a source of greater profitability. Organizations attempt to gain and maintain power over environmental conditions that are of strategic importance to them. In a situation of scarce resources, organizations may also resort to illegal acts such as price-fixing or other activities to restrain trade.[21] Thus, like the development of internal organizational power in which successful coping with strategic contingencies is linked to the development of power, so in its interactions with the environment the organization must be able to cope with and control external strategic and important contingencies.

The discussion thus far has emphasized those external factors that appear to be most crucial for the organization. Ideally, we should be able to trace the exact strength and direction of the influence of each factor, but this is not possible in our present state of knowledge. Turning from the manner in which contemporary conditions affect organizations, we will now look at the ways in which the total social structure affects the organizations within it. This discussion will reinforce the conclusions already reached in regard to the importance of the environment. We will also see the manner in which the social structure affects the emergence of organizations.

THE SOCIAL STRUCTURE AND THE EMERGENCE OF ORGANIZATIONS

Arthur Stinchcombe has examined the interface between organizations and the social structure.[22] In a discussion of organizational development and historical conditions, Stinchcombe maintains that

it seems that in some societies the *rate* at which special purpose organizations take over various social functions (economic production,

[20] Paul M. Hirsch, "Organizational Effectiveness and the Institutional Environment," *Administrative Science Quarterly*, 20, No. 3 (September 1975), 327–44.

[21] Barry M. Staw and Eugene Szawjkowski, "The Scarcity-Munificence Component of Organizational Environments and the Commission of Illegal Acts," *Administrative Science Quarterly*, 20, No. 3 (September 1975), 345–54.

[22] Arthur L. Stinchcombe, "Social Structure and Organizations," in James G. March, ed., *Handbook of Organizations* (Chicago: Rand McNally & Co., 1965), pp. 142–93.

policing, education, political action, military action, etc.) is higher than in other societies, and that within societies some population groups are more likely to found new types of organizations to replace or supplement multiple-purpose groups such as families or geographical communities for certain purposes.[23]

According to this approach, in order to develop a new organization a population must be *aware* of alternative techniques for accomplishing some task or set of tasks in the society. This means that the traditional approaches are at least being questioned, the population concerned is in contact with other ideas, and there are some possibilities for change within the society. The alternative of developing a new form of organization must be viewed as *attractive* in terms of a cost-benefit analysis; that is, the social and economic costs associated with starting a new organization must be less than the benefits it is expected to yield. Stinchcombe also points out that the benefits are expected to go to those engaged in organizational development rather than to other groups in the society. Another important condition is that the people involved have to have sufficient *resources*—such as wealth, power, legitimacy, and strength of numbers—to get the new organization off the ground.[24]

> In societies where most of the land passes through inheritance and is not freely alienable outside the family, where labor's obedience is to its traditional lord rather than to the highest bidder, where wealth stays in bags in the lord's warehouse to be used to support retainers rather than for investment, the rate of organization formation is low.[25]

The final condition is that those seeking to establish the new organization must have the *power* to defeat those interested in maintaining the older system.

These conditions necessary for the start of a new organization have not been distributed randomly throughout history, but they are present in sufficient degrees to allow many new organizations and new organizational forms to develop at many points in time. Stinchcombe notes that new organizations are more likely to survive over time than are new organizational forms. Similarly, new organizations, and more particularly

---

[23] *Ibid.*, p. 143.

[24] See John R. Kimberly, "Environmental Constraint and Organizational Structure: A Comparative Analysis of Rehabilitation Organizations," *Administrative Science Quarterly*, 20, No. 1 (March 1975), 1–9.

[25] Stinchcombe, "Social Structure and Organizations," p. 147.

new organizational forms, have a higher organizational death rate than old organizations or old organizational forms. This "liability of newness" is indicative of the inherently conservative nature of society.

The reasons for the liability of newness are found in the social relations that are part of the larger society and in the behaviors of the members of the new organizations and organizational forms. In the first place, new *roles* have to be learned in new settings. These cannot be the traditional passing on of skills and behaviors; the new organization must rely on general skills possessed by the population. This again means that the nature of the population surrounding the organization is vital for its development and form. If not enough people have the requisite general skills, the new organizations will have extreme difficulties in accomplishing their tasks and thus will probably not survive.

The fact that new roles have to be learned leads to other organizational problems. There is likely to be little of the semiautomatic communication and interaction that characterize mature organizations. In a totally new organization, where the new roles are not yet part of the repertoire of the personnel, the whole system is apt to be barely operative *until the roles and role relationships are learned.* This can be accomplished by the imposition of the organizational structure, but this, too, must be learned and must also coincide in some degree with the behaviors and expectations of the organization members. Stinchcombe notes that if the people coming into the organization have skills and values that are relevant for the organization, the task of developing the organization is simpler. The liability of newness is reduced when there is a "disciplined and responsible work force."[26]

Another characteristic of new organizations is that they involve *social relations among strangers,* without the trust that is generated by long years of association. Here again, the state of the society makes a difference. If the general social relations are characterized by universalistic religious and legal codes that make oaths sacred and laws binding, and by achievement norms that are stronger than kinship ties, the liability of newness will be reduced. Social relations in these situations will be built around the current situation, rather than on past experiences and expectations. Strangers can interact with more trust, allowing the organization to get off the ground more easily.

New organizations suffer another drawback, in that *they do not have established ties with the larger society.* There are no steady customers or clients. If the social system is one in which the use of alternative organizations for common tasks is an accepted thing, new organizations will

26 *Ibid.,* p. 149.

have an easier time establishing themselves. It will not be as unusual for customers and clients to try alternative organizations for supplying their products and services.

This analysis makes it clear that the conditions under which organizations and organizational forms are likely to develop are not constant for all times and places. While the points made are clearest in a cross-cultural and historical perspective, it should also be apparent that within one society and in a relatively short period of time, conditions can change sufficiently to produce intrasocietal differences in the rates of organizational development.

Other Societal Conditions   The conditions just discussed do not exist independent of other societal characteristics. They are in fact intermediate variables between some basic societal characteristics and the rate of organizational development. One major societal determinant of the other variables of organizational development is the general *literacy* and specialized advanced *schooling* of the population. The presence of literacy raises the likelihood that each of the intermediate variables will be sufficiently present for organizational development to occur. Stinchcombe states:

> . . . literacy and schooling raise practically every variable which encourages the formation of organizations and increases the staying power of new organizations. It enables more alternatives to be posed to more people. It facilitates learning new roles with no nearby role model. It encourages impersonal contact with customers. It allows money and resources to be distributed more easily to strangers and over distances. It provides records of transactions so that they can be enforced later, making the future more predictable. It increases the predictability of the future environment of an organization by increasing the available information and by making possible a uniform body of law over a large area.[27]

In addition to the key variable of education and literacy, several other factors are crucial for the conditions permitting organizational formation. *Urbanization* is a second factor identified by Stinchcombe in this regard. He notes that the rate of urbanization should be slow enough to allow the rural migrants to learn and develop routines of urban living. At the same time, the development of urban life is associated with greater heterogeneity of life style, thus providing more alternative working and living arrangements. The urban scene is one of dealing with strangers, and this too assists organizational development, since ascriptive role rela-

[27] *Ibid.*, pp. 150–51.

tionships are likely to be minimized. Impersonal laws are necessary in urban areas just as they are in organizations. Urbanization, like education, increases the organizational capacity of populations, although not to the same degree, according to Stinchcombe.

Another important condition, and one that has long been identified, is the presence of a *money economy*. This sort of economy

> . . . liberates resources so that they can be more easily recruited by new organizations, facilitates the formation of free markets so that customers can transfer loyalties, depersonalizes economic social relations, simplifies the calculation of the advantages of alternative ways of doing things, and allows more precise anticipation of the consequences of future conditions on the organization.[28]

The *political base* of a society is also important. For the creation of a new organization, political revolutions are held to be important because of their rearranging of vested interest groups and power systems. Resources are allocated on bases different from those in the past.

The final societal condition identified by Stinchcombe is the existing level of *organizational density*. The greater the density and the greater the range of organizational alternatives already available, the greater the likelihood that people will have had experience in organizations. This suggests that there is likely to be an exponential growth curve for organizations in a society—assuming, of course, that the other conditions are also present.

Stinchcombe's discussion is concerned with the conditions of the society that are important for the development of new organizations and new organizational forms. These conditions are components of those discussed earlier in this chapter—the contemporary environmental conditions that are important for the life of an organization. While the picture is drawn in broader relief with historical data, the factors identified remain important for analyses at any particular point in time.

Technology and Organizational Form   Stinchcombe's article contains an additional set of ideas that is relevant for our purposes. He maintains that the technological conditions available at the time of the formation of an organization set the limits for the form the organization can take.

> Organizations which have purposes that can be efficiently reached with the socially possible organizational forms tend to be founded during the

[28] *Ibid.*, p. 152.

period in which they become possible. Then, both because they can function effectively with those organizational forms, and because the forms tend to become institutionalized, the basic structure of the organization tends to remain relatively stable.[29]

The emphasis on technology is consistent with the argument here, with the addition that if the newly introduced organizational form is compatible with the technology of the times, it tends to persist over time regardless of gradual changes in technology. This raises the question of whether or not the historical factors based on the technology of the period in which an organizational form develops outweigh later technological developments affecting the same kind of organization.

Tradition vs. Competition   Stinchcombe's answer to this question is illustrative of the interplay among the environmental factors that have been identified. He notes that the development of organizational forms is based on the factors suggested above, such as the availability of money, labor, and so on. These allow the development of the intermediate conditions that in turn permit the development of alternatives from the organizational forms of the past. Once an organizational form is developed, such as, for example, railroads, banks, or universities, the questions are: Do these forms persist over time in the face of changes in the environment, and if so, why? The answers lie in another relationship between organizations and their environment. Stinchcombe notes that organizations develop ideologies by which they can be legitimated in the society. Values are built up around the manner in which the organization operates. These values are transmitted to the external world and become part of the value system of the organizational members.

> Thus, in craft-organized industries, unions can and do appeal to the norms of craftsmanship—the value of the industrial discipline they provide—to defend the closed shop. The powers they use to defend their monopoly in the local labor market they obtained originally because they could in fact provide a skilled labor force on predictable terms. The current effectiveness of their strikes is a function of the degree to which craftsmen are in fact superior to untrained men for the work.[30]

While internal traditions and effective institutionalization provide a basis for the continuation of traditional forms, there is still the element of the competition of new forms within the same general technological

[29] *Ibid.*, p. 153.
[30] *Ibid.*, pp. 167–68.

base. Stinchcombe notes that the family farm and family retail business have largely disappeared in the face of competition from alternative forms. University medical schools have eliminated proprietary medical schools. Countries with common political backgrounds may contain rather different political party forms. If an organization is able to withstand competition or in fact has no competition, the power of tradition carries the day. The railroad industry prior to the emergence of truck, auto, and air transit is probably the most conspicuous example. It existed through time with essentially the same structure with which it began. Competition has forced slow, and in this case, painful, changes to take place. There is thus an interplay between the force of tradition and the demands of competition and new technologies.[31]

A note relating this discussion to the topic of the next chapter is in order here. Since tradition does play an important role in the way an organization operates, and since organizations are unlikely to change unless there is strong external pressure (in competitive, political, technological, or some other form) to change, organizations will tend to maintain their ways. This means that organizations are basically conservative, and they have a stabilizing, conservative, or even reactionary influence on the society around them. Social unrest at any period of history is directed at the organizations of the period—government, private industry, universities, or whatever is viewed by the restive segments of the population as impediments to progress. An understanding of why organizations are unlikely to change is thus a major tool for those who would seek to change the society as a whole. However, the successful development of new organizations and new organizational forms requires certain conditions. Thus, revolution cannot accomplish change without the presence of the appropriate conditions for organizational development.

The examination of the general environmental factors central to organizations has been inconclusive. While the roles of technology, legal patterns, culture, and so on, have been demonstrated to be important, we cannot even assign a ranking to the various factors to indicate their relative importance. The situation is further complicated by the fact that these general environmental factors themselves interact, so that it is difficult to isolate any one thing for analysis. This section must therefore conclude on the note that the relationships between organizations and their environment are complicated, but also crucial.

[31] A slightly modified approach to Stinchcombe's argument is that of Aldrich and Pfeffer, "Environments of Organizations." The basic conclusions remain the same.

THE SPECIFIC ENVIRONMENT—INTERORGANIZATIONAL RELATIONSHIPS

The specific environment is composed of the organizations and individuals with which an organization is in direct interaction. Our analysis will be focused on organizations, because although particular individuals, such as certain politicians or others who independently attack an organization because of real or imagined evils, can be very important, in the vast majority of cases such individuals are representatives of another organization.[32]

The Organization Set

The easiest way to begin the analysis is to introduce the notion of the "organization set."[33] In simple terms, the organization set is composed of organizations in interaction with a focal organization. They provide inputs and receive outputs. The complexity of the organization set can be seen in figures 11-1, 11-2, 11-3, and 11-4. The example is drawn from research on the social-control system for problem youth.[34] Figure 11-1 indicates the organizations in interaction with a focal organization, in this case the police. The frequency of the interaction is also indicated. Figure 11-2 indicates the degree of formalization of the relationship, the figure 11-3 indicates whether it is cooperative or conflictual.

These figures include only a few variables and a few members of the organization set. The complexity of the relationships is indicated by the fact that frequent interactions do not necessarily mean highly formalized or cooperative relations. In addition, it can be seen in Figure 11-3 that cooperation and conflict can exist in the same relationship. The organizations cooperate on some issues but conflict on others.

Another meaning implicit in the idea of the organization set is indicated in Figure 11-4, where the major linkages for the police are seen to be with other law-enforcement agencies.[35] While these relationships are

[32] The most conspicuous recent example of a single individual is Ralph Nader, who attacked and affected General Motors and the entire automobile industry. This sort of example is the exception, rather than the rule.

[33] See William M. Evan, "The Organization-Set: Toward a Theory of Interorganizational Relations," in James D. Thompson, ed., *Approaches to Organizational Design* (Pittsburgh: University of Pittsburgh Press, 1966); and Theodore Caplow, *Principles of Organization* (New York: Harcourt Brace Jovanovich, Inc., 1964), pp. 201–28.

[34] The research was conducted by the author and John P. Clark with support by NIMH Grant #2RO MH17508–03MH8.

[35] This approach to the organizational set is Caplow's, while the one depicted in Figures 11-1 to 11-3 is Evan's approach.

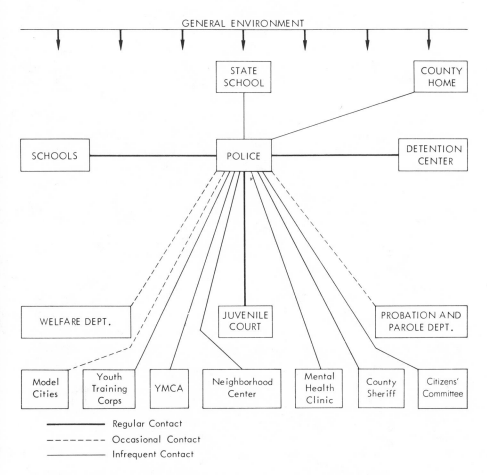

Figure 11-1   The organization set and interaction frequency

based on contacts in regard to law enforcement problems, they are also
a major basis by which the focal police department determines how well
it is doing. Organizations use other organizations of the same type both
for comparison purposes and as a source of new ideas.

The analysis of interorganizational relationships is complex. Not only
does an organization like the police have relationships with the sets of
organizations depicted in Figures 11-1 to 11-4, but they also have multiple
other sets of relationships. Each organization must purchase goods and
services. Many of these organizations have concerns other than problem
youths. The welfare department, for example, also is involved in financial
assistance programs with linkages to federal, state, and local organiza-

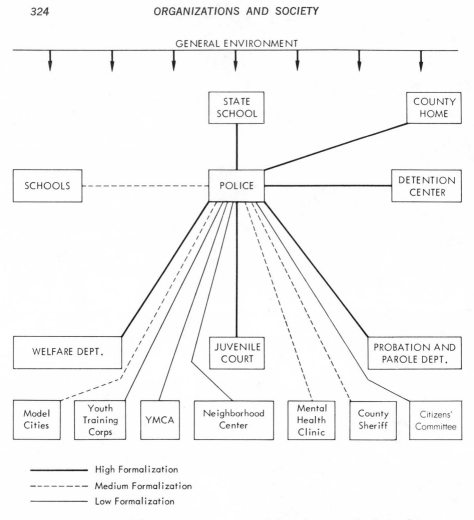

Figure 11-2   The organization set and formalization of relationships

tions as well as citizen's groups. In the discussion that follows, we will attempt to analyze interorganizational relationships so that they are understood in their own right and also in terms of their impact on the organizations involved.

The Importance of Interorganizational Relationships

Some analysts believe that interorganizational relationships are *the* most important aspect of society. They are seen as the key to power in

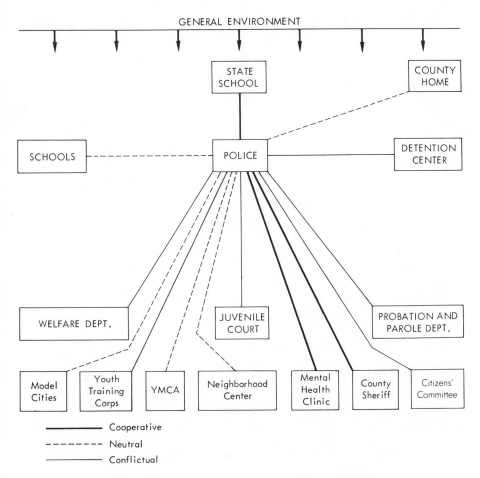

Figure 11-3   The organization set and conflict–cooperation

the society. It has been demonstrated that many business and financial organizations are linked by interlocking directorates;[36] it has been asserted that these interlocking directorates are the key to the military–

36 Joel H. Levine, "The Sphere of Influence," *American Sociological Review,* 37, No. 1 (February 1972), 14–27; Michael Patrick Allen, "The Structure of Interorganizational Elite Cooptation: Interlocking Corporate Directorates," *American Sociological Review,* 39, No. 3 (June 1974), 393–406; and Jeffrey Pfeffer, "Size and Composition of Corporate Boards of Directors: The Organization and its Environment," *Administrative Science Quarterly,* 17, No. 2 (June 1972), 218–28.

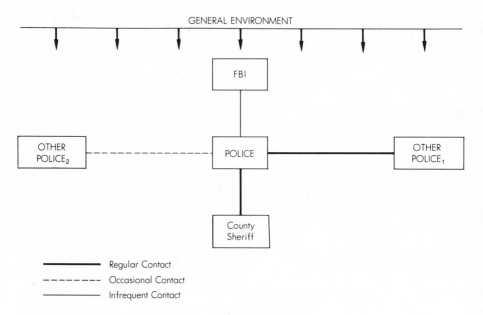

Figure 11-4   Another type of organization set

industrial complex in the United States and elsewhere.[37] It has also been shown that interorganizational linkages form the power bases in local communities, shaping decisions about the direction of the community.[38] It is also clear that interorganizational relationships are important to people in contact with organizations, because clients are often passed or referred from one organization to another.[39] The problems of governing

[37] Maurice Zeitlin, "Corporate Ownership and Control: The Large Corporation and the Capitalist Class," *American Journal of Sociology*, 79, No. 5 (March 1974), 1073–1119; Maurice Zeitlin, Lynda Ann Ewen, and Richard Earl Ratcliff, "New Princes for Old? The Large Corporation and the Capitalist Class in Chile," *American Journal of Sociology*, 80, No. 1 (July 1974), 87–123; and the classic, C. Wright Mills, *The Power Elite* (New York: Oxford University Press, 1957).

[38] Robert Perrucci and Marc Pilisuk, "Leaders and Ruling Elites: The Interorganizational Bases of Community Power," *American Sociological Review*, 35, No. 6 (December 1970), 1040–57.

[39] Yeheskel Hasenfeld and Richard A. English, eds., *Human Service Organizations* (Ann Arbor: The University of Michigan Press, 1974); Peggy C. Giordano, "The Juvenile Justice System: The Client Perspective" (unpublished Ph.D. dissertation, University of Minnesota, 1974); and Daniel Katz, Barbara A. Gutek, Robert L. Kahn, and Eugenia Barton, *Bureaucratic Encounters* (Ann Arbor: Survey Research Center, University of Michigan, 1975).

cities or nations can be viewed as an interorganizational phenomenon, since separate government units act as independent organizations.[40]

The Nature of Interorganizational Relationships

Sets of organizations can be examined and compared, as can total systems or networks.[41] It is also reasonable to focus on the patterns of relationships themselves to determine what leads to patterns of coordination or conflict. Another approach is to examine the relationships between organizational characteristics and interorganizational patterns.[42] But this approach presents a severe conceptual and methodological problem: it is extremely difficult to determine which is the dependent and which is the independent variable. Do organizational characteristics lead to certain patterns of interorganizational relationships, or is it the other way around —interorganizational patterns contribute to organizational characteristics? There is undoubtedly a reciprocal relationship that has been difficult to capture in the research conducted thus far.

Interorganizational relationships occur for several reasons. Probably the dominant one is that individual organizations seek to maximize or improve their own positions by entering into *exchange* relationships with other organizations.[43] If one organization has resources—money, person-

---

[40] David Rogers, *The Management of Big Cities* (Beverly Hills, Ca.: Sage Publications, 1971 ; and Edward C. Banfield, *The Unheavenly City* (Boston: Little, Brown and Company, 1970).

[41] For discussion of the different possible levels of analysis, see Cora Bagley Marrett, "On the Specification of Interorganizational Dimensions," *Sociology and Social Research*, 56, No. 1 (October 1971), 83–99; Andrew Van de Ven, Dennis Emmett, and Richard Koenig, Jr., "Frameworks for Interorganizational Analysis," *Organization and Administrative Sciences*, 5, No. 1 (Spring 1974), 113–29; Roland L. Warren, "The Interorganizational Field as a Focus for Investigation," *Administrative Science Quarterly*, 12, No. 3 (December 1967), 396–419; Joseph P. Morrissey, Patrick Horan, and Patricia Rieker, "Interorganizational Relations: Directions for Further Research" (Chapel Hill, N.C.: University of North Carolina, mimeographed paper, 1975); and Howard Aldrich, "Organization-Sets, Action-Sets, and Networks: Making the Most of Simplicity" (Ithaca, N.Y.: Cornell University, mimeographed paper, 1975).

[42] Michael Aiken and Jerald Hage, "Organizational Interdependence and Organizational Structure," *American Sociological Review*, 33, No. 6 (December 1968), 912–30; and Steven K. Paulson, "Causal Analysis of Interorganizational Relations: An Axiomatic Theory Revised," *Administrative Science Quarterly*, 19, No. 3 (September 1974), 319–37.

[43] Sol Levine and Paul E. White, "Exchange as a Conceptual Framework for the Study of Interorganizational Relationships," *Administrative Science Quarterly*, 5, No. 4 (March 1961), 583–601; and J. Kenneth Benson, "The Interorganizational Network as a Political Economy," *Administrative Science Quarterly*, 20, No. 2 (June 1975), 229–49.

nel, expertise, facilities—that another organization needs, then the organization needing the resources will try to enter an exchange relationship with the resource-holding organization. An exchange of something of equal value can be made, or the resource-needing organization can become dependent on the other organization, increasing the power of the latter.[44] This is part of the explanation of interlocking directorates and the power of financial institutions. Business firms need capital. They ask a director of a bank to sit on their board to give them readier access to capital. While they get their capital, they also lose their independence. The same sort of exchange occurs when organizations like hospitals agree to exchange services; one hospital prepares the food for the other, which in turn does the laundry service for the former.

Once an exchange agreement has been reached, the nature of the interactions between the organizations shifts. The interactions are more regularized and routine. The parties in the relationship give it less attention until a new exchange issue arises.

There is another important basis for interorganizational relationships. They can be required or mandated by law.[45] Most business organizations are required to interact with federal, state and local agencies of one kind or another. Government agencies themselves are required by law or policy to interact. Of the organizations that dealt with youths, for example, the welfare department was required to interact with the juvenile court each time the former decided that a child should be removed from his or her home. Although such legal requirements for interaction do not appear to diminish the potential for coordination among organizations, when coordination does occur it is achieved through different means and may be more difficult to achieve than when exchange is the basis of interaction.[46]

Most analyses of interorganizational relationships have focused on coordination.[47] Coordination can be viewed as an attempt to adapt to the

[44] Richard J. Butler, David J. Hickson, and Arthur E. McCullogh, "Power in the Organization Coalition" (paper delivered to the Eighth World Congress of Sociology, Toronto, 1974).

[45] Richard H. Hall, John P. Clark, Peggy C. Giordano, Paul V. Johnson, and Martha Van Roekel, "Patterns of Interorganizational Relationships" (Minneapolis: University of Minnesota, mimeographed paper, 1976).

[46] Ibid.

[47] See Walter B. Miller, "Inter-Institutional Conflict as a Major Impediment to Delinquency Prevention," Human Organization, 17, No. 3 (Fall 1958), 20–23; William Reid, "Interagency Coordination in Delinquency Prevention and Control," Social Service Review, 38, No. 4 (December 1964), pp. 418–28; and Benjamin Yep, "An Elaboration of the Concept of Coordination in Interorganizational Research" (Ames, Iowa: Iowa State University, mimeographed paper, 1974).

environment or as a specific means of goal attainment. Particularly in the area of human services, coordination has been an active policy goal. There is no evidence that coordination is a universal good, even in the area of human services, since it is quite possible to have well-coordinated but rotten programs.

Another component of interorganizational relationships is conflict.[48] Extreme interorganizational conflict is war. Far less extreme are conflicts over budget allocations among government agencies, conflicts over prices between buyer and seller, and conflicts over domain (sphere of influence or scope of program).[49] Like conflict in general, interorganizational conflict can benefit clients, the organizations involved, and the relationship itself if the conflict does not reach the destructive stage. Also, conflict and coordination can coexist in the same relationship.

Like the relationships among units and individuals within organizations, interorganizational relationships vary in the degree to which they are formalized.[50] Some relationships become so highly standardized that rules and regulations govern each interaction, while others are as casual as two people from different organizations running into each other and having a drink together. Like intraorganizational relationships, formalization of interorganizational relations is contingent upon what is being related and what participants are doing the relating.

The Context of Interorganizational Relationships

Like organizations themselves, interorganizational relationships occur in an environment. We will now briefly consider the context of interorganizational relationships and also consider the organizational characteristics related to them. As suggested earlier, of course, no particular cause-and-effect sequence can be assumed, since it cannot be demon-

[48] Henry Assael, "Constructive Role of Interorganizational Conflict," *Administrative Science Quarterly*, 14, No. 4 (December 1969), 573–82; Howard Aldrich, "Organizational Boundaries and Interorganizational Conflict," *Human Relations*, 26, No. 2 (April 1973), 203–14; and Harold Guetzkow, "Relations among Organizations," in *Studies on Behavior in Organizations*, Raymond V. Bower, ed., (Athens: University of Georgia Press, 1966).

[49] See Marshall W. Meyer, "Organizational Domains" *American Sociological Review*, 40, No. 6 (October 1975), 599–615; James D. Thompson, *Organizations in Action* (New York: McGraw Hill Book Company, 1967).

[50] Eugene Litwak and Lydia Hylton, "Interorganizational Analysis: A Hypothesis on Coordinating Agencies," *Administrative Science Quarterly*, 6, No. 4 (March 1962), 395–420; and Eugene Litwak and Jerald Rothman, "Towards the Theory and Practice of Coordination Between Formal Organizations," in William Rosengren and Mark Lefton, eds., *Organizations and Clients* (Columbus, O.: Charles E. Merrill, 1970).

strated that either organizational or environmental characteristics lead to or result from interorganizational characteristics.

The number or frequency of interorganizational relationships has been shown to be related to such characteristics of urban areas as the scale of the municipal government, the strength of political parties, and the impact of local voluntary organizations.[51] The need for interorganizational relationships in programs such as poverty or health is also related to the initiation of interactions. If there are a small number of organizations in an industry, more movement of personnel between the organizations is likely. (The movement of personnel between organizations is a form of interorganizational relationships that has not received much attention.)[52] In highly uncertain environments, organizations are likely to try to develop as many links to other organizations as possible in order to protect themselves.[53] The same is probably also true in terms of environmental scarcity. Particular interorganizational networks are vitally affected by their linkages to legislative bodies, government bureaus, the political arena, and other sources of control.[54]

Organizational characteristics related to interorganizational relationships resemble what would be expected from earlier discussions. High degrees of formalization and centralization are related to lower levels of interorganizational interaction; and complexity, as indicated by the number of specialized personnel, is related to higher levels of interaction.[55] Personnel in boundary-spanning roles (those in direct interaction with other organizations) have a great potential for obtaining power in the

[51] Herman Turk, *Interorganizational Activation in Urban Communities* (Washington, D.C.: American Sociological Association, 1973).

[52] Jeffrey Pfeffer and Huseyin Leblebici, "Executive Recruitment and the Development of Interfirm Organizations," *Administrative Science Quarterly*, 18, No. 4 (December 1973), 449–61; and Gordon B. Baty, William M. Evan and Terry W. Rothermel, "Personnel Flows as Interorganizational Relations," *Administrative Science Quarterly*, 16, No. 4 (December 1971), 430–43.

[53] Paul M. Hirsch, "Processing Fads and Fashions: An Organization-Set Analysis of Cultural Industry Systems," *American Journal of Sociology*, 72, No. 4 (January 1972), 639–59.

[54] J. Kenneth Benson, "The Interorganizational Network as a Political Economy," *Administrative Science Quarterly*, 20, No. 2 (June 1975), 229–49.

[55] Steven K. Paulson, "Causal Analysis of Interorganizational Relations: An Axiomatic Theory Revised," *Administrative Science Quarterly*, 19, No. 3 (September 1974), 319–37; and Michael Aiken and Jerald Hage, "Interorganizational Dependence and Intraorganizational Structure," *American Sociological Review*, 33, No. 6 (December 1968), 912–30. Paulson found that formalization was positively (and indirectly) related to interorganizational interaction, but Aiken and Hage's original formulation still seems more plausible.

organization.[56] At the same time, the fact that personnel have contact with other organizations is important for the attitudes of the boundary-spanners.[57] Their contacts alter their own perceptions of the environment. Interorganizational contacts at the personal level increase the likelihood of diffusion of innovations and of organizational change.[58] If a person has a friend in another organization and the other organization is trying something new, word of this is likely to spread through informal friendship channels. Key decision makers in the organization are also important. If the key personnel themselves are oriented toward organizational boundaries and are active in such external activities as professional associations or other such cross-organizational groups, they are more oriented toward linkages with other organizations.[59]

Most of the evidence in regard to interorganizational relationships, with the exception of that dealing with interlocking directorates and boards of directors, has come from organizations that deal with human services.[60] There is virtually no information on the interactions of other government organizations or of other forms of interaction among business firms. Given the theoretical and practical importance of such relationships, it is puzzling that so little research in business and government organizations has been conducted.

Interorganizational relationships are obviously critical for organizations. There is some limited evidence that institutionalized interaction among organizational elites is related to organizational effectiveness.[61] Such relationships permit interorganizational transactions to take place more smoothly. This, of course, ignores the issue of who may or may not benefit from increased organizational effectiveness, since organized crime and price-fixing appear to be prime examples of institutionalized cooperation among elites. It should, however, be noted that institutionalized interorganizational affiliations can place some member organizations in

[56] Howard Aldrich and Diane Herker, "Boundary Spanning Roles and Organization Structure," (Ithaca, N.Y.: Cornell University, mimeographed paper, 1974).

[57] Jeffrey Pfeffer, "Interorganizational Influence and Managerial Attitudes," *Academy of Management Journal*, 15, No. 3 (September 1972), 317–30.

[58] John A. Czepiel, "Patterns of Interorganizational Communications and the Diffusion of a Major Technological Innovation in a Competitive Industrial Community," *Academy of Management Journal*, 18, No. 1 (March 1974), 6–24.

[59] John R. Schermerhorn, Jr., "Openness to Interorganizational Cooperation: A Study of Hospital Administrators," *Academy of Management Journal*, forthcoming.

[60] Jerald Hage and Richard H. Hall in separate remarks at the Midwest Sociological Society Annual Meetings, Chicago, 1975.

[61] Charles L. Mulford and Carolyn Marzec Sriram, "Interorganizational Relations and Organizational Effectiveness" (Ames, Iowa: Iowa State University, mimeographed paper, 1973).

jeopardy.[62] The involvement of the National Council of Churches in the civil rights movement cost churches with Southern constituencies both membership and money. Some of the paradoxes in findings such as these are accounted for by the fact that the analysis of interorganizational relationships is in its formative stages.

SUMMARY AND CONCLUSIONS

This chapter has dealt with the critical factors in the environments of organizations. While hampered by inadequate evidence, it should be clear that the general environment in which an organization is operating and the specific environment of other organizations have direct and indirect influences on any organization. The specific details and mechanisms of these impacts are not as well known as we would like, but any organizational analysis must be concerned with environmental factors.

Environmental conditions are important contingencies for organizations about which choices must be made. Its interaction with the environment is a crucial determinant of the viability of an organization. Indeed, the internal structure and process are largely developed in response to the environment, either as a reaction to something that has happened or in anticipation of something that might.

The final chapter will deal with the influence of the organization on the environment. As we have seen in the present chapter, organizations are not just passive recipients of environmental pressures. Organizations are actors in their social system.

[62] James R. Wood, "Unanticipated Consequences of Organizational Coalitions: Ecumenical Cooperation and Civil Rights Policy," *Social Forces*, 50, No. 4 (June 1972), 512–21.

12

organizations and social change

In this final chapter our analysis comes full circle. We return to the topic the book began with: the role of organizations in society, but with the major difference that here our emphasis is on social change and the role of organizations in promoting and resisting change. This dual nature of organizations in their relationship to social change will be examined. We will try to indicate the ways in which organizations contribute to social change, relating this to the nature of the organizations themselves, and then look more closely at the resistance shown by organizations toward the change process. We continue to employ the general perspective that has been taken throughout, namely that organizations act to control the factors that are important to their existence.

It is an evident but frequently ignored fact that social change is dependent upon organizations. At times, people like to believe that the great and small social movements in our past and present society are the consequence of particular individuals with charismatic qualities. One need only point out, however, that such diverse movements as Christianity and communism are at the core organizational movements. So, too, are apparently smaller scale phenomena, such as consumerism, the environmental movement, or any effort in behalf of a newly emergent nation, such as Angola or Vietnam. Counter efforts are also organizationally based.

These self-evident truths must be balanced by another that is less evident: *organizations are great resisters of change.* Again, the perspective of this book has been that organizational structures and processes are developed to serve as predictors and controllers of actions by the organization and its members. Organizations are conservative by their very nature. They resist change and the introduction of new patterns. Anyone who has tried to introduce an innovation into a college or university curriculum, alter hospital admitting procedures, fight city hall, or start or stop a program within a government agency has been brought face to face with organizational conservatism.

A major assumption that will soon be evident is that an organizationally dense society is one in which the change process is both rapid and intense. In the discussion in the previous chapter, it was stated that particular social conditions must be ripe if new organizations and organizational forms are to emerge. In a society in which a wide variety of organizations and organizational forms exists, as in the contemporary United States, social change is also a constant condition.[1] So we will not spend time discussing whether or not social change is a fact for an organizational society.

In this chapter a neutral stance will be taken toward change; that is, no assumption will be made that change is progress. While everyone probably has a pet change that he or she would like to see instituted and others that he or she would resist strongly, it is not the intent here to advocate any kinds of changes as being most beneficial for the society or the organizations involved. Like anyone else, I have ideas about changes I would like to see in the society, some of which I feel may even be necessary for the survival of the society. However, since the appropriateness of such changes can be demonstrated only by a form of evidence different from the one we are considering here, it would be a disservice to the analysis to get into political, economic, or social advocacy. If the examples and analysis make sense, other examples can be inserted at the reader's will.

The same point holds for the discussion of organizations as resisters of change. Bookshelves are filled with both serious and humorous accounts of the persistence of organizations in the face of extreme demands for change. The negative connotation of the term "bureaucracy" indicates the emotional coloration given to organizational unresponsiveness toward change. Here again, a nonevaluative approach will be taken.

Aside from the general scientific norm that calls for objectivity and dispassionate discussions, there are pragmatic reasons for the position of neutrality taken here. The basic reason is the absence of reliable evidence regarding what constitutes a good change, or when an organization is damaging the society around it by its resistance to change. In specific cases, this can be relatively easily determined, but for a total analysis it gets risky. If our knowledge about organizations and social change is at all correct, it should be equally relevant, regardless of the persuasion —left, right, or center—for all organizations, their members, and their publics. The analysis which follows will of necessity shift levels—from

---

[1] Phillip Hauser argues that the tempo of change is accelerated in an organizational society such as ours. See Hauser, "The Chaotic Society: Product of the Social Morphological Revolution," *American Sociological Review*, 34, No. 1 (February 1969), 1–19.

the organization to the society to the individual and to groups. The over-riding thrust of the argument remains that organizations are at the core of any consideration of social change.

THE ORGANIZATION AND THE SOCIAL STRUCTURE

We will begin with the usual caveat that the analysis is hampered by the absence of good data. Most of the information comes from the limited number of published case studies. Examples of attempts to change society typically deal with successful efforts—as in the case of studies of politicians; we know very little about the losers. While we are concerned with change, and ineffective attempts at change therefore are not a central concern, it would be useful to be able to compare successful and unsuccessful efforts.

Organizations are both agents of change and major studies of societal stability. William Dill notes:

> In countries like the United States and Canada, most of the nations of Western Europe, Australia, or Japan, business organizations are the most powerful. They provide the major source of employment and income and some of the major bases for determining social status. They decide in large measure what shall be produced and how much.[2]

In other societies, government organizations perform the same functions. Regardless of the form of the economy, organizations are the major decision makers for the priorities and actualities of the society.

There is another way in which organizations are important for the social structure. Since modern work is almost exclusively organizational work, and since total life styles are decreasingly influenced by the ascriptive components of age, sex, race, ethnicity, or other such factors, occupational roles and the interrelationships between these roles are a major component in determining the overall social structure.[3] The organizations set occupational rewards of all sorts. In addition, they shape their surrounding social structures. We have seen that interorganizational coalitions determine the power structures of local communities. In communities dominated by a single industry—be it a coal mine, a university, the

---

[2] William R. Dill, "Business Organizations," in James G. March, ed., *Handbook of Organizations* (Chicago: Rand McNally & Co., 1965), p. 1101.

[3] For a discussion of this point, see Richard H. Hall, *Occupations and the Social Structure*, 2nd ed. (Englewood Cliffs, N.J.: Prentice-Hall, Inc., 1975).

government itself (Washington, D.C., is an unusual city), or a ski resort—the entire community is dependent on and thus shaped by the particular organization and its policies.

Organizations are change agents in two ways. The first involves internal changes in respect to organizational membership, while the second involves direct attempts by organizations to intervene in the social system.

Internal Change and the Social Structure

Internal organizational changes can affect the social structure in two ways. The first is by changing membership patterns. If an organization alters its stance toward minority group members, women, or the aging, there is a direct impact on the social structure. Moreover, by the hiring of more women or minority-group members (a condition usually brought about by such external pressures as affirmative action programs) the patterns of the surrounding communities are affected as needs for child care facilities are increased or as more minority-group members move into the area. If the minority-group members are at anything other than the low-skill levels, residential patterns are affected, since ghetto residences are not sought by minority professionals or executives. Similarly, the importation of low-skill minority group members has traditionally led to the creation of ghettos.

The second way in which internal changes affect the social structure is through altered patterns of work. Although it is unclear whether or not a person's attitude toward the job work affects his or her outlook on life, or vice versa, there is certainly a relationship.[4] Thus, changes in the manner in which work is performed—such as through programs of participative management, job enlargement or enrichment, or through other such mechanisms—would appear to be related to other important social relationships. Alteration of superior–subordinate patterns such as making them more egalitarian or by otherwise altering the reward structure would appear to have an important carry-over effect for the society. This is said not on the basis of firm evidence, but rather on the basis of our knowledge of the powerful role of organizations in society.

Two additional aspects of the impact of organizations on their members and its relationship with the overall social structure deserve mention. While it is not clear whether a dull or exciting position in an organization leads to a dull or exciting life outside the organization, it is evident that a person's occupation has important consequences for other aspects of personal life. For example, political outlook, patterns of family life, and general life style have been shown to be linked to an individ-

4 *Ibid.*

ual's occupation. Organizations with occupations encouraging dissent and controversy, as opposed to conformity and acceptance of the status quo, would have members who carried this style of life outside the organization. Since organizations affect the way in which their various constituent occupations are oriented, there is an organizational effect on the way people view and act toward the world around them.[5] This effect is balanced by nonorganizational factors as well, but the organization does make a difference. Here again, comparative research is needed to determine exactly how much membership in various forms of organizations contributes to the variance in people's approaches to life.

Voluntary Organizations   The final point in this discussion involves organizations that are *designed* to have an impact on the behaviors and attitudes of their members. The voluntary organization, in most cases, is established to be a force affecting the lives and behaviors of its members. People belong to voluntary organizations because they believe in what the organization stands for and would like to see it promoted. (This ignores that element of voluntary-organization membership that is present for nonnormative reasons.) It is probably very safe to assume that the voluntary-organization membership of an individual is a good indicator of some of his or her salient values. Even when this assumption is made, however, the question remains as to whether the membership itself has any effect on individual attitudes and behaviors. The answer is that such memberships undoubtedly reinforce predispositions already present when the person joins the organization.

This answer is not very useful, however, since there are insufficient indications of the extent to which such memberships are balanced against other facts of the individual's life. Research into the impact of membership in religious organizations, for example, has led to largely inconclusive results regarding the impact of such membership as opposed to that of the persons place in the social stratification system, his or her occupation, place of origin, and so on.[6] Without an extended discussion of the importance of such memberships vis-à-vis other important considerations, it is sufficient for our purposes here to note that voluntary-organization memberships have some consequences for the people involved, but it would appear that such consequences are not as strong as

---

[5] Melvin Kohn, "Bureaucratic Man: A Portrait and Interpretation," *American Sociological Review*, 36, No. 3 (June 1971), 461–74.

[6] See Gerhard Lenski, *The Religious Factor* (Garden City, N.Y.: Doubleday & Company, Inc., Anchor Books, 1963). See also Howard Schuman, "The Religious Factor in Detroit: Review, Replication, and Reanalysis," *American Sociological Review*, 36, No. 1 (February 1971), 30–48; and Gerhard Lenski, "The Religious Factor in Detroit: Revisited," *American Sociological Review*, 36, No. 1 (February 1971), 48–50.

those of other conditions under which the person is living. Voluntary-organization memberships thus appear to be modifiers of attitudes and behaviors formed for the individual through his life history.

THE ORGANIZATION AS A CHANGE AGENT

Besides affecting society (largely unintentionally) through their structuring of social life and impacts on members, organizations are also active participants in the social-change process. This can be most easily seen in the political arena, as organizations lobby and fight for legislation and rulings favorable to their own programs. A favorable decision for one organization leads to programs that in turn affect the society. Whenever a government agency is established to carry out a new program, it becomes a social-change agent. We will begin the analysis of change agents with this point, moving from this rather established, accepted form of social change to a consideration of organizations as revolutionary agents.

A classic example of the organization as a change agent is provided by Selznick's study of the Tennessee Valley Authority (TVA) during its formative years.[7] In addition to its pertinence to the analysis of change, this study is also very important for its contribution to the topic of the last chapter—the environmental impact on the organization. There is a reciprocal relationship between organizations and their environments. Each affects the other as they interact.

The TVA Act was passed by the U.S. Congress in 1933.

A great public power project was envisioned mobilizing the "by-product" of dams built for the purpose of flood control and navigation improvement on the Tennessee River and its tributaries. Control and operation of the nitrate properties, to be used for fertilizer production, was also authorized, although this aspect was subordinated to electricity. . . . A new regional concept—the river basin as an integral unit—was given effect, so that a government agency was created which has a special responsibility neither national nor state-wide in scope.[8]

That the TVA has had an effect on the physical environment is evident. Of greater interest for our purposes here is its effect on the social system

---

[7] Phillip Selznick, *TVA and The Grass Roots* (New York: Harper Torchbook Edition, 1966). Originally published by the University of California Press, Berkeley and Los Angeles, 1949.

[8] *Ibid.*, pp. 4–5.

into which it was placed. An important consideration in understanding the social effects of the TVA is the fact that the organization was designed to be decentralized. Not only were decisions within the organization to be made at the lowest reasonable levels with participation by members, but local organizations and even local citizens were also to be brought into the decision-making process. For example, the agricultural-extension services of the land-grant colleges were intimately involved with the TVA. This, of course, is one of the prime examples of co-optation, or "the process of absorbing new elements into the leadership or policy-determining structure of an organization as a means of averting threats to its stability or existence."[9]

Co-optation, however, is a two-way process. The organization is affected by the new elements brought into its decision-making process; Selznick documents the manner in which some activities of the TVA were deflected from the original goals because of the new elements in the system. At the same time, the co-optation process affects the system from which the elements were co-opted. The presence of the agricultural-extension element from the land-grant colleges gave this part of the local system much more strength than it had had in the past. The American Farm Bureau Federation was also brought into the process at an early point. In both these cases, the inclusion of one group was associated with the exclusion of another. Black colleges and non-Farm Bureau farm organizations either lost power or did not benefit to the degree that co-opted organizations did. In addition, the strength of the Farm Bureau in the decision-making process led to the exclusion from the area of other federal government farm programs. Regardless of their merits, these programs were therefore unavailable to the system. Selznick notes, "This resulted in the politically paradoxical situation that the eminently New Deal TVA failed to support agencies with which it shared a political communion, and aligned itself with the enemies of those agencies."[10] This becomes a rather complex analysis when one considers the fact that the other government programs involved were also part of the same larger organization, so that internal politics in one large organization were affected by the external relationships of some of its component parts.

An organization like the TVA affects the surrounding social organization. Some elements prosper while others suffer. New social relationships arise as alliances among affected individuals and organizations are formed. Thus, an organization specifically designed to be a change agent

9 *Ibid.*, p. 13.
10 *Ibid.*, p. 263.

is exactly that, but in ways that can be most inconsistent with the original intent of the planners. The dynamics of the interactions with the environment affect both the organization and its environment.

In a later reexamination of the study, Selznick notes that the TVA has recently been attacked by conservationists for strip mining.[11] The need for coal for its power productions and the strength of those supporting an expansion of this function within the TVA has led to a further environmental impact. Selznick attributes the current state of the TVA to the internal struggles that occurred in its early history—struggles to obtain environmental support. Since such support is selective, a strong organization such as this rearranges the world around it. If the groups in power in the TVA see the need for a greater capacity for generating electrical power as more important than soil conservation, the internal decision-making process, affected as it is by external pressures, makes a further impact on the social and physical environment.

The Organizational Weapon   In another analysis of organizations as change agents, Selznick studied the bolshevik revolution in Russia.[12] Here he analyzes the nature and role of the "organizational weapon." In defining what he means, Selznick states:

> We shall speak of organizations and organizational practices as weapons when they are used by a power-seeking elite *in a manner unrestrained by the constitutional order of the arena within which the contest takes place.* In this usage, "weapon" is not meant to denote *any* political tool, but one torn from its normal context and unacceptable to the community as a legitimate mode of action. Thus the partisan practices used in an election campaign insofar as they adhere to the written and unwritten rules of the contest—are not weapons in this sense. On the other hand, when members who join an organization in apparent good faith are in fact the agents of an outside elite, then routine affiliation becomes "infiltration."[13]

An important component of the organizational weapon is the *"distinctive competence to turn members of a voluntary association into disciplined and deployable political agents."*[14]

The Organization as the Requisite of Social Change   Before turning to some elements of Selznick's analysis, we must point out that the organizational weapon cannot be regarded as a tactic of the bolsheviks

---

[11] *Ibid.*, pp. xii–xiii.
[12] Phillip Selznick, *The Organizational Weapon* (New York: The Free Press, 1960).
[13] *Ibid.*, p. 2.
[14] *Ibid.*, p. xii.

alone. Indeed, it is the vital component of most major social changes and of change within the organization itself. In other words, in order to achieve change, *there must be organization.* This organization requires the kind of commitment to which Selznick refers. Spontaneous demonstrations or collective emotional responses may be sincere and well-intended, but longer-lasting movements toward change must come about through the organizational mode. And Selznick's reference to "constitutionality" can be translated into the *official* and accepted set of organizational arrangements that make up the "constitution" of any organization. The concern here is thus with the organizational weapon as it seeks to change any ongoing societal or organizational arrangement.

The scope of the organization as a weapon is determined by its aims. Even if the change sought is a limited one and one that will not upset the basic system under attack, the change agent still must be viewed as a weapon, although of less scope than one that seeks total organizational or societal change. The aim of bolshevism was total societal change. The basic means of accomplishing the movement's goal was the "combat party." Cadres of dedicated men are a basic component of such parties. This dedication requires that the individuals be totally committed to the cause, insulated from other concerns, and absorbed in the movement. Once a core of dedicated personnel is available, the party must protect itself from internal dissension, banning power centers that might threaten the official leadership. The party must be capable of mobilization and manipulation; it must be protected from possible isolation from the people it hopes to convert and also from possible liquidation at the hands of the existing authorities; and it must struggle for power in every possible area of action. This struggle can take place through seeking official recognition, as well through conspiratorial or illegal practices. And at all times, the basic ideology must be kept at the forefront of the members' minds.[15]

The operation of these principles can be seen in the history of the movement that Selznick carefully traces. This manifesto for an organizational weapon is potentially applicable at any point in history, in any social setting, and at either the total societal or more microcosmic levels. A revolt of junior high school students exhibits the same characteristics as the bolshevik movement, and so does the history of early Christianity.

For our purposes, the important thing is not the cause being advanced, but rather the fact that having a cause is not enough for social change. The cause must be organized if it is to be successful. The organization can be a successful change agent if it is capable of maintaining dedica-

<hr />

[15] *Ibid.,* pp. 72–73.

tion and gaining power in the system. The specific means of gaining power will depend on the situation. Political or military power is successful only where it is relevant. Selznick says:

> We must conclude, therefore, that in the long view political combat plays only a tactical role. Great social issues such as those which divide communism and democracy are not decided by political combat, perhaps not even by military clashes. They are decided by the relative ability of the contending systems to win and to maintain enduring loyalties.
> Consequently, no amount of power and cunning in the realm of political combat can avail in the absence of measures which rise to the height of the times.[16]

The implication is that the specific tactics used in the bolshevik movement may not be effective in another setting, but that the need for a dedicated membership and the concern for power are central to the change process.

Societal Support   Throughout the analysis in this book, we have stressed the reciprocal nature of the relationship between an organization and its environment. This is seen in clear relief in the consideration of organizations as change agents. The basic processes are the same in all effective change situations; to be successful an organizational weapon must gain power and support in the society it is attempting to change. The pages of history are filled with abortive efforts that did not gather sufficient support from the society they were trying to change. The basic set of ideas underlying the change effort must therefore be compatible—or become compatible—with the values of the population as a whole. These values of the wider community can be altered during the change process to become more congruent with those of the change agent. At the same time, the change agent itself can become altered as it seeks support from the wider community.

The importance of this form of support can be extrapolated from Joseph Gusfield's analysis of the Women's Christian Temperance Union.[17] This organization was highly successful in its attempts to change society through the passage of legislation prohibiting the sale of alcoholic beverages. Its tactics were appropriate for the values of the times, and it succeeded in mobilizing support from a sufficiently large segment of the population. But later, as it became evident that Prohibition was not

---

[16] *Ibid.*, p. 333.

[17] Joseph R. Gusfield, *Symbolic Crusade* (Urbana, Ill.: University of Illinois Press, 1963).

accomplishing what it was intended to do—and indeed had some un-
intended consequences that have lasted until the present—and as the
originally supportive society changed, the WCTU was faced with a
decision regarding its future. It could have altered its stance toward
alcohol to keep it in line with the prevailing opinions or maintained its
position in favor of total abstinence. The latter course was selected as the
result of decisions made within the organization. The consequences of
the decision were to isolate the movement from the population, reducing
it to virtual ineffectiveness as a force in the wider society.

It is difficult to predict what might have happened if the stance had
been altered to one of temperance rather than abstinence. It well might
be that the whole antialcohol movement was one whose time had passed.
It might also be that the WCTU would have had a greater educational
and social impact if its position had shifted with the times. At any rate,
what was once an important social movement became a small, socially
insignificant organization.

The social system around it thus affects the social-change agent as
much as it does any other form of organization. While such organizations
can appear to be revolutionary, deviant, martyred, or to fit any other
emotion-laden category, the fact remains that they are organizations. The
critical aspect is the acceptance of the organization by society. This is
obviously important for any organization, since to survive it must receive
support in one form or another, but for these change-oriented ones it is
even more so. Unfortunately (or fortunately in some cases), because
organizational analysts, decision makers, and politicians have not figured
out exactly how to determine when an idea's time has come, the organization embarking on a change mission is in a precarious position at best.

There are other, more subtle ways in which organizations are change
agents. As Perrow notes:

> We tend to forget, or neglect, the fact that organizations have an enormous
> potential for affecting the lives of all who come into contact with them.
> They control or can activate a multitude of resources, not just land and
> machinery and employees, but police, governments, communications, art,
> and other areas, too. That is, an organization, as a legally constituted entity,
> can ask for police protection and public prosecution, can sue, and can
> hire a private police force with considerably wider latitude and power than
> an individual can command. It can ask the courts to respond to requests
> and make legal rulings. It can petition for changes in other areas of
> government—zoning laws, fair-trade laws, consumer labeling, and protection
> and health laws. It determines the content of advertising, the art work in
> its products and packages, the shape and color of its buildings. It can
> move out of a community, and it selects the communities in which it will
> build. It can invest in times of imminent recession or it can retrench;

support or fight government economic policies or fair employment practices. In short, organizations generate a great deal of power that may be used in a way not directly related to producing goods and services or to survival.[18]

Rather obviously, the power potential of organizations is often used to thwart change, as will be seen in the next section. Even when an organization is an active change agent, if the change is accomplished, the organization tends then to resist further changes. The labor-union movement, which was once considered revolutionary, is now viewed by some as reactionary. National revolutions lead to established governments that in turn are attacked as opponents of social progress. Industries that alter the composition of a society resist new technologies and social patterns.

Constraints   Organizations do not change the society around them at will. All the environmental influences on organizations also constrain it as a change agent. This point is most graphically seen in the case of organizations in developing nations. If development is a national goal, then almost all organizations in such a society are designed to be change agents. A basic problem, however, is that the organizational forms that work in developed societies do not necessarily work in the case of those just developing. For example, R. S. Milne notes that there is a strong tendency for superiors not to delegate authority to subordinates. This is seen as a result of the lack of shared values among the different ranks, differing conceptions of authority, incompetence or lack of training among the subordinates, and the fear of loss of opportunity to earn income corruptly.[19] Similarly, subordinates seem unwilling to accept power. Studies in the Philippines and Latin America have noted the unwillingness of middle-level administrators to make decisions.[20] Milne states that in addition to the shortage of skills, deficiencies in training, lack of resources, and poor communications, the general culture precludes effective administration. Loyalty to the organization, for example, is an alien notion and thus is not present to supplement the formal channels.[21] Milne concludes that effective administration cannot be achieved unless the general cultural conditions also change.

Because of the cultural and other environmental constraints, organizations in developing societies must take a different form from those in

[18] Perrow, *Organizational Analysis*, pp. 170–71.

[19] R. S. Milne, "Mechanistic and Organic Models of Public Administration in Developing Countries," *Administrative Science Quarterly*, 15, No. 1 (March 1970), 57.

[20] *Ibid.*, p. 58.

[21] *Ibid.*, p. 62.

more developed situations.[22] It is generally suggested that such an organization must operate in a less formalized manner, taking into account the particular environment in which it is trying to operate.

But despite the constraints, organizations in developing societies do affect those societies. They do things that were not done before, in terms of yielding goods and services and arranging social relationships, and this simple fact alone affects the surrounding society. Not all such societies will become Westernized or bureaucratized, but they will be different from what they were before the advent of organizations. As in many other situations, the exact direction and extent of the organizational impact is not known, but the impact itself can be seen on the immediate alterations of the social fabric. A more subtle effect one occurs between generations. Each succeeding generation will tend to be more accepting of the presence of organizations, creating generation gaps and also altering the organizational environment. A previously hostile environment may become accepting. Here again, the *reciprocity* of the organizational–societal relationship can be seen.

Before we turn to the discussion of organizations as resisters of change, it should be reiterated that organizations have a wide variety of impacts on the environment. These range from the exciting examples of revolution or pollution to the more mundane but equally important matters of establishing and maintaining equilibrium in the system. In a comprehensive analysis, organizations must be viewed as a major stabilizing factor in society. Each kind of output has an impact on society, from the production of goods to the development of ideas. As we have noted repeatedly, this output must be of some value to the society; but it may also have by-products that are harmful to the society. Since an organizational society contains a multitude of values, it must also be recognized that what is of value to one segment of the society may be violently opposed by another segment. Thus, organizations that provide drugs or prostitutes are still organizations and can only be understood as such.

Because organizations do have outputs that in either intent or effect are opposed to those of other organizations, another point is raised about the organizational impact on society. Organizations are at the source of much of the conflict in society. While individual conflict in the form of fights, debates, shootouts, and so on, are the stuff of which movies and newspaper headlines are made, it is conflict between organizations that really alters the fabric of society. The ability to wage a successful con-

[22] See particularly Fred W. Riggs, *Administration in Developing Countries* (Boston: Houghton Mifflin Company, 1964); and Victor A. Thompson, "Administrative Objectives for Development Administration," *Administrative Science Quarterly*, 9, No. 1 (June 1964), 91–108.

flict is largely tied to the organizational capacities of the parties involved. The outcome of a conflict is usually alteration of the situation that existed before the conflict. Since organizations are such an important component of conflict in society, it follows that organizations are central to social change through this mechanism.

ORGANIZATIONS AS RESISTERS OF CHANGE

An earlier section began with the point that organizations are a major structuring component in society. This structuring takes place through the work roles of the members of the organizations and the values that organizational membership can impart. Organizations are a means of structuring the activities of the members. This in and of itself is a structuring element. Since our concern in this chapter is with change, it is important to go beyond the basic fact of organizational contributions to social stability. Organizations also actively resist change. This resistance is directed toward change introduced from outside the organization. The organization attempts to protect itself. Obviously, changes that are not important to the organization will not bring an organizational response.

Again, organizations by their very nature are conservative. This is seen in the political stances taken and in economic policies. When the focus is shifted to how the organization itself operates, the point becomes even more clear. *Organizations operate conservatively regardless of whether they are viewed as radical or as reactionary by the general population.* Seymour Martin Lipset's analysis of populist rural socialism in Saskatchewan, Canada[23] provides an example of this point. In 1944, the Cooperative Commonwealth Federation (CCF) came to power in the province. The objective was "the social ownership of all resources and the machinery of wealth production to the end that we may establish a Cooperative Commonwealth in which the basic principle regulating production, distribution and exchange will be the supplying of human needs instead of the making of profits."[24] This aim has been only partially realized. One reason has been continued political opposition to the movement; another, consistent with the argument here, is that the movement itself apparently became more conservative as power was achieved. An additional important consideration is the fact that the new socialist government utilized

[23] Seymour Martin Lipset, *Agrarian Socialism* (Berkeley and Los Angeles: University of California Press, 1950).
[24] *Ibid.*, p. 130.

the existing government structures in attempting to carry out its program. In explanation Lipset notes:

> Trained in the traditions of a laissez-faire government and belonging to conservative social groups, the civil service contributes significantly to the social inertia which blunts the changes a new radical government can make. Delay in initiating reforms means that the new government becomes absorbed in the process of operating the old institutions. The longer a new government delays making changes, the more responsible it becomes for the old practices and the harder it is to make the changes it originally desired to institute.[25]

The reason for this blunting is quite simple. The new ruling cabinet had to rely on the system already in operation.

> The administratively insecure cabinet ministers were overjoyed at the friendly response they obtained from the civil servants. *To avoid making administrative blunders* [emphasis added] that would injure them in the eyes of the public and the party, the ministers began to depend on the civil servants. As one cabinet minister stated in an interview, "I would have been lost if not for the old members of my staff. I'm only a beginner in this work. B———— has been at it for twenty years. If I couldn't go to him for advice, I couldn't have done a thing. Why now (after two years in office) I am only beginning to find my legs and make my own decisions. . . . I have not done a thing for two years without advice."[26]

It is important to note that the aims of the movement can be blunted without malice or intent. It is not a personal matter, but an organizational one. Certainly, personal motivations can enter the picture in an important way, but the crucial factor is that the new leaders did not understand the organizations they were to head. The organization itself contained rules and procedures that had to be learned along the way, so that the organization became the instrument that deflected the party in power from its goals.

The organization trains its members to follow a system for carrying out its activities. It would require a complete resocialization before the takeover of a new party if this sort of thing were to be prevented. This, of course, is impossible in government organizations. An alternative

[25] *Ibid.*, pp. 272–73.
[26] *Ibid.*, p. 263.

practice would be to purge the entire system, replacing the original members with ones of the appropriate ideology. This would in essence mean that the organization would have to start *de novo* and that nothing would be done until the organizational roles were learned and linkages to the society were established. Since the organization has clients and customers, as well as a broader constituency in the case of government organizations, the expectations of nonmembers would also have to be altered. For these reasons, the likelihood of success is slim, regardless of the technique selected. The tendency for the organization to operate as it has in the past is very strong.

Most government organizations in Western democracies operate with a civil service system. An extension of Lipset's analysis suggests, therefore, that changes in the party in power will have less impact on the operation of the government agencies than political rhetoric would suggest. In non-Western societies, the same principles seem to hold. The potentiality for major social change through change in government is therefore modified by the organizational realities that exist. Since social systems do change, of course, the organization must be viewed as something that does not change overnight, but will change with time. The changes that occur may not be in phase with the change in political philosophy of the government in power. A "liberal" party in power may over time be able to introduce more of its adherents into the civil service system. These people can remain in office after a change in the party in power, blunting the efforts of a conservative party, but at the same time increasing the "liberalness" of the agencies involved. In whatever political direction a state, county, or nation is moving, organizational conservatism will remain an important consideration.

Examples from outside the political–government arena can also be readily found. In education, schools in urban areas have seen their constituencies change around them,[27] but there is a strong tendency toward maintenance of the educational programs that were appropriate in the past, despite their growing irrelevancy—and the same change could be documented in higher education. In private industry, the plight of U.S. railroads is indicative of the resistance of this organizational form to change. Here the resistance is more than the desire to maximize income; in fact, some suggest that the railroads' persistence in their past practices is in spite of the fact that profits could be increased if practices were altered. Organized religions have similarly resisted change, with apparently damaging results for themselves, both as organizations and as social movements.

[27] For a discussion of this point, see Morris Janowitz, *Institution Building in Urban Education* (New York: Russell Sage Foundation, 1969), pp. 7–10.

These examples could be extended. Probably everyone has a favorite case of an organization swallowing up attempts at what seem to be improvements through the continuation of past practices. The point must be reiterated that this is endemic to the nature of organizations. Organizations can and do change. As has been shown, mechanisms can be set up that help foster change within the organization. Nevertheless, at some point in its history every organization will resist efforts to make it do something it has not been doing. Individuals in the organization are reinforced by their consistent behavior in relationship to the organizational norms. Organizational procedures become fixed and valued. Precedent is part of the organizational legal system. All these factors conspire to make the organizations in a society major resisters of change in that society.

SUMMARY AND IMPLICATIONS

Our analysis is ended. Readers will have to conclude themselves whether or not it was worth it. It should be evident that I consider organizations to be one of the most crucial of all variables affecting our individual and collective lives. It is organizations that contribute to or detract from the quality of life and the quality of our environment. From the perspective taken here, it is naive to view the world as being composed of good and evil men and women and to search for solutions to our problems in the form of new leadership. Men and women are good and evil and leadership is important, but this is only a small portion of the total picture. If our analysis is at all correct, then we should readily see that bringing good people into an organization to replace the old, evil ones is not going to do very much unless the organizational structure is changed, distributions of power altered, and so on. It is unlikely that brave new leadership can turn an organization around, unless the contingencies that the organization faces are changed.

Organizations are the significant actors in our society. Their very complexity makes certain types of conclusions difficult. For example, in Minnesota there has been a long legal fight over the alleged pollution of Lake Superior by a mining company that was given state approval to dump iron mine tailings into the lake. A simplistic analysis would conclude that the corporate hierarchy is composed of people that have no human concerns and that the state's Pollution Control Agency, which is seeking to halt the company's practice, is staffed by virtuous personnel. The analysis would be simplistic, not because it was wrong (it may or may not be), but because it does not identify the root causes of the actions. The company was given permission for such dumping in the past by the state in an attempt to attract the firm in the first place. The firm does supply hundreds of relatively well-paying jobs for people in an otherwise economically weak area (it also makes a good profit from the labor of these people). From the standpoint of this organization, it is more reasonable and rational to continue as it has been doing. As the Pollution Control Agency marshals its forces against this business firm, it undoubtedly pays less attention to other situations. In addition, the sheer fact that it sets up procedures to deal with this firm makes it unlikely that it will rescind its pursuit of the firm. Organizational momentum is not easily halted. The point is simply that the *organization* becomes the actor—hero or villain.

What of the future? Will organizations be more or less humanizing? Will they turn to socially beneficial goals? The future does not encourage optimism, if the arguments presented in this book are valid. For example, if certain technologies are related to particular kinds of organizational structures and the need for routine work continues, it is unlikely that dehumanizing work will disappear. If it is correct that organizations have multiple goals, and one of them is organizational survival, it is unlikely that they will seek to do away with themselves. If one were to want to do away with the hold that organizations have on us, it would require what is perhaps the ultimate paradox—an organized anarchical movement.

index

351